POST-AUGUSTAN POETRY

FROM SENECA TO JUVENAL

POST-AUGUSTAN POETRY

FROM SENECA TO JUVENAL

BY

HAROLD EDGEWORTH BUTLER

Select Bibliographies Reprint Series

BOOKS FOR LIBRARIES PRESS
FREEPORT, NEW YORK

First Published 1909
Reprinted 1969

STANDARD BOOK NUMBER:
8369-5085-2

LIBRARY OF CONGRESS CATALOG CARD NUMBER:
70-99656

PRINTED IN THE UNITED STATES OF AMERICA

PREFACE

I HAVE attempted in this book to provide something of an introduction to the poetical literature of the post-Augustan age. Although few of the writers dealt with have any claim to be called poets of the first order, and some stand very low in the scale of poetry, as a whole the poets of this period have suffered greater neglect than they deserve. Their undeniable weaknesses tend in many cases to obscure their real merits, with the result that they are at times either ignored or subjected to unduly sweeping condemnation. I have attempted in these pages to detach and illustrate their excellences without in any way passing over their defects.

Manilius and Phaedrus have been omitted on the ground that as regards the general character of their writings they belong rather to the Augustan period than to the subsequent age of decadence. Manilius indeed composed a considerable portion of his work during the lifetime of Augustus, while Phaedrus, though somewhat later in date, showed a sobriety of thought and an antique simplicity of style that place him at least a generation away from his contemporaries. The authorities to whose works I am indebted are duly acknowledged in the course of the work. I owe a special debt, however, to those great works of reference, the Histories of Roman Literature by Schanz and Teuffel, to Friedländer's *Sittengeschichte*, and, for the chapters on Lucan and Statius, to Heitland's *Introduction to Haskins's edition of Lucan* and Legras' *Thébaïde de Stace*. I wish particularly to express my indebtedness to Professor Gilbert Murray and Mr. Nowell Smith, who read the book in manuscript and made many valuable suggestions and corrections. I also have to thank Mr. A. S. Owen for much assistance in the corrections of the proofs.

My thanks are owing to Professor Goldwin Smith for permission to print translations from 'Bay Leaves', and to Mr. A. E. Street and Mr. F. J. Miller and their publishers, for permission to quote from their translations of Martial (Messrs. Spottiswoode) and Seneca (Chicago University Press) respectively.

H. E. BUTLER.

November, 1908.

CONTENTS

CHAPTER I

THE DECLINE OF POST-AUGUSTAN POETRY.

CHAPTER II

DRAMA

CHAPTER III

PERSIUS

CHAPTER IV

LUCAN

CHAPTER V

PETRONIUS

CHAPTER VI

MINOR POETRY, 14–69 A.D.

I. DIDACTIC POETRY.

II. CALPURNIUS SICULUS, THE EINSIEDELN FRAGMENTS, AND THE PANEGYRICUS IN PISONEM.

III. ILIAS LATINA.

IV. MINOR POETS.

CHAPTER VII

EMPERORS AND MINOR POETS, 70–117 A.D.

I. EMPERORS AND POETS WHOSE WORKS ARE LOST

II. SULPICIA.

CHAPTER VIII

VALERIUS FLACCUS

CHAPTER IX

STATIUS

CHAPTER X

SILIUS ITALICUS

CHAPTER XI

MARTIAL

CHAPTER XII

JUVENAL

CHAPTER I

THE DECLINE OF POST-AUGUSTAN POETRY

During the latter years of the principate of Augustus a remarkable change in literary methods and style begins to make itself felt. The gradual extinction of the great luminaries is followed by a gradual disappearance of originality and of the natural and easy-flowing style whose phrases and felicities adorn, without overloading or obscuring the sense. In their place comes a straining after effect, a love of startling colour, produced now by over-gorgeous or over-minute imagery, now by a surfeit of brilliant epigram, while controlling good sense and observance of due proportion are often absent and imitative preciosity too frequently masquerades as originality. Further, in too many cases there is a complete absence of moral enthusiasm, close observation, and genuine insight.

What were the causes of this change ? Was it due mainly to the evil influence of the principate or to more subtle and deep-rooted causes ?

The principate had been denounced as the *fons et origo mali*.[1] That its influence was for evil can hardly be denied. But it was rather a symptom, an outward and visible sign of a deep-engrained decay, which it accentuated and brought to the surface, but in no way originated. We are told that the principate ' created around itself the quiet of the graveyard, since all independence was compelled under threat of death to hypocritical silence or subterfuge ; servility alone was allowed to speak ; the rest submitted to what was inevitable, nay, even endeavoured to accommodate their minds to it as much as possible.' Even if this highly coloured statement were true, the influence of

---

[1] See Teuffel and Schwabe, § 272.

such tyrannical suppression of free thinking and free speaking could only have *directly* affected certain forms of literature, such as satire, recent history,[1] and political oratory,
while even in these branches of literature a wide field was
left over which an intending author might safely range.
The *direct* influence on poetry must have been exceedingly
small. If we review the great poets of the Augustan and
republican periods, we shall find little save certain epigrams
of Catullus that could not safely have been produced in
post-Augustan times. Moreover, when we turn to what is
actually known of the attitude of the early emperors towards
literature, the balance does not seriously incline against
them. It may be said without hesitation of the four
emperors succeeding Augustus that they had a genuine
taste and some capacity for literature.

Of two only is it true that their influence was in any
way repressive. The principate of Tiberius is notorious
for the silence of literature ; whether the fact is due as
much to the character of Tiberius as to the temporary
exhaustion of genius following naturally on the brilliance
of the Augustan period, is more than doubtful. But
Tiberius cannot be acquitted of all blame. The cynical
humour with which it pleased him to mark the steady
advance of autocracy, the *lentae maxillae* which Augustus
attributed to his adopted son,[2] the icy and ironic cruelty
which was—on the most favourable estimate—a not inconsiderable element in his character, no doubt all exercised
a chilling influence, not only on politics but on all spon-
taneous expression of human character. Further, we find
a few instances of active and cruel repression. Lampoons
against the emperor were punished with death.[3] Cremutius
Cordus was driven to suicide for styling ' Brutus and Cassius
the last of all the Romans '.[4] Mamercus Scaurus had the
misfortune to write a tragedy on the subject of Atreus in

---

[1] Cf. Tac. *Ann.* i. 1.   Velleius Paterculus is a good example of the
servile historian.   For an example of servile oratory cf. Tac. *Ann.* xvi. 28.

[2] Suet. *Tib.* 21.   [3] Dion. lvii. 22 ; Tac. *Ann.* vi. 39 ; iv. 31.

[4] Tac. *Ann.* iv. 34.

which he advised submission to Atreus in a version of the
Euripidean

$$\tau \grave{a}_{S} \ \tau \hat{\omega} \nu \ \tau \upsilon \rho \acute{a} \nu \nu \omega \nu \ \mathring{a} \mu a \theta \acute{\iota} a_{S} \ \phi \acute{e} \rho \epsilon \iota \nu \ \chi \rho \epsilon \acute{\omega} \nu.^{1}$$

He too fell a victim to the Emperor's displeasure, though
the chief charges actually brought against him were of
adultery with the Princess Livilla and practice of the black
art. We hear also of another case in which *obiectum est
poetae quod in tragoedia Agamemnonem probris lacessisset*
(Suet. *Tib.* 61). It is worthy of notice that actors also
came under Tiberius's displeasure.[2] The mime and the
Atellan farce afforded too free an opportunity for impro-
visation against the emperor. Even the harmless Phaedrus
seems to have incurred the anger of Sejanus, and to have
suffered thereby.[3] Nor do the few instances in which
Tiberius appears as a patron of literature fill us with great
respect for his taste. He is said to have given one Asellius
Sabinus 100,000 sesterces for a dialogue between a mush-
room, a finch, an oyster, and a thrush,[4] and to have
rewarded a worthless writer,[5] Clutorius Priscus, for a poem
composed on the death of Germanicus. On the other hand,
he seems to have had a sincere love of literature,[6] though
he wrote in a crabbed and affected style. He was a purist
in language with a taste for archaism,[7] left a brief autobiography[8] and dabbled in poetry, writing epigrams,[9] a lyric
conquestio de morte Lucii Caesaris,[10] and Greek imitations of
Euphorion, Rhianus, and Parthenius, the learned poets of
Alexandria. His taste was bad : he went even farther
than his beloved Alexandrians, awaking the laughter of his
contemporaries even in an age when obscure mythological
learning was at a premium. The questions which delighted
him were—' Who was the mother of Hecuba ? ' ' What was

---

1 Dion. lviii. 24 μαθὼν οὖν τοῦτο ὁ Τιβέριος, ἐφ᾽ ἑαυτῷ τότε τὸ ἔπος εἰρῆσθαι
ἔφη, ᾽Ατρεὺς διὰ τὴν μιαιφονίαν εἶναι προσποιησάμενος. Tac. *Ann.* vi. 29.
2 ' Pulsi tum Italia histriones,' Tac. *Ann.* iv. 14.

3 III Prol. 38 sqq., Epil. 29 sqq.   4 Suet. *Tib.* 42.
5 Tac. *Ann.* iii. 49 ; Dion. lvii. 20.   6 Suet. *Tib.* 70.
7 Suet. *Tib.* 71.   8 Suet. *Tib.* 61.
9 Suidas, s. v. Καῖσαρ Τιβέριος.   10 Suet. *Tib.* 70.

the name of Achilles when disguised as a girl ? ' ' What
did the sirens sing ? '[1]   Literature had little to learn from
Tiberius, but it should have had something to gain from
the fact that he was not blind to its charms : at the worst
it cannot have required abnormal skill to avoid incurring
a charge of *lèse-majesté*.

The reign of the lunatic Caligula is of small importance,
thanks to its extreme brevity. For all his madness he
had considerable ability ; he was ready of speech to a
remarkable degree, though his oratory suffered from extravagant ornament [2] and lack of restraint.   He had, however,
some literary insight : in his description of Seneca's rhetoric
as *merae commissiones*, 'prize declamations,' and 'sand
without lime ' he gave an admirable summary of that
writer's chief weaknesses.[3]   But he would in all probability
have proved a greater danger to literature than Tiberius.
It is true that in his desire to compare favourably with his
predecessors he allowed the writings of T. Labienus, Cremutius Cordus, and Cassius Severus, which had fallen under
the senate's ban in the two preceding reigns, to be freely
circulated once more.[4]   But he by no means abandoned
trials for *lèse-majesté*.   The rhetorician Carinas Secundus
was banished on account of an imprudent phrase in a
suasoria on the hackneyed theme of tyrannicide.[5]   A writer
of an Atellan farce was burned to death in the amphitheatre [6] for a treasonable jest, and Seneca narrowly escaped
death for having made a brilliant display of oratory in
the senate.[7]   He also seriously meditated the destruction
of the works of Homer.   Plato had banished Homer from
his ideal state.   Why should not Caligula ?   He was with
difficulty restrained from doing the like for Vergil and Livy.
The former, he said, was a man of little learning and less
wit ;[8] the latter was verbose and careless.   Even when he
attempted to encourage literature, his eccentricity carried

---

[1] Suet. *Tib.* 70.   [2] Suet. *Cal.* 53.   [3] Suet. *Cal.* 53.
[4] Suet. *Cal.* 16.   [5] Dion. lix. 20.   [6] Suet. *Cal.* 27.
[7] Dion. lix. 19.
[8] Suet. *Cal.* 34 ' nullius ingenii minimaeque doctrinae '.

him to such extremes that the competitors shrank in horror
from entering the lists.   He instituted a contest at Lugu-
dunum in which prizes were offered for declamations in
Greek and Latin.   The prizes were presented to the victors
by the vanquished, who were ordered to write panegyrics
in honour of their successful rivals, while in cases where
the declamations were decided to be unusually poor, the
unhappy authors were ordered to obliterate their writings
with a sponge or even with their own tongues, under penalty
of being caned or ducked in the Rhone.[1]

Literature had some reason to be thankful for his early
assassination.   The lunatic was succeeded by a fool, but
a learned fool.   Claudius was historian, antiquary, and
philologist.   He wrote two books on the civil war, forty-
one on the principate of Augustus, a defence of Cicero,
eight books of autobiography,[2] an official diary,[3] a treatise
on dicing.[4]   To this must be added his writings in Greek,
twenty books of Etruscan history, eight of Carthaginian,[2]
together with a comedy performed and crowned at Naples
in honour of the memory of Germanicus.[5]   His style, according to Suetonius, was *magis ineptus quam inelegans*.[6]   He
did more than write : he attempted a reform of spelling,
by introducing three new letters into the Latin alphabet.
His enthusiasm and industry were exemplary.   Such indeed
was his activity that a special office,[7] *a studiis*, was established, which was filled for the first time by the influential
freedman Polybius.   Claudius lacked the saving grace of
good sense, but in happier days might have been a useful
professor : at any rate his interest in literature was whole-
hearted and disinterested.   His own writing was too feeble
to influence contemporaries for ill and he had the merit of
having given literature room to move.   Seneca might mock
at him after his death,[8] but he had done good service.

---

[1] Suet. *Cal.* 20.   [2] For his writings generally cf. Suet. *Claud.* 41, 42.
[3] Tac. *Ann.* xiii. 43.   [4] Suet. *Claud.* 33.   [5] Suet. *Claud.* 11.
[6] Suet. *Claud.* 41.   This is borne out by the fragments of the speech
delivered at Lyons on the Gallic franchise.   *C. I. L.* 13, 1668.
[7] Suet. *Claud.* 28.   [8] Sc. in the *Apocolocyntosis*.

Nero, Claudius' successor, was also a liberal, if embarrassing, patron of literature. His tastes were more purely literary. He had received an elaborate and diversified education. He had even enjoyed the privilege of having Seneca—the head of the literary profession—for his tutor. These influences were not wholly for the good : Agrippina dissuaded him from the study of philosophy as being unsuited for a future emperor, Seneca from the study of earlier and saner orators that he might himself have a longer lease of Nero's admiration.[1] The result was that a temperament, perhaps falsely styled artistic,[2] was deprived of the solid nutriment required to give it stability. Nero's great ambition was to be supreme in poetry and art as he was supreme in empire. He composed rapidly and with some technical skill,[3] but his work lacked distinction, connexion of thought, and unity of style.[4] Satirical [5] and erotic [6] epigrams, learned mythological poems on Attis and the Bacchae,[7] all flowed from his pen. But his most famous works were his *Troica*,[8] an epic on the Trojan legend, which he recited before the people in the theatre,[9] and his Ἰλίου ἅλωσις, which may perhaps have been included in the *Troica*, and is famous as having—so scandal ran—been declaimed over burning Rome.[10] But his ambition soared higher. He contemplated an epic on the whole of Roman history. It was estimated that 400 books would be required. The Stoic Annaeus Cornutus justly remarked that no one would read so many. It was pointed out that the Stoic's master, Chrysippus, had written even more. ' Yes,' said Cornutus, ' but they were of some use to humanity.' Cornutus was

---

[1] Suet. *Ner.* 52.   [2] Suet. *Ner.* 49 ' qualis artifex pereo ! '
[3] Suet. *Ner.* 52 ; Tac. *Ann.* xiii. 3.   [4] Tac. *Ann.* xiv. 16.
[5] Suet. *Domit.* 1 ; Tac. *Ann.* xv. 49 ; Suet. *Ner.* 24.
[6] Mart. ix. 26. 9 ; Plin. *N. H.* xxxvii. 50.
[7] Persius is sometimes said to quote from the Bacchae. Cf. Schol. Pers. *Sat.* i. 93–5, 99–102. But see ch. iii, p. 89.
[8] Juv. viii. 221 ; Serv. Verg. *Georg.* iii. 36, *Aen.* v. 370.
[9] Dion. lxii. 29.
[10] Dion. lxii. 18 ; Suet. *Ner.* 38 ; Tac. *Ann.* xv. 39. For fragments of his work see Baehrens, *Poet. Rom. Fragm.*, p. 368.

banished, but he saved Rome from the epic. Nero was
also prolific in speeches and, proud of his voice, often
appeared on the stage. He impersonated Orestes matricida,
Canace parturiens, Oedipus blind, and Hercules mad.[1] It
is not improbable that the words declaimed or sung in these
scenes were composed by Nero himself.[2] For the encourage-
ment of music and poetry he had established quinquennial
games known as the Neronia. How far his motives for so
doing were interested it is hard to say. But there is no
doubt that he had a passionate ambition to win the prize
at the contest instituted by himself. In A.D. 60, on the
first occasion of the celebration of these games, the prize
was won by Lucan with a poem in praise of Nero.[3] Vacca,
in his life of Lucan, states that this lost him Nero's favour,
the emperor being jealous of his success. The story is
demonstrably false,[4] but that Nero subsequently became
jealous of Lucan is undoubted. Till Lucan's fame was
assured, Nero extended his favour to him : then partly
through Lucan's extreme vanity and want of tact, partly
through Nero's jealousy of Lucan's pre-eminence that favour
was wholly withdrawn.[5] Nevertheless, though Nero may
have shown jealousy of successful rivals, he seems to have
had sufficient respect for literature to refrain from persecu-
tion. He did not go out of his way to punish personal
attacks on himself. If names were delated to the senate
on such a charge, he inclined to mercy. Even the introduction into an Atellan farce of jests on the deaths of
Claudius and Agrippina was only punished with exile.[6]
Only after the detection of Piso's conspiracy in 65 did his
anger vent itself on writers : towards the end of his reign
the distinguished authors, Virginius Flavus and the Stoic

---

[1] Suet. Ner. 10, 21.
[2] Philostr. vit. Apoll. iv. 39 ᾄδων τὰ τοῦ Νέρωνος μέλη ... ἐπῆγε μέλη τὰ
μὲν ἐξ Ὀρεστείας, τὰ δ᾽ ἐξ Ἀντιγόνης, τὰ δ᾽ ὁποθενοῦν τῶν τραγῳδουμένων αὐτῷ
καὶ ᾠδὰς ἔκαμπτεν ὁπόσας Νέρων ἐλύγιζέ τε καὶ κακῶς ἔστρεφεν.
[3] Suet. vita Lucani ; see chapter on Lucan, p. 97.
[4] See chapter on Lucan, p. 98.
[5] Suet. Luc. ; Tac. Ann. xv. 49.   [6] Suet. Ner. 39.

Musonius Rufus, were both driven into exile. As for the deaths of Seneca and Lucan, the two most distinguished writers of the day, though both perished at Nero's hands, it was their conduct, not their writings, that brought them to destruction. Both were implicated in the Pisonian conspiracy. If, then, Nero's direct influence on literature was for the bad, it was not because he was adverse : it suffered rather from his favour : the extravagant tastes of the princeps and the many eccentricities of his life and character may perhaps find a reflection in some of the more grotesque extravagances of Lucan, such for instance as the absurdly servile dedication of the *Pharsalia*. But even in this direction his influence was probably comparatively small.

In view, then, of what is known of the attitude of the four emperors of the period most critical for Silver Latin literature, the period of its birth, it may be said that, on the worst estimate, their direct influence is not an important factor in the decline.[1] On the other hand, the indirect influence of the principate was beyond doubt evil. Society was corrupt enough and public life sufficiently uninspiring under Augustus. After the first glow of enthusiasm over the restoration of peace and order, and over the vindication of the Roman power on the frontiers of empire had passed away, men felt how thinly veiled was their slavery. Liberty was gradually restricted, autocracy cast off its mask : the sense of power that goes with freedom dwindled ; little was left to waken man's enthusiasm, and the servility exacted by the emperors became more and more degrading. Unpleasing as are the flatteries addressed to Augustus by Vergil and Horace, they fade into insignificance compared with Lucan's apotheosis of Nero ; or to take later and yet more revolting examples, the poems of the Silvae

---

[1] It may be urged that the damage lies not in the loss of poetry suppressed by the Emperor, but in the generation of a type of court poetry, examples of which survive in their most repulsive form in the *Silvae* of Statius and the epigrams of Martial. The objection has its element of truth, but only affects a very small and comparatively unimportant portion of the poetry of the age.

addressed by Statius to Domitian or his favourites. Further, these four emperors of the Julio-Claudian dynasty set a low standard of private life : they might command flattery, they could hardly exact respect. Two clever lunatics, a learned fool, and a morose cynic are not inspiring.

Nevertheless, however unhealthy its influence may have been—and there has been much exaggeration on this point— it must be remembered that the principate found ready to its hand a society with all the seeds of decay implanted deep within it. Even a succession of sane and virtuous Caesars might well have failed, with the machinery and material at their disposal, to put new and vigorous life into the aristocracy and people of Rome. Even the encroachments of despotism on popular liberty must be attributed in no small degree to the incapacity of what should have been the ruling class at Rome. Despotism was in a sense forced upon the emperors : they were not reluctant, but, had they been so, they would still have had little choice. The primary causes of the decline of literature, as of the decay of life and morals, lie much deeper. The influence of princeps and principate, though not negligible, is *comparatively* small.

The really important causes are to be found first in the general decay of Roman character—far-advanced before the coming of Caesarism, secondly in the peculiar nature of Roman literature, and thirdly in the vicious system of Roman education.

It was the first of these factors that produced the lubricity that defiles and the lack of moral earnestness that weakens such a large proportion of the literature of this age. It is not necessary to illustrate this point in any detail.[1] The record of Rome, alike in home and foreign politics, during the hundred and twenty years preceding the foundation of the principate forms one of the most fascinating, but in many respects one of the most profoundly melancholy pages in history. The poems of Catullus and the speeches

---

[1] See Tacitus, *Dial.* 28 sqq. on the moral training of a young Roman of his day. Also Juv. xiv.

of Cicero serve equally to illustrate the wholesale corruption
alike of public and private morality.   The Roman character
had broken down before the gradual inroads of an alien
luxury and the opening of wide fields of empire to plunder.
It is an age of incredible scandal, of mob law, of *coups
d'état* and proscriptions, saved only from utter gloom by
the illusory light shed from the figures of a few great men
and by the never absent sense of freedom and expansion.
There still remained a republican liberty of action, an inspiring possibility of reform, an outlet for personal ambition,
which facilitated the rise of great leaders and writers.   And
Rome was now bringing to ripeness fruit sprung from the
seed of Hellenism, a decadent and meretricious Hellenism,
but even in its decay the greatest intellectual force of the
world.

Wonderful as was the fruit produced by the graft of
Hellenism, it too contained the seeds of decay.   For Rome
owed too little to early Greek epic and to the golden literature
of Athens, too much to the later age when rhetoric had
become a knack, and

> the love of letters overdone
> Had swamped the sacred poets with themselves.[1]

Roman literature came too late : that it reached such
heights is a remarkable tribute to the greatness of Roman
genius, even in its decline.   With the exception of the
satires of Lucilius and Horace there was practically no
branch of literature that did not owe its inspiration and
form to Greek models.   Even the primitive national metre
had died out.   Roman literature—more especially poetry—
was therefore bound to be unduly self-conscious and was
always in danger of a lack of spontaneity.   That Rome
produced great prose writers is not surprising ; they had
copious and untouched material to deal with, and prose
structure was naturally less rapidly and less radically affected

---

[1] After the death of the great Augustan authors Alexandrian erudition
becomes yet more rampant.   It was a great assistance to men of second-
rate poetical talent.

by Greek influence. That she should have produced a Catullus, a Lucretius, a Vergil, a Horace, and—most wonderful of all—an Ovid was an amazing achievement, rendered not the less astonishing when it is remembered that the stern bent of the practical Roman mind did not in earlier days give high promise of poetry. The marvel is not wholly to be explained by the circumstances of the age. The new sense of power, the revival of the national spirit under the warming influence of peace and hope, that characterize the brilliant interval between the fall of the republic and the turbid stagnation of the empire, are not enough to account for it. Their influence would have been in vain had they not found remarkable genius ready for the kindling.

The whole field of literature had been so thoroughly covered by the great writers of Hellas, that it was hard for the imitative Roman to be original. As far as epic poetry was concerned, Rome had poor material with which to deal : neither her mythology—the most prosaic and business-like of all mythologies—nor her history seemed to give any real scope for the epic writer. The Greek mythology was ready to hand, but it was hard for a Roman to treat it with high enthusiasm, and still harder to handle it with freshness and individuality. The purely historical epic is from its very nature doomed to failure. Treated with accuracy it becomes prosy, treated with fancy it becomes ridiculous. Vergil saw the one possible avenue to epic greatness. He went back into the legendary past where imagination could have free play, linked together the great heroic sagas of Greece with the scanty materials presented by the prehistoric legends of Rome, and kindled the whole work to life by his rich historical imagination and his sense of the grandeur of the Rome that was to be. His unerring choice of subject and his brilliant execution seemed to close to his successors all paths to epic fame. They had but well-worn and inferior themes wherefrom to choose, and the supremacy of Vergil's genius dominated their minds, becoming an obsession and a clog rather than an assistance to such poetic genius as they possessed. The same is true of Horace.

As complete a master in lyric verse as Vergil in heroic, he left the after-comer no possibility of advance. As for Ovid, there could be only one Ovid : the cleverest and most heartless of poets, he at once challenged and defied imitation. Satire alone was left with real chance of success : while the human race exists, there will always be fresh material for satire, and the imperial age was destined to give it peculiar force and scope. Further, satire and its nearest kin, the epigram, were the only forms of literature that were not seriously impaired by the artificial system of education that had struck root in Rome.

Otherwise the tendency to artificiality on the one hand and inadequacy of thought on the other, to which the conditions of its birth and growth exposed Roman literature, were aggravated to an almost incredible extent by the absurd system of education to which the unformed mind of the young Roman was subjected. It will be seen that what Greece gave with the right hand she took away with the left.

There were three stages in Roman education, the elementary, the literary, the rhetorical. The first, in which the *litterator* taught the three R's, does not concern us here. In the second stage the *grammaticus* gave instruction in Greek and Latin literature, together with the elements of grammar and style. The profound influence of Greece is shown by Quintilian's recommendation [1] that a boy should start on Greek literature, and by the fact that boys began with Homer.[2] Greek authors, particularly studied, were Aesop, Hesiod, the tragedians, and Menander.[3] Among Roman authors Naevius, Ennius, Pacuvius, Accius, Afranius, Plautus, Caecilius, and Terence were much read, though there was a reaction against these early authors under the empire, and they were partly replaced by Vergil, Horace, and Ovid.[4] These authors were made vehicles for the

---

[1] Quint. i. 1. 12.   [2] Quint. i. 8. 5 ; Plin. *Ep.* ii. 14.
[3] Quint. i. 9. 2 ; Cic. *Ep. ad Fam.* vi. 18. 5 ; Quint. i. 8. 6 ; Stat. *Silv.* ii. 1. 114 ; Ov. *Tr.* ii. 369.   [4] Cp. Wilkins, *Rom. Education*, p. 60.

teaching of grammar and of style. The latter point alone
concerns us here. The Roman boy was taught to read
aloud intelligently and artistically with the proper modula-
tion of the voice. For this purpose he was carefully taught
the laws of metre, with special reference to the peculiarities
of particular poets. After the reading aloud (*lectio*) came
the *enarratio* or explanation of the text. The educational
value of this was doubtless considerable, though it was
impaired by the importance assigned to obscure mythological
knowledge and unscientific archaeology.[1] The pupil would
be further instructed by exercises in paraphrase and by the
treatment in simple essay form of themes (*sententiae*).
' Great store was set both in speaking and writing on a
command of an abundance of general truths or commonplaces, and even at school boys were trained to commit them
to memory, to expand them, and illustrate them from
history.' [2] Finally they were taught to write verse. Such
at least is a legitimate inference from the extraordinary
precocity shown by many Roman authors.[3] This literary
training contained much that was of great value, but it
also had grave disadvantages. There seems in the first
place to have been too much ' spoon-feeding ', and too little

---

[1] Cp. Juv. vii. 231–6 ; Suet. *Tib.* 70. The result of this type of instruction is visible throughout the poets of the age, whereas Vergil and the best
of the Greek Alexandrians had a true appreciation of the sensuous charm
of proper names and legendary allusions, as in our literature had Marlowe,
Milton, Keats, and Tennyson. Cp. Milton, *Paradise Lost*, Bk. I :

> What resounds
> In fable or romance of Uther's son
> Begirt with British and Armoric knights ;
> And all who since, baptised or infidel,
> Jousted in Aspramont or Montalban,
> Damasco, or Marocco, or Trebisond,
> Or whom Biserta sent from Afric shore,
> When Charlemain with all his peerage fell
> By Fontarabia.

Or compare Tennyson's use of the names of Arthur's battles, ' Agned
Cathregonion ' and the ' waste sand-shore of Trath Treroit.'

[2] Wilkins, *Roman Education*, p. 72.

[3] See Wilkins, op. cit. p. 74.

genuine brain exercise for the pupil.[1] Secondly, the fact
that at this stage boys were nurtured almost entirely on
poetry requires serious consideration. The quality of the
food supplied to the mind, though pre-eminently palatable,
must have tended to be somewhat thin. The elaborate
instruction in mythological erudition was devoid of religious
value ; and indeed of any value, save the training of a purely
mechanical memory. Attention was called too much to
the form, too little to the substance. Style has its value,
but it is after all only a secondary consideration in education.
The effect upon literature of this poetical training was
twofold. It caused an undue demand for poetical colour
in prose, and produced a horrible precocity and *cacoethes
scribendi*[2] in verse, together with an abnormal tendency to
imitation of the great writers of previous generations.[3]

But the rhetorical training which succeeded was responsible for far worse evils. The importance of rhetoric in
ancient education is easily explained. The Greek or Roman
gentleman was destined to play a part in the public life
of the city state. For this purpose the art of speaking
was of enormous value alike in politics and in the law
courts. Hence the universal predominance of rhetoric in
higher education both in Rome and Greece.[4] The main
instrument of instruction was the writing of themes for
declamation. These exercises were divided into *suasoriae*—
deliberative speeches in which some course of action was
discussed—and *controversiae*—where some proposition was
maintained or denied. Pupils began with *suasoriae* and

---

[1] Wilkins, *Roman Education*, p. 75.

[2] The most striking instances of this precocity are Q. Sulpicius Maximus,
who at the age of twelve and a half won the prize for Greek verse at the
Agon Capitolinus A.D. 94 (cp. Kaibel, *Epigr. Gr.* 618), and L. Valerius
L. F. Pudens, aged thirteen, who won the prize for Latin verse in A.D. 106.
Cp. *C. I. L.* ix. 286.

[3] For the importance attached to imitation see Quint. x. 2.

[4] The Greek rhetoricians of this period lay great stress on the importance
of avoiding declamatory rhetoric. They belong to the Attic revival. But
the Attic revival never really ' caught on ' at Rome ; by the time of
Quintilian the mischief was done.

went on to *controversiae*.   Regarded as a mental gymnastic,
these themes may have possessed some value.   But they
were hackneyed and absurdly remote from real life, as
can be judged from the examples collected by the elder
Seneca.   Typical subjects of the *suasoria* are—' Agamemnon deliberates whether to slay Iphigenia '; [1] ' Cicero
deliberates whether to burn his writings, Antony having
promised to spare him on that condition '; [2] ' Three hundred Spartans sent against Xerxes after the flight of troops
sent from the rest of Greece deliberate whether to stand
or fly.' [3]

The *controversia* requires further explanation.   A general
law is stated, e. g. *incesta saxo deiciatur*.   A special case
follows, e. g. *incesti damnata antequam deiceretur invocavit
Vestam : deiecta vixit*.   The special case had to be brought
under the general rule ; *repetitur ad poenam*. [4]   Other

---

[1] Sen. *Suas.* 3.   [2] Ib. 7.

[3] Ib. 2.   I subjoin the text of the last.   The author is Triarius.   ' Non
pudet Laconas ne pugna quidem hostium, sed fabula vinci ?   Magnum
est alumnum virtutis nasci et Laconem : ad certam victoriam omnes
remansissent : ad certam mortem tantum Lacones.   Non est Sparta
lapidibus circumdata : ibi muros habet ubi viros.   Melius revocabimus
fugientes trecenos quam sequemur.   Sed montes perforat, maria contegit.
Nunquam solido stetit superba felicitas et ingentium imperiorum magna
fastigia oblivione fragilitatis humanae conlapsa sunt.   Scias licet non ad
finem pervenisse quae ad invidiam perducta sunt.   Maria terrasque,
rerum naturam statione immutavit sua : moriamur trecenti, ut hic
primum invenerit quod mutare non posset.   Si tam demens placiturum
consilium erat, cur non potius in turba fugimus ? '

[4] Latro is the author of the following treatment of the theme.
' Hoc exspectastis ut capite demisso verecundia se ipsa antequam im-
pelleretur deiceret ?   id enim deerat ut modestior in saxo esset quam in
sacrario fuerat.   Constitit et circumlatis in frequentiam oculis sanctissi-
mum numen, quasi parum violasset inter altaria, coepit in ipso quo vin-
dicabatur violare supplicio : hoc alterum damnatae incestum fuit, damnata
est quia incesta erat, deiecta est quia damnata erat, repetenda est quia
et incesta et damnata et deiecta est, dubitari potest quin usque eo de-
icienda sit, donec efficiatur propter quod deiecta est ?   patrocinium suum
vocat pereundi infelicitatem.   Quid tibi, importuna mulier, precor nisi
ut ne bis quidem deiecta pereas ?   "Invocavi," inquit, "deos ", statuta in
illo saxo deos nominasti, et miraris si te iterum deici volunt ?   si nihil
aliud, loco incestarum stetisti.'   Sen. *Cont.* i. 3.

examples are equally absurd : [1] one and all are ridiculously
remote from real life. It was bad enough that boys' time
should be wasted thus, but the evil was further emphasized
by the practice of recitation. These exercises, duly corrected
and elaborated, were often recited by their youthful authors
to an audience of complaisant friends and relations. Of
such training there could be but one possible result. ' Less
and less attention was paid to the substance of the speech,
more and more to the language ; justness and appropriateness of thought came to be less esteemed than brilliance and
novelty of expression.' [2]

These formal defects of education were accompanied
by a widespread neglect of the true educational spirit.
The development on healthy lines of the *morale* and intellect
of the young became in too many instances a matter of
indifference. Throughout the great work of Quintilian we
have continued evidence of the lack of moral and intellectual
enthusiasm that characterized the schools of his day. Even
more passionate are the denunciations levelled against contemporary education by Messala in the *Dialogus* of Tacitus.[3]
Parents neglect their children from their earliest years : they
place them in the charge of foreign slaves, often of the most
degraded character ; or if they do pay any personal attention to their upbringing, it is to teach them not honesty,
purity, and respect for themselves and their elders, but
pertness, luxurious habits, and neglect alike of themselves
and of others. The schools moreover, apart from their
faulty methods and ideals of instruction, encourage other
faults. The boys' interests lie not in their work, but in

---

[1] e. g. Sen. *Cont.* i. 7 ' Liberi parentes alant aut vinciant: quidam
alterum fratrem tyrannum occidit, alterum in adulterio deprehensum
deprecante patre interfecit. A piratis captus scripsit patri de redemptione.
Pater piratis epistolam scripsit, si praecidissent manus, duplam se daturum.
Piratae illum dimiserunt : patrem egentem non alit.'

[2] For a brilliant description of the evils of the Roman system of education see Tac. *Dial.* 30–5. See also p. 127 for the very similar criticism of
Petronius.

[3] cc. 28–30. Cp. also Quint. i. 2 1–8.

the theatres, the gladiatorial games, the races in the circus—
those ancient equivalents of twentieth-century athleticism.
Their minds are utterly absorbed by these pursuits, and there
is little room left for nobler studies.   ' How few boys will
talk of anything else at home ?   What topic of conversation
is so frequent in the lecture-room ; what other subject so
frequently on the lips of the masters, who collect pupils
not by the thoroughness of their teaching or by giving
proof of their powers of instruction, but by interested visits
and all the tricks of toadyism ? ' [1]   Messala goes on [2] to
denounce the unreality of the exercises in the schools,
whose deleterious effect is aggravated by the low standard
exacted.   ' Boys and young men are the speakers, boys and
young men the audience, and their efforts are received
with undiscriminating praise.'

The same faults that were generated in the schools were
intensified in after-life.   In the law courts the same smart
epigrams, the same meretricious style were required.   No true
method had been taught, with the result that ' frivolity of
style, shallow thoughts, and disorderly structure' prevailed;
orators imitated the rhythms of the stage and actually
made it their boast that their speeches would form fitting
accompaniments to song and dance.   It became a common
saying that ' our orators speak voluptuously, while our
actors dance eloquently '.[3]   Poetical colour was demanded
of the orator, rhetorical colour of the poet.   The literary
and rhetorical stages of education reacted on one another.[4]

---

[1] The schoolmaster was not infrequently, it is to be feared, of doubtful
character.   Cp. the case of the famous rhetorician Remmius Palaemon.
Cp. also Quint. i. 3. 13.

[2] c. 35.   [3] Tac. Dial. 26.

[4] The influence of rhetoric was of course large in the Augustan age.
Vergil and still more Ovid testify to this fact.   But the tone of rhetoric
was saner in the days of Vergil.   Ovid, himself no inconsiderable influence
on the poetry of the Silver Age, begins to show the effects of the new and
meretricious type of rhetoric that flourished under the anti-Ciceronian
reaction, when the healthy influence of the great orators of a saner age
began to give way before the inroads of the brilliant but insincere epigrammatic style.   This latter style was fostered largely by the importance

Further, just as the young poet had to his great detriment been encouraged to recite at school, so he had to recite if he was to win fame for his verse in the larger world. Even in a saner society poetry written primarily for recitation must have run to rhetoric ; in a rhetorical age the result was disastrous. In an enormous proportion of cases the poet of the Silver Age wrote literally for an audience. Great as were the facilities for publication the poet primarily made his name, not by the gradual distribution of his works among a reading public, but by declaiming before public or private audiences. The practice of gathering a circle of acquaintances together to listen to the recitations of a poet is said first to have been instituted by Asinius Pollio, the patron of Vergil. There is evidence to show that all the poets of the Augustan age gave recitations.[1] But the practice gradually increased and became a nuisance to all save the few who had the courage to stand aloof from these mutual admiration societies. Indiscriminate praise was lavished on good and bad work alike. Even Pliny the younger, whose cultivation and literary taste place him high above the average literary level of his day, approves of the increase of this melancholy harvest of minor poetry declaimed by uninspired bards.[2] The effect was lamentable. All the faults of the *suasoria* and *controversia* made their appearance in poetry.[3] The poet had continually to be performing acrobatic feats, now of rhetoric or epigram, now of learning, or again in the description of blood-curdling horrors, monstrous deaths and prodigious sorceries. Each work was overloaded with *sententiae* and purple patches.[4] So only could the author keep the attention of his audience.

---

assigned to the *controversia* and *suasoria* as opposed to the more realistic methods of oratorical training during the last century of the republic.

[1] See Mayor on Juv. iii. 9.

[2] Cp. Juv. i. 1 sqq., iii. 9. For the enormous part played in social life by recitations cp. Plin. *Ep.* i. 13, ii. 19, iv. 5, 27, v. 12, vi. 2, 17, 21, viii. 21.

[3] Cp. especially the speeches of Lucan.

[4] For some very just criticism on this head cp. Quint. viii. 5. 25 sqq.

The results were disastrous for literature and not too satisfactory[1] for the authors themselves, as the following curious
passage from Tacitus (*Dial.* 9) shows :

> Bassus is a genuine poet, and his verse possesses both beauty and
> charm : but the only result is that, when after a whole year, working
> every day and often well into the night, he has hammered out one
> book of poems, he must needs go about requesting people to be
> good enough to give him a hearing : and what is more he has to
> pay for it : for he borrows a house, constructs an auditorium,
> hires benches and distributes programmes. And then—admitting
> his recitations to be highly successful—yet all that honour and
> glory falls within one or two days, prematurely gathered like grass
> in the blade or flowers in their earliest bloom : it has no sure or
> solid reward, wins no friendship or following or lasting gratitude,
> naught save a transient applause, empty words of praise and a
> fleeting enthusiasm.

The less fortunate poet had to betake himself to the
forum or the public baths or some temple, there to inflict
his tawdry wares upon the ears of a chance audience.[2]
Others more fortunate would be lent a room by some rich
patron.[3] Under Nero and Domitian we get the apotheosis
of recitation. Nero, we have seen, established the Neronia
in 60 and himself competed. Domitian established a quin-
quennial competition in honour of Jupiter Capitolinus in 86
and an annual competition held every Quinquatria Minervae
at his palace on the Alban mount.[4] From that time forward
it became the ambition of every poet to be crowned at these
grotesque competitions.

The result of all these co-operating influences will be evident
as we deal with the individual poets. Here we can only
give a brief summary of the general characteristics of this

---

[1] For amusing instances of rudeness on the part of members of the
audience cp. Sen. *Ep.* cxxii. 11 ; Plin. *Ep.* vi. 15.

[2] Petr. 83, 88–91, 115. Mart. iii. 44. 10 ' et stanti legis et legis cacanti. |
in thermas fugio: sonas ad aurem. | piscinam peto: non licet natare. | ad
cenam propero: tenes euntem. | ad cenam venio: fugas sedentem. | lassus
dormio: suscitas iacentem.' Cp. also 3, 50 and passim. Plin. *Ep.* vi.
15 ; Juv. i. 1–21 ; iii. 6–9 ; vii. 39 sqq.

[3] Plin. *Ep.* viii. 12.   [4] Suet. *Dom.* 4.

fantastic literature. We have a striving after originality
that ends in eccentricity : writers were steeped in the great
poets of the Augustan age : men of comparatively small
creative imagination, but, thanks to their education, possessed
of great technical skill, they ran into violent extremes to
avoid the charge of imitating the great predecessors whom
they could not help but imitate ; hence the obscurity of
Persius—the disciple of Horace—and of Statius and Valerius
Flaccus—the followers of Vergil. Hence Lucan's bold
attempt to strike out a new type of epic, an attempt that
ended in a wild orgy of brilliant yet turbid rhetoric.   The
simple and natural was at a discount : brilliance of point,
bombastic description, gorgeous colour were preferred to
quiet power.   Alexandrian learning, already too much in
evidence in the Augustan age, becomes more prominent
and more oppressive. For men of second-rate talent it
served to give their work a spurious air of depth and originality to which it was not entitled. The necessity of patronage
engendered a fulsome flattery, while the false tone of the
schools of rhetoric,[1] aided perhaps by the influence of the
Stoical training so fashionable at Rome, led to a marvellous
conceit and self-complacency, of which a lack of humour
was a necessary corollary. These symptoms are seen at
their worst during the extravagant reign of Nero, though the
blame attaches as much to Seneca as to his pupil and
emperor.   Traces of a reaction against this wild unreality
are perhaps to be found in the literary criticism scattered
up and down the pages of Petronius,[2] but it was not till
the extinction of Nero and Seneca that any strong revolt
in the direction of sanity can be traced.   Even then it is
rather in the sphere of prose than of poetry that it is mani-
fest. Quintilian headed a Ciceronian reaction and was
followed by Pliny the younger and for a time by Tacitus.
But we may perhaps trace a similar Vergilian reaction in
the verse of Silius, Statius, and Valerius.[3] Their faults

---

[1] Tac. *Dial.* 35.   [2] See ch. v.

[3] There had always, it may be noted, existed an archaistic section of

do not nauseate to the same extent as those of their predecessors. But the mischief was done, and in point of
extravagance and meretricious taste the difference is only
one of degree.

Satire alone attains to real eminence : rhetoric and
epigram are its most mordant weapons, and the schools
of rhetoric, if they did nothing else, kept those weapons
well sharpened : the gross evils of the age opened an ample
field for the satirist. Hence it is that all or almost all
that is best in the literature of the Silver Age is satirical
or strongly tinged with satire. Tacitus, who had many of
the noblest qualifications of a poet, almost deserves the
title of Rome's greatest satirist ; the works of Persius and
Juvenal speak openly for themselves, while many of the
finest passages in Lucan are most near akin to satire. It
is true that under the principate satire had to be employed
with caution ; under the first two dynasties it was compelled
to be general in tone : it was not until after the fall of
Domitian, under the enlightened rule of Nerva and Trajan,
that it found a freer scope and was at least allowed to lash
the vices of the present under the names of the past.

It is in satire alone that we find any trace of genuine
moral earnestness and enthusiasm ; and the reason for this
is primarily that the satirists wrote under the influence of
the one force that definitely and steadily made for righteousness. It is the Stoic philosophy that kindles Persius and
Lucan, while Tacitus and Juvenal, even if they make no profession of Stoicism, have yet been profoundly influenced by
its teaching. Their morality takes its colour, if not its form,
from the philosophy of the ' Porch '. The only non-satirical
poetry primarily inspired by Stoicism is the dramatic verse
of Seneca. That its influence here is not wholly for the best

---

literary society. Seneca (*Ep.* cxiv. 13), Persius (i. 76), and Tacitus (*Dial.*
23) deride the imitators of the early poets of the republic. But virtually
no trace of pronounced imitation of this kind is to be observed in the
poetry that has survived. Novelty and what passed for originality were
naturally more popular than the resuscitation of the dead or dying
past.

is due only in part to the intrinsic qualities of its teaching.
It is rather in its application that the fault lies ; it dominates
and crushes the drama instead of suffusing it and lending
it wings; it insists on preaching instead of suggesting. It
is too insistent and aggressive a creed to harmonize with
poetry, unless that poetry be definitely didactic in type and
aim. But it is admirably suited to be the inspiration of
satire, and it is therefore that the satire makes a far stronger
moral appeal than any other form of post-Augustan literature.

Satire apart, the period is in the main an age of *belles
lettres*, of ' the literary *gourmet*, the connoisseur, the *blasé*
and disillusioned man of society, passionately appreciative
of detail, difficulties overcome, and petty felicities of expression.'[1] It is the fashion to despise its works, and the fashion
cannot be described as unhealthy or unjust. Yet it produced
a few men of genius, while even in the works of those who were
far removed from genius, the very fact that there is much
refinement of wit, much triumphing over technical difficulties,
much elaborate felicity of expression, makes them always
a curious and at times a remunerative study. But perhaps
its greatest claim upon us lies in the unexpected service
that it rendered to the cause of culture. In the darkness
of the Middle Ages when Greek was a hidden mystery to
the western world, Lucan and Statius, Juvenal and Persius,
and even the humble and unknown author of the *Ilias
Latina* did their part in keeping the lamp alive and
illumining the midnight in which lay hidden the ' budding
morrow ' of the Renaissance.

---

[1] Boissier, *L'Opposition sous les Césars*, p. 238.

CHAPTER II

DRAMA

I

THE STAGE

THE drama proper had never flourished at Rome. The causes are not far to seek. Tragic drama was dead in Greece by the time Greek influence made itself felt, while the New Comedy which then held the stage was of too quietly realistic a type and of too refined a wit and humour to be attractive to the coarser and less intelligent audiences of Rome. Terence, the *dimidiatus Menander*, as Caesar called him, though he won himself a great name with the cultured classes by the purity and elegance of his Latin and the fine drawing of his characters, was a failure with popular audiences owing to his lack of broad farcical humour. Plautus with his coarse geniality and lumbering wit made a greater success. He had grafted the festive spirit of Roman farce on to the more artistic comedy of Athens. Tragedy obtained but a passing vogue. Ennius, Accius, and Pacuvius were read and enjoyed by not a few educated readers, but for the Augustan age, as far as the stage was concerned, they were practically dead and buried. The Roman populace had by that period lost all taste for the highest and most refined forms of art. The races in the circus, the variety entertainments and bloodshed of the amphitheatre had captured the favour of the polyglot, pampered multitude that must have formed such a large proportion of a Roman audience.

Still, dramatic entertainments had by no means wholly disappeared by the time of the Empire. But what remained was of a degraded type. The New Comedy of Athens, as transferred to the Roman stage, had given ground before the advance of the mime and the *fabula Atellana*. The history of both these forms of comedy belongs to an earlier period. For the post-Augustan age our evidence as to their development is very scanty. Little is known save that they were exceedingly popular. Both were characterized by the broadest farce and great looseness of construction ; both were brief one-act pieces and served as interludes or conclusions to other forms of spectacle.

The Atellan was of Italian origin and contained four stock characters, Pappus the old man or pantaloon, Dossennus the wise man, corresponding to the *dottore* of modern Italian popular comedy, Bucco the clown, and Maccus the fool. It dealt with every kind of theme, parodied the legends of the gods, laughed at the provincial's manners or at the inhabitants of Italian country towns, or depicted in broad comic style incidents in the life of farmer and artisan. Maccus appeared as a young girl, as a soldier, as an innkeeper ; Pappus became engaged to be married ; Bucco turned gladiator ; and in the rough and tumble of these old friends the Roman mob found rich food for laughter.[1]

The mime was of a very similar character, but freer in point of form. It renounced the use of masks and reached, it would seem, an even greater pitch of indecency than the Atellan. The subjects of a few mimes are known to us. Among the most popular were the *Phasma* or *Ghost* [2] and the *Laureolus* [3] of Catullus, a writer of the reign of Caligula. In the latter play was represented the death by crucifixion of the famous brigand ' Laureolus ' ; so degraded was popular taste that on one occasion it is recorded that a criminal was made to take the part of Laureolus and was crucified in grim earnest upon the stage.[4] In another mime of the principate of Vespasian the chief attraction was a performing dog,[5] which, on being given

---

[1] Macrobius (*Sat.* 10. 3) speaks of a revival of the Atellan by a certain Mummius, but gives no indication of the date.

[2] Juv. viii. 185.

[3] Suet. *Calig.* 57 ; Joseph. *Ant.* xix. 1. 13 ; Juv. viii. 187.

[4] Mart. *de Spect.* 7.

[5] Plutarch, *de Sollert. Anim.* xix. 9.

a pretended opiate, went to sleep and later feigned a gradual
revival in such a realistic manner as to rouse the wildest
applause on the part of the audience.

Both Atellan and mime abounded in topical allusions
and spared not even the emperors. Allusion was made to
the unnatural vices attributed to Tiberius,[1] to the deaths
of Claudius and Agrippina,[2] to the avarice of Galba,[3] to the
divorce of Domitian,[4] and on more than one occasion heavy
punishment was meted out to authors and actors alike.[5]

Legitimate comedy led a struggling existence. An inscription at Aeclanum [6] records the memory of a certain
Pomponius Bassulus, who not only translated certain
comedies of Menander but himself wrote original comedies ;
while in the letters of Pliny [7] we meet with Vergilius Romanus,
a writer of comedies of ' the old style ' and of *mimiambi*.
He possessed, so Pliny writes, ' vigour, pungency, and wit.
He gave honour to virtue and attacked vice.' It is to
be feared that such a form of comedy can hardly have been
intended for the public stage, and that Vergilius, like so
many poets of his age, wrote for private performance or
recitation. These two writers are the only authors of
legitimate comedies known to us during the Silver Age.
But both *fabulae palliatae* and *togatae*, that is to say, comedies
representing Greek and Roman life respectively, continued
to be acted on the public stage. The *Incendium* [8] of
Afranius, a *fabula togata*, was performed in the reign of
Nero, and the evidence of Quintilian [9] and Juvenal [10] shows
that *palliatae* also continued to be performed. But true
comedy had been relegated to a back place and the Silver
Age did nothing to modify the *dictum* of Quintilian,[11] *in
comoedia maxime claudicamus.*

As with comedy so with tragedy. Popular taste rejected

---

[1] Suet. *Tib.* 45.   [2] Ib. *Ner.* 39.
[3] Ib. *Galb.* 13.   [4] Ib. *Dom.* 10.
[5] Ib. *Calig.* 27 ; *Nero*, l. c. ; Tac. *Ann.* iv. 14.
[6] *C. I. L.* ix. 1165.   [7] *Ep.* vi. 21.
[8] Suet. *Ner.* 11.   [9] Quint. xi. 3. 178.
[10] Juv. iii. 93.   [11] x. 1, 99.

the Graeco-Roman tragedy as tedious, and it was replaced by a more sensuous and sensational form of entertainment. The intenser passions and emotions were not banished from the stage, but survived in the *salticae fabulae* and a peculiar species of dramatic recitation. Infinitely debased as were these substitutes for true drama, the forms assumed by the decomposition of tragedy are yet curious and interesting. The first step was the separation of the *cantica* from the *diverbia*. Lyric scenes or even important iambic monologues were taken from their setting and sung as solos upon the stage.[1] It was found difficult to combine effective singing with effective gesture and dancing, for music had become more florid and exacting than in the days of Euripides. A second actor appeared who supplied the gesture to illustrate the first actor's song.[2] From this peculiar and to us ridiculous form of entertainment it is a small step to the *fabula saltica*, which was at once nearer the legitimate drama and further from it. It was nearer in that the scenes were not isolated, but formed part of a more or less carefully constructed whole. It was further inasmuch as the actor disappeared, only the dancer remaining upon the stage. The words of the play were relegated to a chorus, while the character, actions, and emotions of the person represented by the words of the chorus were set forth by the dress, gesticulation, and dancing of the *pantomimus*. How the various scenes were connected is uncertain; but it is almost a necessary inference that the connexion was provided by the chorus or, as in modern oratorio, by recitative. To us the mimetic posturing of the *pantomimus* appears an almost ridiculous substitute for drama ; but the dancing of the actors seems to have been extraordinarily artistic and at times to have had a profound effect upon the emotions of the audience,[1] while the brilliant success in our own time of plays in dumb show, such as the famous *Enfant Prodigue*, should be a warning against treating the *pantomimus* with contempt.

This form of entertainment was first introduced at Rome

---

[1] Lucian, *de Salt.* 27.   [2] Suet. *Ner.* 24.   [3] Lucian, *de Salt.* 79.

in 22 B.C. by the actors Pylades and Bathyllus,[1] the former
being famed for his tragic dancing, the latter for a broader
and more comic style, whose dramatic counterpart would
seem to have been the satyric drama.[2] The satyric element
seems, however, never to have become really popular, the
fabula saltica as we know it dealing mainly with tragic or
highly emotional themes. Indeed, to judge from Lucian's
disquisition on the art of dancing, the subjects seem to
have been drawn from almost every conceivable source
both of history and mythology.[3] Many of these *salticae
fabulae* must have been mere adaptations of existing
tragedies. Their literary value was, according to Plutarch,
by no means high ; [4] it was sacrificed to the music and
the dancing, for the emotional effect of which Lucian can
scarcely find sufficiently high terms of praise.[5] The themes
appear to have been drawn from the more lurid passages
in mythology and history. If the libretto was not coarse
in itself, there is abundant evidence to show that the subjects chosen were often highly lascivious, while the movements of the dancers—not seldom men of the vilest character
—were frequently to the last degree obscene.[6] Inadequate
as this substitute for the drama must seem to us, we must
remember that southern peoples were—and indeed are--
far more sensitive to the language of signs, to expressive
gesticulation and the sensuous movements of the body [7]
than are the less quick-witted and emotional peoples of
the North ; and further, even if for the most part these
fabulae salticae had small literary value, distinguished
poets did not disdain to write librettos for popular actors.

---

1 Suet. *ap. Hieronym.* (Roth, p. 301, 25).

2 Plut. *Qu. Conv.* vii. 8. 3 ; Sen. *Contr.* 3. praef. 10.

3 Lucian, op. cit., 37–61.

4 Plut. *Qu. Conv.* iv. 15. 17 ; Libanius (Reiske) iii, p. 381.

5 Lucian, op. cit., 69 sqq.

6 e. g. Pasiphae, Cinyras and Myrrha, Jupiter and Leda. Lucian, l. c.;
Joseph. *Ant. Iud.* xix. 1. 13 ; Juv. vi. 63–6.

7 For the effect of such dancing cp. the interesting stories told by Lucian,
op. cit., 63–6. Cp. also Liban., iii, p. 373. For the importance attached
to gesture in ancient times see Quint. xi. 3. 87 sqq.

Passages from the works of Vergil were adapted for such performances ;[1] Lucan wrote no less than fourteen *fabulae salticae*,[2] while the *Agave* of Statius,[3] written for the dancer Paris, is famous from the well-known passage in the seventh satire of Juvenal. Nothing survives of these librettos to enlighten us as to their literary characteristics, and the other details of the performance do not concern us here.[4] It is sufficient to say that the *pantomimus* had an enormous vogue in the Silver Age, and won a rich harvest by his efforts, and that the factions of the theatre, composed of the partisans of this or that actor, were scarcely less notorious than the factions of the circus for the disturbances to which they gave rise.[5]

Of the musical recitations of portions of existing tragedies or of tragic episodes written for the occasion we possess even less knowledge. The passages selected or composed for this purpose were in all probability usually lyric, but we hear also of the chanting of iambics, as, for instance, in the case of the *Oedipus in Exile*, in which Nero made his last appearance on the stage.[6] Of the part played by the chorus and of the structure of the librettos we know nothing ; they may have been purely episodic and isolated or may, as in the *salticae fabulae*, have been loosely strung together into the form of an ill-constructed play. That they were sometimes written in Greek is known from the fact that the line quoted by Suetonius from the *Oedipus in Exile* mentioned above is in that language. Of the writers of this debased and bastard offspring of drama we know nothing save that Nero, who was passionately fond of appearing in them, seems also to have written them.[7]

The tragic stage had indeed sunk low, when it served almost entirely for exhibitions such as these. Nevertheless

---

[1] Story of Turnus ; Suet. *Ner.* 54. Dido ; Macrob. *Sat.* v. 17. 15.

[2] See p. 100.   [3] Juv. vii. 92.

For the general history of the pantomimus see Friedlaender, *Sittengeschicht*, II. iii. 3, and Lucian, *de Saltatione*.

[5] Dion. liv. 17 ; Tac. *Ann.* i. 54 and 77 ; Dion. lvii. 14.

[6] Suet. *Ner.* 46.   [7] See p. 7 note.

tragedy had not ceased to exist even if it had ceased to
hold the stage.[1]   Varius and Ovid had won fame in the
Augustan age by their Thyestes and Medea, and the post-
Augustan decadence was not without its tragedians.   One
only is mentioned by Quintilian in his survey of Roman
poetry, Pomponius Secundus.   Of him he says (x. 1. 98),
' Of the tragedians whom I myself have seen, Pomponius
Secundus is by far the most eminent ; a writer whom the
oldest men of the day thought not quite tragic enough,
but acknowledged that he excelled in learning and elegance
of style.'   Pomponius was a man of great distinction.[2]
His friendship for Aelius Gallus, the son of Sejanus, had
brought him into disgrace with Tiberius, but he recovered
his position under Claudius.   He attained to the consulship, and commanded with distinction in a war against
the Chatti in A.D. 50.   Of his writings we know but very
little.   Of his plays nothing is left save a brief fragment [3]
from a play entitled *Aeneas* ; whether it dealt with the
deeds of Aeneas in his native land or in the land of his
adoption is uncertain, though it is on the whole probable
that the scene was Italian and that the drama was therefore a *fabula praetexta*.   Whether his plays were performed
on the public stage is not quite clear.   Tacitus tells us of
riots in the theatre in A.D. 44,[4] when ' poems ' by Pomponius
were being recited on the stage.   But the words used by
the historian (*is carmina scaenae dabat*) point rather to the
recitation of a dramatic solo than to a complete tragedy
of the orthodox type.   Pomponius, dramatist and philologist,[5] remains a mere name for us.

---

[1] There is no clear proof of the performance on the Roman stage of
any tragedy in the strict sense of the word during the Silver Age.   The
words used e.g. in Dio Chrys. (19, p. 261 : 23, p. 396), Lucian (*Nigrin.* 8),
Libanius (iii, p. 265, Reiske) may refer merely to the performance of isolated
scenes.   See note on Vespasian's attitude to the theatre, p. 166.

[2] Pliny the elder wrote his life.   Plin. *Ep.* iii. 5.   Cp. also Tac. *Ann.*
v. 8 ; xii. 28 ; Plin. *N. H.* xiii. 83.

[3] Ribbeck, *Trag. Rom. Fr.* p. 268, fr. 1 ; p. 331 (ed. 3).

[4] *Ann.* xi. 13.

[5] Charis, *Gr. Lat.* i. p. 125, 23 ; p. 137, 23.

Another distinguished writer of plays was Curiatius Maternus, a well-known orator ; it is in his house that Tacitus places the scene of the *Dialogus*, and he is the chief character of the conversation. He had written his first tragedy under Nero,[1] and at the time of the *Dialogus* (A.D. 79–81) his *Cato*—a *fabula praetexta*—was the talk of Rome.[2] He had written another historical drama on the ancestor of Nero, L. Domitius Ahenobarbus, the persistent foe of Julius Caesar, who perished on the field of Pharsalia.[3] He had also written plays on the more hackneyed themes of Medea and Thyestes.[3] He had all the opportunities and all the requisite gifts for a successful public career, but his heart was with the Muses, and he resolved to quit public life and to devote himself wholly to poetry, for there, in his estimation, the truest fame was to be found.[4] Here our knowledge ends. Of the details of his life we are as ignorant as of his plays.

A few other names of tragic poets are known to us. Paccius wrote an *Alcithoe*,[5] Faustus a *Thebais* and a *Tereus*,[5] Rubrenus Lappa an *Atreus*,[6] while Scaevus Memor,[7] victor at the Agon Capitolinus and brother of Turnus the satirist, wrote a *Hercules* and a *Hecuba* or *Troades*.[8] Martial (xi. 9) styles him the ' glory of the Roman buskin ', but he too is but the shadow of an empty name. The tragedies of the age are lost to us, all save the tragedies of the philosopher Seneca, plays of which, save for one casual reference[9] in Quintilian, contemporary literature gives no hint, but which, however little they may have deserved it, were destined to have no negligible influence on the subsequent history of the world's drama.

---

[1] Tac. *Dial*. 11.   [2] Ib. 2, 3.   [3] Ib. 3.
[4] Ib. 11.   [5] Juv. vii. 12.   [6] Ib. vii. 72.

[7] He flourished in reign of Domitian. Schol. Vall. Iuv. i. 20 ; Mart. xi. 9 and 10 ; Donat. *Gramm. Lat.* iv. p. 537, 17 ; Apollin. Sid. ix. 266.

[8] In the fragment preserved by Donatus (Ribbeck, *Trag. Rom. Fr.* p. 269) the chorus address Hecuba under the name Cisseis. ' Fulgentius expos. serm. antiq. 25 (p. 119, 5, Helm) says *Memos* (Schopen emends to *Memor*) *in tragoedia Herculis ait : ferte suppetias optimi comites*.'

[9] xi. 2. 8

II

SENECA

Lucius Annaeus Seneca, one of the most striking figures among the great writers of Rome, was born at Cordova [1] about the opening of the Christian era, to be the most remarkable member of a remarkable family. His father, who bore the same name, was the famous rhetorician to whom we have already referred. His elder brother, M. Annaeus Novatus,[2] was adopted by L. Iunius Gallio, whose name he assumed, had a distinguished public career, and is best known to us, in his capacity of governor of Achaea, as the ' Gallio ' of the Acts. The youngest of the family, M. Annaeus Mela,[2] remained in the equestrian order and devoted himself to the acquisition of wealth, regarding this as the safest path to fame. He succeeded to some extent in his object, but his main claim upon our remembrance is as the father of the poet Lucan. Lucius Seneca came to Rome at an early age,[3] and, in spite of the bad health which afflicted him all his life long,[4] soon made his mark as an orator. Indeed, so striking was his success that—although he showed no particular eagerness for a political career—his sheer mastery of the Roman speech wakened the jealousy of Caligula,[5] who only spared his life on the ground that he suffered from chronic asthma and was not likely to live long, and contented himself, therefore, with mordant but not unjust criticism of the style of his intended victim.[6] But though oratory provided Seneca with the readiest means for the gratification of his not inconsiderable vanity, and for the exercise of his marvellous powers of wit and epigram, it was not the pursuit of rhetoric and its prizes that really held the first place in his heart. That

---

[1] Mart. i. 61, 7 ; *Poet. Lat. Min.* iv. p. 62, 19, Baehrens.

[2] Tac. *Ann.* xv. 73 ; xvi. 17.   [3] Sen. *ad Helv. de Cons.* xix. 2.

[4] Sen. *ad Helv.* l. c. ; *Ep.* lxxviii. 1.   Dion. Cass. lix. 19.

[5] Dion. Cass. l. c.   [6] Suet. *Calig.* 53. See ch. i. p. 4.

place was claimed by philosophy. His first love was
Pythagoreanism, which he studied under Sotion[1] of Alexandria, whose influence was sufficient to induce his youthful
pupil to become a convinced vegetarian. But his father,
who hated fads and philosophers, persuaded Seneca without much difficulty to 'dine better', and the doctrines of
Pythagoras were soon displaced by the more fashionable
teaching of the Stoics. From the lips of Attalus[2] he learned
all the principles of that ascetic school. 'I besieged his
class-room,' he writes ; 'I was the first to come, the last
to go ; I would waylay him when out walking and lead him
to discuss serious problems.' Whether he denounced vice
and luxury, or extolled poverty, Attalus found a convinced
disciple in Seneca. His convictions did not possess sufficient
weight to lead him to embrace a life of austere poverty,
but he at least learned to sleep on a hard mattress, and to
eschew hot baths, wine, unguents, oysters, and mushrooms.
How far his life conformed to the highest principles of his
creed, it is hard to say. If we are to believe his detractors,
he was guilty of committing adultery with the Princess
Julia Livilla, was surrounded with all the luxuries that the
age could supply, and drained the life-blood of Italy and
the provinces by extortionate usury.[3] During his long
exile in Corsica he could write a consolatory treatise to his
mother on the thesis that the true philosopher is never an
exile ;[4] wherever he is, there he is at home ; but little more
than a year later he writes another consolatory treatise to
the imperial freedman Polybius, full of the most grovelling
flattery of Polybius himself and of the Emperor Claudius,[5]
the same Claudius whom he afterwards bespattered with
the coarse, if occasionally humorous, vulgarity of the

---

[1] *Ep.* cviii. 17 sqq. ; Hieronym. *ad ann.* 2029. That he knew and never
lost his respect for the teaching of Pythagoras is shown by the frequency
with which he quotes him in the letters.

[2] *Ep.* cviii. 3 sqq.

[3] Cp. the speech of Suillius, Tac. *Ann.* xiii. 42 ; Dion. Cass. lxi. 10.

[4] *ad Helv. de Cons.* 6 sqq.

[5] *ad Polyb. de Cons.*

Apocolocyntosis.[1] He was tutor to the young Nero, but had
not the strength to check his vices. He sought to control
him by flattery and platitudes rather than by the high
example of the philosophy which he professed.[2] The
composition of the treatise *ad Neronem de Clementia* was
a poor reply to Nero's murder of Britannicus.[3] He could
write eloquently of Stoic virtue, but when he himself was
confronted with the hard facts of life over which Stoicism
claimed to triumph, he proved no more than a ' lath painted
to look like iron '. Such is the case against Seneca. That
it can be rebutted entirely it is impossible to claim.
But we must remember the age in which he lived. Its
love of debauchery was only equalled by its prurient love
of scandal. Seneca's banishment on the charge of an
intrigue with Livilla is not seriously damaging. The
accusation *may* have been true : it is at least as likely to
have been false, for it was instigated by Messalina. That
he lived in wealth and luxury is undoubted : his only
defence was that he was really indifferent to it ; he could
face any future ; he had, therefore, a right to enjoy the
present.[4] That he ground down the provincials by his
usury is possible ; the standard in such matters was low,
and the real nature of his extortions may never have come
home to him ; he must have depended largely on his
agents. With regard to his management of the young
princeps the case is different. Seneca was given an almost
impossible task. Neither his nature nor his surroundings

---

1 The *Apocolocyntosis*—almost undoubtedly by Seneca—hardly falls
within the scope of this work. Such intrinsic importance as it possesses
is due to the prose portions. In point of form it is an example of the
Menippean Satire, that strange medley of prose and verse. The verse
portions form but a small proportion of the whole and are insipid and
lacking in interest.

2 He was forbidden by Agrippina to give definite philosophical instruction. Cp. Suet. *Nero*, 52.

3 Cp. *ad Ner. de Clem.* ii. 2 ; Henderson, *Life of Nero*, Notes, p. 459.

4 For what may be regarded as an academic *apologia pro vita sua*, cp.
Ep. 5; 17; 20; *de Ira*, iii. 33 ; *de Const. Sap.* 1–4, 10–13 ; *de Vit. Beat.*
17–28, &c.

made Nero a suitable subject for moral instruction. Seneca must have been hampered at every turn. He must either bend or break. At least he won the respect of his pupil, and the good governance of the empire during the first five years of Nero's reign was due largely to the fact that the power was really in the hands of Seneca and Burrus.[1] Many of the weaknesses of his character may be accounted for by physical debility, and we must further remember that a Stoic of the age of Nero found himself in a most difficult position. He could not put his principles into full practice in public life without incurring the certain displeasure of the emperor. The stricter Stoic, therefore, like Thrasea, retired to the seclusion of his estates ' condemning the wicked world of Rome by his absence from it '.[2] Seneca, weaker, but possessed of greater common sense, chose the *via media*. He was content to sacrifice something of his principles to the service of Rome—and of himself. It is not necessary to regard him as wholly disinterested in his conduct ; it is unjust and absurd to regard him as a glorified Tartuffe.[3] Such a supposition is adequately refuted by his writings. It is easy for a writer at once so fluent and so brilliant to give the impression of insincerity ; but the philosophical works of Seneca ring surprisingly true. We cannot doubt his faith, though his life may at times have belied it. He reveals a warmth of human feeling, a richness of imagination, a comprehension of human failings and sorrows, that make him rank high among the great preachers of the world. Even here, it is true, he has his failings ; he repeats himself, has little constructive talent, and fails at times to conceal a passion for the obvious beneath the brilliance of his epigram. But alike in the spheres of politics and literature he is the greatest man of

---

[1] Dion. Cass. lxi. 4. 5.   [2] Tac. *Ann.* xvi. 28.

[3] This is Dion's view, lxi. 10.   For an ingenious view of Seneca's character see Ball, *Satire of Sen. on apotheosis of Claudius*, p. 34. ' It may be that Seneca cared less for the realization of high ideals in life than for the formulation of the ideals as such. Sincerity and hypocrisy are terms much less worth controversy in some minds than others.'

his age.   In literature he stands alone : he is a prose Ovid,
with the saving gift of moral fervour.   His style is terse
and epigrammatic, but never obscure ; it lacks the roll of
the continuous prose of the Augustan age, but its phrases
have a beauty and a music of their own : at their best they
are touched with a genuine vein of poetry, at their worst
they have a hard brilliance against the attractions of which
only the most fastidious eye is proof.   He towered over
all his contemporaries.   In him were concentrated all the
excellences of the rhetorical schools of the day.   Seneca
became the model for literary aspirants to copy.   But he
was a dangerous model.   His lack of connexion and rhythm
became exaggerated by his followers, and the slightest
lack of dexterity in the imitator led to a flashy tawdriness
such as Seneca himself had as a rule avoided.   He was
too facile and careless a composer to yield a canon for style.
The reaction came soon.   Involved, whether justly or not,
in the Pisonian conspiracy of 65 A.D., he was forced to
commit suicide.   He died as the Stoics of the age were
wont to die, cheerfully, courageously, and with self-conscious
ostentation.[1]   Within a few years of his death the great
Ciceronian reaction headed by Quintilian began.   The very
vehemence with which the Senecan style was attacked,
now by Quintilian[2] and later by Fronto,[3] shows what
a commanding position he held.

   He was poet as well as philosopher.   Quintilian tells us
that he left scarcely any branch of literature untouched.
' We possess,' he says, ' his speeches, poems, letters, and
dialogues.'[4]   Two collections of poems attributed to Seneca
have come down to us, a collection of epigrams and a collection of dramas.   There is strangely little external evidence
to support either attribution, but in neither case can there
be any serious doubt as to the general correctness of the
tradition.

---

[1] Tac. *Ann.* xv. 61-4.   [2] Quint. x. 1. 125-9.   [3] Fronto, p. 155, N.
[4] Quint. x. 1. 129.   Over and above his writings on moral philosophy
we possess seven books *ad Lucilium naturalium quaestionum.*

The *Anthologia Latina*, compiled at Carthage in the sixth
century, opens with seventy-three epigrams, of which three
are attributed by the MSS. to Seneca (*Poet. Lat. Min.* 1–3,
Baehrens). The first is entitled *de qualitate temporis* and
descants on the ultimate destruction of the world by fire—
a well-known Stoical doctrine. The second and third are
fierce denunciations of Corsica, his place of exile. The rest
are nameless. But there are several which can only be
attributed to Seneca. The ninth is entitled *de se ad patriam,*
and is addressed to Cordova by one plunged in deep misfortune—a clear reference to his banishment in Corsica,
The fifty-first is a prayer that the author's two brothers
may be happier than himself, and that ' the little Marcus
may rival his uncles in eloquence '. The brothers are
described one as older, the other as younger than the author.
It is an obvious inference that the brothers referred to are
Gallio and Mela, while it is possible that the little Marcus
is no other than the gifted son of Mela, Marcus Annaeus
Lucanus, the epic poet.[1] The fifteenth represents him as
an exile in a barren land : he appeals to a faithful friend
named Crispus, probably the distinguished orator Passienus
Crispus, the younger, who was consul for the second time in
44 A. D.[2] There are also other epigrams which, though
less explicit, suit the circumstances of Seneca's exile. The
fifth is written in praise of the quiet life. The author has
two brothers (l. 14), and at the opening of the poem cries,
' let others seek the praetorship ! ' In this connexion it
is noteworthy that at the time of his banishment Seneca
had held no higher office than the quaestorship. The
seventeenth and eighteenth are on the same subject, and
contain a solemn warning against *regum amicitiae,* appropriate enough in the mouth of the victim of a court intrigue.
Epigrams 29–36 are devoted to the praises of Claudius
for his conquest of Britain. Claudius had banished him

---

[1] *Patruos duos* more naturally, however, refers to Gallio and Mela,
in which case Marcus is the son of Seneca himself.

[2] Cp. *P. L. M.* iv. 15, 8; Plin. *N. H.* xvi, 242,

and was a suitable subject for flattery. For the rest the
poems are largely of the republican character so fashionable
in Stoic circles during the first century of the empire.   There
are many epigrams on Cato [1] and the Pompeys.   Others,
again, are of a rhetorical nature, dealing with scholastic
themes ; [2] others of an erotic and even scandalous character.
We can claim no certainty for the view that all these poems
are by Seneca, but there is a general resemblance of style
throughout, and probability points to the whole collection
being by the same author.   The fact that the same theme
is treated more than once scarcely stands in the way.   We
cannot dictate the amusements of a weary exile.   It would
be rash even to deny the possibility of his being the author
of the erotic poems.[3]   Philosopher as he was, he had been
banished on a charge of adultery : without in any way
admitting the truth of that accusation, we may readily believe that he stooped to one of the fashionable amusements
of the day, the composition of pointed and unsavoury verse ;
for the standard of morality in writing was far lower than
the standard of morals in actual life.[4]

The poems repay reading, but call for little comment.
They lack originality.   The thought is thin, the expression
neat, though scarcely as pointed as we might expect from
such an author, while the metre is graceful : the treatment
of the elegiac is freer than that of Ovid, but pleasing and
melodious.   At times powerful lines flash out.

> qua frigida semper   [1]
> praefulget stellis Arctos inocciduis (xxxvi. 6)

shines out from the midst of banal flattery of the emperor
with astonishing splendour.   The poem *de qualitate temporis*

---

[1] Where the cold constellation of the heaven gleams ever with un-
setting stars.

---

1 For these cp. *Ep.* xiv. 13 ; ib. civ. 29.
2 e. g. 71 'de Atho monte', 57 'de Graeciae ruina', 50 'de bono quietae
vitae', 47, 48 'morte omnes aequari', 25 'de spe'.
3 There is, in fact, direct evidence that he wrote such verses. Plin.
Ep. v. 3. 5.   4 Cp. p. 263.

(4) closes with four fine lines with the unmistakable Senecan ring about them—

> quid tam parva loquor ? moles pulcerrima caeli   [1]
> ardebit flammis tota repente suis.
> omnia mors poscit. lex est, non poena, perire :
> hic aliquo mundus tempore nullus erit.

Cato (9) deliberates on suicide with characteristic rhetoric, artificial in the extreme, but not devoid of dignity—

> estne aliquid, quod Cato non potuit ?   [2]
> dextera, me vitas ? durum est iugulasse Catonem ?
> sed, quia liber erit, iam puto, non dubitas.
> fas non est vivum cuiquam servire Catonem :
> quinetiam vivit nunc Cato, si moritur.

Cleverest of all is the treatment of the rhetorical theme of the two brothers who meet in battle in the civil war (72). The one unwittingly slays the other, strips the slain, and discovers what he has done—

> quod fuerat virtus, factum est scelus. haeret in hoste [3]
> miles et e manibus mittere tela timet.
> inde ferox : ' quid, lenta manus, nunc denique cessas ?
> iustius hoste tibi qui moriatur adest.
> fraternam res nulla potest defendere caedem ;
> mors tua sola potest : morte luenda tua est,
> scilicet ad patrios referes spolia ampla penates ?
> ad patrem victor non potes ire tuum,

[1] Why speak of things so small ? The glorious vault of heaven one day shall blaze with sudden self-kindled flame. Death calls for all creation. 'Tis a law, not a penalty to perish. The universe itself shall one day be as though it had never been.

[2] Is there then that which Cato had not the heart to do ? Right-hand, dost thou shrink from me ? Is it hard to slay Cato ? Nay, methinks thou dost hesitate no more, for thou shalt set Cato free. 'Tis a crime that Cato should live to be any man's slave ; nay, Cato truly lives if Cato die.

[3] What had been valour now is made a crime. The soldier halts by his foe and fears to launch his shafts. Then his courage rekindled. ' What ! coward hand, dost thou delay *now* ? There is one here whom thou shouldst slay sooner than the foe. Naught can assoil of the guilt of a brother's blood save only death; 'tis thy death must atone. Shalt thou bear home to thy father's halls rich spoil of war ? Nay, victor thus, thou

sed potes ad fratrem : nunc fortiter utere telo !
  impius hoc telo es, hoc potes esse pius.
vivere si poteris, potuisti occidere fratrem !
  nescisti : sed scis : haec mora culpa tua est.
viximus adversis, iaceamus partibus isdem
  (dixit et in dubio est utrius ense cadat).
ense meo moriar, maculato morte nefanda ?
  cui moreris, ferrum quo moriare dabit.'
dixit et in fratrem fraterno concidit ense :
  victorem et victum condidit una manus.[1]

This is not poetry of the first class, if indeed it is poetry
at all.   But it is trick-rhetoric of the most brilliant kind
without degenerating into bombastic absurdity.   There is, in
fact, a restraint in these epigrams which provides a remarkable contrast with the turgid extravagance that defaces
so much of the dramas.   This is in part due to the difference
of the moulds into which the rhetoric is run, but it is hard
to resist the belief that the epigrams—written mainly
during the exile in Corsica—are considerably later than
the plays.   They are in themselves insignificant ; they
show no advance in dexterity upon the dramas, but they
do show a distinct increase of maturity.

The plays are ten in number ; they comprise a *Hercules
Furens, Troades, Phoenissae* (or *Thebais*), *Medea, Phaedra*
(or *Hippolytus*), *Oedipus, Agamemnon, Thyestes, Hercules
Oetaeus*, and—sole example of the *fabula praetexta*—the

---

canst not go to meet thy sire.   But victor thou canst go to meet thy brother ;
now use thy weapon bravely.   This weapon stained thee with crime, 'tis
this weapon shall make thee clean.   If thou hast heart to live, thou hadst
the heart to slay thy brother ; thou *hadst* no such murderous thought,
but *now* thou hast ; this thy tarrying brings thee guilt.   We have lived
foes, let us lie united in the peace of the grave.'   He ceased and doubted
on whose sword to fall.   ' Shall I die by mine own sword, thus foul with
shameful murder.   He for whom thou diest shall give thee the steel
wherewith to die.'   He ceased, and fell dead upon his brother, slain by
his brother's sword.   The same hand slew both victor and vanquished.

[1] Cp. the not dissimilar situation in Sen. *Oed.* (936), where Oedipus meditates in very similar style, as to how he may expiate his guilt.   The
couplet *vivere si poteris*, &c., is nothing if not Senecan.

Octavia. Despite the curious silence of Seneca himself and of his contemporaries, there can be little doubt as to the general correctness of the attribution which assigns to Seneca the only Latin tragedies that grudging time has spared us. The *Medea, Hercules Furens, Troades, Phaedra, Agamemnon,* and *Thyestes* are all cited by late writers, while Quintilian[1] himself cites a line from the Medea as the work of Seneca. The name Seneca, without any further specification, points as clearly to Seneca, the philosopher, as the name Cicero to the great orator. The absence of any further or more explicit reference on the part of Quintilian to Seneca's achievements as a tragedian is easily explained on the supposition that the critic regarded them as but an insignificant portion of his work. Yet stronger confirmation is afforded by the internal evidence. The verse is marked by the same brilliant but fatiguing terseness, the same polish and point, the same sententiousness, the same succession of short stabbing sentences, that mark the prose works of Seneca.[2] More remarkable still is the close parallelism of thought. The plays are permeated through and through with Stoicism, and the expression given to certain Stoical doctrines is often almost identical with passages from the philosophical works.[3] Against

---

[1] Quint. viii. 3. 31 ('memini iuvenis admodum inter Pomponium ac Senecam etiam praefationibus esse tractatum, an "gradus eliminet" in tragoedia dici oportuisset') shows Seneca as critic of dramatic diction; there is no evidence to show what these *praefationes* were, but they *may* have been prefaces to tragedies. The *Medea* (453) is cited by Quintilian ix. 2. 8. For later quotations from the tragedies, cp. Diomedes, *gr. Lat.* i. p. 511, 23; Terentianus Maurus, ibid. vi. p. 404, 2672; Probus, ibid. iv. p. 229, 22, p. 246, 19; Priscian, ibid. ii. p. 253, 7 and 9; Tertullian, *de An.* 42, *de Resurr.* 1; Lactantius, *Schol. Stat. Theb.* iv. 530.

[2] Cp. also the iambic translation of Cleanthes, *Ep.* cvii. 11:—

duc, o parens celsique dominator poli,
quocunque placuit: nulla parendi mora est.
adsum impiger. fac nolle, comitabor gemens
malusque patiar, facere quod licuit bono.
ducunt volentem fata, nolentem trahunt.

[3] Some of the more remarkable parallels have been collected by Nisard (*Études sur les poètes latins de la décadence*, i. 68–91), e.g. *Med.* 163

these evidences the silence of Seneca himself counts for
little. We may charitably suppose that he rated his plays
at their just value. In any case a poet is under no compul-
sion to quote his own verses, or even to refer to them, in
works of a totally different nature.[1]

A more serious question is whether Seneca is the author
of all the plays transmitted to us under his name. The
authenticity of four of these dramas has been seriously
questioned. That the *Octavia* is by a later hand may be
regarded as certain. Seneca could hardly have dared to
write a play on so dangerous a theme—the brutal treatment
by Nero of his young wife Octavia. Moreover, Seneca
himself is one of the dramatis personae, and there are clear
references to the death of Nero, while the style is simple
and restrained, and wholly unlike that of the other plays.
It is the work of a saner and less flamboyant age.[2] The
Agamemnon and the *Oedipus* have been suspected on the
ground that certain of the lyric portions are written in a

'qui nil potest sperare, desperet nihil'. *Ep.* v. 7 'desines timere, si
sperare desieris'. *Oed.* 705 'qui sceptra duro saevus imperio regit, timet
timentes : metus in auctorem redit'. *Ep.* cv. 4 'qui timetur, timet :
nemo potuit terribilis esse secure'. *de Ira*, ii. 11 'quid quod semper in
auctores redundat timor, nec quisquam metuitur ipse securus?'—*Oed.*
980 sqq.; *de Prov.* v. 6 sqq.; *Phoen.* 146–53 ; *Ep.* xii. 10 ; *de Prov.* vi. 7 ;
Herc. F. 463, 464 ; *Ep.* xcii. 14.

[1] The arguments against the Senecan authorship are of little weight.
It has been urged (*a*) that the MSS. assign the author a *praenomen* Marcus.
No Marcus Seneca is known, though Marcus was the *praenomen* of both
Gallio and Mela, and of Lucan. Mistakes of this kind are, however, by
no means rare (cp. the 'Sextus Aurelius Propertius Nauta' of many MSS.
of that poet : both 'Aurelius' and 'Nauta' are errors). (*b*) Sidonius
Apollinaris (ix. 229) mentions three Senecas, philosopher, tragedian, and
epic writer (i.e. Lucan). But Sidonius lived in the fifth century A. D.,
and may easily have made a mistake. Such a mistake actually occurs
(S. A. xxiii. 165) where he seems to assert that Argentaria Polla, Lucan's
faithful widow, subsequently married Statius. The mistake as regards
Seneca is probably due to a misinterpretation of Martial i. 61 'duosque
Senecas unicumque Lucanum | facunda loquitur Corduba'. Not being
acquainted with the works of the elder Seneca the rhetorician, Sidonius
invented a new author, Seneca the tragedian.

[2] See ch. on Octavia, p. 78.

curious patchwork metre of a character fortunately unique in Latin lyric verse. The *Agamemnon* further has two choruses.[1] But in all other respects the language, technique, and metre closely resemble the other dramas. Neither objection need carry any weight. There is no reason why Seneca should not have introduced a double chorus or have indulged in unsuccessful metrical experiments.[2] Far more difficult is the problem presented by the *Hercules Oetaeus*. It presents many anomalies, of which the least are a double chorus and a change of scene from Oechalia to Trachis. Imitations and plagiarisms from the other plays abound, and the work has more than its fair share of vain repetitions and tasteless absurdities. On the other hand, metre and diction closely recall the dramas accepted as genuine. It is hard to give any certain answer to such a complicated problem, but it is noteworthy that all the worst defects in this play (which among its other peculiarities possesses abnormal length) occur after l. 705, while the earlier scenes depicting the jealousy of Deianira show the Senecan dramatic style almost at its best. Even in the later portion of the play there is much that may be by the hand of Seneca. It is impossible to brand the drama as wholly spurious. The opening lines (1–232) may not belong to the play, but may form an entirely separate scene dealing with the capture of Oechalia : there is no reason to suppose that they are not by Seneca, and the same statement applies to the great bulk of ll. 233–705. The remainder has in all probability suffered largely from interpolation, but its general resemblance to Seneca in style and diction is too strongly marked to permit us to reject it *en bloc*. The problem is too obscure to repay detailed discussion.[3] The most probable

---

[1] Leo, *Sen. tragoed.* i. 89–134.

[2] It is not even necessary to suppose with Leo that these were the earliest of the plays and that these metrical experiments were youthful indiscretions which failed and were not repeated. Leo, i. p. 133.

[3] For a detailed treatment see Leo, i. p. 48. Melzer, *de H. Oetaeo Annaeano*, Chemnitz, 1890; *Classical Review*, 1905, p. 40, Summers.

solution of the question would seem to be that the work was left in an unfinished condition with inconsistencies, self-plagiarisms, repetitions, and absurdities which revision would have removed ; this unfinished drama was then worked over and corrected by a stupid, but careful student of Seneca.

There is such a complete absence of evidence as to the period of Seneca's life during which these dramas were composed, that much ingenuity has been wasted in attempts to solve the problem. The view most widely held—why it should be held is a mystery—is that they were composed during Seneca's exile in Corsica (41–9 A.D.).[1] Others, again, hold that they were written for the delectation of the young Nero, who had early betrayed a taste for the stage. This view has nothing to support it save the accusation mentioned by Tacitus,[2] to the effect that the patronage and approval of Nero led Seneca to write verse more frequently than his wont. Direct evidence there is none, but the general crudity of the work, coupled with the pedantic hardness and rigidity of the Stoicism which pervades the plays, points strongly to an early date, considerably earlier than the exile in Corsica. There is no trace of the mature experience and feeling for humanity that characterize the later philosophical works. On the contrary, these plays are just what might be expected of a young man fresh from the schools of rhetoric and philosophy.[3] As to the order in which the plays were written there is practically nothing to guide us.[4] The *Hercules Oetaeus* is probably

---

[1] See p. 39 on relation of epigrams to dramas.   [2] *Ann.* xiv. 52.

[3] See also note on p. 42 for Leo's ingenious, but inconclusive theory for the dates of the *Agamemnon* and *Oedipus*.

[4] There is but one passage that can be held to afford the slightest evidence for a later date, *Med.* 163 ' qui nil potest sperare, desperet nihil ' seems to be an echo of *Ep.* v. 7 ' sed ut huius quoque diei lucellum tecum communicem, apud Hecatonem nostrum inveni . . . " desines ", inquit, " timere, si sperare desieris " .' This aphorism is quoted as newly found. The letters were written 62–5 A.D. This passage would therefore suggest a very late date for the *Medea*. But Seneca had probably been long familiar with the works of Hecato, and the epigram is not of such profundity that it might not have occurred to Seneca independently.

the latest, for in it we find plagiarisms from the *Hercules Furens, Oedipus, Thyestes, Phoenissae, Phaedra,* and *Troades.* Even here, however, there is an element of uncertainty, for it is impossible to ascertain whether any given plagiarism is due to Seneca or to his interpolators.

Leaving such barren and unprofitable ground, what can we say of the plays themselves ? Even after making due allowance for the hopeless decline of dramatic taste and for the ruin wrought by the schools of rhetoric, it is hard to speak with patience of such productions, when we recall the brilliance and charm of the prose works of Seneca. We can forgive him being rhetorical when he speaks for himself ; when he speaks through the lips of others he is less easily tolerable.

Drama is a reading of human life : if it is to hold one's interest it must deal with the feelings, thought, and action of genuine human beings and represent their complex inter-action : the characters must be real and must differ one from the other, so that by force of contrast and by the continued play of diverse aspects and developments of the human soul, the significance, the pathos, and the power of the fragment of human life selected for representation may be fully brought out and set before our eyes. If these characteristics be absent, the drama must of necessity be an artistic failure by reason of its lack of truth. But it requires also plot, with a logical growth leading to some great climax and developing a growing suspense in the spectator as to what shall be the end. It is true that plot without reality may give us a successful melodrama, that truth of character-drawing with a minimum of plot may move and interest us. But in neither case shall we have drama in its truest and noblest form.

Seneca gives us neither the half nor the whole. The stage is ultimately the touchstone of dramatic excellence. But if it is to be such a touchstone, it must have an audience with a penetration of intelligence and a soundness of taste such as had long ceased to characterize Roman audiences. The Senecan drama has lost touch with the stage and lacks

both unity and life. Such superficial unity as his plots
possess is due to the fact that they are ultimately imitations of Greek [1] drama. A full discussion of the plots is
neither necessary here nor possible. A few instances of
Seneca's treatment of his material must suffice.[2] He has
no sense of logical development ; the lack of sequence
and of proportion traceable in the letters is more painfully
evident in the tragedies.

The *Hercules Furens* supplies an excellent example of
the weakness of the Senecan plot. It is based on the
'Ηρακλῆς μαινόμενος of Euripides, and such unity as it
possesses is in the main due to that fact. It is in his chief
divergences from the Euripidean treatment of the story
that his deficiencies become most apparent. Theseus
appears early in the play merely that he may deliver a long
rhodomontade on the appearance of the underworld, whence
Hercules has rescued him ; and, worst of all, the return of
Hercules is rendered wholly ineffective. Amphitryon hears

---

[1] For comparative analyses of Seneca's tragedies and the corresponding Greek dramas see Miller's *Translation of the Tragedies of
Seneca*, p. 455.

[2] The *Phaedra* of Seneca is interesting as being modelled on the lost
Hippolytus Veiled of Euripides. Phaedra herself declares her passion to
Hippolytus, with her own lips reveals to Theseus the pretended outrage
to her honour, and slays herself only on hearing of the death of Hippolytus.
Cp. Leo, *Sen. Trag.* i. 173. The *Phoenissae* presents a curious problem.
It is far shorter than any of the other plays and has no chorus. It falls
into two parts with little connexion. I. (*a*) 1–319. Oedipus and Antigone
are on their way to Cithaeron. Oedipus meditates suicide and is dissuaded by Antigone. (*b*) 320–62. An embassy from Thebes arrives
begging Oedipus to return and stop the threatened war between his sons.
He refuses, and declares the intention of hiding near the field of battle
and listening joyfully to the conflict between his unnatural sons. II. The
remaining portion, on the other hand, seems to imply that Oedipus is still
in Thebes (553, 623), and represents a scene between Jocasta and her
sons. It lacks a conclusion. These two different scenes can hardly have
belonged to one and the same play. They may be fragments of two
separate plays, an *Oedipus Coloneus* and a *Phoenissae*, or may equally
well be two isolated scenes written for declamation without ever having
been intended for embodiment in two completed dramas. Cp. Ribbeck,
Gesch. Röm. Dichtung, iii. 70.

the approaching steps of Hercules as he bursts his way to
the upper world and cries (523)—

est est sonitus Herculei gradus.

The chorus then, as if they had heard nothing, deliver themselves of a chant that describes Hercules as still a prisoner
in Hades.   When Hercules at last is allowed to appear,
he appears alone, and delivers a long ranting glorification
of himself (592–617) before he is joined by his father, wife,
and children.   As Leo has remarked,[1] this episode has been
tastelessly torn into two fragments merely to give Hercules
an opportunity for turgid declamation.

The *Medea*, again, is, on the whole, Euripidean in form,
though it probably owes much to the influence of Ovid.[2]
It is, moreover, the least tasteless and best constructed of
his tragedies.   It loses comparatively little by the omission
of the Aegeus episode, but suffers terribly by the insertion
of a bombastic description of Medea's incantations.   The
love of the Silver Age for rhetoric has converted Medea
into a skilful rhetorician, its love for the black art has
degraded her to a vulgar sorceress.   Nothing, again, can be
cruder or more awkward than the manner in which the news
of the death of Creon and his daughter is announced.   After
an interval so brief as scarcely to suffice even for the con-
veyance of the poisoned gifts to the palace, in rushes a
messenger crying (879)—

> periere cuncta, concidit regni status.   [1]
> nata atque genitor cinere permixto iacent.
> *Cho.* qua fraude capti ? *Nunt.* qua solent reges capi,
> donis. *Cho.* in illis esse quis potuit dolus ?
> *Nunt.* et ipse miror vixque iam facto malo
> potuisse fieri credo ; quis cladis modus ?

----

[1] All is lost ! the kingdom's fallen ! Father and daughter lie in
mingled dust !
Ch. By what snare taken ?
Mess. By gifts, the snare of kings.
Ch. What harm could lurk in them ?
Mess. Myself I marvel, and scarce though the deed is done can I believe

----

1 *Sen, Trag.* i. 161,   2 Leo, op. cit., i. 166 sqq.

avidus per omnem regiae partem furit
ut iussus ignis : iam domus tota occidit,
urbi timetur. *Cho.* unda flammas opprimat.
Nunt. et hoc in ista clade mirandum accidit,
alit unda flammas, quoque prohibetur magis,
magis ardet ignis : ipsa praesidia occupat.

That is all : if we had not read Euripides we should scarcely
understand the connexion between the gifts and the
mysterious fire.   Seneca, with the lack of proportion dis-
played in nearly all his dramas, has spent so much time
in describing the wholly irrelevant and absurd details of
Medea's incantations that he finds no room to give what
might be a really dramatic description of the all-important
catastrophe in which Medea's vengeance finds issue.   There
is hardly a play which will not provide similar instances
of the lack of genuine constructive power.   In the *Oedipus*
we get the same long narrative of horror that has disfigured
the *Hercules Furens* and the *Medea.*   Creon describes to
us the dark rites of incantation used to evoke the shade
of Laius.[1]   In the *Phaedra* we find what at first would
seem to be a clever piece of stagecraft.   Hippolytus, scandalized at Phaedra's avowal of her incestuous passion,
seizes her by the hair and draws his sword as though to
slay her.   He changes his purpose, but the nurse has seen
him and calls for aid, denouncing Hippolytus' violence and
clearly intending to make use of it as damning evidence
against him.   But the chorus refuse to credit her, and the

it possible. How died they ? Devouring flames rage through all the
palace as at her command. Now the whole house is fallen and men fear
for the city.
Ch. Let water quench the flames.
Mess. Nay, in this overthrow is this added wonder. Water feeds the
flames and opposition makes the fire burn fiercer. It hath seared even
that which should have stayed its power.

[1] 530–658. The *Oedipus* is based on the *O. Rex* of Sophocles, but
is much compressed, and the beautiful proportions of the Greek are lost.
In Seneca out of a total of 1,060 lines 330 are occupied by the lyric measures
of the chorus, 230 by descriptions of omens and necromancy.

incident falls flat.[1] Everywhere there is the same casual
workmanship. If we stop short of denying to Seneca the
possession of any dramatic talent, it is at any rate hard
to resist the conviction that he treated the plays as a
parergon, spending little thought or care on their *ensemble*,
though at times working up a scene or scenes with an
elaboration and skill as unmistakable as it is often misdirected.

The plays are, in fact, as Nisard has admirably put it,
drames de recette. The recipe consists in the employment
of three ingredients—description, declamation, and philosophic aphorism. There is room for all these ingredients
in drama as in human life, but in Seneca there is little else :
these three elements conspire together to swamp the drama,
and they do this the more effectively because, for all their
cleverness, Seneca's description and declamation are radically bad. It is but rarely that he shows himself capable of
simple and natural language. If a tragic event enacted
off the stage requires description, it must outdo all other
descriptions of the same type. And seeing that one of the
chief uses of narrative in tragedy is to present to the imagination of the audience events which are too horrible for their
eyes, the result in Seneca's hands is often little less than
revolting. For example, the self-blinding of Oedipus is set
forth with every detail of horror, possible and impossible,
till the imagination sickens.

(961)   gemuit et dirum fremens
          manus in ora torsit, at contra truces

---

1 It is also to be noted that the nurse does not make use of this device
till after Hippolytus has left the stage, although to be really effective her
words should have been uttered while Hippolytus held Phaedra by the
hair. The explanation is, I think, that the play was written for recitation,
not for acting. Had the play been acted, the nurse's call for help and
her accusation of Hippolytus could have been brought in while Hippolytus was struggling with Phaedra. But being written for recitation
by a single person there was not room for the speech at the really
critical moment, and therefore it was inserted afterwards—too late.
See p. 73,

oculi steterunt et suam intenti manum
ultro insequuntur, vulneri occurrunt suo.
scrutatur avidus manibus uncis lumina,
radice ab ima funditus vulsos simul
evolvit orbes; haeret in vacuo manus
et fixa penitus unguibus lacerat cavos
alte recessus luminum et inanes sinus
saevitque frustra plusque quam satis est furit.

The last line is an epitome of Seneca's methods of description. Yet more revolting is the speech of the messenger
describing the banquet, at which Atreus placed the flesh
of Thyestes' murdered sons before their father (623–788).
Nothing is spared us, much that is impossible is added.[1]
At times, moreover, this love of horrors leads to the introduction of descriptions wholly alien to the play. In the
Hercules Furens the time during which Hercules is absent
from the scene, engaged in the slaying of the tyrant Lycus,
is filled by a description of Hades from the mouth of
Theseus, who is fresh-come from the underworld. The
speech is not peculiarly bad in itself; it is only very long [2]
(658–829) and very irrelevant.

The effect of the declamation is not less unhappy.
Seneca's dramatis personae rarely speak like reasoning
human beings : they rant at one another or at the audience
with such overwrought subtleties of speech and rhetorical
perversions that they give the impression of being no
more than mechanical puppets handled by a crafty but
inartistic showman. All speak the same strange language, a
language born in the rhetorical schools of Greece and Rome.
Gods and mortals alike suffer the same melancholy fate.
Juno, when she declares her resolve to afflict Hercules
with madness, addresses the furies who are to be her
ministers as follows (*H. F.* 105) :

---

[1] Similarly, Medea, being a sorceress, must be represented engaged in
the practice of her art. Hence lurid descriptions of serpents, dark invoca-
tions, &c. (670–842).

[2] Seneca never knows when to stop. Undue length characterizes
declamations and lyrics alike.

concutite pectus, acrior mentem excoquat   [1]
quam qui caminis ignis Aetnaeis furit :
ut possit animo captus Alcides agi
magno furore percitus, nobis prius
insaniendum est—Iuno, cur nondum furis ?
me me, sorores, mente deiectam mea
versate primam, facere si quicquam apparo
dignum noverca ; vota mutentur mea :
natos reversus videat incolumes precor
manuque fortis redeat : inveni diem
invisa quo nos Herculis virtus iuvet.
me vicit et se vincat et cupiat mori
ab inferis reversus. . . .
                             pugnanti Herculi
tandem favebo.

She is clearly a near relative of that Oedipus who, in the
Phoenissae, begs Antigone to lead him to the rock where
the Sphinx sat of old (120) :

                         dirige huc gressus pedum,   [2]
hic siste patrem.   dira ne sedes vacet,

---

[1]   Distract his heart with madness : let his soul
        More fiercely burn than that hot fire which glows
        On Aetna's forge. But first, that Hercules
        May be to madness driven, smitten through
        With mighty passion, I must be insane.
        Why rav'st thou not, O Juno ?   Me, oh, me,
        Ye sisters, first of sanity deprive,
        That something worthy of a stepdame's wrath
        I may prepare. Let all my hate be change
        To favour. Now I pray that he may come
        To earth again, and see his sons unharmed ;
        May he return with all his old time strength.
        Now have I found a day when Hercules
        May help me with his strength that I deplore.
        Now let him equally o'ercome himself
        And me ; and let him, late escaped from death,
        Desire to die . . . And so at last I'll help
        Alcides in his wars.   MILLER.

[2]   Direct me thither, set thy father there.
        Let not that dreadful seat be empty long,

monstrum repone maius. hoc saxum insidens
obscura nostrae verba fortunae loquar,
quae nemo solvat.

       . . . saeva Thebarum lues
luctifica caecis verba committens modis
quid simile posuit ? quid tam inextricabile ?
avi gener patrisque rivalis sui
frater suorum liberum et fratrum parens ;
uno avia partu liberos peperit viro,
sibi et nepotes. monstra quis tanta explicat ?
ego ipse, victae spolia qui Sphingis tuli,
haerebo fati tardus interpres mei.

There is no need to multiply instances ; each play will
supply many. Only in the *Troades* [1] and the *Phaedra*
does this declamatory rhetoric rise to something higher
than mere declamation and near akin to true poetry. In
these plays there are two speeches standing on a different
plane to anything else in Seneca's iambics. In the *Troades*
Agamemnon is protesting against the proposed sacrifice of
Polyxena to the spirit of the dead Achilles (255).

But place me there a greater monster still.
There will I sit and of my fate propose
A riddle dark that no man shall resolve.

.   .   .   .

What riddle like to this could she propose,
That curse of Thebes, who wove destructive words
In puzzling measures ? What so dark as this ?
He was his grandsire's son-in-law, and yet
His father's rival ; brother of his sons,
And father of his brothers : at one birth
The grandame bore unto her husband sons,
And grandsons to herself. Who can unwind
A tangle such as this ? E'en I myself,
Who bore the spoils of triumph o'er the Sphinx,
Stand mute before the riddle of my fate.

                            MILLER.

[1] As a whole the *Troades* fails, although, the play being necessarily
episodic, the deficiencies of plot are less remarkable. But compared
with the exquisite *Troades* of Euripides it is at once exaggerated and
insipid.

quid caede dira nobiles clari ducis   [1]
aspergis umbras ? noscere hoc primum decet,
quid facere victor debeat, victus pati.
violenta nemo imperia continuit diu,
moderata durant ; . . .
                 magna momento obrui
vincendo didici. Troia nos tumidos facit
nimium ac feroces ? stamus hoc Danai loco,
unde illa cecidit. fateor, aliquando impotens
regno ac superbus altius memet tuli ;
sed fregit illos spiritus haec quae dare
potuisset aliis causa, Fortunae favor.
tu me superbum, Priame, tu timidum facis.
ego esse quicquam sceptra nisi vano putem
fulgore tectum nomen et falso comam
vinclo decentem ? casus haec rapiet brevis,
nec mille forsan ratibus aut annis decem.
. . . fatebor . . . affligi Phrygas
vincique volui ; ruere et aequari solo
utinam arcuissem.

The thought is not deep : the speech might serve for a
model for a *suasoria* in the schools of rhetoric. But there
is a stateliness and dignity about it that is most rare in
these plays. At last after dreary tracts of empty rant we
meet Seneca, the spiritual guide of the epistles and the
treatises.

---

[1] Why besmirch with murder foul the noble shade of that renowned
chief ? First must thou learn the bounds of a victor's power, of the
vanquished's suffering. No man for long has held unbridled sway ; only
self-control may endure . . . I myself have conquered and have learned
thereby that man's mightiness may fall in the twinkling of an eye. Shall
Troy o'erthrown exalt our pride and make us overbold ? Here we the
Danaans stand on the spot whence she has fallen. Of old, I own, I have
borne myself too haughtily, self-willed and proud of my power. But Fortune's favour, which had made another proud, has broken my pride. Priam,
thou makest me proud, thou makest me tremble. I count the sceptre
naught save a glory bright with worthless tinsel that sets the vain splendour
of a crown upon my brow. All this the chance of one short hour may take
from me without the aid of a thousand ships and ten long years of siege. . . .
I will own my fault . . . I desired to crush and conquer Troy. Would
I had forbidden to lay her low and raze her walls to the ground !

Far more striking, however, from the dramatic standpoint, are the great speeches in the *Phaedra*, where the
heroine makes known her passion for Hippolytus (600 sqq.).
They are frankly rhetorical, but direct, passionate, and to
the point. They contain few striking lines or sentiments,
but they are clear and comparatively free from affectation.
Theseus has maddened Phaedra by his infidelities, and has
long been absent from her, imprisoned in the underworld.
An uncontrollable passion for her stepson has come upon
her. She appeals to the unsuspecting Hippolytus for pity
and protection (619) :

> muliebre non est regna tutari urbium ;   [1]
> tu qui iuventae flore primaevo viges
> cives paterno fortis imperio rege,
> sinu receptam supplicem ac servam tege.
> miserere viduae. *Hipp.* Summus hoc omen deus
> avertat. aderit sospes actutum parens.

Phaedra then begins to show her true colours. ' Nay ! '
she replies, ' he will not come. Pluto holds him fast, the
would-be ravisher of his bride, unless indeed Pluto, like
others I wot of, is indifferent to love.' Hippolytus attempts
to console her : he will do all in his power to make life
easy for her :

> et te merebor esse ne viduam putes   [2]
> ac tibi parentis ipse supplebo locum.

These innocent words are as fuel to Phaedra's passion.
She turns to him again appealing for pity, pity for an ill
she dare not name—

> quod in novercam cadere vix credas malum.

He bids her speak out. She replies, ' Love consumes me

---

[1] 'Tis no woman's task to rule cities. Do thou, strong in the flower of
thy first youth, flinch not, but govern the state by the power thy father
held. Take me and shield me in thy bosom, thy suppliant and thy slave !
Pity thy father's widow.

Hipp. Nay, high heaven avert the omen. Soon shall my father return
unscathed.

[2] I shall prove me worthy of thee : so thou shalt not deem thyself
a widow. I will fill up my absent father's room.

with an all-devouring flame.' He still fails to catch her meaning, supposing that the passion of which she speaks is for the absent Theseus. She can restrain herself no longer : ' Aye, 'tis for Theseus ! ' she cries (646) :

Hippolyte, sic est ; Thesei vultus amo [1]   [1]
illos priores quos tulit quondam puer,
cum prima puras barba signaret genas
monstrique caecam Cnosii vidit domum
et longa curva fila collegit via.
quis tum ille fulsit ! presserant vittae comam
et ora flavus tenera tinguebat pudor ;
inerant lacertis mollibus fortes tori ;
tuaeque Phoebes vultus aut Phoebi mei,
tuusque potius—talis, en talis fuit
cum placuit hosti, sic tulit celsum caput :
in te magis refulget incomptus decor ;
est genitor in te totus et torvae tamen
pars aliqua matris miscet ex aequo decus :
in ore Graio Scythicus apparet rigor.
si cum parente Creticum intrasses fretum,
tibi fila potius nostra nevisset soror.
te te, soror, quacumque siderei poli

---

[1] Even so, Hippolytus ; I love the face that Theseus wore, in the days of old while yet he was a boy, when the first down marked his bright cheeks and he looked on the dark home of the Cretan monster and gathered the long magic thread along the winding way. Ah ! how then he shone upon my eyes. A wreath was about his hair and his delicate cheeks glowed with the golden bloom of modesty. Strong sinews stood out upon his shapely arms and his countenance was the countenance of the goddess that thou servest or of mine own bright sun-god ; nay, rather 'twas as thine own. Even so, even so looked he when he won the heart of her that was his foe, and lofty was his carriage like to thine. But in thee still brighter shines an artless glory, and on thee is all thy father's beauty. Yet mingled therewith in equal portion is something of thy wild mother's fairness. On thy Greek face is seen the fierceness of the Scythian. Hadst thou sailed o'er the sea with thy sire to Crete, for thee rather had my sister spun the magic thread. On thee, on thee, my sister, I call where'er

---

[1] Cp. Apul. *Met.* x. 3, where a step-mother in similar circumstances defends her passion with the words, 'illius (sc. patris) enim recognoscens imaginem in tua facie merito te diligo.'

in parte fulges, invoco ad causam parem :
domus sorores una corripuit duas,
te genitor, at me natus. en supplex iacet
adlapsa genibus regiae proles domus,
respersa nulla labe et intacta, innocens
tibi mutor uni. certa descendi ad preces :
finem hic dolori faciet aut vitae dies.
miserere amantis.[1]

Then the storm of Hippolytus' anger breaks. Here at
least Seneca has used his great rhetorical gifts to good
effect. The passion may be highly artificial when compared with the passion of the genuinely human Phaedra
of Euripides, but it is nevertheless passion and not bombast : crudity there may be, but there is no real irrelevance.

There is less to praise and more to wonder at in Seneca's
dialogue. Instead of rational conversation or controversy,
he gives us a brilliant but meretricious display of epigram,
the mechanical nature of which is often emphasized by
a curious symmetry of structure. For line after line one
character takes up the words of another and turns them
against him with dexterity as extraordinary as it is monotonous. The resulting artificiality is almost incredible. It
appears in its most extravagant form in the *Thyestes*.[2]
Scarcely less strained, though from the nature of the subject
the extravagance is less repellent, is a passage in the *Troades*.
Achilles' ghost has demanded the sacrifice of Polyxena.
Agamemnon hesitates to give orders for the sacrifice.

thou shinest in the starry heaven, on thee I call to aid my cause.
Lo ! sisters twain hath one house brought to naught—thee did the
father ruin, me the son. Lo ! suppliant at thy knees I fall, the daughter
of a king, stainless and pure and innocent. For thee alone I swerve
from my course. I have steeled my soul and stooped to beg of thee.
To-day shall end either my sorrow or my life. Pity, have pity, on her
that loves thee.

[1] This speech is closely imitated by Racine in his *Phèdre*.
[2] Cp. esp. 995–1006 : the *agnosco fratrem* of Thyestes is perhaps the
most monstrous stroke of rhetoric in all Seneca. Better, but equally
revolting, are ll. 1096–1112 from the same play.

Pyrrhus, Achilles' son, enumerates the great deeds of his father, and asks, indignantly, if such glory is to win naught save neglect after death. Agamemnon has sacrificed his own daughter, why should he not sacrifice Priam's? Agamemnon—in the speech quoted above—refuses indignantly. ' Sacrifice oxen if you will : no human blood shall be shed ! ' Pyrrhus replies (306) :

> hac dextra Achilli victimam reddam suam.   [1]
> quam si negas retinesque, maiorem dabo
> dignamque quam det Pyrrhus; et nimium diu
> a caede nostra regia cessat manus
> paremque poscit Priamus. *Agam.* haud equidem nego
> hoc esse Pyrrhi maximum in bello decus,
> saevo peremptus ense quod Priamus iacet,
> *supplex paternus. Pyrrh. supplices* nostri *patris*
> hostesque eosdem novimus. Priamus tamen
> praesens rogavit; tu gravi pavidus metu,
> nec ad rogandum fortis Aiaci preces
> Ithacoque mandas clausus atque hostem tremens.

Agamemnon retorts, ' What of your father, when he shirked the toils of war and lay idly in his tent ? '—

---

[1]   By this right hand he shall receive his own.
           And if thou dost refuse and keep the maid,
           A greater victim will I slay, and one
           More worthy Pyrrhus' gift: for all too long
           From royal slaughter hath my hand been free,
           And Priam asks an equal sacrifice.

Agam.   Far be it from my wish to dim the praise
           That thou dost claim for this most glorious deed—
           Old Priam slain by thy barbaric sword,
           Thy father's suppliant.

Pyrrh.   I know full well
           My father's suppliants—and well I know
           His enemies. Yet royal Priam came
           And made his plea before my father's face ;
           But thou, o'ercome with fear, not brave enough
           Thyself to make request, within thy tent
           Did trembling hide, and thy desires consign
           To braver men, that they might plead for thee.
                                   MILLER.

                  levi canoram verberans plectro chelyn.   [1]
Pyrrh. tunc magnus Hector, arma contemnens tua,
          cantus Achillis timuit et tanto in metu
          navalibus pax alta Thessalicis fuit.
Agam.   nempe isdem in *istis Thessalis navalibus*
          pax alta rursus Hectoris patri *fuit.*
Pyrrh. est *regis* alti *spiritum* regi dare.
Agam.   cur dextra *regi spiritum* eripuit tua ?
Pyrrh. mortem *misericors* saepe pro vita dabit.
Agam.   et nunc *misericors* virginem busto petis ?
Pyrrh. iamne immolari virgines credis nefas ?
Agam.   praeferre patriam liberis regem decet.
Pyrrh. *lex nulla* capto parcit aut poenam impedit.
Agam.   quod non vetat *lex*, hoc vetat fieri pudor.
Pyrrh. quodcumque *libuit* facere victori *licet.*
Agam.   minimum decet *libere* cui multum *licet.*

The cleverness of this is undeniable : individual lines (e.g.
the last) are striking.   Taken collectively they are ineffective ; we feel, moreover, that the cleverness is mere knack :
the continued picking up of the adversary's words to be
used as weapons against himself is wearisome.   It would
be nearly as great a strain to listen to such a dialogue as
to take part in it : the atmosphere is that of the school

------

[1]   Idly strumming on his tuneful lyre.
Pyrrh. Then mighty Hector, scornful of thy arms,
         Yet felt such wholesome fear of that same lyre,
         That our *Thessalian ships* were left in *peace.*
Agam. An equal *peace* did Hector's father find,
         When he betook him to Achilles' *ships.*
Pyrrh. 'Tis regal thus to spare a *kingly life.*
Agam. Why then didst thou a *kingly life* despoil ?
Pyrrh. But *mercy* oft doth offer death for life.
Agam. Doth *mercy* now demand a maiden's blood ?
Pyrrh. Canst thou proclaim such sacrifice a sin ?
Agam. A king must love his country more than child.
Pyrrh. No *law* the wretched captive's life doth spare.
Agam. What *law* forbids not, yet may shame forbid.
Pyrrh. 'Tis victor's right to do whate'er he *will.*
Agam. Then should he *will* the least, who most can do.
                                          MILLER.

of rhetoric, an atmosphere in which sensible and natural dialogue is impossible.[1]

The characters naturally suffer from this continued display of declamatory rhetoric. They have but one voice and language ; they differ from one another only in their clothes and the situations in which they are placed. It is true that some of them are patterns of virtue and others monsters of iniquity. But strip off the coating of paint, and within the limits of these two types—for there are but two—the puppets are precisely the same. There is none of the play of light and shade so essential to drama : all is agonizingly crude and lurid. This is not due to the rhetoric alone, there is another influence at work. The plays are permeated by a strong vein of Stoicism. Carried to its logical conclusion Stoicism lays itself open to taunts such as Cicero levels at his friend Cato in the *pro Murena*,[2] where he delivers a humorous *reductio ad absurdum* of its tenets. Such a philosophy is fatal to the drama. It allows no room for human sentiment or human weakness ; the most virtuous affections are chilled and robbed of their attractiveness : there are no gradations of temperament, intellect, or character : pathos disappears. The Stoic ideal was a being in whom the natural impulses and desires should be completely subjected to the laws of pure reason. It tends in its intensity to a narrowness, an abstract unreality which is unfavourable to the development of the more human virtues. What it gave with one hand the more rigid Stoic philosophy took away with the other. It

---

[1] For other examples of dialogue cp. esp. *Medea*, 159–76, 490–529 (perhaps the most effective dialogue in Seneca), *Thyestes*, 205–20 ; *H. F.* 422–38, for which see p. 62.

[2] *Pro M.* 61 ' Fuit enim quidam summo ingenio vir, Zeno, cuius inventorum aemuli Stoici nominantur : huius sententia et praecepta huiusmodi : sapientem gratia nunquam moveri, nunquam cuiusquam delicto ignoscere ; neminem misericordem esse nisi stultum et levem : viri non esse neque exorari neque placari : solos sapientes esse, si distortissimi sint, formosos, si mendicissimi, divites, si servitutem serviant reges,' &c. He goes on to put a number of cases where the Stoic rules break down.

preached the brotherhood of man and took away half the
value of sympathy. And here in the plays there is nothing
of the *mitis sapientia*, the concessions to mortal weakness,
the humanity, which characterize the prose works of Seneca
and have won the hearts of many generations of men.
There the hardness of Stoicism is softened by ripe experience
and a tendency to eclecticism, and the doctrinaire stands
less sharply revealed. ' Sous l'austérité du philosophe, on
trouve un homme.' The most noteworthy result of this
hard Stoicism upon the plays is the almost complete absence
of pathos springing from the tenderer human affections.
Seneca's tragedy may sometimes succeed in horrifying us,
as in the ghastly rhetoric of the *Thyestes* or the *Medea*.
He moves us rarely.

But there are a few striking exceptions to the rule, notably
the beautiful passage of the *Troades*, where Andromache
bids her companions in misfortune cease from useless
lamentation [1] (409) :

> quid, maesta Phrygiae turba, laceratis comas   [1]
> miserumque tunsae pectus effuso genas
> fletu rigatis ? levia perpessae sumus,
> si flenda patimur. Ilium vobis modo,
> mihi cecidit olim, cum ferus curru incito
> mea membra raperet et gravi gemeret sono
> Peliacus axis pondere Hectoreo tremens.
> tunc obruta atque eversa quodcumque accidit
> torpens malis rigensque sine sensu fero.
> iam erepta Danais coniugem sequerer meum,

[1] Why, ye sad Phrygian women, do ye rend your hair and beat your
woeful breasts and bedew your cheeks with streaming tears ? But light
is our sorrow, if it lies not too deep for tears. For you Ilium but now
has fallen, for me it fell long ago, when the cruel wheels of the swift car
of Peleus' son dragged in the dust the limbs of him I loved, and groaned
loud as they quivered beneath the weight of Hector dead. Then was
I overthrown, then cast to utter ruin, and since then I bear whatso falleth
upon me, with a heart that is numb with grief, chilled and insensible, and
long since had I snatched myself from the hands of the Greeks and followed

---

[1] Cp. Eurip. *Andr.* 453 sqq.

nisi hic teneret : hic meos animos domat
morique prohibet ; cogit hic aliquid deos
adhuc rogare—tempus aerumnae addidit.

Even here the pathos is the calm and reasoned pathos of
hopelessness, the pathos of a Stoic who preaches endurance
of evils against which his philosophy is not proof.   Here,
too, we find the Stoic attitude towards death.   Death is
the end of all ; there is naught to dread ; death puts an
end to hope and fear : to die is to be as though we had
never been (394) :

post mortem nihil est, ipsaque mors nihil,   [1]
velocis spatii meta novissima ;
spem ponant avidi, solliciti metum.
tempus nos avidum devorat et chaos :
mors individua est, noxia corpori
nec parcens animae : Taenara et aspero
regnum sub domino limen et obsidens
custos non facili Cerberus ostio
rumores vacui verbaque inania
et par sollicito fabula somnio.
quaeris quo iaceas post obitum loco ?
quo non nata iacent.

Death brings release from sorrow : the worst of torture is
to be forced to live on in the midst of woe—

-----

my husband, did not my child keep me among the living : he checks my
purpose and forbids me to die ; he constrains me still to make supplication
to heaven and prolongs my anguish.

Since naught remains, and death is naught
But life's last goal, so swiftly sought :
Let those who cling to life abate
Their fond desires, and yield to fate ;
Soon shall grim time and yawning night
In their vast depths engulf us quite ;
Impartial death demands the whole—
The body slays nor spares the soul.
Dark Taenara and Pluto fell,
And Cerberus, grim guard of hell—
All these but empty rumours seem,
The pictures of a troubled dream.
Where then will the departed spirit dwell ?
Let those who never came to being tell.   MILLER.

mors votum meum—cries Hecuba—(1171)   [1]
infantibus violenta, virginibus venis,
ubique properas, saeva : me solam times.

So, too, Andromache, in the passage quoted above, almost
apologizes for not having put an end to her existence.
Polyxena meets death with exultation (*Tro.* 945, 1152–9) :
even the little Astyanax is infected with Stoic passion for
suicide (1090) :

nec gradu segni puer   [2]
ad alta pergit moenia. ut summa stetit
pro turre, vultus huc et huc acres tulit
intrepidus animo. . . .
non flet e turba omnium
qui fletur ; ac, dum verba fatidici et preces
concipit Vlixes vatis et saevos ciet
ad sacra superos, sponte desiluit sua
in media Priami regna.

The enthusiasm for death is carried too far.[1] Even the
agony of the *Troades* fails really to stir us : it depresses
us without wakening our sympathy. So, too, with other
scenes : in the *Hercules Furens* we have the virtuous Stoic—
in the persons of Megara and Amphitryon—confronting
the *instans tyrannus* in the person of Lycus : it is the hackneyed theme of the schools of rhetoric,[2] but derives its
inspiration from Stoicism (426) :

---

[1]   O death, my sole desire, for boys and maids
Thou com'st with hurried step and savage mien :
But me alone of mortals dost thou fear.

MILLER.

[2] And with no lingering pace the boy climbed the lofty battlements, and
all about him cast his keen gaze with dauntless soul . . . But he alone
of all the throng who wept for him wept not at all, and, while Ulysses
' uttered in priestly wise the words of fate and prayed ' and called the
cruel gods to the sacrifice, the boy of his own will cast himself down to
death on the fields that Priam ruled.

---

[1] For still greater exaggeration cp. *Phoen.* 151 sqq. ; *Oed.* 1020 sqq.
[2] Cp. Sen. *Contr.* ii. 5 ; ix. 4.

Lyc. cogere. *Meg.* cogi qui potest nescit mori. [1]
Lyc. effare potius, quod novis thalamis parem
    regale munus. *Meg.* aut tuam mortem aut meam.
Lyc. moriere demens. *Meg.* coniugi occurram meo.
Lyc. sceptrone nostro famulus est potior tibi ?
Meg. quot iste famulus tradidit reges neci.
Lyc. cur ergo regi servit et patitur iugum ?
Meg. imperia dura tolle : quid virtus erit ?[1]
Lyc. obici feris monstrisque virtutem putas ?
Meg. virtutis est domare quae cuncti pavent.
Lyc. tenebrae loquentem magna Tartareae premunt.
Meg. non est ad astra mollis e terris via.[2]

So, too, a little later (463) Amphitryon crushes Lycus with
a true Stoic retort :—

Lyc.   quemcumque miserum videris, hominem scias. [2]
Amph. quemcumque fortem videris, miserum neges.[3]

Admirable as are the sentiments expressed by these virtuous
and calamitous persons, they leave us cold : they are too
self-sufficient to need our sympathy. Pain and death have
no terrors for them ; why should we pity them ? But it
would be unjust to lay the blame for this absence of pathetic

---

[1]   *Lyc.* Thou shalt be forced.
  Meg. He can be forced, who knows not how to die.
  Lyc. Tell me what gift I could bestow more rich
      Than royal wedlock ? *Meg.* Or thy death or mine.
  Lyc. Then die, thou fool. *Meg.* 'Tis thus I'll meet my lord.
  Lyc. Is that slave more to thee than I, a king ?
  Meg. How many kings has that slave given to death !
  Lyc. Why does he serve a king and bear the yoke ?
  Meg. Remove hard tasks, and where would valour be ?
  Lyc. To conquer monsters call'st thou valour then ?
  Meg. 'Tis valour to subdue what all men fear.
  Lyc. The shades of Hades hold that boaster fast.
  Meg. No easy way leads from the earth to heaven.

                                               Miller.
[2] *Lyc.* Whoe'er is wretched, him mayst thou know for mortal.
  Amph. Whoe'er is brave, thou mayst not call him wretched.

---

[1] Cp. Sen. *de Prov.* iv. 6 ' calamitas virtutis occasio est '.
[2] Cp. Sen. *Ep.* xcii. 30, 31 ' magnus erat labor ire in caelum '.
[3] Cp. Sen. *Ep.* xcii. 16 sqq.

power entirely on the influence of Stoicism. The scholastic
rhetoric is not a good vehicle for pathos, and must bear
a large portion of the blame, though even the rhetoric
is due in no small degree to the Stoic type of dialectic.
As Seneca himself says, speaking of others than himself,
'Philosophia quae fuit, facta philologia est.'[1]   And it must
further be remembered that of the few flights of real poetry
in these plays some of the finest were inspired by Stoicism.
The drama cannot flourish in the Stoic atmosphere, poetry
can. Seneca was sometimes a poet. His best-known
chorus, the famous *regem non faciunt opes* of the *Thyestes*
(345), is directly inspired by Stoicism. The speeches of
Agamemnon and Andromache, together with the chorus
already quoted from the *Troades*, all bear the impress of
the Stoic philosophy. The same is true of the scarcely
inferior chorus on fate from the *Oedipus* (980).

But there are other passages of genuine poetry where
the Stoic is silent. The chorus in the *Hercules Furens*
(838), giving the conventional view of death, will stand
comparison with the chorus of the *Troades*, giving the
philosophic view. The chorus on the dawn (*H. F.* 125)
brings the fresh sounds and breezes of early morning into
the atmosphere of the rhetorician's lecture-room. The
celebrated

> venient annis saecula seris   [1]
> quibus Oceanus vincula rerum
> laxet et ingens pateat tellus
> Tethysque novos detegat orbes
> nec sit terris ultima Thule (*Med.* 375)

has acquired a fictitious importance since the discovery
of the new world, but shows a fine imagination, even if—
as has been maintained—it is merely a courtly reference
to the British expedition of Claudius. And the invocation

---

[1] Late in time shall come an age, when Ocean shall unbar the world,
and the whole wide earth be revealed, and Tethys shall show forth a new
world, nor Thule be earth's limit any more.

---

[1] *Ep.* cviii. 24.

to sleep in the *Hercules Furens* proved worthy to provide
an inspiration for Shakespeare [1] (1063):

> solvite tantis animum monstris   [1]
> solvite superi, caecam in melius
> flectite mentem. tuque, o domitor
> Somne malorum, requies animi,
> pars humanae melior vitae,
> volucre o matris genus Astraeae,
> frater durae languide Mortis,
> veris miscens falsa, futuri
> certus et idem pessimus auctor,
> pax errorum, portus vitae,
> lucis requies noctisque comes,
> qui par regi famuloque venis,
> pavidum leti genus humanum
> cogis longam discere noctem :
> placidus fessum lenisque fove,
> preme devinctum torpore gravi.

But the poetry is confined mainly to the lyrics. In them,
though the metre be monotonous and the thought rarely
more than commonplace, the feeling rings true, the expression
is brilliant, and the never absent rhetoric is sometimes

---

[1] Save him, ye gods, from monstrous madness, save him, restore his
darkened mind to sanity. And thou, O sleep, subduer of ill, the spirit's
repose, thou better part of human life, swift-winged child of Astraea, drowsy
brother of cruel death, mixing false with true, prescient of what shall be,
yet oftener prescient of sorrow, peace mid our wanderings, haven of man's
life, day's respite, night's companion, that comest impartially to king
and slave, thou that makest trembling mankind to gain a foretaste of the
long night of death ; do thou bring gentle rest to his weariness, and sweet
balm to his anguish, and overwhelm him with heavy stupor.

---

[1] Cp. *Macbeth* ii. 2. 36, Macbeth does murder sleep, &c. For other
Shakespearian parallels, cp. *Macbeth*, Canst thou not minister to a
mind diseased ? *H. F.* 1261 ' nemo polluto queat | animo mederi.'
Macbeth, I have lived long enough. . . . And that which should accompany
old age, As honour, love, obedience, troops of friends, I must not look to
have. *H. F.* 1258 ' Cur animam in ista luce detineam amplius | morerque
nihil est ; cuncta iam amisi bona, | mentem, arma, famam, coniugem,
natos, manus.' J. Phil. vi. 70. Cunliffe, *Influence of Seneca on
Elizabethan Tragedy*.

transmuted to a more precious substance with a far-off
resemblance to true lyrical passion.   In the iambics, with
the exception of the passages already quoted from the
Troades and the *Phaedra*, touches of genuine poetry are
most rare.[1]   In certain of the long descriptive passages
(*H. F.* 658 sqq., *Oed.* 530 sqq.) we get a stagey picturesqueness, but no more. It is for different qualities that we read
the iambics of Seneca, if we read them at all.

Even in its worst moments the rhetoric is capable of
extorting our unwilling admiration by its sheer cleverness
and audacity.   A good example is to be found in the passage
of the *Thyestes*, where Atreus meditates whether he shall
call upon his sons Menelaus and Agamemnon to aid him
in his unnatural vengeance on Thyestes.   He has doubts
as to whether he is their father, for Thyestes had seduced
their mother Aerope (327) :—

> prolis incertae fides   **[1]**
> ex hoc petatur scelere : si bella abnuunt
> et gerere nolunt odia, si patruum vocant,
> pater est. eatur.

---

[1]   And by this test of crime,
           Let their uncertain birth be put to proof:
           If they refuse to wage this war of death
           And will not serve my hatred ; if they plead
           He is their uncle—then he is their sire.
           So to my work !
                  MILLER's translation slightly altered.

---

1 An exception might be made in favour of the beautiful simile describing
Polyxena about to die, notable as giving one of the very few allusions to
the beauty of sunset to be found in ancient literature (*Troad.* 1137) :

> ipsa deiectos gerit
> vultus pudore, sed tamen fulgent genae
> magisque solito splendet extremus decor,
> ut esse Phoebi dulcius lumen solet
> iamiam cadentis, astra cum repetunt vices
> premiturque dubius nocte vicina dies.

Fine, too, are the lines describing the blind Oedipus (*Oed.* 971) :

> attollit caput
> cavisque lustrans orbibus caeli plagas
> noctem experitur.

Equally ingenious is the closing scene between Atreus and Thyestes after the vengeance is accomplished and Thyestes has feasted on the flesh of his own sons (1100):

Thy. quid liberi meruere ? *Atr.* quod fuerant tui. [1]
Thy. natos parenti— *Atr.* fateor et, quod me iuvat,
    certos. *Thy.* piorum praesides testor deos.
Atr. quin coniugales ? *Thy.* scelere quid pensas scelus ?
Atr. scio quid queraris : scelere praerepto doles,
    nec quod nefandas hauseris angit dapes ;
    quod non pararis : fuerat hic animus tibi
    instruere similes inscio fratri cibos
    et adiuvante liberos matre aggredi
    similique leto sternere—hoc unum obstitit :
    tuos putasti.

These passages are as unreal as they are repulsive, but they are diabolically clever. Seneca's rhetoric is, however, as we have already seen, capable of rising to higher things, and even where he does not succeed, as in the passages quoted above from the *Phaedra* and *Troades*,[1] in introducing a genuine poetic element, he often produces striking

---

[1] *Thy.* What was my children's sin ?
  Atr. This, that they were thy children.
  Thy.   But to think
  That children to the father ——
  Atr.   That indeed,
  I do confess it, gives me greatest joy,
  That thou art well assured they were thy sons.
  Thy. I call upon the gods of innocence——
  Atr. Why not upon the gods of marriage call ?
  Thy. Why dost thou seek to punish crime with crime ?
  Atr. Well do I know the cause of thy complaint :
  Because I have forestalled thee in the deed.
  Thou grievest, not because thou hast consumed
  This horrid feast, but that thou wast not first
  To set it forth. This was thy fell intent,
  To arrange a feast like this unknown to me,
  And with their mother's aid attack my sons,
  And with a like destruction lay them low.
  But this one thing opposed—thou thought'st them thine.
                                MILLER.

---

[1] pp. 52 sqq., 59.

declamatory effects. The exit of the blind Oedipus, as he goes forth into life-long banishment, bringing peace to Thebes at the last, is highly artificial in form, but, given the rhetorical drama, is not easily surpassed as a conclusion—

> mortifera mecum vitia terrarum extraho.   [1]
> violenta Fata et horridus Morbi tremor,
> Maciesque et atra Pestis et rabidus Dolor,
> mecum ite, mecum. ducibus his uti libet (1058).

So likewise the last despairing cry of Jason, as Medea sails victoriously away in her magic car—

> per alta vade spatia sublimi aethere,   [2]
> testare nullos esse qua veheris deos

forms a magnificent ending to a play which, for all its unreality, succeeds for more than half its length (1–578) in arresting our attention by its ingenious rhetoric and its comparative freedom from mere bombast. Excellent, too, is the speech (*Phoen.* 193) in which Antigone dissuades her father from suicide. 'What ills can time have in store for him compared to those he has endured?'—

> qui fata proculcavit ac vitae bona   [3]
> proiecit atque abscidit et casus suos
> oneravit ipse, cui deo nullo est opus,
> quare ille mortem cupiat aut quare petat?
> utrumque timidi est: nemo contempsit mori
> qui concupivit. cuius haut ultra mala

---

[1] With me to exile lead I forth 'all pestilential humours of the land. Ye blasting fates', ye trembling agues, famine and deadly plague and maddened grief, go forth with me, with me! My heart rejoices to follow in your train.

[2] Sail on through the airy depths of highest heaven, and bear witness that, where thou soarest, no gods can be.

[3]   Who tramples under foot his destiny,
Who disregards and scorns the goods of life,
And aggravates the evils of his lot,
Who has no further need of Providence:
Wherefore should such a man desire to die,
Or seek for death? Each is the coward's act.
No one holds death in scorn who seeks to die.
The man whose evils can no further go

exire possunt, in loco tuto est situs.
quis iam deorum, velle fac, quicquam potest
malis tuis adicere ? iam nec tu potes
nisi hoc, ut esse te putes dignum nece—
non es nec ulla pectus hoc culpa attigit.
et hoc magis te, genitor, insontem voca,
quod innocens es dis quoque invitis. . . .
. . . . . . quidquid potest
auferre cuiquam mors, tibi hoc vita abstulit.

It is, however, in isolated lines and striking *sententiae*
that Seneca's gift for rhetorical epigram is seen at its best.
Nothing could be better turned than

quaeris Alcidae parem ?   [1]
nemo est nisi ipse : (*H. F.* 84).
curae leves loquuntur, ingentes stupent (*Phaedra* 607). [2]
fortem facit vicina libertas senem (*Phaedra* 139).   [3]
qui genus iactat suum,
aliena laudat (*H. F.* 340).
fortuna fortes metuit, ignavos premit (*Med.* 159).
fortuna opes auferre, non animum potest (*Med.* 176).
maius est monstro nefas :   [4]
nam monstra fato, moribus scelera imputes (*Phaedra* 143).

Is safely lodged. Who of the gods, think'st thou,
Grant that he wills it so, can add one jot
Unto thy sum of trouble ? Nor canst thou,
Save that thou deem'st thyself unfit to live.
But thou art not unfit, for in thy breast
No taint of sin has come. And all the more,
My father, art thou free from taint of sin,
Because, though heaven willed it otherwise,
Thou still art innocent. . . .
Whatever death
From any man can take, thy life hath taken.   MILLER.
[1] Cp. Theobald : None but himself can be his parallel.
[2] Cp. Sir W. Raleigh : Passions are best compared with floods and
streams, The shallow murmur but the deep are dumb.
[3]   For dawning freedom makes the aged brave.   MILLER.
[4]   For thy impious love is worse
Than her unnatural and impious love.
The first you would impute to character,
The last to fate.   MILLER.

If nothing had survived of Seneca's plays but a collection
of *sententiae*, we might have regretted his loss almost as
we regret the loss of Menander.

Here his merits, such as they are, end : they fail to
justify us in placing him high as a dramatist ; and he
has many faults over and above those incidental to his
style and modes of thought. While freer than most of his
contemporaries from the vain display of obscure erudition,
he falls into the common vice of introducing ' catalogues '.
They are dull in epic : in drama they are worse than
dull. The *Hercules Furens* is no place for a matter-of-fact
catalogue of the hero's labours, set forth (210–248) in
monotonous iambics from the mouth of Amphitryon. If
they are to be described at all, they demand the decora-
tive treatment of lyric verse,[1] nor is a catalogue of the
herbs used by Medea to poison the robe destined for her
rival any more excusable.[2] Again, like his contemporaries,
he shows a lack of taste and humour which in its
worst manifestations passes belief. Not a few of the
passages already quoted serve to illustrate the point.
But for fatuity it would be hard to surpass the words
with which Amphitryon interrupts Theseus' account of
the horrors of the underworld :

> estne aliqua tellus Cereris aut Bacchi ferax ? (*H. F.* 697.)

Scarcely less absurd is the chorus in the *Phaedra*, who,
when hymning the power of love, give a long list of
animals subject to such passion : the catalogue culminates
with the statement that even whales and elephants fall in
love (351) :

> amat insani belua ponti
> Lucaeque boves.

But all such instances pale before the conclusion of the
Phaedra. Not content with giving a ghastly and exaggerated account of the death of Hippolytus, Seneca must needs

---

[1] Cp. Eur. *H. F.* 438 sqq.
[2] For further examples cp. *H. F.* 5–18, *Troades* 215–19.

bring the fragments of his mutilated body upon the scene.
Theseus, at the suggestion of the chorus, attempts to put
them together again. The climax comes when, finding
an unidentifiable portion, he cries (1267) :

> quae pars tui sit dubito, sed pars est tui !

The actual language of the plays is pure and classical.
There is no trace of provincialism, nothing to suggest that
Seneca was a Spaniard. Its vices proceed from the false
mould in which it has been cast. There is a lack of connecting particles, and we proceed by a series of short rhetorical
jerks.[1] It is the style that Seneca himself condemns in
his letters (114. 1). Its faults are further aggravated by
the metre : taken line by line, the iambics of Seneca are
impressive : taken collectively they are monotonous in
the extreme. The ear suffers a continual series of stabs,
which are not the less unpleasant because none of them
go deep. The verse seems formed, one might almost say
punched out, by a relentless machine. It is never modified
by circumstances ; it is the same in narrative and dialogue,
the same in passion and in calm, if indeed Seneca can ever
be said to be either passionate or calm. Its pauses come
with monotonous regularity at the end of the line, diversified
only by an occasional break at the caesura in the third
foot. Nor does the rule [2] observed by Seneca, that only
a spondee or anapaest is permitted in the fifth foot, tend
to relieve the monotony, though it does much to give the
individual lines such weight as they possess. A more
complete contrast with the iambics of the early Latin
Tragedies cannot be imagined. What has been gained

---

[1] This terse stabbing rhetoric is characteristic of Stoicism ; the same
short, jerky sentences reappear in Epictetus. Seneca is doubtless influenced
by the declamatory rhetoric of schools as well, but his philosophical training probably did much to form his style.

[2] Exceptions are so few as to be negligible. The effect of this rule
is aggravated by the fact that in nine cases out of ten the accent of the
word and the metrical ictus ' clash ', this result being obtained ' by most
violent elisions, such as rarely or never occur in the other feet of the verse '.
Munro, J. Phil. 6, 75.

in polish has been lost in dignity. Whence the Senecan
iambic is derived, is a question which cannot be answered
with certainty. It is wholly unlike the early Roman
tragic iambic. Elision is rare, and there is little variety.
Instead of the massive and rugged measure of Pacuvius
or Accius, we have a finished and elegant monotony. In
all likelihood it is the lineal descendant of the iambic of
Ovid.[1] In view of Seneca's great admiration for Ovid—
he quotes him continually in his prose works—of Ovid's
mastery of rhetoric and epigram, and yet more of the distinct parallels traceable between the *Phaedra* and *Medea* of
Seneca and the corresponding *Heroides* of Ovid, it becomes
a strong probability that the Senecan iambic was deeply
influenced—if not actually created—by the iambic style of
the earlier poet's lost drama, the famous *Medea*.[2]

As to the models to which he is indebted for his treatment
of choric metres we know nothing. In spite of the fact
that he employs a large variety of metres, and that his
choruses at times stray from rhetoric into poetry of a high
order, there is in them a still more deadly monotony than
in his iambics. The chorus are devoid of life ; they are there
partly as a concession to convention, but mainly to supply
incidental music. Their inherent dullness is not relieved
by the metre. Of strophic arrangement there is no clear
trace ; in a large proportion of cases the choruses are written
in one fixed and rigid metre admitting of no variety : even
where different metres alternate, the relaxation is but
small, for the same monotony reigns unchecked within
the limits of each section. The strange experiments in
mixed metres in the *Agamemnon* and *Oedipus* show Seneca's
technique at its worst : they are composed of fragments
of Horatian metres, thinly disguised by inversions and
resolutions of feet : they lack all governing principle and
are an unqualified failure. Of the remaining metres the
Anapaestic, Asclepiad, Sapphic, and Glyconic predominate.

---

[1] The older and more rugged iambic survives in the fables of Phaedrus,
written at no distant date from these plays, if not actually contemporary.

[2] Cp. Leo, op. cit. i. 166, 174.

He is, perhaps, least unsuccessful in his treatment of the Anapaest : the lines do not lack melody, and the natural flexibility of the metre saves them from extreme monotony, though they would have been more successful had he employed the paroemiac line as a solemn and resonant close to the march of the dimeter. But one wearies soon of the eternal Asclepiads and Glyconics which he often allows to continue in unbroken and unvaried series for seventy or eighty lines together. He rarely allows any variation within the Glyconic and never makes use of it to break the monotony of the Asclepiad. Still worse are his Sapphics. Abandoning the usual arrangement in stanzas of three lesser Sapphics followed by an Adonic verse, his Sapphic choruses consist almost entirely of the lesser Sapphic varied by a very occasional Adonic. The continual succession of these lines without so much as an occasional change of caesura to diversify the rhythm is at times almost intolerable. At the close of such choruses we feel as though we had jogged at a rapid trot for long miles on a very hard and featureless road.

Language and metre work hand in hand with rhetoric to make these strange plays dramatically ineffective. So strange are they and in many ways so unlike anything else in Classical literature, that the question as to the purpose with which they were written and the place they occupied in the literature of their day affords an interesting subject for speculation. Were they written for the stage ? Decayed as was the taste for tragedy, tragedies may occasionally have been acted.[1] But there are considerations which suggest doubt as to whether the plays of Seneca were written with any such purpose. Even under Nero it is scarcely credible that the introduction of the mangled fragments of Hippolytus upon the stage would be possible or palatable.[2]

---

[1] See p. 29.

[2] These horrors go beyond the crucifixion scene in the Laureolus (see p. 24), and the tradition of genuine tragedy was all against such presentation. As far as the grotesqueness and bombast of the plays go, the age of Nero might have tolerated them. We must remember that seven-

Medea kills her children *coram populo*, and, not content with
killing them, flings their bodies at Jason from her magic
chariot high in air.   Hercules kills his children in full
view of the audience, not within the house as in the corresponding drama of Euripides.   Such scenes suggest that
the plays were written not for the stage but for recitation
with musical interludes from a trained choir.   Indications
that this was the case are to be found in the *Hercules
Furens*.   While the hero is engaged in slaying his children,
Amphitryon, in a succession of short speeches, gives the
details of the murder.   This would be ridiculous and
unnecessary were the scene actually presented on the stage,
whereas they become absolutely necessary on the assumption that the play was written for recitation.[1]   This
assumption has the further merit of being charitable ;
skilful recitation would cover many defects that would
be almost intolerable on the stage.

   It is improbable, however, that the drama of Seneca
occupied an important position in the literature of their
day.   The golden age of tragedy was past, and it is hard
to believe that these plays are favourable specimens even
of their own age.   The authors of the Silver Age virtually
ignore their existence, and, with the exception of two references in Tertullian and one in Apollinaris Sidonius, they
are quoted only by scholars and grammarians.

   They have small intrinsic value : but they afford interesting evidence for the taste [2] of their own day, and their
influence on modern drama has been enormous.   In the
Renaissance at the dawn of the drama's revival, Seneca

---

teenth-century England enjoyed the brilliant bombast of Dryden (e.g. in
Aurungzebe) and that the eighteenth delighted in the crude absurdities
of such plays as *George Barnwell*.

[1] Cp. also *Phaedra* 707, where Hippolytus' words, ' en impudicum crine
contorto caput | laeva reflexi,' can only be justified as inserted to explain
to the hearers what they could not see.   See also p. 48, note.

[2] They have been influenced by the pantomimus and the dramatic
recitation so fashionable in their day, inasmuch as they lack connexion,
and, though containing effective episodes, are of far too loose a texture to
be effective drama.

was regarded as a dramatist of the first order. Scaliger
ranked him above Euripides : it was to him men turned
to find models for tragedy. Everywhere we see traces of
the Senecan drama.[1] It is a tribute to the dexterity of
his rhetoric that his influence should have been so enormous,
but it is to be regretted in the interests of the drama.
For to Seneca more than to any other man is due the
excessive prominence of declamatory rhetoric, which has
characterized the drama throughout Western Europe from
the Renaissance down to the latter half of the nineteenth
century, and has proved a blemish to the work of all save
a few great writers who recognized the value of rhetoric,
but never mistook the shadow for the substance.

III

THE ' OCTAVIA '

A tragedy with this title is included by the MSS. among
the plays of Seneca. Its chief interest lies in the fact that it
is the one surviving example of a *fabula praetexta*, or tragedy,
drawn from Roman life. It deals with a tragic incident
of Nero's reign, the final extinction of the Claudian house.
Octavia, daughter of Claudius and Messalina, is the heroine.
Her life was one long tragedy. Her childhood was darkened
by the disaster that befell her unworthy mother, her maturer
years by her marriage to Nero. She was a mere pawn in
the game of politics. The marriage was brought about
by the designs of Agrippina, to render Nero secure of the
principate. To effect this end her betrothed Silanus was

---

[1] See R. Fischer, *Die Kunstentwicklung der englischen Tragödie* ;
J. W. Cunliffe, *Influence of Seneca on Elizabethan Tragedy* ; J. E. Manly,
Introductory Essay to Miller's *Translation of the Tragedies of Seneca*. The
Senecan drama finds its best modern development in the tragedies of
Alfieri. Infinitely superior in every respect as are the plays of the modern
dramatist, he yet reveals in a modified form not a few of Seneca's faults.
There is often a tendency to bombast, an exaggeration of character,
a hardness of outline, that irresistibly recall the Latin poet.

killed, Claudius, her father, and Britannicus, her brother,
dispatched by poison. Soon her own wedded life turned
to tragedy. Nero fell madly in love with Poppaea, and
resolved to put away Octavia. At Poppaea's instigation
she was accused of a base intrigue. The plot failed ; the
false charge could not be pressed home ; she was divorced
on the ground of sterility, and imprisoned in a town of
Campania. A rumour arose that she was to be reinstated ;
the mob of Rome declared itself in her favour and gave
wild expression to its joy. Poppaea's statues were cast
down, Octavia's replaced. Poppaea was furious. She laid
siege to Nero and won him to her will. The old false
charge of adultery was trumped up ; a complaisant freedman was found to confess himself Octavia's lover. She
was banished to Pandataria and slain (June 9, 62 A.D.).

The play gives us a compressed version of the tragedy.
It opens with a speech by Octavia's nurse, setting forth
the sorrows of her young mistress. The speech over, she
leaves the stage to be succeeded by Octavia, who, in a lament
closely modelled on the lament of the Sophoclean Electra,[1]
bewails the sorrows of her house, the deaths of Messalina,
Claudius, and Britannicus. The nurse reappears, attempts
to console her, and counsels submission to fate. Octavia
changes her strain and prays for death. After a lament
from the chorus, Nero and Seneca enter on the scene.
Seneca urges moderation and sets forth his ideal of mon-
archy. Nero is quite his match in argument, rejects his
advice, and, concluding with the words

> desiste tandem, iam gravis nimium mihi,   [1]
> instare : liceat facere quod Seneca improbat (588).

declares his intention of marrying Poppaea without delay.
An interesting chorus follows, describing how Rome of

---

[1]   Have done at last,
        For wearisome has thine insistence grown ;
        One still may do what Seneca condemns . . .
                                        MILLER.

---

[1] The debt is as good as acknowledged, ll. 58 sqq.

old expelled the kings for their crimes. Nero has sinned
even more than they. Has he not slain even his mother ?
There follows a long and interesting description of the
murder,[1] which serves as an introduction to the entrance of
the ghost of Agrippina in the guise of an avenging fury,
prophesying the dethronement and death of her unnatural
son. She is succeeded on the stage by Octavia, resigned
to the surrender of her position and content to be no more
than Nero's sister ; once more the chorus bewail her fate.
At last her rival Poppaea appears in conversation with
her nurse. The nurse congratulates her, but Poppaea has
been terrified by visions of the night and is ill at ease. Her
rival is not yet removed and her own place is still insecure.
At this point comes the one ray of hope that illumines this
sombre drama. A messenger arrives with the news that
the people have risen in Octavia's favour. But the reader is
not left in suspense for a moment. Nero appears and orders
the suppression of the *émeute* and the execution of Octavia.
The chorus mourn the fate of the beloved of the Roman
people. Their power and splendour is but brief : Octavia
perishes untimely, like Gracchus and Livius Drusus. She
herself appears in the hands of soldiers, being dragged off
to execution and death. Like Cassandra,[2] she compares
her fate with that of the nightingale, to whom the gods
gave a new life of peace full of sweet lamentation as a close
to her troubled human existence. One more song of con-
dolence from the chorus, one more song of sorrow from
Octavia, and she is taken from our sight, and the play
closes with a denunciation by the chorus of the hardness
of heart and the insatiate cruelty of Rome.

It is not hard to summarize the general effect of this
curious drama. Its author has read the Greek tragedians
carefully and to some purpose ; he has studied the characters
of Electra, Cassandra, and Antigone with diligence, if without
insight. He clearly feels deep sympathy for Octavia, and
to some extent succeeds in communicating this sympathy

---

[1] ll. 310 sqq.   [2] l. 915.

to the audience. His heroine speaks in character : she is
never a male Stoic, flaunting in female garb, she is a genuine
woman, a gentle, lovable creature broken down by misfortune. The other characters are uninteresting. Nero is
an academic tyrant, Seneca an academic adviser, Poppaea
is little more than a lay figure. The most that can be said
for them is that they do not rant. The chorus are on the
whole a fairly satisfactory imitation of a chorus of sympa-
thetic Greek women.[1] There is nothing forced or unnatural
about them ; they are real human beings ; their sympathy
is genuine, and its expression appropriate. But they are
dull ; monotonous lamentation in monotonous anapaests
is the height of their capacity. The play is a failure :
the subject is not in itself dramatic ; if it had been, it
would have been spoiled by the treatment it receives.
We are never in suspense ; Octavia has never the remotest
chance of escape ; our pity for her is genuine enough,
but her character lacks both grandeur and psychological
interest : the pathos of her situation will not compensate
us for the absence of a dramatic plot. The fall of the
house of Claudius compares ill with the tragedy of the
Pelopidae. And the treatment of the story, from the
dramatic standpoint, is childish. The play is scarcely
more than a series of melancholy monologues interspersed
with not less melancholy dirges from the chorus. The
most we can say of it is that it is simple and unaffected :
if it lacks brilliance, it also lacks exaggeration. Thought
and diction are commonplace and uninspired, but they
are never absurd—an extraordinary merit in a poet of the
Silver Age.

It will have been sufficiently evident from this brief
sketch that the *Octavia* is in all respects very different
indeed from the other plays that claim Seneca for their
author. It is free from their faults and their merits alike.
It never sinks to their depths, but it never rises to their

---

[1] There is no direct evidence of the sex of the chorus in the *Octavia*. In
Greek drama they would almost certainly have been women.

heights. Apart, however, from these general considerations,[1] there is evidence amounting almost to certainty that the *Octavia* is not by Seneca. The tragedy takes place in the lifetime of Seneca. Seneca himself figures in the play. The story is of such a nature that it could hardly have been written, much less published, in the reign of Nero. Yet more conclusive is the fact that the ghost of Agrippina prophesies the fate of Nero in such a way as to make it certain that the author outlived the emperor and was acquainted with the facts of his death.[2]

Who then was the author ? When did he write ? Evidence is almost absolutely lacking. From its comparative sanity and simplicity and its intense hatred of Nero it may reasonably be conjectured that it is the work of the Flavian age ; the age of the anti-Neronian reaction and of the return to saner models in life and literature. But there is no certainty ; it may have been written under Nerva, Trajan, or Hadrian. It stands detached and aloof from the literature of its age.

---

[1] The diction is wholly un-Senecan. There is no straining after epigram ; the dialogue, though not lacking point (e.g. the four lines 185–8, or 451–60), does not bristle with it, and is far less rhetorical and more natural. The chorus confines itself to anapaests, is simpler and far more relevant. The all-pervading Stoicism is the one point they have in common.

[2] The imitation of Lucan in 70, 71 ' magni resto nominis umbra,' is also strong evidence against the Senecan authorship.

CHAPTER III

PERSIUS

It is possible to form a clearer picture of the personality of Aulus Persius Flaccus, the satirist, than of any other poet of the Silver Age. Not only are the essential facts of his brief career preserved for us in a concise, but extremely relevant biography taken from the commentary of the famous critic Valerius Probus, but there are few poets whose works so clearly reveal the character of their author.

Persius was born at the lofty hill-town of Volaterrae, in Tuscany, on the 4th of December, 34 A. D.[1] He was scarcely six years old when he lost his father, a wealthy Roman knight, named Flaccus. His mother, Fulvia Sisennia, married again, but her second husband, a knight named Fusius, died after a few years of wedded life. Persius was educated at home up to the age of twelve, when he was taken to Rome to be taught literature by Remmius Palaemon and rhetoric by Verginius Flavus. Of the latter nothing is known save that he wrote a much-approved textbook on rhetoric and was exiled by Nero;[2] the former was a freedman whose remarkable talents were only equalled by his gross vices; he had a prodigious memory, was a skilful *improvvisatore*, and the most distinguished teacher of the day.[3] At the age of sixteen, shortly after his assumption of the *toga virilis*, the young Persius made the friendship which was to be the ruling influence of his life. He learned to know and love the great Stoic teacher, Cornutus, with an attachment that was broken only by death. It was from

---

[1] *Probus, vita.* 'A. Persius Flaccus natus est pridie non. Dec. Fabio Persico, L. Vitellio coss.' Hieronym. ad ann. 2050 = 34 A. D. 'Persius Flaccus Satiricus Volaterris nascitur.' Where not otherwise stated the facts of Persius' life are drawn from the biography of Probus.

[2] Quint. vii. 4, 40; Tac. *Ann.* xv. 71.

[3] Suet. *de Gramm.* 23.

Cornutus that he imbibed the principles of Stoicism, and at his house that he met the Greek philosophers, Petronius Aristocrates of Magnesia and the Lacedaemonian physician, Claudius Agathurnus, whose influence upon his character was only less than that of Cornutus. Among his intimates he counted Calpurnius Statura, who died in early youth, and the famous lyric poet, Caesius Bassus,[1] who was destined long to survive his friend and to do him the last service of editing the satires, which his premature death left unpublished and unfinished. Lucan also was one of his fellow students in the house of Cornutus,[2] while at a later date he made the acquaintance of Seneca, the leading writer of the day, although he never felt the seductive attractions of his fluent style and subtle intellect. More important influences were his almost filial respect and affection for the distinguished orator,[3] M. Servilius Nonianus, and his close companionship with Thrasea Paetus, the leader of the Stoic opposition.[4] At one time Persius, if the scholiast may be believed,[5] contemplated a military career. The statement is scarcely probable in view of the contempt and dislike with which he invariably speaks of soldiers, nor is it easy to conceive a profession less suited to the temperament of the quiet and retiring poet. Whatever his original intentions may have been, he actually chose the secluded life of study, the *vita umbratilis*, as the Romans called it, remote from the dust and heat of the great world. That he was wise we cannot doubt. It was the only life possible in those days for a man of his character. ' Fuit

[1] Bassus was many years his senior—addressed as *senex* in Sat. vi. 6, written late in 61 or early in 62 A.D.—and perished in the eruption of Vesuvius, 79 A.D. Cp. Schol. *ad Pers.* vi. 1.

[2] Lucan was five years his junior. Cp. p. 97.

[3] Cp. Tac. *Ann.* xiv. 19; *Dial.* 23; Quint. x. 1. 102.

[4] This friendship lasted ten years, presumably the last ten of Persius' life; cp. *Prob. vit.*

The second satire is addressed to Plotius Macrinus, who, according to the scholiast, was a learned man, who ' loved Persius as his son, having studied with him in the house of Servilius Nonianus.'

[5] See O. Jahn's ed., p. 240.

morum lenissimorum, verecundiae virginalis, pietatis erga
matrem et sororem et amitam exemplo sufficientis : fuit
frugi, pudicus.' Even in a saner, purer, and less turbulent
age, such a one would have been more fitted for the paths
of study than for any branch of public life. He died of
a disease of the stomach on the 24th of November, 62 A.D.,
in his villa on the Appian Way, some eight miles south of
Rome,[1] leaving behind him a valuable library, a small
amount of unpublished verse, and a considerable fortune,
amounting to 2,000,000 sesterces. The whole of this fortune
he bequeathed to his mother and sister, only begging them
to give to his friend Cornutus a sum of 100,000 sesterces,
twenty pounds weight of silver plate, and the whole of his
library, containing no less than 700 volumes by the Stoic
Chrysippus. Cornutus accepted the books, but refused
the rest, showing that indifference to wealth that was to
be looked for, though not always to be found, in professors
of the Stoic philosophy. The literary work left by the
dead poet was submitted by his mother to the judgement
of Cornutus, himself a poet.[2] The bulk of the work was
not great. Persius had in his boyhood written a *praetexta*
or tragedy with a Roman plot, a book of poems describing
his journeys with Thrasea,[3] and a few verses on his kins-
woman Arria, the wife of Caecina Paetus, immortalized
by her devotion to her husband and her heroic death.[4] As
the work of his maturer years he left his satires. Cornutus
recommended that all save the satires should be destroyed ;
they alone, unfinished though they might be, were worthy
of the memory of his dead friend. He began the task of
correcting them for publication, but transferred it to Caesius
Bassus, at the latter's earnest entreaty. Of the nature

---

[1] *Prob. vit.* 'decessit VIII Kal. Dec. P. Mario, Afinio Gallio coss.' Hieronym. ad ann. 2078 = 62 A.D. ' Persius moritur anno aetatis XXVIII.'

[2] *Prob. vit.*

[3] Such at least is a plausible inference. Probus tells us that he used
to travel abroad with Thrasea. It is a natural conjecture that these
hodoeporica were in the style of Horace's journey to Brundisium.

[4] Cp. Mart. i. 13 ; Plin. *Ep.* iii. 16. She was the mother of the wife
of Thrasea.

of the correction and editing required we are ignorant,
save for the statement of Probus that a few lines were
removed from the end of the book to give it an appearance
of completion.[1] The poems met with instant success ;[2]
they excited both wonder and criticism; that they continued
to be read is shown by the existence of copious scholia,
which must, indeed, have been almost necessary for such
continuance of their popularity.[3]

The slender volume of Persius' works is composed of
six satires in hexameter verse and a prologue written in
choliambi. The first deals with the corruption of literature ;
the second, addressed to Macrinus on his birthday, treats
of the right and wrong objects of prayer ; the third is an
appeal to an indolent young man for energy and earnestness ; the fourth, almost a continuation of the third, attacks
the lack of ' self-reverence, self-knowledge, self-control ', in
public men ; the fifth, addressed to his friend and teacher
Cornutus, maintains the Stoic doctrine that all the world
are slaves ; only the righteous man attains to freedom;
in the sixth, addressed to Caesius Bassus, the poet claims
the right to spend his wealth in reasonable enjoyment,
and denounces the grasping and unseemly selfishness of an
imaginary heir to his fortune. In the prologue—or epilogue
as it is sometimes regarded [4]—he sarcastically disclaims

---

[1] This may mean that the last satire was actually incomplete, but that
the omission of a few lines at the end gave it an appearance of completion ;
or that a few lines intended for the opening of a seventh satire were
omitted.

[2] So Probus. Cp. also Quint. x. 1. 94 ' multum et verae gloriae quamvis
uno libro meruit.' Mart. iv. 29. 7.

[3] Hieronym. *in apol. contra Rufin.* i. 16 ' puto quod puer legeris . . .
commentarios . . . aliorum in alios, Plautum videlicet, Lucretium, Flaccum,
Persium atque Lucanum.' The high moral tone of the work, coupled
perhaps with the smallness of its bulk, is in the main responsible for its
survival. Scholia from different sources have come down to us under the
title of *Cornuti commentum.* Whether such a person as the commentator
Cornutus existed or not is uncertain. The name may have been attached
to the scholia merely to give them a spurious importance as though
possessing the imprimatur of the friend and teacher of the poet.

[4] The choliambi are placed after the satires by two of the three best

any pretensions to poetic inspiration, and hints ironically
that, in view of the number of poets who write merely to
win their bread, inspiration may be regarded as unnecessary.

The ambition to win fame as a satirist was first fired
in Persius by his reading the tenth book of the satires
of Lucilius. If we may believe Probus, he imitated the
opening of that book in his first satire, beginning like Lucilius
by detracting from himself and proceeding to attack other
authors indiscriminately.[1] Not enough of the tenth book
of Lucilius has survived to enable us to check the accuracy
of this statement, though it finds independent testimony
in a remark of the scholiast on Horace, that the tenth book
of Lucilius contained free criticisms of the early poets of
Rome.[2] Further, the third satire is said by the scholiast
to have been modelled on the fourth book of Lucilius,
and there is a certain amount of evidence for supposing
the choliambi of the epilogue to be an imitation of a Lucilian
model.[3] We have, however, no means of testing the truth
of these assertions : the debt of Persius to Lucilius must be
taken on trust. Of his enormous indebtedness to Horace
we have, on the other hand, the clearest evidence. It is
hard to conceive two poets with less in common as regards
ideals, temperament, and technique ; and yet throughout
Persius we are startled by strange, though unmistakable,
echoes of Horace.

MSS., but before them by the scholia and inferior MSS. It is of little
importance which we follow. But it seems probable that Probus (see
below) regarded the choliambi as a prologue. Such at least is my interpretation of *sibi primo* (i.e. in the prologue) *mox omnibus detrectaturus.*
The lines have rather more force if read first and not last.

[1] *Prob. vit.* ' sed mox ut a schola magistrisque devertit, lecto Lucili
libro decimo vehementer saturas componere studuit; cuius libri principium
imitatus est, sibi primo, mox omnibus detrectaturus, cum tanta recentium
poetarum et oratorum insectatione,' &c. This can only refer to the
prologue and the first satire, and seems to point to its having been the
first to be composed. According to the scholiast the opening line is taken
from the first satire of Lucilius.

[2] Porphyr.' *ad Hor. Sat.* i. 10. 53 ' facit autem Lucilius hoc cum alias
tum vel maxime in tertio libro, . . . et nono et decimo.

[3] Cp. Nettleship's note ad loc., and Petron. 4.

He knows his Horace by heart, and Horace has become a veritable obsession. He is not content with giving his characters Horatian names.[1] That might be convention, not plagiarism. But phrase after phrase calls up the Horatian original. He runs through the whole gamut of plagiarism. There is plagiarism, simple and direct.

> O si
> sub rastro crepet argenti mihi seria, dextro
> Hercule! (2. 10)

is undisguisedly copied from Horace (*Sat.* ii. 6. 10).

> O si urnam argenti fors quae mihi monstret, ut illi,
> thesauro invento, qui mercennarius agrum
> illum ipsum mercatus aravit, dives amico
> Hercule!

But as a rule, since he cannot keep Horace out, he strives to disguise him. The familiar

> si vis me flere, dolendum est
> primum ipsi tibi

of the *Ars Poetica* (102) reappears in the far less natural

> verum nec nocte paratum [2]
> plorabit, qui me volet incurvasse querela (*Pers.* i. 91).

He speaks of his verses so finely turned and polished—

> ut per leve severos [3]
> effundat iunctura unguis (i. 64).

In this fantastically contorted and affected phrase we may espy an ingenious blending of two Horatian phrases,

---

[1] O that I could hear a crock of silver chinking under my harrow, by the blessing of Hercules. CONINGTON.

[2] A man's tears must come from his heart at the moment, not from his brains overnight, if he would have me bowed down beneath his piteous tale. CONINGTON.

[3] So that the critical nail runs glibly along even where the parts join. CONINGTON.

---

1 e. g. Dama, Davus, Natta, Nerius, Craterus, Pedius, Bestius.

> totus teres atque rotundus,
> externi ne quid valeat per leve morari (*Sat.* ii. 7. 86),

and the simple

> ad unguem factus

of *Sat.* i. 5. 32.[1]

There is no need to multiply instances. Horace appears
everywhere, but *quantum mutatus ab illo !* As the result of
this particular method of borrowing, assisted by affectations
and obscurities which are all his own, Persius attains to
a kind of spurious originality of diction, which often degenerates into sheer eccentricity. In spite of the fact that the
original text can almost everywhere be reconstructed with
certainty, he is almost the most obscure of Latin poets
to the modern reader. A few instances will suffice. There
were, it appears, three ways of mocking a person behind his
back : one might tap the fingers against the lower portion
of the hand in imitation of a stork's beak, one might imitate
a donkey's ears, or one might put out one's tongue. When
Persius wishes to say ' Janus, I envy you your luck, for no
one can mock at you behind your back! ' he writes (i. 58) :

> O Iane, a tergo quem nulla ciconia pinsit,   [1]
> nec manus auriculas imitari mobilis albas,
> nec linguae, quantum sitiat canis Apula, tantae.

The obscurity of the first line springs in part from the
fact that the custom is not elsewhere spoken of. The
second line may pass. The third defies literal translation.
It means ' no long tongues thrust out like the tongue of
a thirsty Apulian bitch '. But the omission of all mention
both of ' protrusion ' and of the ' dog days' makes the Latin
almost without meaning. The epithet *Apula* becomes

---

[1] Happy Janus, whom no stork's bill batters from behind, no nimble
hand quick to imitate the ass's white ears, no long tongues thrust out like
the tongue of a thirsty Apulian bitch.

---

1 Instances might be almost indefinitely multiplied. The whole of
Pers. i, but more especially the conclusion, is strongly influenced by Hor.
Sat. i. 10. Cp. also Pers. ii. 12, Hor. *Sat.* ii. 5. 45 ; Pers. iii. 66, Hor. *Ep.* i.
18. 96 ; Pers. v. 10, Hor. *Sat.* i. 4. 19, &c., &c.

absurd. A 'thirsty Apulian dog' is barely sufficient to
suggest the midsummer drought of Apulia. This is an
extreme case ; it is perhaps fairer to quote lines such as

> si puteal multa cautus vibice flagellas (iv. 49),

'if in your zeal for the main chance you flog the exchange
with many a stripe,' a mysterious passage generally supposed to mean 'if you exact exorbitant usury'. A little
less enigmatic, but fully as forced and unnatural is

> dum veteres avias tibi de pulmone revello (v. 92),

'while I pull your old grandmotherly views from your
heart,' or the extraordinarily harsh metaphor of the first
satire (24)—

> quo didicisse, nisi hoc fermentum et quae semel intus [1]
> innata est rupto iecore exierit caprificus ?

which means nothing more than 'What is the good of study
unless a man brings out what he has in him ? ' A far more
serious source of obscurity, however, is his obscurity of
thought. Even when the sense of individual lines has
been discovered, it is often difficult to see the drift of the
passage as a whole. Logical development is perhaps not
to be expected in the 'hotch-potch' of the 'satura'.
But one has a right to demand that the transitions should
be easy and the drift of the argument clear. This Persius
refuses us. The difficulties which he presents are—as in
the case of Robert Browning—in part due to his adoption
of the traditional dramatic form in satire, a form in which
clearness of expression is as difficult as it is desirable. But
we cannot excuse his obscurity as we sometimes can in
Browning—either as being to some extent a realistic representation of the discursiveness and lack of method that
characterize the reasonings of the average intelligent man,
or on the other hand as springing from the intensity of
the poet's thought. It is not the case with Persius that

---

[1] What is the good of past study, unless this leaven—unless the wild
fig-tree which has once struck its root into the breast, break through and
come out ? CONINGTON.

his thoughts press so thick and quick upon him, or are
of so deep and complicated a character, as to be incapable
of simple and lucid expression.   It is sheer waywardness
and perversity springing from the absence of true artistic
feeling to which we must attribute this cardinal defect.
For his thought is commonplace, and his observation of
the minds and ways of men is limited.

The qualities that go to the making of the true satirist
are many.   He must be dominated by a moral ideal, not
necessarily of the highest kind, but sufficiently exalted
to lend dignity to his work and sufficiently strongly realized
to permeate it.   He must have a wide and comprehensive
knowledge of his fellow men.   A knowledge of the broad
outlines of the cardinal virtues and of the deadly sins is
not sufficient.   The satirist must know them in their
countless manifestations in the life of man, as they move
our awe or our contempt, our admiration or our terror,
our love or our loathing, our laughter or our tears.   He
must be able to paint society in all its myriad hues.   He
must have a sense of humour, even if he lacks the sense
of proportion ; he must have the gift of laughter, even
though his laughter ring harsh and painful.   He must
have the gift of mordant speech, of epigram, and of rhetoric.
He must drive his points home with directness and lucidity.
Mere denunciation of vice is not enough.   Few prophets
are satirists ; few satirists are prophets.

Of these qualities Persius has all too few.   The man
who has become the pupil of a Cornutus at the age of sixteen, who has shunned a public career, and is characterized
by a *virginalis verecundia*, is not likely, even in a long life,
to acquire the knowledge of the world required for genuine
satire.   The satirist, it might almost be said, must not only
have walked abroad in the great world, but must have
passed through the fire himself, and in some sense experienced
the vices he has set himself to lash.   But Persius is young
and, as far as might be in that age, innocent.   His outlook
is from the seclusion of literary and philosophic circles,
and his satire lacks the peculiar vigour that can only be

got from jostling one's way in the wider world. In conse-
quence the picture of life which he presents lacks vividness.
A few brilliant sketches there are ; but they are drawn
from but a narrow range of experience. There is nothing
better of its kind than the description in the first satire
of the omnipresent poetaster of the reign of Nero, with
his affected recitations of tawdry, sensuous, and soulless
verse (15) :

> Scilicet haec populo pexusque togaque recenti   [1]
> et natalicia tandem cum sardonyche albus
> sede leges celsa, liquido cum plasmate guttur
> mobile conlueris, patranti fractus ocello.
> tunc neque more probo videas nec voce serena
> ingentis trepidare Titos, cum carmina lumbum
> intrant et tremulo scalpuntur ubi intima versu.

A few lines later comes a similar and equally vivid picture
(30) :

> ecce inter pocula quaerunt   [2]
> Romulidae saturi, quid dia poemata narrent.
> hic aliquis, cui circum umeros hyacinthina laena est,
> rancidulum quiddam balba de nare locutus,
> Phyllidas Hypsipylas, vatum et plorabile siquid,
> eliquat ac tenero subplantat verba palato.

Here the poet is describing what he has seen ; in the world
of letters he is at home. He can laugh pungently enough
at the style of oratory prevailing in the courts—

---

[1] Yes—you hope to read this out some day, got up sprucely with
a new toga, all in white, with your birthday ring on at last, perched up
cn a high seat, after gargling your supple throat by a liquid process of
tuning, with a languishing roll of your wanton eye. At this you may see
great brawny sons of Rome all in a quiver, losing all decency of gesture
and command of voice, as the strains glide into their very bones, and the
marrow within is tickled by the ripple of the measure. CONINGTON.

[2] Listen. The sons of Rome are sitting after a full meal, and inquiring
in their cups, ' What news from the divine world of poesy ? ' Hereupon
a personage with a hyacinth-coloured mantle over his shoulders brings
out some mawkish trash or other, with a snuffle and a lisp, something
about Phyllises or Hypsipyles, or any of the many heroines over whom
poets have snivelled, filtering out his tones and tripping up the words
against the roof of his delicate mouth. CONINGTON.

nilne pudet capiti non posse pericula cano   [1]
pellere, quin tepidum hoc optes audire ' decenter '.
' fur es ', ait Pedio.   Pedius quid ?   crimina rasis
librat in antithetis, doctas posuisse figuras
laudatur, ' bellum hoc ? ' (i. 83).

He can parody the decadent poets with their effeminate
rhythms and their absurdities of speech.[1] He can mock
the archaizer who goes to Accius and Pacuvius for his
inspiration.[2] He can give an admirable summary of the
genius of Lucilius and Horace—

        secuit Lucilius urbem,   [2]
te Lupe, te Muci, et genuinum fregit in illis ;
omne vafer vitium ridenti Flaccus amico
tangit et admissus circum praecordia ludit,
callidus excusso populum suspendere naso (i. 114).

---

[1] Are you not ashamed not to be able to plead against perils threatening your grey hairs, but you must needs be ambitious of hearing mawkish
compliments to your ' good taste'?   The accuser tells Pedius point blank,
' You are a thief.' What does Pedius do ?   Oh, he balances the charges
in polished antitheses—he is deservedly praised for the artfulness of his
tropes. Monstrous fine that !   CONINGTON.

[2] Lucilius bit deep into the town of his day, its Lupuses and Muciuses,
and broke his jaw-tooth on them.   Horace, the rogue, manages to probe
every fault while making his friend laugh ; he gains his entrance and
plays about the heartstrings with a sly talent for tossing up his nose and
catching the public on it.   CONINGTON

---

[1] i. 92–102.   According to the scholiast the last four lines—

    torva Mimalloneis implerunt cornua bombis,
    et raptum vitulo caput ablatura superbo
    Bassaris et lyncem Maenas flexura corymbis
    euhion ingeminat, reparabilis adsonat echo (i. 99)—

are by Nero. But it is incredible that Persius should have had such
audacity as openly to deride the all-powerful emperor.   The same remark
applies to other passages where the scholiast and some modern critics
have seen satirical allusions to Nero (e.g. prologue and the whole of Sat. iv).
The only passage in which it is possible that there was a covert allusion
to Nero is i. 121, which, according to the scholiast, originally ran *auriculas
asini Mida rex habet.* Cornutus suppressed the words *Mida rex* and substi-
tuted *quis non.* For an ingenious defence of the view that Persius hits
directly at Nero see Pretor, *Class. Rev.*, vol. xxi, p. 72.

[2] i. 76 'Est nunc Brisaei quem venosus liber Acci, | sunt quos Pacuvius-
que et verrucosa moretur | Antiopa, aerumnis cor luctificabile fulta.'

But the first satire stands alone *qua* satire. It is not, perhaps, the most interesting to the modern reader. It mocks at empty literary fashions, which have comparatively small human interest. But it is in this satire that Persius comes nearest the true satirist. The obscurity and affectation of its language is its one serious fault ; otherwise it shows sound literary ideals, close observation, and a pretty vein of humour. Elsewhere there is small trace of keen observation[1] of actual life ; he calls up before his reader no vision of the varied life of Rome, whether in the streets or in the houses of the rich. Instead, he laboriously tricks out some vice in human garb, converses with it in language such as none save Persius ever dreamed of using, or scourges it with all the heavy weapons of the Stoic armoury. There is at times a certain violence and even coarseness[2] of description which does duty for realism, but the words ring hollow and false. The picture described or suggested is got at second-hand. He lacks the vivacity, realism, and common sense of Horace, the cultured man of the world, the biting wit, the astonishing descriptive power, and the masterly rhetoric of Juvenal. We care little for the greater part of Persius' disquisition[3] on the trite theme of the schools, ' what should be the object of man's prayers to heaven ? ' when we have read the tenth satire of Juvenal. There is the same commonplace theme in both, and there is perhaps less originality to be found in the general treatment applied to it by Juvenal. But Juvenal makes us forget the triteness of the theme by his extraordinary gift of style. Like Victor Hugo, he has the gift of imparting richness and splendour to the obvious by the sheer force and glory of his declamatory power. Similarly the fifth satire, where Persius descants on the theme that only the good man is free, while all the rest are slaves, compares ill as a whole

---

[1] The description of the self-indulgent man who, feeling ill, consults his doctor and then fails to follow his advice (iii. 88), is a possible exception. It is noteworthy that in Sat. iv he addresses a young aspirant to a political career as though free political action was still possible at Rome.

[2] e. g. iv. 41.   [3] But see below, p. 91.

with the dialogue between Horace and Davus on the same subject (*Sat.* ii. 7). There is such a harshness, an angularity and bitterness about it, that he wholly fails of the effect produced by the easy dignity of the earlier poet. It is abrupt, violent, and obscure ; and for this reason the austere Stoic makes less impression than his more engaging and easy-going predecessor. Horace knew how to press home his points, even while he played about the hearts of men. Persius has neither the persuasiveness of Horace nor the force of Juvenal.

But Persius, if he falls below his great rivals in point of art, is in one respect immeasurably their superior. He is a better and a nobler man. In his denunciations of vice his eyes are set on a more exalted ideal, an ideal from which he never wanders. There is a world of difference between the ' golden mean ' of Horace, and the worship of virtue that redeems the obscurities of Persius. There is a still greater gulf between the high scorn manifested by Persius for all that is base and ignoble, and the fierce, almost petulant, indignation of Juvenal, that often seems to rend for the mere delight of rending, and is at times disfigured by such grossness of language that many an unsympathetic reader has wondered whether the indignation was genuine. Neither Horace nor Juvenal ever rose to the moral heights of the conclusion of the second satire (61):

> O curvae in terris animae et caelestium inanes, [1]
> quid iuvat hoc, templis nostros immittere mores
> et bona dis ex hac scelerata ducere pulpa ?
> haec sibi corrupto casiam dissolvit olivo
> et Calabrum coxit vitiato murice vellus,
> haec bacam conchae rasisse et stringere venas
> ferventis massae crudo de pulvere iussit.

---

[1] O ye souls that cleave to earth and have nothing heavenly in you ! How can it answer to introduce the spirit of the age into the temple-service and infer what the gods like from this sinful pampered flesh of ours ? The flesh it is that has got to spoil wholesome oil by mixing casia with it—to steep Calabrian wool in purple that was made for no such use ; that has made us tear the pearl from the oyster, and separate the veins of the glowing ore from the primitive slag. It sins—yes, it sins ; but it

peccat et haec, peccat, vitio tamen utitur. at vos
dicite, pontifices, in sancto quid facit aurum ?
nempe hoc quod Veneri donatae a virgine pupae.
quin damus id superis, de magna quod dare lance
non possit magni Messalae lippa propago ?
compositum ius fasque animo sanctosque recessus
mentis et incoctum generoso pectus honesto :
haec cedo ut admoveam templis et farre litabo.

This is real enthusiasm, though the theme be trite, and it
is noteworthy that the enthusiasm has clarified the language, which goes straight to the point without obscurity
or circumlocution. Here alone does the second satire of
Persius surpass the more famous tenth satire of Juvenal.
Yet even this fine outburst is surpassed by the deservedly
well-known passage of the third satire, in which Persius
appeals to a young man ' who has great possessions ' to
live earnestly and strenuously (23) :

udum et molle lutum es, nunc nunc properandus et acri [1]
fingendus sine fine rota. sed rure paterno
est tibi far modicum, purum et sine labe salinum
(quid metuas ?) cultrixque foci secura patella est.
hoc satis ? an deceat pulmonem rumpere ventis,
stemmate quod Tusco ramum millesime ducis,
censoremve tuum vel quod trabeate salutas ?
ad populum phaleras, ego te intus et in cute novi.

---

takes something by its sinning ; but you, reverend pontiffs, tell us what
good gold can do in a holy place. Just as much or as little as the dolls
which a young girl offers to Venus. Give *we* rather to the gods such an
offering as great Messala's blear-eyed representative has no means of
giving, even out of his great dish—duty to God and man well blended in
the mind—purity in the shrine of the heart, and a manly flavour of noble-
ness pervading the bosom. Let me have these to carry to the temple,
and a handful of meal shall win me acceptance. CONINGTON.

[1] You are moist soft earth, you ought to be taken instantly, instantly,
and fashioned without end by the rapid wheel. But you have a paternal
estate with a fair crop of corn, a salt-cellar of unsullied brightness (no fear
of ruin surely !), and a snug dish for fireside service. Are you to be satisfied
with this ? or would it be decent to puff yourself and vapour because your
branch is connected with a Tuscan stem, and you are thousandth in the
line, or because you wear purple on review days and salute your censor ?
Off with your trappings to the mob ! I can look under them and see

non pudet ad morem discincti vivere Nattae.
sed stupet hic vitio et fibris increvit opimum
pingue, caret culpa, nescit quid perdat, et alto
demersus summa rursus non bullit in unda.
    magne pater divum, saevos punire tyrannos
haut alia ratione velis, cum dira libido
moverit ingenium ferventi tincta veneno :
virtutem videant intabescantque relicta.
anne magis Siculi gemuerunt aera iuvenci,
et magis auratis pendens laquearibus ensis
purpureas subter cervices terruit, ' imus,
imus praecipites ' quam si sibi dicat et intus
palleat infelix quod proxima nesciat uxor ?

The man who wrote this has ' loved righteousness and
hated iniquity '. In the work of Persius' rivals it is scarcely
an exaggeration to say that it is the hatred of iniquity
that is most prominent; the love of righteousness holds
but a secondary place.

Persius is uncompromising ; he is the true Stoic with
the motto ' all or nothing '. But he has nothing of the
stilted Stoicism that is such a painful feature of the plays
of Seneca ; nor, however perverse and affected he may be
in diction, do we ever feel that his Stoicism is in some
respects no better than a moral pose, a distressing feeling
that sometimes afflicts as we read Seneca's letters or consolatory treatises. He speaks straight from the heart. His
faults are more often the faults of the school of philosophy

---

your skin. Are you not ashamed to live the loose life of Natta ? But he
is paralysed by vice ; his heart is overgrown by thick collops of fat ; he
feels no reproach ; he knows nothing of his loss ; he is sunk in the depth
and makes no more bubbles on the surface. Great Father of the Gods,
be it thy pleasure to inflict no other punishment on the monsters of
tyranny, after their nature has been stirred by fierce passion, that has
the taint of fiery poison—let them look upon virtue and pine that they
have lost her for ever ! Were the groans from the brazen bull of Sicily
more terrible, or did the sword that hung from the gilded cornice strike
more dread into the princely neck beneath it, than the voice which whispers
to the heart, ' We are going, going down a precipice,' and the ghastly
inward paleness, which is a mystery, even to the wife of our heart ?
CONINGTON.

than of the schools of rhetoric. The young Lucan is said
to have exclaimed, after hearing a recitation given by
Persius :[1] 'That is real poetry, my verses are mere *jeux
d'esprit.*'

If we take Persius at his noblest, Lucan's criticism is
just. In these passages not only is the thought singularly
pure and noble, and the expression felicitous, but the
actual metre represents almost the high-water mark of
the post-Vergilian hexameter. Here, as in other writers
of the age, the influence of Ovid is traceable in the increase
of dactyls and the avoidance of elision. But the verse
has a swing and dignity, together with a variety, that can
hardly be found in any other poetry of the Silver Age. It
is the existence of passages such as these, and the high
unswerving moral enthusiasm characterizing all his work,
that have made Persius live through the centuries. It is
fashionable for the critic to say, 'We lay down Persius
with a sigh of relief.' That is true, but we feel the better
for reading him. He is one of the few writers of Rome
whose personality awakens a feeling of warm affection.
He was a rigid Stoic, yet not proud or cold. In an age
of almost universal corruption he kept himself unspotted
from the world. He had a rare capacity for whole-hearted
friendship. If his teacher Cornutus had never made another
convert, and his preaching had been vain, it would have
been ample reward to have won such a tribute of affection
and gratitude as the lines in which Persius pours forth
his soul to him (v. 21):

> tibi nunc hortante Camena [1]
> excutienda damus praecordia, quantaque nostrae
> pars tua sit, Cornute, animae, tibi, dulcis amice,
> ostendisse iuvat. pulsa dinoscere cautus

[1] It is to you, at the instance of the muse within me, that I would offer
my heart to be sifted thoroughly ; my passion is to show you, Cornutus,
how large a share of my inmost being is yours, my beloved friend ; strike
it, use every test to tell what rings sound, and what is the mere plaster of

[1] *Prob. vita Persii.*

quid solidum crepet et pictae tectoria linguae.
hic ego centenas ausim deposcere fauces,
ut quantum mihi te sinuoso in pectore fixi,
voce traham pura, totumque hoc verba resignent,
quod latet arcana non enarrabile fibra.

   cum primum pavido custos mihi purpura cessit
bullaque subcinctis Laribus donata pependit,
cum blandi comites totaque inpune Subura
permisit sparsisse oculos iam candidus umbo,
cumque iter ambiguum est et vitae nescius error
deducit trepidas ramosa in compita mentes,
me tibi supposui. teneros tu suscipis annos
Socratico, Cornute, sinu. tunc fallere sollers
adposita intortos extendit regula mores,
et premitur ratione animus vincique laborat
artificemque tuo ducit sub pollice vultum.
tecum etenim longos memini consumere soles,
et tecum primas epulis decerpere noctes.
unum opus et requiem pariter disponimus ambo,
atque verecunda laxamus seria mensa.
non equidem hoc dubites, amborum foedere certo
consentire dies et ab uno sidere duci :

---

a varnished tongue. An occasion indeed it is for which I may well venture
to ask a hundred voices, that I may bring out in clear utterance how
thoroughly I have lodged you in the very corners of my breast, and unfold
in words all the unutterable feelings which lie entwined deep down among
my heart-strings. When first the guardianship of the purple ceased to awe
me and the band of boyhood was hung up as an offering to the quaint
old household gods, when my companions made themselves pleasant,
and the folds of my gown, now white, the stripe of purple gone, left me free
to cast my eyes at will over the whole Subura—just when the way of life
begins to be uncertain, and the bewildered mind finds that its ignorant
ramblings have brought it to a point where roads branch off—then it was
that I made myself your adopted child. You at once received the young
foundling into the bosom of a second Socrates ; and soon your rule, with
artful surprise, straightens the moral twists that it detects, and my spirit
becomes moulded by reason and struggles to be subdued, and assumes
plastic features under your hand. Aye, I mind well how I used to wear
away long summer suns with you, and with you pluck the early bloom
of the night for feasting. We twain have one work and one set time for
rest, and the enjoyment of a moderate table unbends our gravity. No,
I would not have you doubt that there is a fixed law that brings our
lives into one accord, and one star that guides them. Whether it be in

nostra vel aequali suspendit tempora libra
Parca tenax veri, seu nata fidelibus hora
dividit in geminos concordia fata duorum,
Saturnumque gravem nostro Iove frangimus una :
nescio quod certe est quod me tibi temperat astrum.

There is a sincerity about these beautiful lines that is as
rare as it is welcome in the poetry of this period. Much
may be forgiven to the poet who could write thus, even
though rarely. And it must be remembered that Persius
is free from the worst of the besetting sins of his age, the
love of rhetorical brilliance at the expense of sense, a failing
that he criticizes with no little force in his opening satire.
His harshness and obscurity are due in part to lack of
sufficient literary skill, but still more to his attempt to
assert his originality against the insistent obsession of
the satires of Horace. As in the case of so many of his
contemporaries, his literary fame must depend in the main
on his ' purple patches '.

But he does what few of his fellow poets do ; he leaves
a vivid impression of his personality, and reveals a genuine
moral ardour and nobility of character that refuse to be
clouded or hidden by his dark sayings and his perverse
obscurity.

---

the equal balance that truthful Destiny hangs our days, or whether the
birth-hour sacred to faithful friends shares our united fates between
the Heavenly Twins, and we break the shock of Saturn together by
the common shield of Jupiter, some star, I am assured, there is which
fuses me with you.   CONINGTON.

CHAPTER IV

LUCAN

MARCUS ANNAEUS LUCANUS,[1] the poet who more than any other exhibits the typical excellences and defects of the Silver Age, was born at Cordova on November 3, in the year 39 A. D.[2] He came of a distinguished line. He was the son of M. Annaeus Mela, brother of Seneca the philosopher and dramatist, and son of Seneca the rhetorician. Mela was a wealthy man,[3] and in 40 A. D. removed with his family to Rome. His son (whose future as a great poet is said to have been portended by a swarm of bees that settled on the cradle and the lips of the bard that was to be [2]) received the best education that Rome could bestow. He showed extraordinary precocity in all the tricks of declamatory rhetoric, soon equalling his instructors in skill and far out-distancing his fellow pupils.[2] Among his preceptors was his kinsman, the famous Stoic, L. Annaeus Cornutus, well known as the friend and teacher of Persius.[4] His first appearance before the public was at the Neronia in 60 A. D., when he won the prize for Latin verse with a poem in praise of Nero.[5] Immediately afterwards he seems to have proceeded to Athens. But his talents had attracted the attention and patronage of Nero. He was recalled to Rome,[6] and at the nomination of the

---

[1] Our chief authorities for Lucan's life are the 'lives' by Suetonius (fragmentary) and by Vacca (a grammarian of the sixth century).

[2] Vacca.   [3] Tac. *Ann.* xvi. 1′.

[4] The young Lucan is said to have formed a friendship with the satirist at the school of Cornutus ; Persius was some five years his senior. *Vita Persii* (p. 58, Bücheler).

[5] Suetonius and Vacca. The latter curiously treats this victory as one of the causes of Nero's jealousy. Considering that the poem was a panegyric of the emperor, and that it was Lucan's first step in the imperial favour, the suggestion deserves small credit.

[6] Sueton. There is an unfortunate hiatus in the Life by Suetonius, occurring just before the mention of the visit to Athens. As the text stands

princeps became Quaestor, although he had not yet attained
the requisite age of twenty-five.[1] He was also admitted
to the College of Augurs, and for some time continued to
enjoy Nero's friendship. But it was not to last. Lucan
had been educated in Stoic surroundings. Though his own
relatives managed to combine the service of the emperor
with their Stoic principles, Lucan had not failed to imbibe
the passionate regret for the lost liberty of the republic
that was so prominent a feature in Stoic circles. It was
not a mere pose that led him to select the civil war as
the subject of his poem. His enthusiasm for liberty may
have been literary rather than political in character. But
when we are dealing with an artistic temperament we must
bear in mind that the ideals which were primarily inspiration
for art may on slight provocation become incentives to
action. And in the case of Lucan that provocation was
not lacking. As his fame increased, Nero's friendship was
replaced by jealousy. The protégé had become too serious
a rival to the patron.[2] Lucan's vanity was injured by
Nero's sudden withdrawal from a recitation.[3] From servile
flattery he turned to violent criticism : he spared his former
patron neither in word nor deed. He turned the sharp
edge of his satire against him in various pungent epigrams,
and was forbidden to recite poetry or to plead in the law
courts.[4] But it would be unjust to Lucan to attribute
his changed attitude purely to wounded vanity. Seneca
was at this very moment attempting to retire from public
life. The court of Nero had become no place for him.
Lucan cannot have been unaffected by the action of his
uncle, and it is only just to him to admit the possibility
that the change in his attitude may have been due, at any

---

it suggests that the visit to Athens occurred after the victory at the
Neronia. Otherwise it would seem more probable that Lucan went to
Athens somewhat earlier (e.g. 57 A. D.) to complete his education.

[1] Sueton., Vacca.

[2] Vacca; Tac. *Ann.* xv. 49 ; Dion. lxii. 29.

[3] Vacca.   [4] Suetonius.

rate in part, to a change in character, an awakening to the
needs of the State and the needs of his own soul. There is
no need to question the genuineness of his political enthusiasm, even though it tended to be theatrical and may have
been largely kindled by motives not wholly disinterested.
The Pisonian conspiracy found in him a ready coadjutor.
He became one of the ringleaders of the plot ('paene
signifer coniurationis'), and in a bombastic vein would
promise Nero's head to his fellow-conspirators.[1]   On the
detection of the plot, in 65 A. D., he, with the other chiefs
of the conspiracy, was arrested. For long he denied his
complicity ; at last, perhaps on the threat or application
of torture, his nerve failed him; he descended to grovelling
entreaties, and to win himself a reprieve accused his innocent
mother, Acilia, of complicity in the plot.[2] His conduct
does not admit of excuse. But it is not for the plain, matter-
of-fact man to pass judgement lightly on the weakness of
a highly-strung, nervous, artistic temperament ; the artist's
imagination may transmute pain such as others might
hope to bear, to anguish such as they cannot even imagine.
There lies the palliation, if palliation it be, of Lucan's crime.
But it availed him nothing : the reprieve was never won ;
he was condemned to die, the manner of his death being
left to his free choice. He wrote a few instructions for
his father as to the editing of his poems, partook of a sumptuous dinner, and then, adopting the fashionable form of
suicide, cut the arteries of his arms and bled to death. He
died declaiming a passage from his own poetry in which
he had described the death of a soldier from loss of blood.[3]
It was a theatrical end, and not out of keeping with his
life.

He lived but a little over twenty-five years and five

---

[1] Suetonius.

[2] Sueton. ; Tac. *Ann.* xv. 56.

[3] Vacca ; Sueton. ; Tac. *Ann.* xv. 70. Various passages in the *Pharsalia*
have been suggested as suitable for Lucan's recitation at his last gasp,
iii. 638–41, vii. 608–15, ix. 811.

months, but he left behind him a vast amount of poetry
and an extraordinary reputation.   His earliest work[1] seems
to have been the *Iliacon*, describing the death of Hector,
his ransom and burial.   Next came the *Catachthonion*,
a short work on the underworld.   This was followed by
the *laudes Neronis*, to which reference has already been
made, and the *Orpheus*, which was extemporized in a competition with other poets.[2]   If we follow the order given
by Statius, his next work was the prose declamation on the
burning of the city (64 A.D.) and a poem addressed to his
wife Polla (*adlocutio ad Pollam*).   Then comes his *chef
d'œuvre*, the *Pharsalia*, to which we shall return.   Of the
other works mentioned by Vacca, the *Silvae* must have
been, like the *Silvae* of Statius, trifles thrown off hurriedly
for the gratification of friends or for the celebration of
some great occasion.[3]   The *salticae fabulae* were *libretti*
written for the *pantomimus*,[4] while the *Saturnalia* were
light verse sent as presents to friends on the festival of

---

[1] Statius, in his *Genethliacon Lucani* (*Silv.* ii. 7. 54), seems to indicate the
order of the poems :

> ac primum teneris adhuc in annis
> ludes Hectora Thessalosque currus
> et supplex Priami potentis aurum,
> et sedes reserabis inferorum ;
> ingratus Nero dulcibus theatris
> et noster tibi proferetur Orpheus,
> dices culminibus Remi vagantis
> infandos domini nocentis ignes,
> hinc castae titulum decusque Pollae
> iucunda dabis adlocutione.
> mox coepta generosior iuventa
> albos ossibus Italis Philippos
> et Pharsalica bella detonabis.

Cp. also Vacca, 'extant eius complures et alii, ut Iliacon, Saturnalia,
Catachthonion, Silvarum x, tragoedia Medea imperfecta, salticae fabulae
xiv, et epigrammata (MSS. *appamata* sive *ippamata*), prosae orationes
in Octavium Sagittam et pro eo, de incendio Urbis, epistularum ex
Campania, non fastidiendi quidem omnes, tales tamen ut belli civili
videantur accessio.'

[2] Vacca.   [3] See chapter on Statius.
[4] See chapter on Drama.

Saturn.[1] Of these works nothing has come down to us
save a few scanty fragments, not in any way calculated
to make us regret their loss.[2] Even Vacca can find no
very high praise for them. Judging alike from the proba-
bilities of the case and from the *Pharsalia* itself, they must
have suffered from Lucan's fatal gift of fluency.

It was the *Pharsalia* that won Lucan undying fame.
Three books of this ambitious historical epic were finished
and given to the world during the poet's lifetime.[3] These
the poet had, at any rate in part, recited in public, calling
attention, with a vanity worthy of himself and of the age,
to his extreme youth ; he was younger than Vergil when
he composed the *Culex* ![4] The remaining seven books
never had the benefit of revision, owing to the poet's untimely
end,[5] though curiously enough they show no special signs
of lack of finish, and contain some of the finest passages
in the whole work. The composition of all ten books
falls between 60 and 65 A.D. Lucan had chosen for his
theme the death-struggle of the republic. It was a daring
choice for more reasons than one. There were elements of
danger in singing the praises of Pompey and Cato under the
principate. To that the fate of Cremutius Cordus bore
eloquent testimony.[6] But Nero was less sensitive about the

---

[1] Cp. Mart., bks. xiii and xiv.

[2] There are two fragments from the *Iliacon*, two from the *Orpheus*, one
from the *Catachthonion*, two from the *Epigrammata*, together with a few
scanty references in ancient commentators and grammarians : see Post-
gate, *Corp. Poet. Lat.*

[3] Vacca, ' ediderat . . . tres libros, quales videmus.'

[4] Sueton. ' civile bellum . . . recitavit ut praefatione quadem aetatem et
initia sua comparans ausus sit dicere, "quantum mihi restat ad Culicem ".'
Cp. also Stat. *Silv.* ii. 7. 73 :—

> haec (Pharsalia) primo iuvenis canes sub aevo
> ante annos Culicis Maroniani.

Vergil was twenty-six when he composed the *Culex*. Cp. Ribbeck, *App.
Verg.* p. 19.

[5] Vacca, ' reliqui septem belli civilis libri locum calumniantibus tanquam
mendosi non darent; qui tametsi sub vero crimine non egent patrocinio :
in iisdem dici, quod in Ovidii libris praescribitur, potest : emendaturus, si
licuisset, erat.'   [6] See p. 4.

past than Tiberius. The republic had never become officially
extinct. Tyrannicide was a licensed and hackneyed theme
of the schools of rhetoric ; in skilful hands it might be
a subtle instrument of flattery. Moreover, Nero was descended in direct line from Domitius Ahenobarbus, who
had fought and died for Pompey on the field of Pharsalus.
In the books published during Lucan's lifetime there is
not a line that could have given personal offence to the
princeps, while the fulsome dedication would have covered
a multitude of indiscretions.[1] Far more serious were the
difficulties presented by the nature of the story itself.
Historical epic rarely admits of artistic treatment, and the
nearer the date of the events described, the more insoluble
is the problém.

Two courses were open to Lucan : he might treat the
story with comparative fidelity to truth, avoiding all
supernatural machinery, save such as was justified by
historical tradition ; on the other hand he might adopt
the course subsequently pursued by Silius Italicus in his
poem on the Punic War, and introduce all the hackneyed
interventions of Olympus, sanctioned by Vergil and followed
by many a poet since. The latter method is obviously
only suited for a purely legendary epic, though even the
legendary epic can well dispense with it, and it might have
been supposed that an age so sceptical and careless of the
orthodox theology, as that into which Lucan was born,
would have felt the full absurdity of applying such a device
to historical epic. Lucan was wise in his choice, and left

---

[1] Boissier, L'Opposition sous les Césars (p. 279), sees some significance in
the fact that the list of Nero's ancestors always stops at Augustus. But
there was no reason why the list should go further than the founder of
the principate. It is noteworthy that Lucan's uncle Seneca wrote a
number of epigrams in praise of the Pompeii and Cato. The
famous lines,

               quis iustius induit arma
    scire nefas : magno se iudice quisque tuetur,
    victrix causa deis placuit, sed victa Catoni (i. 126),

are supremely diplomatic. Without sacrificing his principles, Lucan avoids
giving a shadow of offence to his emperor.

Olympus severely alone. But his choice roused contemporary criticism. In the *Satyricon* of Petronius we find
a defence of the old conventional mechanism placed in
the mouth of a shabby and disreputable poet named Eumolpus (118). He complains ' that young men plunge headlong
into epic verse thinking that it requires no more skill than
a showy declamation at the school of rhetoric. They do
not realize that to be a successful poet one must be steeped
in the great ocean of literature. They do not recognize
that there is such a thing as a special poetic vocabulary,[1]
or that the commonplaces of rhetoric require to be inter-
woven with, not merely tacked on to, the fabric of their
verse, and so it comes about that the writer who would
turn the Civil War into an epic is apt to stumble beneath
the burden he takes upon his shoulders, unless indeed he
is permeated through and through with literature. You
must not simply turn history into verse : historians do
it better in prose. Rather the poet should sweep on his
way borne by the breath of inspiration and untrammelled
by hard fact, making use of cunning artifice and divine
intervention, and interfusing his " commonplaces " with
legendary lore ; only so will his work seem to be the fine
frenzy of an inspired bard rather than the exactitude of
one who is giving sworn evidence before a judge '. He then
proceeds in 295 verses to deal, after the manner he has
prescribed, with the events contained in the first three
books of the *Pharsalia*, the only books that had been made
public at the time when Petronius' romance was composed.
Pluto inspires Caesar to the crime of civil war. Peace,
Fidelity, and Concord fly from the earth at his approach.
The gods range themselves on this side and on that. Discord
perched high on Apennine incites the peoples of Italy
to war. The verse is uninspired, the method is impossible,
the remedy is worse than the disease. The last hope of
our taking the poem seriously has departed. Yet this
passage of Petronius contains much sound criticism. Mili-

---

[1] See p. 116.

tary and political history does *not* admit of being turned
into genuine poetry ; an epic on an historic war must depend
largely on its purple patches of description and rhetoric : it
almost demands that prominence of epigram and ' commonplace ' that Eumolpus condemns.[1] Petronius sees the weakness of Lucan's epic ; he fails because, like Silius Italicus,
he thinks he has discovered a remedy. The faults of
Lucan's poem are largely inherent in the subject chosen ;
they will stand out clearly as we review the structure and
style of the work.

In taking the whole of the Civil War for his subject Lucan
was confronted with a somewhat similar problem to that
which faced Shakespeare in his *Julius Caesar*. The problem
that Shakespeare had to meet was how to prolong and
sustain the interest of the play after the death of Caesar
and the events that centre immediately round it. The
difficulty was surmounted triumphantly. The obstacles
in Lucan's path were greater. The poem is incomplete,
and there must be some uncertainty as to its intended
scope. That it was planned to include the death of Cato
is clear from the importance assigned him in the existing
books. But could the work have concluded on such a
note of gloom as the death of the staunchest champion
of the republic ? The whole tone of the poem is republican
in the extreme. If the republic must perish, it should not
perish unavenged. There are, moreover, many prophetic
allusions to the death of Caesar,[2] which point conclusively
to Lucan's intention to have made the vengeance of Brutus
and Cassius the climax of his poem. The problem which
the poet had to resolve was how to prevent the interest
from flagging, as his heroes were swept away before the
triumphant advance of Caesar. He concentrates our
attention at the outset on Pompey. Throughout the first
eight books it is for him that he claims our sympathy.
And then he is crushed by his rival and driven in flight

---

[1] Petron., loc. cit.

[2] v. 207, vii. 451, 596, 782, x. 339–42, 431.

to die an unheroic death. It is only at this point that
Cato leaps into prominence. But though he has a firmness
of purpose and a grandeur of character that Lucan could
not give Pompey, he never has the chance to become the
protagonist. Both Pompey and Cato, for all the fine rhetoric
bestowed on them, fail to grip the reader, while from the
very facts of history it is impossible for either of them to
lend unity to the plot. Both are dwarfed by the character
of Caesar. Caesar is the villain of the piece ; he is a monster
athirst for blood, he will not permit the corpses of his enemies
(over which he is made to gloat) to be buried after the great
battle, and when on his coming to Egypt the head of his
rival is brought him, his grief and indignation are represented
as being a mere blind to conceal his real joy. The successes
are often merely the result of good fortune. Lucan is
loth to admit even his greatness as a general. And yet,
blacken his character as he may, he feels that greatness.
From the moment of his brilliant characterization of Caesar
in the first book [1] we feel we have a man who knows what
he desires and will shrink from nothing to attain his ends ;
he ' thinks naught yet done while aught remains to do ',[2]
he ' strikes fear into men's hearts because he knows not
the meaning of fear ',[3] and through all the melodramatic
rhetoric with which he addresses his soldiers, there shines
clear the spirit of a great leader of men. Whoever was
intended by the poet for his hero, the fact remains that
Caesar dominates the poem as none save the hero should
do. He is the hero of the *Pharsalia* as Satan is the hero
of *Paradise Lost*.[4] It is through him above all that Lucan
retains our interest. The result is fatal for the proper
proportion of the plot. Lucan does not actually alienate
our sympathies from the republic, but, whatever our moral
judgement on the conflict may be, our interest centres on
Caesar, and it is hardly an exaggeration to say that the

---

[1] i. 143–57.
[2] ii. 657 nil actum credens cum quid superesset agendum.
[3] v. 317 meruitque timeri non metuens.
[4] See Shelley, *Prometheus Unbound*, Preface.

true tragedy of the epic would have come with his death. The *Pharsalia* fails of its object as a republican epic ; its success comes largely from an unintended quarter.

What the exact scale of the poem was meant to be it is hard to say. Vergil had set the precedent for an epic of twelve books, and it is not improbable that Lucan would have followed his example. On the other hand, if Cato and Caesar had both to be killed in the last two books, great compression would have been necessary. In view of the diffuseness of Lucan's rhetoric, and the rambling nature of his narrative, it is more than probable that the epic would have exceeded the limit of twelve books and been a formidable rival in bulk to the *Punica* of Silius Italicus. On the other hand, the last seven books of the existing poem are unrevised, and may have been destined for abridgement. There is so much that is irrelevant that the task would have been easy.

But it is not for the plot that Lucan's epic is read. It has won immortality by the brilliance of its rhetoric, its unsurpassed epigrams, its clear-cut summaries of character, its biting satire, and its outbursts of lofty political enthusiasm. These features stand out pre-eminent and atone for its astounding errors of taste, its strained hyperbole, its foolish digression. Lucan fails to make his actors live as they move through his pages ; their actions and their speeches are alike theatrical ; he has no dramatic power. But he can sum up their characters in burning lines that live through all time and have few parallels in literature. And these pictures are in all essentials surprisingly just and accurate. His affection for Pompey and the demands of his plot presented strong temptations to exalt his character at the expense of historical truth. Yet what can be more just than the famous lines of the first book, where his character is set against Caesar's ? (129) :

> vergentibus annis   [1]
> in senium longoque togae tranquillior usu

---

[1]   One aged grown
      Had long exchanged the corselet for the gown :

dedidicit iam pace ducem : famaeque petitor
multa dare in volgus ; totus popularibus auris
inpelli plausuque sui gaudere theatri ;
nec reparare novas vires, multumque priori
credere fortunae, stat magni nominis umbra :
qualis frugifero quercus sublimis in agro
exuvias veteres populi sacrataque gestans
dona ducum : nec iam validis radicibus haerens
pondere fixa suo est, nudosque per aera ramos
effundens trunco non frondibus efficit umbram.

Even the panegyric pronounced on him by Cato on hearing the news of his death is as moderate as it is true and
dignified (ix. 190) :

civis obit, inquit, multum maioribus inpar   [1]
nosse modum iuris, sed in hoc tamen utilis aevo,
cui non ulla fuit iusti reverentia ; salva
libertate potens, et solus plebe parata
privatus servire sibi, rectorque senatus,
sed regnantis, erat.

     . . . invasit ferrum, sed ponere norat ;

In peace forgotten the commander's art,
And learned to play the politician's part,—
To court the suffrage of the crowd, and hear
In his own theatre the venal cheer ;
Idly he rested on his ancient fame,
And was the shadow of a mighty name.
Like the huge oak which towers above the fields
Decked with ancestral spoils and votive shields.
Its roots, once mighty, loosened by decay,
Hold it no more : weight is its only stay ;
Its naked limbs bespeak its glories past,
And by its trunk, not leaves, a shade is cast.
                   PROF. GOLDWIN SMITH.

[1]   A man, he said, is gone, unequal far
To our good sires in reverence for the law,
Yet useful in an age that knew not right,
One who could power with liberty unite,
Uncrowned 'mid willing subjects could remain,
The Senate rule, yet let the Senate reign.

.   .   .   .   .   .

He drew the sword, but he could sheathe it too,

praetulit arma togae, sed pacem armatus amavit ;
iuvit sumpta ducem, iuvit dimissa potestas.

Elsewhere he is as one of the ' strengthless dead ', here
he lives. Elsewhere he may be invested with the pathos
that must cling to the shadow of a mighty name, but he
is too weak and ineffective to be interesting. His wavering
policy in his last campaign is unduly emphasized.[1] When
he is face to face with Caesar at Pharsalus and exhorts his
men, he can but boast, he cannot inspire.[2] When the battle
turns against him he bids his men cease from the fight,
and himself flies, that he may not involve them in his
own disaster.[3] No less convincing portrait could be drawn.
The material was unpromising, but Lucan emphasizes all
his weaknesses and wholly fails to bring out his nobler
elements. He is unworthy of the line

nec cinis exiguus tantam compescuit umbram.

So, too, in a lesser degree with Caesar. For a moment
in the first book he flashes upon us in his full splendour (143) :

sed non in Caesare tantum   [1]
nomen erat nec fama ducis : sed nescia virtus
stare loco, solusque pudor non vincere bello.
acer et indomitus, quo spes quoque ira vocasset,
ferre manum et numquam temerando parcere ferro,
successus urgere suos, instare fauori
numinis, inpellens quidquid sibi summa petenti
obstaret, gaudensque viam fecisse ruina.

War was his trade, yet he to peace inclined,
Gladly command accepted—and resigned.—Prof. Goldwin Smith.

[1] Not such the talisman of Caesar's name,
But Caesar had, in place of empty fame,
The unresting soul, the resolution high
That shuts out every thought but victory.
Whate'er his goal, nor mercy nor dismay
He owned, but drew the sword and cleft his way ;
Pressed each advantage that his fortune gave ·
Constrained the stars to combat for the brave ;
Swept from his path whate'er his rise delayed,
And marched triumphant through the wreck he made.
                     Prof. Goldwin Smith.

---

[1] vii. 45–150.   [2] vii. 342.   [3] vii. 647–727.

Here at any rate is Caesar the general : in such a poem
there is no room for Caesar the statesman. But from this
point onward we see no true Caesar. Henceforward, save
for a few brief moments, he is a figure for the melodramatic
stage alone, a ' brigand chief ', a master hypocrite, the
favourite of fortune. And yet, for all his unreality, Lucan
has endowed him with such impetuous vigour and such
a plenitude of power that he dwarfs the other puppets
that throng his pages even more, if possible, than in real
life he overtopped his contemporaries.

Cato, the third great figure of the *Pharsalia*, was easier
to draw. Unconsciously stagey in life, he is little stagier
in Lucan. And yet, in spite of his absurdity, he has a
nobility and a sincerity of purpose which is without parallel
in that corrupt age. He was the hero of the Stoic republi-
cans [1] of the early principate, the man of principle, stern
and unbending. He requires no fine touches of light and
shade, for he is the perfect Stoic. But from the very rigidity
of his principles he was no statesman and never played
more than a secondary part in politics.

Lucan's task is to exalt him from the second rank to
the first. But it is no easy undertaking, since it was not
till after the disaster of Pharsalus that he played any
conspicuous part in the Civil War. He first appears as
warrant for the justice of the republican cause (i. 128).
We next see him as the hope of all true patriots at Rome
(ii. 238). Pompey has fled southward. Cato alone remains
the representative of all that is noblest and best in Rome.
He has no illusions as to Pompey's character. He is not
the leader he would choose for so sacred a cause ; but
between Pompey and Caesar there can be no wavering. He
follows Pompey. Not till the ninth book does he reappear
in the action. Pompey is fallen, and all turn to Cato as
their leader. The cause is lost, and Cato knows it well ;
but he obeys the call of duty and undertakes the hopeless

---

[1] Cp. the epigrams attributed to Seneca, *P. L. M.* iv, *Anth. Lat.*
7, 8, 9.

enterprise undismayed.   He is a stern leader, but he shares
his men's hardships to the full, and fortifies them by his
example.   He is in every action what the real Cato only
was at Utica.   On him above all others Lucan has lavished
all his powers ; and he has succeeded in creating a character
of such real moral grandeur that, in spite of its hardness
and austerity, it almost succeeds in winning our affection
(ii. 380) :

> hi mores, haec duri inmota Catonis   [1]
> secta fuit, servare modum finesque tenere
> naturamque sequi patriaeque inpendere vitam
> nec sibi sed toti genitum se credere mundo.

Here is a man indeed worthy to be the hero of a republican
epic, did history permit it.   Our chief reason—at moments
there is a temptation to say ' our only reason '—for regretting
the incompletion of the *Pharsalia* is that Lucan did not
live to describe Cato's death.   *There* was a subject which
was worthy of his pen and would have been a labour of
love.   With what splendour of rhetoric he might have
invested it can only be conjectured from the magnificent
passage where Cato refuses to inquire into his fate at
Ammon's oracle (ix. 566) :

> quid quaeri, Labiene, iubes ?   an liber in armis   [2]
> occubuisse velim potius quam regna videre ?
> an sit vita nihil, sed longa ?   an differat aetas ?
> an noceat vis ulla bono, fortunaque perdat

---

[1]   'Twas his rule
      Inflexible to keep the middle path
      Marked out and bounded ; to observe the laws
      Of natural right ; and for his country's sake
      To risk his life, his all, as not for self
      Brought into being, but for all the world.
                                          SIR E. RIDLEY.
[2]   What should I ask ?   Whether to live a slave
      Is better, or to fill a soldier's grave ?
      What life is worth drawn to its utmost span,
      And whether length of days brings bliss to man ?
      Whether tyrannic force can hurt the good,
      Or the brave heart need quail at Fortune's mood ?

opposita virtute minas, laudandaque velle
sit satis, et numquam successu crescat honestum ?
scimus, et hoc nobis non altius inseret Hammon.
haeremus cuncti superis, temploque tacente
nil facimus non sponte dei ; nec vocibus ullis
numen eget, dixitque semel nascentibus auctor
quidquid scire licet, steriles nec legit harenas,
ut caneret paucis, mersitque hoc pulvere verum.
estque dei sedes, nisi terra et pontus et aer
et caelum et virtus ? superos quid quaerimus ultra ?
Iuppiter est quodcumque vides quodcumque moveris.
sortilegis egeant dubii semperque futuris
casibus ancipites ; me non oracula certum,
sed mors certa facit. pavido fortique cadendum est ;
hoc satis est dixisse Iouem.

One Cato will not lend life to an epic, and history, to the
great loss of art, forbids him to play a sufficiently important
rôle.   It is unnecessary to comment on the lesser personages
of the epic ; if the leading characters lack life, the minor
characters lack individuality as well.[1] Lucan has nothing of
the dramatic vitalising power that is so necessary for epic.

> Whether the pure intent makes righteousness,
> Or virtue needs the warrant of success ?
> All this I know : not Ammon can impart
> Force to the truth engraven on my heart.
> All men alike, though voiceless be the shrine,
> Abide in God and act by will divine.
> No revelation Deity requires,
> But at our birth, all men may know, inspires.
> Nor is truth buried in this desert sand
> And doled to few, but speaks in every land.
> What temple but the earth, the sea, the sky,
> And heaven and virtuous hearts, hath deity ?
> As far as eye can range or feet can rove
> Jove is in all things, all things are in Jove.
> Let wavering souls to oracles attend,
> The brave man's course is clear, since sure his end.
> The valiant and the coward both must fall
> This when Jove tells me, he has told me all.
>   PROF. GOLDWIN SMITH.

[1] The one exception is Curio, see iv. 799.

He is equally defective in narrative power. He can
give us brilliant pictures as in the lines describing the
vision of Caesar at the Rubicon [1] or Pompey's last sight
of Italy.[2] But such passages are few and far between.
Of longer passages there are not perhaps more than three
in the whole work where we get any sustained beauty of
narrative—the parting of Pompey and his wife,[3] Pompey's
dream before Pharsalus,[4] and a description of a Druid
grove in Southern Gaul.[5] The first of these is noticeable
as being one of the few occasions on which Lucan shows any
command of simple pathos unmarred by tricks of tawdry
rhetoric. The whole episode is admirably treated. The
speeches of both husband and wife are commendably and
unusually simple and direct, but the climax comes after
Cornelia's speech, where the poet describes the moment
before they part. With the simplest words and the most
severe economy of diction, he produces an effect such as
Vergil rarely surpassed, and such as was never excelled
or equalled again in the poetry of Southern Europe till
Dante told the story of Paolo and Francesca (v. 790) :

sic fata relictis   [1]
exsiluit stratis amens tormentaque nulla

---

[1] So spake she, and leaped frenzied from the couch, loth to put off

[1] i. 185:
     ut ventum est parvi Rubiconis ad undas,
ingens visa duci patriae trepidantis imago,
clara per obscuram voltu maestissima noctem
turrigero canos effundens vertice crines
caesarie lacera nudisque adstare lacertis
et gemitu permixta loqui : 'quo tenditis ultra ?
quo fertis mea signa, viri ? si iure venitis,
si cives, huc usque licet.'

[2] iii. 1:
     propulit ut classem velis cedentibus Auster
incumbens mediumque rates movere profundum,
omnis in Ionios spectabat navita fluctus ;
solus ab Hesperia non flexit lumina terra
Magnus, dum patrios portus, dum litora numquam
ad visus reditura suos tectumque cacumen
nubibus et dubios cernit vanescere montes.

[3] v. 722–end.   [4] vii. 6–44.   [5] iii. 399–425.

vult differre mora. non maesti pectora Magni
sustinet amplexu dulci, non colla tenere,
extremusque perit tam longi fructus amoris,
praecipitantque suos luctus, neuterque recedens
sustinuit dixisse ' vale ', vitamque per omnem
nulla fuit tam maesta dies ; nam cetera damna
durata iam mente malis firmaque tulerunt.

It is faulty and monotonous in rhythm, but one would
gladly have more from Lucan of the same poetic quality,
even at the expense of the same blemishes. The dream
of Pompey is scarcely inferior (vii. 7) :

at nox, felicis Magno pars ultima vitae,   [1]
sollicitos vana decepit imagine somnos.
nam Pompeiani visus sibi sede theatri
innumeram effigiem Romanae cernere plebis
attollique suum laetis ad sidera nomen
vocibus et plausu cuneos certare sonantes ;
qualis erat populi facies clamorque faventis,
olim cum iuvenis primique aetate triumphi

. . . .

sedit adhuc Romanus eques ; seu fine bonorum
anxia venturis ad tempora laeta refugit,
sive per ambages solitas contraria visis
vaticinata quies magni tulit omina planctus,

---

the pangs of parting by the least delay. She cannot bear to cast her arms
about sad Magnus' bosom, or clasp his neck in a last sweet embrace ; and
thus the last delight, such long love as theirs might know, is cast away :
they hasten their own agony ; neither as they parted had the heart
to say farewell ; and while they lived they knew no sadder day than
this. All other losses they bore with hearts hardened and steeled by
misery.

[1] But night, the last glad hours that Magnus' life should know,
beguiled his anxious slumbers with vain images of joy. He seemed
to sit in the theatre himself had built, and to behold the semblance
of the countless Roman multitude, and hear his name uplifted to
the stars by joyous voices, and all the roaring benches vying in their
applause. Even so he saw the people and heard their cheers in the
days of old, when still a youth, in the hour of his first triumph . . . he sat
no more as yet than a knight of Rome ; whether it was that at thy fortune's
close thy sleep, tormented with the fears of what should be, fled back to
happier days, or riddling as 'tis wont, foretold the contrary of thy dreams and

seu vetito patrias ultra tibi cernere sedes
sic Romam fortuna dedit. ne rumpite somnos,
castrorum vigiles, nullas tuba verberet aures.
crastina dira quies et imagine maesta diurna
undique funestas acies feret, undique bellum.

The scene is well and naturally conceived ; there is no rant
or false pathos ; it is an oasis in a book which, though in
many ways the finest in the *Pharsalia*, yet owes its impres-
siveness to a rhetoric which, for all its brilliance and power,
will not always bear more than superficial examination.
The last passage, with its description of the Druid's grove
near Massilia,[1] is on a different plane. It gives less scope
to the higher poetical imagination ; it describes a scene
such as the Silver Age delighted in,[2] a dark wood, whereto
the sunlight scarce can penetrate ; altars stand there stained
with dark rites of human sacrifice ; no bird or beast will
approach it ; no wind ever stirs its leaves ; if they rustle,
it is with a strange mysterious rustling all their own : there
are dark pools and ancient trees, their trunks encircled
by coiling snakes ; strange sounds and sights are there,
and when the sun rides high at noon, not even the priest
will approach the sanctuary for fear lest unawares he come
upon his lord and master. While similar descriptions may
be found in other poets of the age, there is a strength
and simplicity about this passage that rivets the attention,
whereas others leave us cold and indifferent. But Lucan
does not always exercise such restraint, and such passages
are as rare as they are welcome. The reason for this is
obvious : the narrative must necessarily consist in the main

brought thee omens of mighty woe ; or whether, since ne'er again thou
mightest see thy father's home, thus even in dreams fortune gave it to
thy sight. Break not his slumbers, guardians of the camp ; let not the
trumpet strike his ears at all. Dread shall to-morrow's slumbers be, and,
haunted by the sad image of the disastrous day, shall bring before his eyes
naught save war and armies doomed to die.

[1] iii. 399.
[2] Cp. Seneca, *Oed.* 530 sqq. The description of a grove was part of the
poetic wardrobe. Cp. Pers. i. 70.

of military movements. In the words of Petronius,[1] that
is better done by the historians. The adventures on the
march are not likely as a rule to be peculiarly interesting ;
there are no heroic single combats to vary and glorify
the fighting. Conscious of this inevitable difficulty, and
with all the rhetorician's morbid fear of being commonplace, Lucan betakes himself to desperate remedies, hyperbole and padding. If he describes a battle, he must invent
new and incredible horrors to enthral us ; his sea-fight at
Massilia is a notable instance ; [2] death ceases to inspire
horror and becomes grotesque. If a storm arises he must
outdo all earlier epic storms. Vergil had attempted to
outdo the storms of the *Odyssey*. Lucan must outdo
Vergil. Consequently, in the storm that besets Caesar on
his legendary voyage to Italy in the fisherman's boat [3]
that ' carried Caesar and his fortunes ', strange things
happen. The boat rocks helplessly in mid-sea—

> Its sails in clouds, its keel upon the ground,
> For all the sea was piled into the waves
> And drawn from depths between laid bare the sand.[4]

In the same tempest—

> The sea had risen to the clouds
> In mighty mass, had not Olympus' chief
> Pressed down its waves with clouds.[4]

If he is concerned with a march through the African desert,
he must introduce the reader to a whole host of apocryphal
serpents, with details as to the nature of their bites.[5] So
terrible are these reptiles that it is a positive relief to the
army to enter the region of lions.[6] Before such specimens as this the hyperbole of Seneca seems tame and insignificant.

The introduction of irrelevant episodes would be less

---

[1] See p. 103.

[2] iii. 509–762. For a still more grotesque fight, cp. vi. 169–262 ; also
ii. 211–20 ; iv. 794, 5.

[3] v. 610–53. Cp. also ix. 457–71.

[4] Sir E. Ridley's trans.   [5] ix. 619–838.   [6] ix. 946, 7.

reprehensible were it not that such episodes are for the most part either dull or a fresh excuse for bombast or (worse still) a display of erudition.[1] He devotes no less than 170 lines in the first book to a description of the prodigies that took place at Rome on the outbreak of the Civil War, and of the rites performed to avert their omens.[2]

In the next book a hundred and sixty-six lines are given to a lurid picture of the Marian and Sullan proscriptions,[3] and forty-six to a compressed geography of Italy.[4] In the fifth book we are given the tedious story of how a certain obscure Appius consulted the Delphian oracle[5] and how he fared, merely, we suspect, that Lucan may have an opportunity for depicting the frenzies of the Pythian prophetess. Similarly, at the close of the sixth book, Pompey's son consults a necromancer as to the result of the war.[6] The scene is described with not a little skill and ingenuity, but it has little *raison d'être* save the gratification of the taste for witchcraft which Lucan shared with his audience and his fellow poets.

Apart from these weaknesses of method and execution, Lucan's style is unsuited to epic whether historical or legendary. He has not sufficient command of a definitely poetical vocabulary to enable him to captivate the reader by pure sensuous charm. He is, as Quintilian says, ' magis oratoribus quam poetis imitandus.' He cannot shake himself free from the influence of his rhetorical training. It is a severe condemnation of an epic poet to deny him,

---

1 For examples of erudition, cp. ix. loc. cit., where the origin of serpents of Africa is given, involving the story of Perseus and Medea, iv. 622 sqq. The arrival of Curio in Africa is signalized by a long account of the slaying of Antaeus by Hercules.

2 i. 523–end.   3 ii. 67–220.

4 ii. 392–438. Cp. the geography of Thessaly, coupled with a description of its witches, vi. 333–506.

5 v. 71–236.

6 vi. 507–830. It is noteworthy, also, that incidents not necessarily irrelevant in themselves are treated with a monstrous lack of proportion, e.g. the siege of Massilia is not irrelevant ; but it is given 390 lines (iii. 372–762), and Lucan forgets to mention that Caesar captured it.

as we have denied, the gifts of narrative and dramatic
power. Yet much of Lucan is more than readable, to
some it is even fascinating. He has other methods of meeting
the difficulties presented by historical epic. The work is
full of speeches, moralising, and apostrophes. He will
not let the story tell itself ; he is always harping on its
moral and political significance. As a result, we get long
passages that belong to the region of elevated political
satire. They are not epic, but they are often magnificent.
It is in them that Lucan's political feeling appears at
its truest and strongest.[1] The actual fortunes of the republican armies, as recounted by Lucan, must fail to rouse the
emotions of the most ardent anti-Caesarian, and it is doubtful
whether they would have responded to more skilful treatment. But in the apostrophes grief and indignation can find
a voice and stir the heart. They may reveal a monstrous
lack of the sense of historical proportion. To attribute the
depopulation of the rural districts of Italy to the slaughter
at Pharsalus is absurd. That Lucan does this is undeniable,
but his words have a deeper significance. It was at Pharsalus, above all other battles, that the republic fell to ruin,
and the poet is justified in making it the symbol of that
fall.[2] And even where the sentiment is at bottom false,
there is such an impetuosity and vigour in the lines, and
such a depth of scorn in each epigram, that the reader
is swept off his balance and convinced against his will.
We hardly pause to think whether Pharsalus, or even the
whole series of civil wars, really prevented the frontiers of
Rome being conterminous with the limits of the inhabited
globe, when we read such lines as (vii. 419)—

> quo latius orbem   [1]
> possedit, citius per prospera fata cucurrit.
> omne tibi bellum gentes dedit omnibus annis :

[1] The wider she lorded it o'er the world, the swifter did she run through
her fair fortunes. Each war, each year, gave thee new peoples to rule ;

[1] e.g. iv. 799–end, vii. 385–459, 586–96, 617–46, 847–72, viii. 542–60.
793–end.   [2] vii. 385–459.

te geminum Titan procedere vidit in axem ;
haud multum terrae spatium restabat Eoae,
ut tibi nox, tibi tota dies, tibi cur.eret aether,
omniaque errantes stellae Romana viderent.
sed retro tua fata tulit par omnibus annis
Emathiae funesta dies. hac luce cruenta
effectum, ut Latios non horreat India fasces.
nec vetitos errare Dahas in moenia ducat
Sarmaticumque premat succinctus consul aratrum,
quod semper saevas debet tibi Parthia poenas,
quod fugiens civile nefas redituraque numquam
libertas ultra Tigrim Rhenumque recessit
ac totiens nobis iugulo quaesita vagatur,
Germanum Scythicumque bonum, nec respicit ultra
Ausoniam.

But this famous apostrophe closes on a truer note with
six lines of unsurpassed satire (454)—

                           mortalia nulli   [1]
sunt curata deo. cladis tamen huius habemus
vindictam, quantam terris dare numina fas est :
bella pares superis facient civilia divos ;
fulminibus manes radiisque ornabit et astris,
inque deum templis iurabit Roma per umbras.

---

thee did the sun behold advancing towards either pole ; little remained
to conquer of the Eastern world ; so that for thee, and thee alone, night
and day and heaven should revolve, and the planets gaze on naught that
was not Rome's. But Emathia's fatal day, a match for all the bygone
years, has swept thy destiny backward. This day of slaughter was the cause
that India trembles not before the lictor-rods of Rome, and that no
consul, with toga girded high, leads the Dahae within some city's wall, forbidden to wander more, and in Sarmatia drives the founder's plough.
This day was the cause that Parthia still owes thee a fierce revenge, that
freedom flying from the crimes of citizens has withdrawn behind Tigris
and the Rhine, ne'er to return, and, sought so oft by us with our life's blood,
wanders the prize of German and of Scyth, and hath no further care for
Ausonia.
  [1] No god has a thought for the doings of mortal men : yet for this
overthrow this vengeance is ours, so far as gods may give satisfaction to
the earth : civil wars shall raise dead Caesars to the level of the gods
above ; and Rome shall deck the spirits of the dead with rays and thunderbolts and stars, and in the temples of the gods shall swear by the name of
shades.

Noblest of all are the lines that close another apostrophe
on the same subject a little later in the same book (638)—

> maius ab hac acie quam quod sua saecula ferrent   [1]
> volnus habent populi ; plus est quam vita salusque
> quod perit ; in totum mundi prosternimur aevum,
> vincitur his gladiis omnis quae serviet aetas.
> proxima quid suboles aut quid meruere nepotes
> in regnum nasci ? pavide num gessimus arma
> teximus aut iugulos ? alieni poena timoris
> in nostra cervice sedet. post proelia natis
> si dominum, Fortuna, dabas, et bella dedisses.

These are the finest of not a few[1] remarkable expressions
of Lucan's hatred for the growing autocracy of the principate :
it is noteworthy that almost all occur in the last seven
books. They can hardly be regarded as mere abstract
meditations ; they have a force and bitterness which justify
us in regarding them as evidence of his changed attitude
towards Nero. The first three books were published while
he yet basked in the sunshine of court favours. Then
came the breach between himself and Nero. His wounded
vanity assisted his principles to come to the surface.[2]

The speeches, with very few exceptions,[3] scarcely rank

---

[1] A deeper wound than their own age might bear was dealt the peoples
of this earth in this battle : 'tis more than life and safety that is lost :
for all future ages of the world are we laid low : these swords have vanquished generations yet unborn, and doomed them to eternal slavery.
What had the sons and grandsons of those who fought that day deserved
that they should be born into slavery ? Did we bear our arms like cowards,
or screen our throats from death ? Upon our necks is riveted the doom
that we should live in fear of another. Nay, Fortune, since thou gavest
a tyrant to those born since the war, thou shouldst have given them also
the chance to fight for freedom.

---

[1] There is nothing in these last seven books that can be regarded as in
any way written to please Nero, save the description of the noble death
of Domitius Ahenobarbus, Nero's great-great-grandfather (vii. 597–616).
On the contrary there are many passages which Lucan would hardly have
written while he was enjoying court favour : e. g. iv. 821–3, v. 385–402,
vi. 809, vii. 694–6, x. 25–8.

[2] See p. 98.

[3] e. g. the two speeches of Cato quoted above.

with the apostrophes.   Like the speeches in the plays of
Seneca, they are little more than glorified *suasoriae*.   They
are, for the most part, such speeches as—after making the
most liberal allowance for rhetorical licence—no human
being outside a school of rhetoric could have uttered.
Caesar's soldiery would have stared aghast had they been
addressed by their general in such language as Lucan makes
him use to inspire them with courage before Pharsalus.
They would have understood little, and cared less, had
Caesar said (vii. 274)—

> civilia paucae   [1]
> bella manus facient; pugnae pars magna levabit
> his orbem populis Romanumque obteret hostem;

or (279)—

> sitque palam, quas tot duxit Pompeius in urbem   [2]
> curribus, unius gentes non esse triumphi.

They would have laughed at exaggerations such as (287)—

> cuius non militis ensem   [3]
> agnoscam? caelumque tremens cum lancea transit,
> dicere non fallar quo sit vibrata lacerto.

And yet beneath all this fustian there is much that stirs
the blood.   Lines such as (261)—

> si pro me patriam ferro flammisque petistis,   [4]
> nunc pugnate truces gladiosque exsolvite culpa.

---

[1]   Not in civil strife
Your blows shall fall—the battle of to-day
Sweeps from the earth the enemies of Rome.
                                        SIR E. RIDLEY.

[2]   Make plain to all men that the crowds who decked
Pompeius' hundred pageants scarce were fit
For one poor triumph.
                                        SIR E. RIDLEY.

[3]   When the sword
Of each of you shall strike, I know the hand:
The javelin's flight to me betrays the arm
That launched it hurtling.
                                        SIR E. RIDLEY.

[4] If for my sake you sought your fatherland with fire and sword, fight
fierce to-day, and by victory clear your swords from guilt. No hand is

nulla manus belli mutato iudice pura est.
non mihi res agitur, sed vos ut libera sitis
turba precor, gentes ut ius habeatis in omnes.
ipse ego privatae cupidus me reddere vitae
plebeiaque toga modicum compomere civem,
omnia dum vobis liceant, nihil esse recuso.
invidia regnate mea;

or (290)—

quod si signa ducem numquam fallentia vestrum   [1]
conspicio faciesque truces oculosque minaces,
vicistis,

though they are not the words of the historical Caesar,
have a stirring sincerity and force. But the speeches
fail because all speak the same artificial language. A
mutineer can say of Caesar (v. 289)—

Rheni mihi Caesar in undis   [2]
dux erat, hic socius. facinus quos inquinat aequat;

or threaten with the words (292)—

quidquid gerimus fortuna vocatur.   [3]
nos fatum sciat esse suum.

The lines are brilliant and worthy of life : in their immediate
context they are ridiculous. Epigrams have their value,
however, even when they suit their context ill, and neither
Juvenal nor Tacitus has surpassed Lucan in this respect,

---

guiltless judged by a new arbiter of war. The struggle of to-day does
naught for me ; but for you, so runs my prayer, it shall bring freedom
and dominion o'er the world. Myself, I long to return to private life, and,
even though my garb were that of the common people, to be a peaceful
citizen once more. So be it all be made lawful for you, there is naught
I would refuse to be : for me the hatred, so be yours the power.

[1] Nay, if I behold those signs that ne'er deceived your leader, fierce
faces and threatening eyes, you are already conquerors.

[2] Caesar was my leader by the waves of Rhine, here he is my comrade. The stain of crime makes all men equal.

[3]   As fortune's gift
He takes the victory which our arms have won :
But *we* his fortunes are, his fates are ours
To fashion as we will.

SIR E. RIDLEY.

or been more often quoted.   He is, says Quintilian, *sententiis clarissimus*.   Nothing can surpass (iv. 519)—

      victurosque dei celant, ut vivere durent,   [1]
      felix esse mori.

or (viii. 631–2)—

              mutantur prospera vitae,   [2]
      non fit morte miser ;

or (i. 32)—

      alta sedent civilis volnera dextrae ;   [3]

or (ix. 211)—

      scire mori sors prima viris, sed proxima cogi.   [4]

Lines such as (i. 281)—

      semper nocuit differre paratis,   [5]

or (v. 260)—

      quidquid multis peccatur, inultum est   [6]

are commonplace enough in thought but perfect in expression.   Of a different character, but equally noteworthy, are sayings such as iv. 819—

      momentumque fuit mutatus Curio rerum ;   [7]

or (iv. 185)—

      usque adeone times, quem tu facis ipse timendum ?   [8]

---

[1] And the gods conceal from those who are doomed to live how happy it is to die.   Thus only may they endure to live.

[2]   Life may bring defeat,
      But death no misery.

                                      SIR E. RIDLEY.

[3] Deep lie the wounds that civil war hath made.

[4]   Best gift of all
      The knowledge how to die : next, death compelled.

                                      SIR E. RIDLEY.

[5] To pause when ready is to court defeat.

                                    SIR E. RIDLEY.

[6] The crime is free where thousands bear the guilt.

                                    SIR E. RIDLEY.

[7] The change of Curio turned the scale of history.

[8]   Dost fear him so
      Who takes his title to be feared from thee ?

                        SIR E. RIDLEY, *slightly altered.*

Lucan's gift for epigram is further enhanced by the nature of his metre. Ponderous in the extreme, it is ill-suited for epic, though in isolated lines its very weight gives added force. But he had a poor ear for rhythm : his hexameter is monotonous as the iambics of Seneca. There is a want of variety in pauses ; he will not accommodate his rhythm to circumstances ; line follows line with but the slightest rhythmical variation, and there is far too[1] sparing a use of elision. This failing is in part due to his desire to steer clear of the influence of Vergil and strike out on a line of his own. Faint echoes of Vergil, it is true, occur frequently throughout the poem, but to the untrained eye Lucan is emphatically un-Vergilian. His affinity to Ovid is greater. Both are rhetorical, and Lucan is indebted to Ovid for much mythological detail. And it is probable that he owes his smoothness and monotony of metre largely to the influence of the *Metamorphoses*. His ponderosity is all his own.[2]

Lucan is the child of his age, but he is almost an isolated figure in literature. He has almost every conceivable defect in every conceivable degree, from the smallest detail to the general conception of his poem. And yet he triumphs over himself. It is a hateful task to read the *Pharsalia* from cover to cover, and yet when it is done and the lapse of time has allowed the feeling of immediate repulsion to evaporate, the reader can still feel that Lucan is a great writer. The absurdities slip from the memory, the dreariness of the narrative is forgotten, and the great passages of lofty rhetoric, with their pungent epigram and their high political enthusiasm, remain deeply engraven on the mind.

---

[1] He is, moreover, very careless in his repetition of the same word, cp. i. 25, 27 urbibus, iii. 436, 441, 445 silva, &c. ; cp. Haskins, ed. lxxxi. (Heitland's introd.)

[2] He is far less dactylic than Ovid. For the relation between the various writers of epic in respect of metre, see Drobisch, *Versuch üb. die Formen des lat. Hex.* 140. The proportion of spondees in the first four feet of hexameters of Roman writers is there given as follows : Catullus 65·8 %, Silius 60·6 %, Ennius 59·5 %, Lucretius 57·4 %, Vergil 56 %, Horace 55 %, Lucan 54·3 %, Statius 49·7 %, Valerius 46·2 %, Ovid 45·2 %.

It is they that have given Lucan the immortality which he promised himself. The *Pharsalia* is dead, but Lucan lives.

It is useless to conjecture what might have been the fate of such remarkable gifts in a less corrupt age. This much, however, may be said, Lucan never had a fair chance. The circle in which he moved, the education which he received, suffered only his rhetorical talent to develop, and to this were sacrificed all his other gifts, his clearness of vision, his sense of proportion, his poetical imagination. He was spoilt by admiration and his own facility. Moreover, Seneca was his uncle : a comparison shows how profoundly the elder poet influenced the younger. There is the same self-conscious arrogance begotten of Stoicism, the same brilliance of wit and absence of humour. Their defects and merits alike reveal them as kindred, though Lucan stands worlds apart as a poet from Seneca, the ranting tragedian. He was but twenty-five when he died. Age might have brought a maturity and dignity of spirit which would have made rhetoric his servant and not his master, and refined away the baser alloys of his character. Even as it was he left much that, without being pure gold, yet possessed many elements and much of the brilliance of the true metal. Dante's judgement was true when he set him among the little company of true poets, of which Dante himself was proud to be made one.

CHAPTER V

PETRONIUS

THE most curious and in some respects the most remarkable work that the Silver Age has bequeathed to us is a fragment of a novel, the *Satyricon* of Petronius Arbiter. Its author is generally identified with Titus Petronius, the friend and victim of Nero. Tacitus has described him in a passage, remarkable even among Tacitean portraits for its extraordinary brilliance. ' His days he passed in sleep, his nights in the business and pleasures of life. Indolence had raised him to fame, as energy raises others, and he was reckoned not a debauchee and spendthrift, like most of those who squander their substance, but a man of refined luxury. And indeed his talk and his doings, the freer they were, and the more show of carelessness they exhibited, were the better liked for their look of a natural simplicity. Yet as proconsul of Bithynia and soon afterwards as consul, he showed himself a man of vigour and equal to business. Then, falling back into vice or affecting vice, he was chosen by Nero to be one of his few intimate associates, as a critic in matters of taste (*elegantiae arbiter*). The emperor thought nothing charming or elegant in luxury unless Petronius had expressed his approval. Hence jealousy on the part of Tigellinus, who looked on him as a rival, and even his superior, in the science of pleasure. And so he worked on the prince's cruelty, which dominated every other passion : charging Petronius with having been the friend of Scaevinus, bribing a slave to turn informer, robbing him of the means of defence, and hurrying into prison the greater part of his domestics. It happened at the time that the emperor was on his way to Campania, and that Petronius, after going as far as Cumae, was there detained. He bore no longer the suspense of fear or of hope. Yet he did not fling away life with precipitate haste, but having made an incision in his veins and then according to his humour bound them up, he again opened them, while he conversed with his friends, not in a serious strain or on topics that might win him the glory of courage. He listened to them as they repeated, not thoughts on the immortality of the soul or on the theories of philosophers, but light poetry and playful verses. To some of his slaves he gave liberal presents, to others a flogging. He dined, indulged himself in sleep, that death, even though forced, might have a natural appearance. Even in his will he did not, as did many in their last moments, flatter Nero or Tigellinus, or any other of the men in power. On the contrary, he described fully the prince's shameful excesses, with the names of his male and female companions and their novelties in debauchery, and sent the account under seal to Nero. Then he broke his signet-ring, that it might not be available to bring others into peril.'[1]

There is nothing definitely to bring this ingenious and brilliant debauchee into connexion with the Petronius Arbiter of the *Satyricon*. But the character of Titus Petronius is exactly in keeping with the tone of the novel ; the novelist's cognomen Arbiter, though in itself by no means extraordinary, may well have sprung from or given rise to the title *elegantiae arbiter* ; and finally the few indications of date in the novel all point to a period not far from the reign of Nero. There is the criticism of Lucan,[2] which certainly loses point if not written during Lucan's lifetime ; there is the criticism of the rhetorical training of the day,[3] which finds a remarkable echo in the criticism of Vipstanus Messala in the *Dialogus* of Tacitus, a work which, whatever the date of its actual composition, certainly refers to a period less than ten years after the death of T. Petronius ; there is the style of the work itself ; wherever the writer abandons the colloquial Latin, in which so much of the work is written, we find a finished diction, whether

---

[1] Tac. *Ann.* xvi. 18, 19 (Church and Brodribb's trans.).
[2] c. 118 sq.   [3] cc. 1-5,

in prose or verse, which no unprejudiced judge could place later than the accession of Trajan, and which has nothing in it to prevent its attribution to the reign of Nero. In that reign there is but one Petronius to whom we can assign the *Satyricon*, the Petronius immortalized by Tacitus.[1]

Of the work as a whole this is no place to speak. The fragments which survive are in the main in prose. But the work is modelled on the Menippean satires of Varro, and belongs to the same class of writing as the *Apocolocyntosis* of Seneca. In the form of a loosely-strung and rambling novel we have a satirical commentary on human life ; the satire is cynical and pungent, rather than mordant, makes no pretence of logic, and proceeds not from a moral sense but from a sense of humour. Wild and indecent as Petronius' laughter often is, it springs from one who is a real artist, possessing a sense of proportion as well as the sense of contrast that is the source and fount of humour. This is most strongly evident in that portion of his satire which concerns us here, inasmuch as it is directed against contemporary literary tendencies. We must beware of fastening on the words of the characters in the novel as necessarily expressing the thoughts of its author. But it is noteworthy that all his literary criticism points in the same direction ; it is above all conservative. Through the mouths of Encolpius, the dissolute hero of the story, and the rhetorician Agamemnon [2] he denounces the flamboyant rhetoric of the day, its remoteness from reality, the lack of sanity and industry on the part both of pupil and instructor. ' As boys they pass their time at school at what is no better than play, as youths they make themselves ridiculous in the forum, and, worst of all, when they grow old they refuse to acknowledge the faults acquired by their education.' Study is necessary, and above all the study of good models. Sophocles, Euripides, Pindar, the great lyricists, Plato, Demo-

---

[1] The first reference in literature to the *Satyricon* is in Macrobius, in *Somn. Scip.* i. 2, 8.

[2] cc. 1–5.

sthenes, Thucydides, Hyperides, all the great classics, these
are the true models for the young orator. Agamemnon
cannot restrain himself and even bursts into verse in the
course of this disquisition on the decadence of oratory :

> artis severae si quis ambit effectus   [1]
> mentemque magnis applicat, prius mores
> frugalitatis lege poliat exacta.
> nec curet alto regiam trucem vultu
> cliensve cenas impotentium captet
> nec perditis addictus obruat vino
> mentis calorem, neve plausor in scaenam
> sedeat redemptus histrionis ad rictus.
> sed sive armigerae rident Tritonidis arces,
> seu Lacedaemonio tellus habitata colono
> Sirenumve domus, det primos versibus annos
> Maeoniumque bibat felici pectore fontem.
> mox et Socratico plenus grege mittat habenas
> liber et ingentis quatiat Demosthenis arma.
> hinc Romana manus circumfluat et modo Graio
> ·exonerata sono mutet suffusa saporem.
> interdum subducta foro det pagina cursum
> et cortina ¹ sonet celeri distincta meatu ;
> dein ² epulas et bella truci memorata canore

---

[1] If any man court success in the lofty art of letters and apply his
mind to great things, he must first perfect his character by simplicity's stern
law ; he must care naught for the haughty frown of the fierce tyrant
that lords it in his palace, nor seek client-like for invitations to the board
of the profligate, nor deliver himself over to the company of debauchees
and drown the fire of his understanding in wine, nor sit in the theatre
the hired applauder of the mouthing actor. But whether the citadel of
panoplied Minerva allure him with its smile, or the land where the Spartan
exile came to dwell, or the Sirens' home, let him devote his early years to
poesy, and let his spirit drink in with happy omen a draught from the
Maeonian fount. Thereafter, when his soul is full of the lore of the Socratic
school, let him give himself free rein and brandish the weapons of great
Demosthenes. Next let the band of Roman authors throng him round,
and, but newly freed from the music of Greece, suffuse his soul and change
its tone. Meanwhile, let his pen run its course withdrawn from the forum,
and let Apollo's tripod send forth a voice rhythmic and swift : next let
him roll forth in lordly speech the tale of heroes' feasting and wars, set
forth in fierce strain and lofty language, such as fell from the lips of daunt-

---

¹ MS. fortuna.   ² MS. dent.

> grandiaque indomiti Ciceronis verba minetur.
> his animum succinge bonis : sic flumine largo
> plenus Pierio defundes pectore verba.

This is not inspired poetry ; but its advice is sound, and its point of view just. Nor is this criticism a mere *jeu d'esprit* ; it is hard to resist the conclusion that the author is putting his own views into the mouths of his more than shady characters. For, *mutatis mutandis*, the same attitude towards literary art is revealed in the utterances of the poet Eumolpus.[1] It is a curious fact that while none of the characters in Petronius are to be taken seriously, their speech at times soars from the reeking atmosphere of the brothel and the clamour of the streets to clearer and loftier regions of thought, if not of action. The first appearance of Eumolpus is conceived in a broadly comic vein. ' While I was thus engaged a grey-haired old man entered the picture gallery. He had a troubled countenance, which seemed to promise some momentous utterance. His dress was lamentable, and showed that he was clearly one of those literary gentlemen so unpopular with the rich. He took his stand by my side. " I am a poet," he said, " and no mean one, if any trust is to be placed in wreaths of honour, which are so often bestowed even on those who least deserve them." " Why, then, are you so ill-clad ? " I asked. " Just for that very reason. Devotion to art never brought any one wealth "—

> qui pelago credit magno se faenore tollit ;   [1]
> qui pugnas et castra petit, praecingitur auro ;
> vilis adulator picto iacet ebrius ostro,
> et qui sollicitat nuptas, ad praemia peccat :

---

less Cicero. Prepare thy soul for joys such as these ; and, steeped in the plenteous stream of letters, thou shalt give utterance to the thoughts of thy Pierian soul.

[1] He who entrusts his fortunes to the sea, wins a mighty harvest ; he who seeks the camp and the field of war, may gird him with gold : the vile flatterer lies drunken on embroidered purple ; the gallant who courts

---

[1] c. 83.

sola pruinosis horret facundia pannis
atque inopi lingua desertas invocat artes.[1]

'There's no doubt as to the truth of it. If a man has a
detestation of vice and chooses the paths of virtue, he
is hated on the ground that his morals are eccentric. No
one approves of ways of life other than his own. Then
there are those whose sole care is the acquisition of wealth ;
they are unwilling that anything should be thought to be
a superior good to that which they themselves possess. And
so they persecute lovers of literature with all their might.'
This *vitiorum omnium inimicus* then proceeds to tell a story
which casts a startling light upon his ' eccentric morality '.
Its undoubted humour can hardly be said to redeem its
amazing grossness. He has scarcely finished the narration
of his own shame when he is back again in another world
—the world of letters. He laments the decay of art and
philosophy. ' The passion for money-making has brought
ruin in its train. While virtue went bare and was a welcome
guest, the noble arts flourished, and men vied with one
another in the effort to discover anything that might be
of service to mankind.' He quotes the examples of Demo-
critus, Eudoxus, Chrysippus in the world of science, of
Myron in art. ' We have given ourselves up to wine and
women, and take no pains to become acquainted even
with the arts already discovered. We traduce antiquity
by teaching and learning its vices only. Where is dialectic ?
Where is astronomy ? Where is philosophy ? ' He sees
that Encolpius is not listening, but is absorbed in the con-
templation of a picture representing the sack of Troy,
and seizes the opportunity of reciting a poem of his own
upon the subject. The lines are for the most part neither
original nor striking ; they form a kind of abstract in
iambics of the second Aeneid, from the appearance of Sinon
to the emergence of the Greeks from the Trojan horse.

---

the favours of wedded wives, wins wealth by his sin : eloquence alone
shivers in frosty rags and invokes the neglected arts with pauper tongue.

---

[1] Cp. Juv. *Sat.* 7 ; Tac. *Dial.* 9.

But the work is finished and elegant,[1] and the simile which describes the arrival of the serpents that were to slay Laocoon is not unworthy of a more successful poet than Eumolpus is represented to have been :

> ecce alia monstra ; celsa qua Tenedos mare   [1]
> dorso replevit, tumida consurgunt freta
> undaque resultat scissa tranquillo minans [2]
> qualis silenti nocte remorum sonus
> longe refertur, cum premunt classes mare
> pulsumque marmor abiete imposita gemit.
> respicimus ; angues orbibus geminis ferunt
> ad saxa fluctus, tumida quorum pectora
> rates ut altae lateribus spumas agunt.

The picture is at once vivid and beautiful, and we feel almost regretful at the fate which his recitation brought on the unhappy poet. ' Those who were walking in the colonnade began to throw stones at Eumolpus as he recited. He recognized this method of applauding his wit, covered his head with his cloak and fled from the temple. I was afraid that he would denounce me as a poet. And so I followed him till I came to the sea-shore and was out of range. " What do you mean," I said, " by inflicting this disease of yours upon us ? You have been less than two hours in my company, and you have more often spoken like a poet than a man. I'm not surprised that people throw stones at you. I'm going to fill my own pockets with stones, and the moment you begin to unburden yourself,

---

[1] Lo ! a fresh portent ; where the ridge of lofty Tenedos filled the sea, there breaks a swelling surge, and the broken waves rebound and threaten the calm : as when in the silent night the sound of oars is borne afar, when navies burden the main and the smitten deep groans beneath its freight of pine. We looked round : the waves bear towards the rocks two coiling snakes, whose swelling breasts, like tall ships, drive the water in foam along their sides.

---

[1] c. 89. It has been suggested that this poem is a parody of Nero's *Troiae halosis !* But the poem shows *no* signs of being a parody. It is obviously written in all seriousness.

[2] MS. *minor.* I suggest *minans* as a possible solution of the difficulty.

I'm going to break your head." His face revealed a painful
emotion. "My good youth," said he, "to-day is not the
first occasion on which I have suffered this fate. Nay,
I have never entered a theatre to recite, without attracting
this kind of welcome. But as I don't want to quarrel
with you, I will abstain from my daily food for the whole
day." ' Eumolpus did not keep this promise; but the poem
with which he broke it is of small importance and need
not detain us.[1] It is a little disquisition on the refinements
of luxury now prevalent, and has but one notable line—
the last—

> quidquid quaeritur optimum videtur.   [1]

But later he has another outbreak. Encolpius and his
friends have been shipwrecked near Croton. On their way
to the town Eumolpus beguiles the tedium of the climb by
the criticism of Lucan and the attempt to improve on the
Pharsalia, which have been discussed in the chapter on Lucan.
If neither his poetry nor his criticism as a whole are sound,
they are at least meant seriously. Here, again, we have a
plea for earnest study, and for the avoidance of mere tricks
of rhetoric. As for the rhetorician Agamemnon, so for
Eumolpus, the great poets of the past are Homer and the
lyric poets; and nearer home are the 'Roman Vergil' and
Horace. If there was nothing else in this passage than
the immortal phrase 'Horatii curiosa felicitas', it would
redeem it from the commonplace. Petronius is a 'classicist';
the friend of Nero, he protests against the flamboyance of the
age as typified in the rhetorical style of Seneca and Lucan.
If the work was written at the time when Seneca and Lucan
first fell from the Imperial favour, such criticism may well
have found favour at court. If, with the brilliant whimsicality that characterizes all his work, Petronius has placed
these utterances in the mouth of disreputable and broadly
comic figures, that does not impair the value or sincerity

---

[1] Whatever must be sought for, that seems best.

---

[1] c. 93.

of the criticism. Eumolpus' complaint of the decline of the arts and the baneful effect of the struggle for wealth is no doubt primarily inspired by the fact that he is poor and can find no patron nor praise for his verse, but must put up with execrations and showers of stones. But that does not affect the truth of much that he says, nor throw doubt upon the sincerity of Petronius himself.

The same whimsicality is shown elsewhere in the course of the novel. It contains not a few poems which, detached from their context, are full of grace and charm, though their application is often disgusting in the extreme. Such are the hexameters towards the close of the work in which Encolpius describes the scene of his unhappy love affair with a certain Circe :

> Idaeo quales fudit de vertice flores   [1]
> terra parens, cum se concesso iunxit amori
> Iuppiter et toto concepit pectore flammas :
> emicuere rosae violaeque et molle cyperon,
> albaque de viridi riserunt lilia prato :
> talis humus Venerem molles clamavit in herbas,
> candidiorque dies secreto favit amori (127);

> nobilis aestivas platanus diffuderat umbras   [2]
> et bacis redimita Daphne tremulaeque cupressus
> et circum tonsae trepidanti vertice pinus.
> has inter ludebat aquis errantibus amnis
> spumeus et querulo vexabat rore lapillos.
> dignus amore locus : testis silvestris aedon

---

[1] As the flowers poured forth by mother earth from Ida's peak, when she yielded to Jove's embrace and the god's soul was filled with passionate flame ; the rose, the violet, and the soft iris flashed forth, and white lilies gleamed from the green meadow ; so shone the earth when it called our love to rest upon the soft grass, and the day, brighter than its wont, smiled on our secret passion.

[2] A noble plane tree and the bay tree with its garland of berries, and the quivering cypress and the trim pine with its tremulous top, spread a sweet summer shade abroad. Amid them a foaming river sported with wandering waters and lashed the pebbles with its peevish spray. Meet was the place for love, with the woodland nightingale and the town-haunting swallow

> atque urbana Procne, quae circum gramina fusae
> ac molles violas cantu sua furta colebant (131).

The unpleasing nature of the context cannot obscure the fact that here we have genuine poetry of great delicacy and beauty.[1]

Of the satirical epigrams contained in the novel little need be said. They are not in any way pointless or feeble, but they lack the ease and grace, and, it may be added, the sting, of the best work of Martial. The themes are hackneyed and suffer from the absence of the personal note. But it is at least refreshing to find that Petronius does not attempt, like Martial and others, to excuse his obscenity on the ground that his actual life is chaste. He speaks out frankly. ' Why hide what all men know ? '

> quid me constricta spectatis fronte Catones   [1]
>   damnatisque novae simplicitatis opus ?
> sermonis puri non tristis gratia ridet,
>   quodque facit populus, candida lingua refert (132).

A more interesting collection of poems, probably Petronian, remains to be discussed. In addition to the numerous fragments of poetry included in the surviving excerpts from the *Satyricon*, a considerable number of epigrams, attributed with more or less certainty to Petronius, are preserved in the fragments of the *Anthologia Latina*.[2] Immediately following on the epigrams assigned to the authorship of Seneca, the Codex Vossianus Q. 86 gives sixteen epigrams,[3] each headed by the word *item*. Of these two are quoted by Fulgentius as the work of Petronius.[4] There is, therefore,

---

for witness, that, flitting all about the grass and the soft violets, told of their loves in song.

[1] Why gaze at me, ye Catos, with frowning brow, and damn the fresh frankness of my work ? my speech is Latin undefiled, and has grace unmarred by gloom, and my candid tongue tells of what all Rome's people do.

---

1 Cp. also 128 and the spirited epic fragment burlesquely used in 108.
2 See p. 36.
3 Baehrens, *P. L. M.* iv. 74–89.
4 Nos. 76 and 86. Cp. Fulg. *Mythol.* i. 1, p. 31 ; Lactant. *ad Stat. Theb.* iii. 661 ; Fulg. *Mythol.* iii. 9, p. 126.

especially in view of the fact that they all bear a marked
family resemblance to one another, a strong presumption
that all are by the author of the *Satyricon*. Further, there
are eleven epigrams[1] published by Binet in his edition of
Petronius[2] from a MS. originally in the cathedral library
of Beauvais, but now unfortunately lost. The first of the
series is quoted by Fulgentíus[3] as being by Petronius, and
there is no reason for doubting the accuracy of Binet or his
MS.[4] as to the rest. These poems are followed by eight
more epigrams,[5] the first two of which Binet attributes to
Petronius on stylistic grounds, but without any MS. authority.[6] Lastly, four epigrams are preserved by a third MS.
(Cod. Voss. F. 111) under the title *Petronii*.[7] Of these the
first two are found in the extant portions of the *Satyricon*.
The evidence for the Petronian authorship of these thirty-
seven poems is not conclusive. Arguments based on
resemblance or divergence in points of style are somewhat
precarious in the case of an author like Petronius, writing
with great variety of style on a variety of subjects. But
there are some very marked resemblances between certain
of these poems and verses surviving in the excerpts from
the *Satyricon*,[8] and the evidence *against* the Petronian
authorship is of the slightest. A possible exception may
be made in the case of the last eight epigrams preserved
by Binet, though even here Binet is just enough in pointing
out the resemblance of the first two of these to what is
admittedly the work of Petronius. But with regard to
the rest we shall run small risk in regarding them as selected
from the lost books of the *Satyricon*.

---

[1] Baehrens, *P. L. M.* iv. 90–100.

[2] Poitiers, 1579 A. D.   [3] Fulg. *Mythol.* i. 12, p. 44.

[4] That the attribution to Petronius rests on the authority of the lost MS.
is a clear inference from Binet's words, cp. Baehrens, *P. L. M.* iv. 101–8,
' sequebantur ista, sed sine Petronii titulo, at priores illi duo Phalaecii
vix alius fuerint quam Petronii.'

[5] Baehrens, *P. L. M.* iv. 101–8.   [6] See note 4.

[7] Petr. cc. 14, 83 ; Baehrens, *P. L. M.* iv. 120, 121.

[8] Cp. *Satyr.* 127, 131 ; *P. L. M.* iv. 75 ; *S.* 128 ; *P. L. M.* iv. 121 ;
S. 108 ; *P. L. M.* iv. 85 ; *S.* 79, iv. 101.

These poems are very varied in character and as a whole reach a higher poetical level than most of those preserved in the existing fragments of the *Satyricon*.[1] The most notable features are simplicity and unaffected grace of diction coupled with a delicate appreciation of the beauties of nature. There is nothing that is out of keeping with the classicism on which we have insisted as a characteristic of Petronius, there is much that is worthy of the best writers of the Augustan age. The five lines in which he describes the coming of autumn have much in common with the descriptions of nature already quoted from the *Satyricon*. The last line in particular has at once a conciseness and a wealth of suggestion that is rare in any post-Ovidian poet :

> iam nunc algentes autumnus fecerat umbras   [1]
> atque hiemem tepidis spectabat Phoebus habenis,
> iam platanus iactare comas, iam coeperat uvas
> adnumerare suas defecto palmite vitis :
> ante oculos stabat, quidquid promiserat annus.[1]

Equally charming and sincere in tone is the description of the delights of the simple life :

> parvula securo tegitur mihi culmine sedes   [2]
> uvaque plena mero fecunda pendet ab ulmo.
> dant rami cerasos, dant mala rubentia silvae
> Palladiumque nemus pingui se vertice frangit.
> iam qua diductos potat levis area fontes,
> Corycium mihi surgit olus malvaeque supinae
> et non sollicitos missura papavera somnos.

---

[1] Now autumn had brought its cool shades, Phoebus' reins glowed less hot and he was looking winterward. The plane was beginning to shed her leaves, the vine to count its clusters, and its fresh shoots were withered. Before our eyes stood all the promise of the year.

[2] My cottage is sheltered by a roof that fears no ill; the grape, bursting with wine, hangs from the fertile elm ; cherries hang by the bough and my orchard yields its rosy apples, and the tree that Pallas loves breaks beneath the rich burden of its branches. And now, where the garden bed's light soil drinks in the runnels of water, rises for me Corycian kale and low-growing mallow, and the poppy that grants easy slumber. More-

---

[1] *P. L. M.* iv. 75.

> praeterea sive alitibus contexere fraudem
> seu magis inbelles libuit circumdare cervos
> aut tereti lino pavidum subducere piscem,
> hos tantum novere dolos mea sordida rura.
> i nunc et vitae fugientis tempora vende
> divitibus cenis ! me qui manet exitus olim,
> hic precor inveniat consumptaque tempora poscat.[1]

These lines may be no more than an academic exercise on a commonplace theme, but there can be no doubt of their artistic success. We find the same simplicity in Columella, but not the same art. Compare them with the work of Petronius' contemporary, Calpurnius Siculus, and there is all the difference between true poetry and mere poetising. More passionate and more convincing is the elegiac poem celebrating the poet's return to the scene of former happiness :

> o litus vita mihi dulcius, o mare ! felix,   [1]
>   cui licet ad terras ire subinde tuas !
> o formosa dies ! hoc quondam rure solebam
>   naidas alterna [2] sollicitare manu.
> hic fontis lacus est, illic sinus egerit algas :
>   haec statio est tacitis fida cupidinibus.
> pervixi ; neque enim fortuna malignior umquam
>   eripiet nobis, quod prior aura dedit.[3]

---

over, whether 'tis my pleasure to set snares for birds or hem in the timid deer, or on fine-meshed net to draw up the affrighted fish, this is all the guile known to my humble lands. Go to, now, and waste the flying hours of life on sumptuous feasts ! I pray, that my destined end may find me here, and here demand an account of the days I have lived.

[1] O shore, O sea, that I love more than life ! Happy is he that may straightway visit the lands ye border. O fairest day ! 'Twas here that once I was wont to swim and vex the sea-nymphs with my hands' alternate strokes. Here is a stream's deep pool, there the bay casts up its seaweed : here is a spot that can faithfully guard the secret of one's love. I have lived my life to the full ; nor can grudging fortune ever rob me of that which her favouring breeze once gave me.

---

[1] *P. L. M.* iv. 81.

[2] The MS. is hopelessly corrupt at this point. I suggest *naidas alterna manu* as a possible correction of the MS. *Iliadas armatas s. manus.*

[3] *P. L. M.* iv. 84.

But Petronius can attain to equal success in other veins.
Now we have a fragment in the epic style containing a
simile at once original and beautiful :

> haec ait et tremulo deduxit vertice canos   [1]
> consecuitque genas ; oculis nec defuit imber,
> sed qualis rapitur per vallis improbus amnis,
> cum gelidae periere nives et languidus auster
> non patitur glaciem resoluta vivere terra,
> gurgite sic pleno facies manavit et alto
> insonuit gemitu turbato murmure pectus.[1]

Elsewhere we find him writing in satirical vein of the
origin of religion,[2] on the decay of virtue,[3] on the hardship
of the married state[4] :

> ' uxor legis onus, debet quasi census amari.' [2]
> nec censum vellem semper amare meum.

But it is in a love-poem that he reaches his highest
achievement :

> lecto compositus vix prima silentia noctis   [3]
> carpebam et somno lumina victa dabam :
> cum me saevus Amor prensat sursumque capillis
> excitat et lacerum pervigilare iubet.
> ' tu famulus meus,' inquit, ' ames cum mille puellas,
> solus, io, solus, dure, iacere potes ? '
> exsilio et pedibus nudis tunicaque soluta
> omne iter incipio, nullum iter expedio.

---

[1] He spake, and rent the white hair on his trembling head and tore his
cheeks, and his eyes streamed with a flood of tears. As when a resistless
river sweeps down the valley when the chill snows have melted and the
languid south wind thaws the earth and suffers not the ice to remain, even
so his face streamed with a torrent of weeping and his breast groaned loud
with a confused murmur of sorrow.

[2] ' One should love one's wife as one loves one's fortune.' Nay, I
desire not always to love even my fortune.

[3] I lay on my bed and began to enjoy the silence of the night scarce yet
begun, and was yielding my wearied eyes to sleep, when fierce Love laid
hold of me, and, seizing me by the hair, aroused me, tore me, and bade me
wake. ' Canst thou, my servant,' he cried, ' the lover of a thousand girls,
lie thus alone, alone, hard-hearted ? ' I leapt from my couch, and barefoot,
with dishevelled robe, started on my errand, yet never accomplished it.

---

[1] *P. L. M.* iv. 85. [2] Ib. 76. [3] Ib. 82. [4] Ib. 78.

nunc propero, nunc ire piget, rursumque redire
paenitet et pudor est stare via media.
ecce tacent voces hominum strepitusque viarum
et volucrum cantus turbaque fida canum :
solus ego ex cunctis paveo somnumque torumque
et sequor imperium, magne Cupido, tuum.[1]

If this is not great poetry, it is at least one of the most
perfect specimens of conventional erotic verse in all ancient
literature. If we except a very few of the best poems of
Propertius, Latin Elegiacs have nothing to show that com-
bines such perfection of form with such exquisite sensuous
charm. It breathes the fragrance of the Greek anthology.

The general impression left by the poetical work of
Petronius is curiously unlike that left by any Latin poet.
Sometimes dull, he is never eccentric ; without the originality of the greatest artists, he has all the artist's sensibility
for form. He writes not as one inspired, but as one steeped
in the best literature. Many were greater stylists, but few
were endowed with such an exquisite sense of style. As a
poet he is a *dilettante*, and his claim to greatness lies in the
brilliant and audacious humour of his ' picaresque novel '.
But his verse at its best has a charm and fragrance of its
own that is almost unique in Latin, and reveals a combination of grace and facility, to find a parallel for which among
writers of the post-Augustan age we must turn to the pages
of Martial.

Now I hurry forward, now am loth to go ; now repent me that I have
returned, and feel shame to stand thus aimless in mid-street. So the
voices of men, the murmur of the streets, the song of birds, and the trusty
watchdogs all are silent ; and I alone dread the slumbers of my couch
and follow thy behest, great god of love.

---

[1] *P. L. M.* iv. 99. Cp. also 92 and 107.

CHAPTER VI

MINOR POETRY, 14–70 A.D.

I

DIDACTIC POETRY

ONLY two didactic poems of this period have survived, the poem of Columella on gardening, and the anonymous work on Mount Etna, setting forth a theory of volcanic action.

i

THE ' AETNA '

The *Aetna* is a hexameter poem, 646 lines in length. The author laments the indifference shown by poets to the natural phenomena of his day. They waste their time on the description of the marvels of art, the spectacular side of human civilization, and the surface-beauties of Nature.[1] They write trivial epics on the voyage of Argo, the sack of Troy, Niobe, Thyestes, Cadmus, Ariadne, the Battle of the Giants.[2] They tell of the terrors of the underworld,[3] and the loves of the gods :[4] they seek the false rather than the true, they neglect the genuine wonders of Nature, the laws that govern heavenly and terrestrial phenomena.

He will be wiser. But there is no need to travel far. He will not soar skyward to treat of the stars in their courses, of the seasons and signs of the weather, to the neglect of the marvels of mother earth.[5] The greatest of miracles is close at hand, Etna, the home of eternal fire. Deep in the heart of earth dwell two irresistible forces, wind and fire.[6] It is their conflict that causes the outbursts of flame and molten rock that devastate the slopes of Etna. It is no smithy of the gods, no Titan's prison. The causes are natural, water

---

[1] 569 sqq.
[2] 17–22, 43 sqq. He falls into the same error himself (203).
[3] 76 sqq.   [4] 88 sqq.   [5] 220 sqq.   [6] 96 sqq.

and wind and fire. He has seen Etna ; he describes the crater,[1] the volcanic rock that can imprison fire,[2] the clouds that continually veil the mountain's crest,[3] the flames that burst from its summit, the subterranean rumblings,[4] the terrors of the lava stream. He concludes with the touching story of the Catanian brothers who, neglecting all else, sought only to save their aged parents from the flames. Their piety had its reward ; they, and they alone, escaped from the lava ; their neighbours, who sought to save their chattels and their wealth, perished in the stream, encumbered by their belongings.

Of the poet's theory of volcanic action we need not speak ; it was the current scientific theory of the day, and has no value for us ; nor has the author any claim to originality. As to the style and composition of the work, brief comment will suffice. We may give the author credit for a real enthusiasm, and for a just contempt of the prevailing themes that engaged the attention of the minor poets of the day. But he has no gifts for poetry. His theme, although it gave considerable opportunities for episodic display, was one of great difficulty. Much dry scientific detail was necessarily required. If Lucretius is sometimes tedious and prosaic in spite of the vastness of his theme, the magnificence of his moral background, and his inspired enthusiasm, what can be expected of a poem on a minor scientific theme such as Etna ? Volcanoes can hardly compete with the universe as a theme for poetry. The subject is one that might have fascinated an Alexandrian poet and found skilful treatment at his hands. But the author of the *Aetna* had not the stylistic gifts of the Alexandrian. The actual arrangement of his matter is good, but, even when due allowance is made for the corruption of our text, his obscurity is intolerable, his imagery confused, his language cumbrous and wooden. He has, moreover, no poetic imagination. *Aetna*, not the poet, provides the fire. Even the beautiful story of the Catanian brothers, which forms by far the best

---

[1] 178 sqq.   [2] 400 sqq.   [3] 333 sqq.   [4] 294.

portion of the poem, never rises to the level of pure poetry. It is illumined neither by the fire of rhetoric nor by the lambent light of sensuous diction and rich imagination. A few lines may be quoted to show its general character (605):

Nam quondam ruptis excanduit Aetna cavernis,   [1]
et velut eversis penitus fornacibus ingens
evecta in longum est rapidis fervoribus unda.

. . . .

ardebant agris segetes et mollia cultu
iugera cum dominis, silvae collesque rubebant.

. . . .

tum vero ut cuique est animus viresque rapinae
tutari conantur opes. gemit ille sub auro,
colligit ille arma et stulta cervice reponit,
defectum raptis illum sua carmina tardant,
hic velox minimo properat sub pondere pauper.

. . . .

. . . haec nullis parsura incendia pascunt,
vel solis parsura piis. namque optima proles
Amphinomus fraterque pari sub munere fortes,
cum iam vicinis streperent incendia tectis,
aspiciunt pigrumque patrem matremque senecta
eheu defessos posuisse in limine membra.
parcite, avara manus, dulces attollere praedas :
illis divitiae solae materque paterque :
hanc rapient praedam. mediumque exire per ignem

---

[1] For once Etna burst its caves and, glowing with fire, cast forth all that its furnaces contained ; a vast wave, swift and hot with fire, streamed forth afar. . . . Crops blazed along the fields, rich acres with their masters were consumed, forest and hill glowed rosy red. . . . Then each man, as he had courage and strength to bear away his goods, strove to protect his wealth. One groans beneath a weight of gold, another collects his weapons and slings them on his foolish neck. Another, unable to carry away what he has snatched up, wastes time in repeating charms, while there the poor man moves swift beneath his slender burden. . . . The fire feeds on all it meets : nought will it spare, or, if aught it spares, only the pious. For Amphinomus and his brother, the best of sons, brave in the toil they shared, when the fires roared loud and were already nigh their home, behold their father and their mother fall fainting on the threshold fordone with years. Cease, greedy folk, to shoulder the spoil of your fortunes that are so dear to you : for these men father and mother are their sole wealth ; this only is the spoil that they would save. They hasten to escape through the midst of the fire, which itself gave them

ipso dante fidem properant. o maxima rerum
et merito pietas homini tutissima virtus !
erubuere pios iuvenes attingere flammae
et, quacumque ferunt illi vestigia, cedunt
felix illa dies, illa est innoxia terra.
dextra saeva tenent, laevaque incendia fervent ;
ille per obliquos ignes fraterque triumphant
tutus uterque pio sub pondere : suffugit illa
et circa geminos avidus sibi temperat ignis,
incolumes abeunt tandem et sua numina secum
salva ferunt. illos mirantur carmina vatum,
illos seposuit claro sub nomine Ditis
nec sanctos iuvenes attingunt sordida fata,
securas cessere domus et iura piorum.

The narrative is clear, and the story delightful. But the
telling of it, though free from affectation, is dull, prosaic,
and uninspired. And it must be remembered that this
passage shows the author in his most favourable aspect. In
his more technical passages the clearness and simplicity is
absent, the prosiness and lack of imagination remain,
nakedly hideous.

The author of the poem is unknown, the very date is
uncertain. The conception of the work is Lucretian, but
in point of style, while full of reminiscences of Lucretius, the
poem owes most to Vergil, whose hexameter has undoubtedly
been taken for a model, though it has lost all its music.
Except in the avoidance of elision there is no trace of the
influence of Ovid. The poem might easily have been written

confidence. O piety, greatest of all that man may possess, of all virtues
that which most saves the righteous. The flames blushed to touch the
pious youths, and yield a path wherever they turn their steps. Blest was
that day ; the ground they trod was unharmed. The fierce burning holds
all things on their right and blazes on their left. The brethren move
triumphant on their path aslant the flame, each saved by his pious burden :
the fire shuns their path and restrains its greedy hunger where pass the
twain ; scatheless they escape at length and bear those whom they worship
to a place of safety. The songs of poets hymn their praise and the underworld gives them a glorious resting-place apart, nor does any unworthy
fate befall these youths that lived so holy. They have passed away to
dwell among the blessed, and sorrow cometh not nigh their dwelling-place.

in the latter half of the reign of Augustus.[1] The obscurity is due to the lack, not the excess of art, and the poem has no special affinity with the Silver Age. Servius and Donatus, indeed, both seem to ascribe the poem to Vergil,[2] while it is found in the MSS. which give us the *Appendix Vergiliana*. But there are considerations which have inclined editors to place it later, in the reign of Nero, or in the opening years of the principate of Vespasian. In one of his letters (Sen. 79) Seneca, writing to his friend Lucilius Junior, urges him to ' describe Etna in his poem, and by so doing treat a topic common to all poets'. The fact that Vergil had already treated it was no obstacle to Ovid's essaying the task, nor was Cornelius Severus deterred by the fact that both Vergil and Ovid had handled the theme. Later he adds, ' If I know you aright, the subject of Aetna will make your mouth water.' Lucilius was procurator in Sicily, and had sung the story of the Syracusan nymph Arethusa.[3] It has been suggested that he[4] wrote the *Aetna*. But Lucilius was an imitator of Ovid,[5] and Seneca advises him *not* to write a didactic poem on Etna, but to treat it episodically (*in suo carmine*), as Vergil and Ovid[6] had done. It is conceivable that he may have written a didactic poem on the subject, but Seneca's remarks yield absolutely no evidence for the fact.

Others have made Cornelius Severus the author,[7] though it is practically certain that his description of the volcano must have occurred in his poem *On the Sicilian War*.[8] But

---

1 So Ellis (*Corp. Poet. Lat.*, vol. ii. pref.); Baehrens, *P. L. M.* ii. pp. 29 sqq.

2 Serv. *ad Verg. Aen.* praef. Donatus, *vita Verg.*, p. 58 R (' Scripsit etiam de qua ambigitur Aetnam ').

3 Sen. *Nat. Quaest.* iii. 26. 5. He also wrote in verse on philosophical subjects; cp. Sen. *Ep.* 24. 19–21.

4 So Wernsdorf, von Jacob, Munro (edd.), Wagler *de Aetna quaest. crit.*, Berlin, 1884.

5 Sen. *Nat. Quaest.* iv. 2. 2.   6 Sen. *Ep.* 79. 5.

7 So many Italian scholars of sixteenth and seventeenth centuries, among them Scaliger.

8 Cornelius Severus wrote a poem on the Sicilian War of Octavian and Sext. Pompeius ; cp. Quint. x. 1. 89.

the fact that Seneca makes no reference to the existence of
any learned didactic poem on the subject carries a little more
weight, and there are marked parallels between Seneca's
'quaestiones Naturales' and passages in the *Aetna*.[1] Further, the very badness of the poem makes us hesitate to
place it in the Augustan period. That age, no doubt, produced much bad work as well as good, but a poem so obscure
and inartistically prosaic as the *Aetna* was more likely to
be produced and more likely to survive in an imitative and
uninspired age such as that which followed on the death of
Augustus. But for the evidence of Seneca we should place
the poem in the prosaic reign of Tiberius ; the considerations adduced from Seneca lead us, though with the utmost
hesitation, to place it somewhere between 57 and 79 A.D.[2]
Of the lower limit there can be no doubt. The fires of the
Phlegraean plains are extinct,[3] therefore the poem was
composed before the eruption of Vesuvius in 79 A. D.[4] The
question of the authorship of the *Aetna* has necessarily been
treated at greater length than the merits of the poem deserve.
It is a work of small importance ; its chief value is to show
how low it was possible for Roman didactic poetry to sink.
In the *Aetna* it sinks lower than epic in the *Punica* of Silius
Italicus. That poem, for all its portentous dullness, shows
a certain ponderous technical skill and literary facility.
The author of the *Aetna*, though clearly a man of culture, is
never at his ease, the verse is laboured and lacking flexibility,
and there is no technical dexterity to compensate for a total

---

[1] Cp. *Nat. Quaest.* iii. 16. 4, *Aetna*, 302 and 303. But this may be due
to the fact that both Seneca and the author of *Aetna* get their information
from the same source, perhaps Posidonius ; cp. Sudhaus, introd. to his
edition, p. 75.

[2] It is not improbable that in 293 sqq. the poet refers to the mechanical
Triton shown at the Naumachia on the Fucine Lake at a festival given
by Claudius in honour of Nero's adoption in 50 A. D.

[3] 425–34.

[4] Baehrens would put the lower limit at 63 A. D., the year in which severe
earthquakes first indicated the reviving activity of Phlegraean fields.
But earthquakes, though often caused by volcanic action, do not necessarily
produce volcanoes.

absence of genius. The terror and beauty of the mountain
crowned with snow and fire find no adequate expression in
these monotonous lines. There remains a conglomerate of
unoriginal and unsound physical speculation.

ii

COLUMELLA

The *Aetna* is a Lucretian poem decked out in a Vergilian
dress. In the tenth book of Columella we have a didactic
poem modelled on the *Georgics* of Vergil. The author was
of Spanish origin, a native of Gades,[1] and the contemporary
of his great compatriot the younger Seneca.[2] He had served
in a military capacity in Syria,[3] but his real passion was
agriculture. His ambition was to write a really practical
farmers' manual.[4] He had written nine books in prose,
covering the whole range of farming, from the tillage of the
soil to the breeding of poultry and cattle, and concluding
with a disquisition on wild animals and bee-keeping. But
in the tenth book, yielding to the solicitation of his friend
Publius Silvinus,[5] he set himself a more exalted task, no
less than the writing of a fifth Georgic on gardening. Vergil,
in his fourth Georgic (148), had left the theme of gardens for
another's singing. Columella takes him at his word. The
tenth book is manifestly intended as the crown and conclusion of his work. But later he changed his plan. Another
friend, Claudius Augustalis,[6] demanded a paraphrase, or

---

[1] viii. 16. 9 ; 10. 185.

[2] iii. 3. 3 'his certe temporibus Nomentana regio celeberrima fama est
illustris, et praecipue quam possidet Seneca, vir excellentis ingenii atque
doctrinae'. He is quoted by Pliny, not infrequently. Columella was an
old man when he wrote ; cp. 12 ad fin. 'nec tamen canis natura dedit
cunctarum rerum prudentiam'.

[3] Cp. *C. I. L.* ix. 235 'L. Iunio L. F. Gal. Moderato Columellae Trib.
mil. leg. VI. Ferratae'. That this refers to the poet is borne out by two
facts. (1) Gades belonged to the Tribus Galeria. (2) At this date the
legio VI. Ferrata was stationed in Syria ; cp. Col. ii. 10. 18 'Ciliciae
Syriaeque regionibus ipse vidi'.

[4] Cp. i. 1. 7. He speaks as a practical farmer; cp. ii. 8. 5 ; 9. 1 ; 10. 11 ;
iii. 9. 2; 10. 8, &c. He writes primarily for Italy, not for Spain; cp. iii. 8. 5.

[5] Cp. x. praef.: also ix. 16. 2, which tells us that Gallio, Seneca's brother,
had added his entreaties.   [6] xi. praef.

rather an amplification in prose.   This resulted in an eleventh
book, in which the care of the garden and the duties of the
villicus are described, while the work was finally concluded
in a twelfth book setting forth the duties of the *villica*.[1]

It may be doubted whether Columella was well advised
when he yielded to the entreaties of his friend Silvinus and
wrote his tenth book in verse.   He had no great poetic
talent, nor did he possess the sleight of hand of Calpurnius,
the imitator of the *Eclogues*.   But he possesses qualities
which render his work far more attractive than that of Calpurnius.   He is a genuine enthusiast, with a real love of the
countryside and a charming affection for flowers.   And as
a stylist he is modest.   He makes no attempt at display,
no contorted striving after originality.   His verse is clear
and simple as his tastes.   He is content to follow humbly in
the footsteps of his great master, the 'starry' Vergil.[2]   He
imitates and even plagiarizes[3] because he loves, not because
it is the fashion.   He shows no appreciation of the more
intimate harmonies of the Vergilian hexameter ;   like so
many contemporaries, he realizes neither the value of judicious elision nor varied pauses ;   but his verse, in spite of its
monotony and lack of life and movement, is not unmelodious.
The poem is a sober work, uninspired in tone, straightforward and simple in plan.   It need not be described in
detail ;   its advice is obvious, setting forth the times and
seasons to be observed by the gardener, the methods of pre-
paring the soil, the choice of flowers, with all the customary
mythological allusions.[4]   At its worst, with its tedious lists
of the names of flowers, it reads like a seedsman's catalogue,[5]

---

[1] He also wrote a treatise against astrologers (cp. xi. 1. 131) and a treatise
on religious ceremonies connected with agriculture (cp. ii. 21. 5).   This
latter work was perhaps never completed (cp. ii. 21. 6).   In any case both
treatises were lost.   There survives a book on arboriculture which is not an
isolated monograph, but portion of a larger work, at least three books
long, for it alludes to a 'primum volumen de cultu agrorum' (ad init.).   It
probably consisted of four books, since Cassiodorus (*div. lect.* 28) speaks
of the sixteen books of Columella.

[2] siderei Maronis, 434.   Cp. esp. 196 sqq.
[4] Cp. 130 sqq., 320 sqq., 344 sqq.   [5] 102 sqq.

at its best it is lit up with a quaint humour, a love of colour, and a homely yet vivid imagination.   Mother earth—'sweet earth' he calls her—is highly personified; that she may be adorned anew, her green locks must be torn from their tangle by the plough, her old raiment stripped from her, her thirst quenched by irrigation, her hunger satisfied with fertilizing manure.[1]   The garden is to be no rich man's park for the display of statues and fountains.   Its one statue shall be the image of the garden god, its patron and its protector.[2]   Its splendour shall be the varied hue of its flower-beds and its wealth in herbs that serve the use of man :

> verum ubi iam puro discrimine pectita tellus   [1]
> deposito squalore nitens sua semina poscet,
> pingite tunc varios, terrestria sidera, flores,
> candida leucoia et flaventia lumina caltae
> narcissique comas et hiantis saeva leonis
> ora feri calathisque virentia lilia canis,
> nec non vel niveos vel caeruleos hyacinthos,
> tum quae pallet humi, quae frondens purpurat auro,
> ponatur viola et nimium rosa plena pudoris (94).

He loves the return of spring with as deep a love as Vergil's, though he must borrow Vergil's language to describe its coming and its power.[3]   But his painting of its harvest of colour is his own :

> quin et odoratis messis iam floribus instat :   [2]
> iam ver purpureum, iam versicoloribus anni
> fetibus alma parens pingi sua tempora gaudet.

---

[1] But when earth, with parted locks combed clear, gleams, all soilure cast aside, and demands the seeds that are her due, call forth the varied hues of flowers, earth's constellations, the white snowflake and the marigold's golden eyes, the narcissus-petals and the blossom that apes the fierce lion's gaping maw; the lily, too, with calix shining white amid its green leaves, the hyacinths white and blue; plant also the violet lying pale upon the ground or purple shot with gold among its leafage, and the rose with its deep shamefaced blush.

[2] Nay, more, the harvest-time draws near for sweet-scented flowers. The purple spring has come, and kindly mother earth rejoices that her brows are painted bright with all the many-coloured offspring of the year.

---

[1] 45–94.   [2] 29–34.   [3] 196 sqq.

iam Phrygiae loti gemmantia lumina promunt
et coniventis oculos violaria solvunt (255).

All the glories of an Italian spring are in the lines in which
a little later he describes the joy of living when the year is
young, and the wasting heat of summer is still far off, when
it is sweet to be in the sun and watch the garden with its
rainbow colours :

nunc ver egelidum, nunc est mollissimus annus,   [1]
dum Phoebus tener ac tenera decumbere in herba
suadet et arguto fugientes gramine fontes
nec rigidos potare iuvat nec sole tepentes,
iamque Dionaeis redimitur floribus hortus,
iam rosa mitescit Sarrano clarior ostro.
nec tam nubifugo Borea Latonia Phoebe
purpureo radiat vultu, nec Sirius ardor
sic micat aut rutilus Pyrois aut ore corusco
Hesperus, Eoo remeat cum Lucifer ortu,
nec tam sidereo fulget Thaumantias arcu
quam nitidis hilares conlucent fetibus horti (282).

These are the words of an enthusiast and a poet, and these
few outbursts of song redeem the poem from dullness.
There is wafted from his pages the perfume of the countryside, and the fresh air breathes welcome amid the hothouse
cultures of contemporary poets.   And he is almost the only
poet of the age that can be read without a wince of pain.
He is at least as good a laureate of the garden as Thomson
of the seasons, and he has all the grace of humility.   Even
when the artist fails us, we love the man.

Now the Phrygian lotus puts forth its jewelled orbs and the violet beds
open their winking eyes.

[1] Now cool spring is come, the gentlest season of the year, while
Phoebus yet is young and bids us recline in the young herbage, and 'tis sweet
to drink the rill that flows among the murmuring grass, with waters neither
icy cold nor warm with the sun's heat.   Now, too, the garden is crowned
with the flowers Dione loves, and the rose ripens brighter than Tyrian
purple.   Not so brightly does Phoebe, Leto's daughter, shine with radiant
face when Boreas has dispersed the clouds, nor glows hot Sirius so, nor
ruddy Pyrois, nor Hesperus with shining countenance when he returns as
the daystar at the break of dawn, not so fair gleams Iris with her starry
bow, as shines the joyous garden with its bright offspring.

II

CALPURNIUS SICULUS. THE EINSIEDELN FRAGMENTS AND THE 'PANEGYRICUS IN PISONEM'

It may be said of pastoral poetry, without undue disrespect, that it is the most artificial and the least in touch with reality of all the more important forms of poetic art. Even in the hands of a master like Theocritus, invested as it is with an incomparable charm, and distinguished in many respects by an astonishing truth and fidelity, it is never other than highly artificial. For its birth an age was required in which the class whence the majority of poets and their audience are drawn had largely lost touch with country life, or had at any rate developed ideals that can only spring up in town society. This does not imply that men have ceased altogether to appreciate the value of the country life or the beauty of country surroundings, only that they have lost much of their understanding of them ; and so their appreciation takes new forms. They love the country as a half-forgotten paradise, they fly back to it as a refuge from the artificiality of town life, but they take much of that artificiality with them. From the time of Theocritus pastoral poetry pure and simple has steadily declined. Great poems have been written with exquisite pastoral elements or even cast in pastoral form. But they have never owed their greatness entirely, or even chiefly, to the pastoral element. That element has merely provided a charming setting for scenes or thoughts that have nothing genuinely pastoral about them.

Of the small amount of pastoral poetry extant in Latin it need hardly be said that the *Bucolica* of Vergil stand in a class by themselves. And yet for all their beauty they are unsatisfactory to those who know and love Theocritus. Their charm is undeniable, but they are immature and too obviously imitative. But Vergil was at least country-born and had a deep sympathy for country life.

When we come to the scanty relics of his successors and
imitators we are conscious of a lamentable falling away.
If Vergil's imitations of Theocritus fail to ring as true as
their original, what shall be said of the imitators of Vergil's
imitations ? Even if they had been true poets, their verse
must have rung false. But the poets with whom we have
to deal, Calpurnius Siculus and the anonymous author of
two poems known as the Einsiedeln fragments, were not
genuine poets. They had little of the intimacy with nature
and unsophisticated man that was demanded by their self-
chosen task. That they possessed some real affection for the
country is doubtless true, but it was not the prime inspiration of their verse. They had the ambition to write poetry
rather than the call ; a slight bent towards the country,
heightened by a vague dissatisfaction and weariness with
the artificial luxury of Rome, led them to choose pastoral
poetry. They make up for depth of observation by a
shallow minuteness. In the seven eclogues of Calpurnius
may be found a larger assortment of vegetables, of agri-
cultural implements and operations, than in the *Bucolics*
of Vergil, but there is little poetry, pastoral or otherwise.
The ' grace of all the Muses ' and the breath of the country
are fled for ever ; the dexterous phrasing of a laborious
copyist reigns in their stead.

Of the life of Calpurnius Siculus nothing is known and
but little can be conjectured. Of his date there can be
little doubt. We learn from the evidence of the poems
themselves that they were written in the principate of
a youthful Caesar (i. 44 ; iv. 85, 137 ; vii. 6), beautiful to
look upon (vii. 84), the giver of splendid games (vii. 44), the
inaugurator of an age of peace, liberty and plenty (i. 42–88 ;
iv *passim*). This points strongly to the opening of Nero's
reign. The young Nero was handsome and personally
popular, and the opening years of his reign (*quinquennium
Neronis*) were famous for good government and prosperity.
But there are two further pieces of internal evidence
which clinch the argument. A comet is mentioned (i. 77)
as appearing in the autumn, an appearance which would

tally with that of the comet observed shortly before the death of Claudius in 54 A.D., while the line

maternis causam qui vicit Iulis (i. 45

seems clearly to refer to the speech delivered by the young Nero for the people of Ilium,[1] from whom the Iuli, Nero's ancestors on the mother's side, claimed to trace their descent. It may therefore safely be assumed that the poems were written early in the reign of Nero. A most ingenious attempt has been made to throw some light on the identity of their author.[2] He speaks of himself as Corydon, and he has a patron whom he styles Meliboeus. He prays that Meliboeus may bring him before Caesar's notice as Pollio brought Vergil (iv. 157 sqq. ; also i. 94). It has been suggested with some plausibility that Meliboeus is no other than C. Calpurnius Piso, the distinguished noble round whom in 65 A.D. centred the great conspiracy against Nero. The evidence rests on the existence of a poem entitled *panegyricus in Pisonem*,[3] in which a nameless poet seeks by his laudations to win Piso for a patron. The style of the poem has a marked resemblance to that of Calpurnius. If, as is possible, it should be assigned to his authorship, it becomes fairly certain that he was a dependent of Piso, and the name Calpurnius would suggest that he may have been the son of one of his freedmen.

The eclogues of Calpurnius are seven in number.[4] The first is in praise of the Golden Age, with special reference to the advent of the young princeps. Though given a different setting it is clearly modelled on the fourth eclogue

---

[1] Tac. *Ann.* xii. 58.

[2] M. Haupt, *Opusc.* i. 391 ; Lachm. *Comm. on Lucret.* 1855, p. 326 Schenkl (ed. Calp. Sic., p. ix).

[3] Or *de laude Pisonis*. See Baehrens, *Poet. Lat. Min.* iii. 1. For the question of authorship see p. 159.

[4] It was long believed that there were eleven, but the last four eclogues of the collection are shown by their style to be of later date, and there can be little doubt that the MSS. which attribute them to Nemesianus of Carthage are right. We know of a Nemesianus who lived about 290 A.D. and wrote a *Cynegetica*, a portion of which survives. Comparison with these four eclogues shows a marked resemblance of style.

of Vergil.   The second, describing a contest of song between
two shepherds before a third as judge, follows Vergil even
more closely.[1]   Parallels might be further elaborated, but
it is sufficient to say here that only two of the poems show
any originality, namely, the fifth and the seventh.   In the
former we have the advice given by an aged farmer to his
son, to whom he is handing over his farm.   It is inclined
to be prosy, but is simple and pleasing in tone, and the
old countryman may be forgiven if he sometimes seems to
be quoting the Georgics.   The seventh is a more ambitious
effort.   A rustic describes the great games that he has
seen given in the amphitheatre at Rome.   The language,
though characteristically decadent in its elaboration, shows
considerable originality.   The amphitheatre is, for instance,
thus described (vii. 30) :

> qualiter haec patulum concedit vallis in orbem   [1]
> et sinuata latus resupinis undique silvis

---

[1] Even as this vale rounds to a wide circle, and with bending sides and
slanting woods on every side makes a curved hollow amid the unbroken

---

1 Verg. *Ecl.* vii. 1 :

> forte sub arguta consederat ilice Daphnis,
> compulerantque greges Corydon et Thyrsis in unum,
> Thyrsis oves, Corydon distentas lacte capellas,
> ambo florentes aetatibus, Arcades ambo,
> et cantare pares et respondere parati.

Calp. ii. 1 :

> intactam Crocalen puer Astacus et puer Idas,
> Idas lanigeri dominus gregis, Astacus horti,
> dilexere diu, formosus uterque nec impar
> voce sonans.

The conclusion is borrowed from Vergil, *Ecl.* iii. 108 :

> non nostrum inter vos tantas componere lites.
> et vitula tu dignus et hic et quisquis amores
> aut metuet dulces aut experietur amaros.
> claudite iam rivos, pueri ; sat prata biberunt.

Calp. ii. 95–100 :

> 'iam resonant frondes, iam cantibus obstrepit arbos :
> i procul, o Doryla, rivumque reclude canali
> et sine iam dudum sitientes irriget hortos '
> vix ea finierant, senior cum talia Thyrsis,
> 'este pares . . .'

inter continuos curvatur concava montes,
sic ibi planitiem curvae sinus ambit arenae
et geminis medium se molibus alligat ovum.
. . . .
balteus en gemmis, en illita porticus auro
certatim radiant ; nec non, ubi finis arenae
proxima marmoreo praebet spectacula muro,
sternitur adiunctis ebur admirabile truncis
et coit in rotulum, tereti qui lubricus axe
impositos subita vertigine falleret ungues
excuteretque feras. auro quoque torta refulgent
retia, quae totis in arenam dentibus extant,
dentibus aequatis : et erat (mihi crede, Lycota,
si qua fides) nostro dens longior omnis aratro.

In its defence it may be urged that the very nature of
the subject demands elaboration, and that the resulting
picture has the merit of being vivid despite its elaborate
ingenuity. It is in this poem that Calpurnius is seen at
his best. Elsewhere his love for minute and elaborate
description is merely wearisome. It would be hard, for
instance, to find a more tiresomely circuitous method of
claiming to be an authority on sheep-breeding than (ii. 36)—

me docet ipsa Pales cultum gregis, ut niger albae   [1]
terga maritus ovis nascenti mutet in agna
quae neque diversi speciem servare parentis
possit et ambiguo testetur utrumque colore.

---

hills, so there the circle of the curving arena surrounds its level plain
and locks either side of its towering structure into an oval about itself. . . .
See how the gangway's parapet studded with gems and the colonnade
plated with gold vie with each other's brightness ; nay more, where the
arena's bound sets forth its shows close to the marble wall, ivory is over-
laid in wondrous wise on jointed beams and is bent into a cylinder, which,
turning nimbly on its trim axle, may cheat with sudden whirl the wild
beast's claws and cast them from it. Nets, too, of twisted gold gleam forth,
hung out into the arena on tusks in all their length and of equal size, and—
believe me, Lycotas, if you can—each tusk was longer than our plough-
share.

[1] Pales herself teaches me how to breed my flocks and tells me how the
black ram transforms the fleece of the white ewe in the lamb that comes
to birth, that cannot reproduce the colour of its sire, so different from
that of its dam, and by its ambiguous hue testifies to either parent.

It is difficult to give a poetic description of the act of rumination, but

> et matutinas revocat palearibus herbas (iii. 17)   [1]

is needlessly grotesque. And the vain struggle to give life to old and outworn themes leads to laboured lines such as (iii. 48)—

> non sic destricta marcescit turdus oliva,   [2]
> non lepus extremas legulus cum sustulit uvas,
> ut Lycidas domina sine Phyllide tabidus erro.

Calpurnius yields little to compensate for such defects. He meanders on through hackneyed pastoral landscapes haunted by hackneyed shepherds. It is only on rare occasions that a refreshing glimmer of poetry revives the reader. In lines such as (ii. 56)—

> si quis mea vota deorum   [3]
> audiat, huic soli, virides qua gemmeus undas
> fons agit et tremulo percurrit lilia rivo
> inter pampineas ponetur faginus ulmos;

or, in the pleasant description of the return of spring (v. 16),

> vere novo, cum iam tinnire volucres   [4]
> incipient nidosque reversa lutabit hirundo,
> protinus hiberno pecus omne movebis ovili.
> tunc etenim melior vernanti germine silva
> pullat et aestivas reparabilis incohat umbras,
> tunc florent saltus viridisque renascitur annus,[1]

---

[1] And recalls to its dewlaps the grass of its morning's meal.

[2] Not so does the thrush pine when the olives are plucked, not so does the hare pine when the vintager has gathered the last grapes, as I, Lycidas, droop while I roam apart from my mistress Phyllis.

[3] If any of the gods hear my prayer, to his honour, and his alone, shall his beechwood statue be planted amid my vine-clad elms, where the jewelled stream rolls its green wave and with rippling water runs through the lilies.

[4] When spring is young and the birds begin to pipe once more, and the swallow returns to plaster its nest anew, then move all your flock from its winter fold. For then the wood sprouts in fresh glory with its spring shoots and builds anew the shades of summer, then all the glades are bright with flowers and the green year is born again.

---

[1] Cp. also v. 50 sqq.

we seem to catch a glimpse of the real countryside; but
for the most part Calpurnius paints little save theatrical
and *manière* miniatures. Of such a character is the clever
and not unpleasing description of the tame stag in the
sixth eclogue (30). He shows a pretty fancy and no more.

The metre is like the language, easy, graceful, and correct. But the pauses are poorly managed ; the rhythm is
unduly dactylic ; the verse trips all too lightly and becomes
monotonous.

The total impression that we receive from these poems
is one of insignificance and triviality. The style is perhaps
less rhetorical and obscure than that of most writers of
the age ; as a result, these poems lack what is often the
one saving grace of Silver Latin poetry, its extreme cleverness. To find verse as dull and uninspired, we must turn
to Silius Italicus or the *Aetna*.

The two short poems contained in a MS. at Einsiedeln
and distinguished by the name of their place of provenance
are also productions of the Neronian age. The first, in the
course of a contest of song between Thamyras and Ladas,
with a third shepherd, Midas, as arbiter, sets forth the
surpassing skill of Nero as a performer on the *cithara*.[1]
The second celebrates the return of the Golden Age to the
world now under the beneficent guidance of Nero. Neither
poem possesses the slightest literary importance ; both are
polished but utterly insipid examples of foolish court flattery. The author is unknown. An ingenious suggestion [2]
has been made that he is no other than Calpurnius Piso,
the supposed Meliboeus of Calpurnius Siculus. The second
of these eclogues begins, ' Quid tacitus, Mystes ? ' The fourth
eclogue of Calpurnius Siculus begins (Meliboeus loquitur),
' Quid tacitus, Corydon ? ' Is Meliboeus speaking in person
and quoting his own poem ? It may be so, but the evidence
is obviously not such as to permit any feeling of certainty.

---

[1] See Baehrens, *Poet. Lat. Min.* vol. iii. p. 60. The first poem is unfinished, the award of Midas being missing.

[2] Bücheler, *Rhein. Mus.* xxvi, p. 235.

But it is at least probable that the poet had access to the court and had been praised by Nero. Such is the most plausible interpretation of a passage in the first eclogue, where Ladas, in answer to Thamyras, who claims the prize on the ground that his song shall be of Caesar, replies (16, 17):

> et me sidereo respexit Cynthius ore   [1]
> laudatamque chelyn iussit variare canendo.[1]

Whether the author be Piso or another, the poems do him small credit.

The *Panegyricus in Pisonem* remains to be considered. Attributed to Vergil by one MS.,[2] to Lucan by another,[3] the poem is certainly by neither. Quite apart from stylistic evidence, which is convincing against its attribution to Lucan, it is almost certain that the name of Lucan has been wrongly inserted for that of Vergil. That it is not by Vergil would be clear from the very inferior nature of the verse, but it can further be shown that the Piso addressed is the Calpurnius Piso of the reigns of Claudius and Nero to whom we have alluded above. If the account of Piso given by Tacitus be compared with the characteristics described in the *Panegyricus*, it will be found that both alike refer in strong terms to his eloquence in the law courts so readily exercised in defence of accused persons, and also to his affability and capacity for friendship.[4] Further, we have the evidence of a scholium on Juvenal as to his

---

[1] On me, too, has the Cynthian god cast his starry glance and bidden me accompany the lyre he praised with diverse song.

[1] So Bücheler, loc. cit. *respexit* is a mere conjecture : *corrumpit*, the MS. reading, is meaningless, and no satisfactory alternative has been suggested. The lines may merely refer to Apollo, but *et me* suggests strongly that Ladas retorts, ' I, too, have Caesar's favour.' Cp. *L.* 37, where *hic vester Apollo est !* clearly refers to Nero.

[2] In a MS. at Lorsch, now lost ; but used by Sechard for his edition of Ovid, Basle, 1527.

[3] In Parisinus 7647 (Florileg.). See Baehrens, *P. L. M.* i, p. 222.

[4] Tac. *Ann.* xv. 48 ' facundiam tuendis civibus exercebat, largitionem adversum amicos et ignotis quoque comi sermone et congressu.'

skill in the game of draughts.[1]　He played so well that
crowds would throng to see him.　One of the chief points
mentioned in the *Panegyricus* is the skill of Piso at the
same game.[2]　Nor is it a mere casual allusion ; on the
contrary, the writer treats this portion of his eulogy with
even greater elaboration than the rest.　There can, therefore, be little doubt as to the date of the poem.　It is
addressed to Calpurnius Piso after his rise to fame (i.e.
during the latter portion of the principate of Claudius,
or during the earlier part of the reign of Nero).　The poet
prays that Piso may be to him what Maecenas was to
Vergil.　It is hardly possible for a poem of this type to
possess any real interest for others than the recipient of
the flattery and its author.　But in this case the poet
has done his work well.　The flattery never becomes outrageous and is expressed in easy flowing verse and graceful
diction.　At times the language is genuinely felicitous.
Any great man might be proud to receive such a tribute
as (129)—

> tu mitis et acri　　　　[1]
> asperitate carens positoque per omnia fastu
> inter ut aequales unus numeraris amicos,
> obsequiumque doces et amorem quaeris amando.

There is, moreover, little straining after effect and little
real obscurity.　The difficulties of the description of Piso's
draught-playing are due to our ignorance of the exact
nature of the game.[3]　The actual language is at least as
lucid as Pope's famous description of the game of ombre
in *The Rape of the Lock*.　The verse is of the usual post-
Augustan type, showing strongly the primary influence of
Vergil modified by the secondary influence of Ovid.　It is

---

[1] Mild is thy temper and free from sharp harshness.　Thou layest aside
thy pride in thy every act, and among thy friends thou art counted a friend
and equal, thou teachest men to follow thee and seekest to be loved by
loving.

---

1 Schol. Vall. *ad Iuv.* v. 109 ' in latrunculorum lusu tam perfectus et
callidus, ut ad eum ludentem concurreretur.'
2 Cp. ll. 190 sqq.

light and easy and not ill-suited to its subject. It has distinct affinities, both in metre and diction, with the verse of Calpurnius Siculus, and may be by the same hand ; but the resemblance is not so close as to afford anything approaching positive proof. Minor poets, lacking all individuality, the victims and not the controlling forces of the tendencies of the age, are apt to resemble one another. There are, however, two noteworthy passages which point strongly to the identity of the author of the *Panegyricus* with the Bucolic poet. The former, addressing Piso as his patron (246), says :

mea vota [1]
si mentem subiere tuam, memorabilis olim
tu mihi Maecenas tereti cantabere versu.

The latter, addressing his patron Meliboeus and begging him to commend him to Caesar, exclaims (iv. 152) :

o mihi quae tereti decurrent carmina versu [2]
tunc, Meliboee, meum si quando montibus istis (i.e. at Rome)
dicar habere larem.

Is it a mere coincidence, a plagiarism, or a direct allusion ? There is no certainty, but the coincidence is—to say the least—suggestive. If the identity of authorship be assumed as correct, it is probable that the eclogues are the later production. To place one's patron among the *dramatis personae* of an eclogue argues a nearer intimacy than the writing of a formal panegyric. That the poet is more at home as a panegyrist than as a writer of idylls does not affect the question. In such an age such a result was to be expected.

---

[1] If my prayers reach thy mind, thou shalt be sung of as Maecenas in my slender verse, and future ages shall tell of thy glory.

[2] O how shall my songs trip in slender verse then, Meliboeus, if ever men shall say of me ' He has a house on yonder mountain '.

III

THE ILIAS LATINA

Latin poetry may almost be said to have begun with Livius Andronicus' translation of the *Odyssey* into the rude Saturnian metre. This translation had great vogue as a school book. But the *Iliad* remained untranslated, and it was only natural that later authors should try their hand upon it. Translations were produced in Republican times by Cn. Matius[1] and Ninnius Crassus,[2] but neither work attained to any popularity.

With the growth of the knowledge of Greek and its increasing use as a medium of instruction in the schools on the one hand, and the appearance of Vergil and the rise of the Aeneas saga on the other, the demand for a translation of the *Iliad* naturally became less. The Silver Age arrived with the problem unsolved. It was a period when writers abounded who would have been better employed on translation than on any attempt at original work. Further, in spite of the general knowledge of Greek, a translation of Homer would have its value in the schools both as a handbook for the subject-matter and as a 'crib'.

Three works of the kind seem to have been produced between the reigns of Tiberius and Nero.

Attius Labeo[3] translated not only the *Iliad* but also the *Odyssey* into hexameters. But it was a poor performance. It was a baldly literal translation, paying small attention to the meaning of the original.[4] Persius pours scorn upon

---

[1] Baehrens, *Fragm. Poet. Rom.* p. 281.

[2] Priscian, *Gr. Lat.* i. 478.

[3] Persius derides a certain Labeo (i. 4) and a writer named Attius (i. 50) for his translation of *Iliad*. On this last passage the scholiast says, 'Attius Labeo poeta indoctus fuit illorum temporum, qui Iliadem Homeri foedissime composuit.' The names are found combined in an inscription from Corinth, Joh. Schmidt, *Mitt. des deutsch. archäol. Inst. in Athen*, vi (1882), p. 354.

[4] Schol. *ad Pers.* i. 4 (p. 248, Jahn).

it, and one verse has survived to confirm our worst suspicions [1]—

crudum manduces Priamum Priamique pisinnos.

Polybius, the well-known freedman of Claudius, also produced a work, which is praised by Seneca as having introduced Homer and Vergil to a yet larger public than they already enjoyed, and as preserving the charm of the original in an altered form.[2] As Polybius had dealt with Vergil as well as Homer, it may be conjectured that the work praised by Seneca was a prose paraphrase. Lastly, there is the *Ilias Latina*, which has been preserved to the present day. It is written in graceful hexameter verse, and is an abridgement rather than a translation. It consists of 1,070 lines, of which the first five books in fact claim a little more than half. The author wearied of his task and finished off the remaining nineteen books in summary fashion. While the twenty-second occupies as much as sixty lines, the abridgements of the thirteenth and seventeenth are reduced to a meagre seven and three lines respectively.

That such work is of small importance is obvious. It must have been useless from its birth save as a handbook for the schools, and even for this purpose its value must have been greatly impaired by its lack of proportion. Its survival can only be accounted for on the assumption that it was written and employed as a textbook. In fact, during the Middle Ages, when the original was a sealed book, there is definite evidence that it was so used.[3] The work is trivial, but might well have been worse. The language is clear and often vigorous, and there is an easy grace about the verse which shows that the author was a man of culture, knowing his Vergil well and his Ovid better. The date cannot be proved with certainty, but there can be no doubt that it was written before the death of Nero.

---

[1] Schol. *ad Pers.* i. 4, ex cod. Io. Tillii Brionensis episc., cited by El. Vinetus.   [2] Sen. *ad Polyb. de Cons.* viii. 2, and xi. 5.

[3] Vualtherus Spirensis Vs. 93. X cent. (ed. Harster, Munich, 1878, p. 22). Eberhard Bethunensis, *Labyr. Tract.* iii. 45.

The lines (899),

> quem (Aenean) nisi servasset magnarum rector aquarum [1]
> ut profugus laetis Troiam repararet in arvis,
> augustumque genus claris submitteret astris,
> non carae gentis nobis mansisset origo,

can only have been written under the Julian Dynasty.

The work is clearly post-Ovidian and must therefore be attributed to the principates of Tiberius, Gaius, Claudius, or Nero. Further evidence of date is entirely wanting. No meaning can be attached to the heading Pindarus found in certain MSS.[1] There is, however, an interesting though scarcely more fruitful problem presented by the possible existence of two acrostics in the course of the poem.[2] The initial letters of the first nine lines spell the name ' Italices ', while the last eight lines yield the word ' scqipsit '. Baehrens, by a not very probable alteration in the eighth line, procures the name 'Italicus', while a slighter and more natural change yields 'scripsit' at the close.[3] Further, a late MS. gives Bebius Italicus as the name of the author.[4] On these

----

[1] Unless the ruler of the mighty deep had preserved Aeneas to found in exile a new Troy in happier fields, and beget a line of princes to shine among the stars, the stock of the race we love would not have endured to bless us.

----

[1] This apparent confusion between Homer and Pindar is first found in Benzo, episc. Albensis (*Monum. Germ.* xi. 599) circa 1087. In Hugo Trimbergensis (thirteenth century) Pindar is the translator : ' Homero, quem Pindarus philosophus fertur transtulisse.' Cp. L. Müller, *Philol.* xv, p. 475. So, too, in Cod. Vat. Reg. 1708 (thirteenth and fourteenth centuries) ; in Vat. Pal. 1611 (end of fourteenth century), he is styled Pandarus. See Baehrens, *P. L. M.* iii. 4.

[2] Seyffert, in Munk, *Geschichte der Röm. Litt.* ii, p. 242. Bücheler, *Rhein. Mus.* 35 (1880), p. 391.

[3] Baehrens (*P. L. M.* iii) reads (7) *ut primum tulerant* for *ex quo pertulerant.* The corruption is unlikely, especially since the corresponding line in the *Iliad* (i. 6) begins ἐξ οὗ. In line 1065, for *quam cernis paucis . . . remis*, he reads *remis quam cernis . . . paucis*, a distinct improvement. Some of those who retain MSS. in (7) attempt to explain *Italice* as a vocative or adverb. But *ex nihilo nihil fit.* For a summary of these unprofitable and generally absurd speculations, cp. Schanz, *Gesch. Röm. Lit.* § 394.

[4] Vindobon. 3509 (fifteenth or sixteenth centuries).

grounds the poem has been attributed to Silius Italicus. But Martial makes no reference to the existence of this work in any of his references to Silius, and indeed suggests that Silius only took to writing poetry after his withdrawal from public life.[1] This would make the poem post-Neronian, which, as we have seen, is most improbable. Further, the style of the verse is very different from that of the *Punica*. When, over and above these considerations, it is remembered that the acrostics can only be produced by emendation of the text, the critic has no course open to him but to abandon the attribution to Silius and to give up the problem of the acrostics as an unprofitable curiosity of literature.

IV

LOST MINOR POETS

In addition to the poets of whom we have already treated as writing under the Julian Dynasty there must have been many others of whom chance or their own insignificance has deprived us. But few names have survived,[2] and only two of these lost poets merit mention here, the erotic poet Lentulus Gaetulicus and the lyric writer Caesius Bassus.

Gnaeus Cornelius Lentulus Gaetulicus was consul in 26 A.D.,[3] and for ten years was legatus in Upper Germany, where his combination of firmness and clemency won him great popularity.[4] He conspired against Caligula while holding this command, and was put to death.[5] Pliny the younger speaks of him as the writer of sportive and lascivious erotic verse, and Martial writes of him in very similar terms.[6] His mistress was named Caesennia, and was herself a poetess.[7] It is possible that the poems in the Greek

---

[1] Mart. vii. 63.

[2] Vagellius, Sen. *N. Q.* vi. 2. 9. Antistius Sosianus, Tac. *Ann.* xiii. 28. C. Montanus, ib. xvi. 28. 29. Lucilius junior, see p. 144.

[3] Tac. *Ann.* iv. 46 ; *C. I. L.* ii. 2093.

[4] Dion. lix. 22 ; Tac. *Ann.* vi. 30.

[5] Dion. loc. cit. ; Suet. *Claud.* 9.

[6] Plin *Ep.* v. 3. 5 ; Mart. i. praef.   [7] Ap. Sid. *Ep.* ii. 10. 6.

Anthology under the title Γαιτουλικοῦ [1] may be from his pen, but the only fragment of his Latin poems which survives is from a work in hexameters, and describes the geographical situation of Britain.[2]

More important is the lyric poet Caesius Bassus,[3] whose loss is the more to be regretted because of the very scanty remains of Roman lyric verse that have survived to modern times. Statius attempted with but indifferent success to imitate the Sapphics and Alcaics of Horace, while the plays of Seneca provide a considerable quantity of lyric choruses of varying degrees of merit. But of lyric writers pure and simple there is scarcely a trace. That they existed we know from Quintilian. If we may trust him, certain of his contemporaries [4] attained to considerable distinction in this branch of poetry—that is to say, they surpassed all Roman lyric poets subsequent to Horace. But when all is said, it is scarcely possible to go beyond Quintilian's emphatic statement, that of Roman lyricists Horace alone repays reading. If any other name deserves mention it is that of Caesius Bassus, but he is inferior to Quintilian's own contemporaries. Caesius Bassus is best known to us as the editor of the satires of Persius. The sixth satire is actually addressed to him:

> admovit iam bruma foco te, Basse, Sabino ?   [1]
> iamne lyra et tetrico vivunt tibi pectine chordae ?
> mire opifex numeris veterum primordia vocum
> atque marem strepitum fidis intendisse Latinae,

---

[1] Has winter made you move yet to your Sabine fireside, dear Bassus ? Are your lyre and its strings and the austere quill that runs over them yet in force ? Marvellous artist as you are at setting to music the primitive antiquities of our language, the manly utterance of the Latian harp, and

---

1 v. 16; vi. 190, 331 ; vii. 71, 244, 245, 275, 354 ; xi. 409.

2 Baehrens, *Poet. Rom. Fragm.* p. 361.

3 Quint. x. 1.96 ' at lyricorum Horatius fere solus legi dignus : . . . si quem adicere velis, is erit Caesius Bassus, quem nuper vidimus ; sed eum longe praecedunt ingenia viventium '.

4 e. g. perhaps Martial, Sulpicia, and some of Pliny's poet friends, see pp. 170 sqq.

> mox iuvenes agitare iocos et pollice honesto
> egregius lusisse senex.[1]

The only information yielded by this passage is that
Bassus had a Sabine villa, that he was already advanced
in years, that he affected 'the simple and manly versification
of antiquity', and that he dealt also with erotic themes.
But few other facts are known to us.   He wrote a treatise
on metre—a portion of which has been preserved to the
present day,[2] and he perished at his Campanian villa in
79 A.D., during the great eruption of Vesuvius.[3]   The
fragments of verse enshrined in his metrical treatise suggest
that he wrote in a large variety of metres,[4] but they may
be no more than examples invented solely to illustrate
metres unfamiliar in Latin.   The one quotation that is
explicitly made from his lyrical poems is, curiously enough,
a hexameter line.   As to his literary merits or defects, it is
now impossible even to guess.

---

then showing yourself excellent in your old age at wakening young loves
and frolicking over the chords with a virtuous touch.

CONINGTON.

---

[1] See p. 80.
[2] See Teuffel and Schwabe, *Hist. Rom. Lit.* § 304 ; Schanz, *Gesch. Röm.
Lit.* 384 a.
[3] Schol. *Pers.* vi. 1.
[4] Ithyphallicum, Archebulium, Philicium, Paeonicum, Proceleusma-
ticum, Molossicum.   Baehrens, *Poet. Rom. Fragm.* p. 364.

CHAPTER VII

THE EMPERORS FROM VESPASIAN TO TRAJAN AND MINOR POETS

I

THE EMPERORS AND POETS WHOSE WORKS ARE LOST

AFTER the death of Nero and the close of the Civil War a happier era, both for literature and the world at large, was inaugurated by the accession of Vespasian in 69 A.D. A man of low birth and of little culture, he yet had a true appreciation of art and literature. Of his own writing we know nothing save that he left behind him memoirs.[1] But we have abundant evidence that he showed himself a liberal patron of the arts. He gave rich rewards to poets and sculptors,[2] effected all that was possible to repair the great loss of works of art occasioned by the burning of the Capitol,[3] and did what he could for the stage, perhaps even attempting to revive the legitimate drama.[4] Above all, he set aside a large sum annually for the support of Greek and Latin professors of rhetoric,[5] the first instance in the history of Rome of State endowment of education. Against this we must set his expulsion from Italy of philosophers and astrologers, an intemperate and presumably ineffective act, prompted by reasons of State and probably without any appreciable influence on literature.[6] His sons, however, had received all the advantages of the highest education. Of Titus' (79–81 A.D.) achievements in literature we have no information save that he aspired to be both orator and

---

[1] Ioseph. *vita* 65.
[2] Suet. *Vesp.* 17, 18. [3] Ib. 8.
[4] Ib. 19 ' vetera quoque acroamata revocaverat '. [5] Ib. 18.
[6] Dion. lxvi. 13, in 71 A.D. That this act was ineffectual is shown by Domitian's action in 89–93 A.D.

poet. The language used in praise of his efforts by Pliny the elder, our one authority on this point, is so extravagant as to be virtually meaningless.[1] Of the literary exploits of his brother Domitian (81–96 A.D.) there is more to be said. It pleased him to lay claim to distinction both in prose and verse.[2] His only prose work of which any record remains was a treatise on the care of the hair;[3] his own baldness rankled in his mind and turned the *calvus Nero* of Juvenal into a hair specialist. As to his poems it is almost doubtful if he ever wrote any. He professed an enthusiasm for poetry, an art which, according to Suetonius, he had neglected in his youth and despised when he came to the throne. But Quintilian, Valerius Flaccus, and Martial[4] all load him with praise of various degrees of fulsomeness, though, reading between the lines of Quintilian, it is easy to see that Domitian's output must have been exceedingly small. The evidence of these three authors goes to show that he had contemplated, perhaps even begun, an epic on the achievements of his brother Titus in the Judaic War. Whether these *caelestia carmina belli*, as Martial calls them, ever existed, save in the imagination of courtiers and servile poets, there is nothing to show. If they did exist there seems no reason to regret their loss.

Domitian's chief service to literature, if indeed it was a true service, was the establishment of the Agon Capitolinus in 86, a quinquennial festival at which prizes were awarded not only for athletics and chariot-racing, but for declamations in verse and prose,[5] and the institution of a similar, though annual, contest at his own palace on the Alban Mount, which took place as often as the great festival of Minerva, known as the Quinquatria, came round.[6] But his interest in literature was only superficial ; he had no originality and

---

[1] Plin. *N. H.* praef. 5 and 11.
[2] Suet. *Dom.* 2 ; Tac. *Hist.* iv. 86 ; Quint. x. 1. 91.
[3] Suet. *Dom.* 18.
[4] Quint. loc. cit. ; Val. Fl. i. 12 ; Mart. v. 5. 7.
[5] Suet. *Dom.* 4.
[6] Stat. *Silv.* iv. 2. 65, v. 3. 227.

read nothing save the memoirs and edicts of Tiberius.[1] His capricious cruelty extended itself to artists and authors ; [2] twice (in 89 and 93 A.D.), following his father's example, he banished philosophers and astrologers from Rome ; [3] the crime of having written laudatory biographies of the Stoics Thrasea and Helvidius Priscus brought Arulenus Rusticus and Herennius Senecio to their deaths.[4] But Domitian's tyranny had little effect on *belles-lettres*, however adverse it may have been to free-spoken philosophy, rhetoric, or history. Valerius Flaccus, Silius, Statius, and Martial, all wrote during his reign, and the works of the last-named poet and Quintilian give ample evidence of widespread literary activity. The minor poet replenished the earth, and the prizes for literature awarded at the Agon Capitolinus and the festival of the Alban Mount must have been a real stimulus to writing, even though the type of literature produced by such a stimulus may have been scarcely worth producing. The worst feature of the poetry of the time is the almost incredibly fulsome flattery to which the tyranny of Domitian gave rise. As a compensation we have in the two succeeding reigns the biting satire of Juvenal and Tacitus, rendered all the keener by its long suppression under the last of the Flavian dynasty.

But, however impossible it may have been to write really effective satire during the Flavian dynasty, of poets there was no lack. It was, moreover, under the Flavians that there sprang up that reaction towards a saner style to which we have already referred as finding its expression in the Ciceronianism of Quintilian, and to a lesser degree in the Vergilianism of Valerius, Statius, and Silius. Of lesser luminaries there were enough and to spare. Serranus and Saleius Bassus are both warmly commended by Quintilian

---

[1] Suet. *Dom.* 20. This may have been creditable to him as ruler of the empire, though Suetonius undoubtedly wishes us to regard Tiberius' memoirs as a manual of tyranny.

[2] Suet. *Dom.* 10.

[3] Suet. loc. cit.; Hieronym. ad ann. 89 and 95 A.D. The latter date is wrong : cp. Mommsen, *Hermes*, iii (1869), p. 84.

[4] Tac. *Agr.* 2.

for their achievements in Epic. The former died young, before his powers had ripened to maturity, but showed great soundness of style and high promise.[1] Of Saleius Quintilian [2] says, 'He had a vigorous and poetic genius, but it was not mellowed by age.' That is to say, he died young, like Serranus. In the *Dialogus* of Tacitus he is spoken of as the best of men and the most finished of poets. He won Vespasian's favour and received a gift from him of five hundred thousand sesterces. His poems brought him no material profit ; both Tacitus and Juvenal emphasize this point :

> contentus fama iaceat Lucanus in hortis
> marmoreis ; at Serrano tenuique Saleio
> gloria quantalibet quid erit, si gloria tantum est.[3]

Statius' father, a distinguished teacher of rhetoric at Naples, had written a poem on the burning of the Capitol in 69 A.D., and was only prevented by death [4] from singing the great eruption of Vesuvius. Arruntius Stella of Patavium,[5] the friend of Statius and Martial, wrote elegies to his wife Violentilla. Turnus,[6] like Juvenal the son of a freedman, attained considerable success as a satirist, while the two distinguished soldiers, Verginius Rufus [7] and Vestricius Spurinna,[8] wrote light erotic verse and lyrics respectively. In addition to these there are a whole host of minor poets mentioned by Statius and Martial. In fact the writing of verse was the most fashionable occupation for the leisure time of a cultivated gentleman.

With Nerva and Trajan the happiest epoch of the principate set in. Nerva (96–98 A.D.) sprung from a line of distinguished jurists, was celebrated by Martial as the Tibullus

---

[1] Quint. x. 1. 89. There is no clear indication of his date, but he is coupled with Saleius Bassus by Juvenal (vii. 80), a fact which suggests that he belonged to the Flavian period.

[2] x. 1. 90.   [3] Juv. vii. 79.   [4] Stat. *Silv.* v. 3 .

[5] Stat. *Silv.* i. 2. 253 ; Mart. iv. 6. 4, i. 7, vii. 14.

[6] Schol. Vall. *ad Iuv.* i. 20 ; Mart. xi. 10 ; Rut. Nam. i. 603 ; Schol. *Iuv.* i. 71.   For his brother Scaevus Memor see p. 30.

[7] Plin. *Ep.* v. 3. 5, vi. 10. 4.   [8] Ib. iii. 1. 11, ii. 7. 1

of his time,[1] and is praised by the younger Pliny for the excellence of his light verses.[2] Trajan, his successor (98–117 A. D.), though a man of war, rather than a man of letters, wrote a history of the Dacian wars,[3] and possessed—as his letters to Pliny testify—a remarkable power of expressing himself tersely and clearly. He was, like Vespasian, a generous patron to rhetoric and education,[4] and the founder of the important library known as the *Bibliotheca Ulpia*.[5] But the great service which he and his predecessor rendered to literature was, as Pliny and Tacitus bear eloquent witness, the gift of freedom. This did more for prose than for poetry, save for one important fact—it was the means of enriching the world with the satires of Juvenal. If the quantity of the literature surviving from the principates of Nerva and Trajan is small, its quality is unmistakable. Pliny the younger, Tacitus, and Juvenal form a trio whose equal is to be found at no other period of the post-Augustan principate, while the letters of Pliny give proof of the existence of a highly cultivated society devoted to literature of all kinds. Poets were numerous even if they were not good. Few names, however, survive, and those have but the slightest interest for us. It will suffice to mention three of them : Passennus Paulus, Sentius Augurinus, and the younger Pliny. With the dramatic poets, Pomponius Bassulus and Vergilius Romanus, we have already dealt.[6] Pliny shall speak for himself and his friends.

' Passennus Paulus,' he writes,[7] ' a distinguished Roman knight of great learning, is a writer of elegies. This runs in the family ; for he is a fellow townsman of Propertius and indeed counts him among his ancestors.' In a later letter [8] he speaks with solicitude of his failing health, and goes on

---

[1] Mart. viii. 70. 7.   [2] Plin. *Ep.* v. 3. 5.

[3] Priscian, *Gr. Lat.* ii, p. 205, 6.

[4] Plin. *Paneg.* 47 ; *Ep.* iii. 18. 5.

[5] Dion. lxviii. 16 ; Gellius xi. 17. 1.

[6] See p. 25. Other names are Octavius Rufus, Plin. *Ep.* i. 7 ; Titinius Capito, *C. I. L.* 798, Plin. *Ep.* i. 17. 3 ; viii. 12. 4 ; Caninius Rufus, Plin. *Ep.* viii. 4. 1 ; Calpurnius Piso, Plin. *Ep.* v. 17. 1.

[7] *Ep.* vi. 15.   [8] *Ep.* ix. 22.

to describe the characteristics of his work. ' In his verse he imitates the ancients, paraphrases them, and reproduces them, above all Propertius, from whom he traces his descent. He is a worthy scion of the house, and closely resembles his great ancestor in that sphere in which he of old excelled. If you read his elegies you will find them highly polished, possessed of great sensuous charm, and quite obviously written in the house of Propertius. He has lately betaken himself to lyric verse, and imitates Horace with the same skill with which he has imitated Propertius. Indeed, if kinship counts for anything in the world of letters, you would deem him Horace's kinsman as well.' Pliny concludes with a warm tribute to Passennus' character. The picture is a pleasant one, but it is startling and significant to find Pliny awarding such praise to one who was frankly imitative, if he was not actually a plagiarist.[1]

Pliny is not less complimentary to Sentius Augurinus. ' I have been listening,' he writes,[2] ' to a recitation given by Sentius Augurinus. It gave me the greatest pleasure, and filled me with the utmost admiration for his talent. He calls his verses " trifles " (*poematia*). Much is written with great delicacy, much with great elevation of style ; many of the poems show great charm, many great tenderness ; not a few are honey-sweet, not a few bitter and mordant. It is some time since anything so perfect has been produced.' The next clause, however, betrays the reason, in part at any rate, for Pliny's admiration. In the course of his recitation he had produced a small hendecasyllabic poem in praise of Pliny's own verses. Pliny proceeds to quote it with every expression of gratification and approval. It is certainly neatly turned and well expressed, but it is such as any cultivated gentleman who had read his Catullus and Martial might produce, and can hardly have been of interest to any

---

[1] Gaius Passennus Paulus Propertius Blaesus was his full title. He derives his chief interest from the fact that the inscription at Assisi which preserves his name is our most conclusive evidence for the birthplace of Propertius. Haupt, opusc. i. p. 283, Leipz. (1875).

[2] *Ep.* iv. 27.

one save Augurinus and Pliny. Pliny was, in fact, with all
his admirable gifts, one of the principal and most amiable
members of a highly cultivated mutual admiration society.
He was a poet himself, though only a few lines of the poems
praised by Augurinus have survived to undergo the judgement of a more critical age. Pliny has, however, given an
interesting little sketch of his poetical career in the fourth
letter of the seventh book. ' I have always had a taste for
poetry,' he tells his friend Pontius ; ' nay, I was only fourteen when I composed a tragedy in Greek. What was it like?
you ask. I know not ; it was called a tragedy. Later,
when returning from my military service, I was weather-
bound in the island of Icaria, and wrote elegiac poems in
Latin about that island and the sea, which bears the same
name. I have occasionally attempted heroic hexameters,
but it is only quite recently that I have taken to writing
hendecasyllables. You shall hear of their origin and of the
occasion which gave them birth. Some writings of Asinius
Gallus were being read aloud to me in my Laurentine
villa ; in these works he was comparing his father with
Cicero ; we came upon an epigram of Cicero dedicated to
his freedman Tiro. Shortly after, about noon—for it was
summer—I retired to take my siesta, and finding that I
could not sleep, I began to reflect how the very greatest
orators have taken delight in composing this style of verse,
and have hoped to win fame thereby. I set my mind to it,
and, quite contrary to my expectations after so long desue-
tude, produced in an extremely short space of time the
following verses on that very subject which had provoked
me to write.'

Thirteen hexameter verses follow of a mildly erotic
character. They are not peculiarly edifying, and are
certainly very far from being poetry. He continues :

' I then turned my attention to expressing the same
thoughts in elegiac verse ; I rattled these off at equal speed,
and wrote some additional lines, being beguiled into doing so
by the fluency with which I wrote the metre. On my return
to Rome I read the verses to my friends. They approved.

Then in my leisure moments, especially when travelling,
I attempted other metres. Finally, I resolved to follow the
example of many other writers and compose a whole separate
volume in the hendecasyllabic metre; nor do I regret having
done so. For the book is read, copied, and even sung ; even
Greeks chant my verses to the sound of the *cithara* or the
lyre ; their passion for the book has taught them to use the
Latin tongue.' It was this volume of hendecasyllables
about which Pliny displays such naïve enthusiasm that led
Augurinus to compare Pliny to Calvus and Catullus. Pliny's
success had come to him comparatively late in life ; but it
emboldened him to the composition of another volume of
poems [1] in various metres, which he read to his friends. He
cites one specimen in elegiacs [2] which awakens no desire for
more, for it is fully as prosy as the hexameters to which we
have already referred. Of the hendecasyllables nothing survives, but Pliny tells us something as to their themes and the
manner of their composition.[3] ' I amuse myself by writing
them in my leisure moments at the bath or in my carriage.
I jest in them and make merry, I play the lover, I weep,
I make lamentation, I vent my anger, or describe something
or other now in a pedestrian, now in a loftier vein.' As this
little catalogue would suggest, these poems were not always
too respectable. The good Pliny, like Martial, thinks it
necessary to apologize [4] for his freedom in conforming to the
fashionable licence of his age by protesting that his muse
may be wanton, but his life is chaste. We can readily believe
him, for he was a man of kindly heart and high ideals, whose
simple vanity cannot obscure his amiability. But it is
difficult to believe that the loss of his poetry is in any way
a serious loss to the world.[5] We have given Pliny the poet
more space than is his due ; our excuse must be the interest
of his engaging self-revelations.

In spite of Pliny's enthusiasm for his poet friends, there is

---

[1] viii. 21. 14.   [2] vii. 9. 10.   [3] iv. 14. 2.   [4] iv. 14. 4.

[5] He also translated the Greek epigrams of Arrius Antoninus. Cp. *Ep.*
iv. 3. 3, and xviii. 1. One of these translations is preserved, Baehrens,
P. L. M. iv. 112.

no reason to suppose that the reign of Trajan saw the production of any poetry, save that of Juvenal, which even ap-
proached the first rank.   With the accession of Hadrian we
enter on a fresh era, characterized by the rise of a new prose
style and the almost entire disappearance of poetry.   Rome
had produced her last great poet.   The *Pervigilium Veneris*
and a few slight but beautiful fragments of Tiberianus are all
that illumine the darkness till we come upon the interesting
but uninspired elegiacs of Rutilius Namatianus, the curiously
uneven and slipshod poetry of Ausonius, and the graceful,
but cold and lifeless perfection of the heroic hexameters of
Claudian.

II

SULPICIA

Poetesses were not rare at Rome during the first century
of our era ; the *scribendi cacoethes* extended to the fair sex
sufficiently, at any rate, to evoke caustic comment both from
Martial [1] and Juvenal.[2]   By a curious coincidence, the only
poetesses of whose work we have any record are both named
Sulpicia.   The elder Sulpicia belongs to an earlier age ; she
formed one of the Augustan literary circle of which her uncle
Messala was the patron, and left a small collection of elegiac
poems addressed to her lover, and preserved in the same
volume as the posthumous poems of Tibullus, to whose
authorship they were for long attributed.[3]

The younger Sulpicia was a contemporary of the poet
Martial, and, like her predecessor, wrote erotic verse.   Frank
and outspoken as was the earlier poetess, in this respect at
least her namesake far surpassed her.   For the younger
Sulpicia's plain-speaking, if we may judge from the comments
of ancient writers [4] and the one brief fragment of her love-

---

[1] ii. 90. 9.   [2] In the sixth Satire.

[3] See Schanz, *Gesch. Röm. Lit.* § 284.

[4] Apoll. Sid. ix. 261 ' quod Sulpiciae iocos Thalia scripsit blandiloquum
suo Caleno '.   Auson. *Cento. Nupt.*, 4 ' meminerint prurire opusculum
Sulpiciae, frontem caperrare '.   Fulgentius, *Mythol.* 1 (p. 4, Helm.) ' Sul-
picillae procacitas '

poems that has survived,[1] was of a very different character
and must at least have bordered on the obscene.   But her
work attracted attention ; her fame is associated with her
love for Calenus, a love that was long [2] and passionate.
She continued to be read even in the days of Ausonius and
Sidonius Apollinaris.   Martial compares her with Sappho,
and her songs of love seem to have rung true, even though
their frankness may have been of a kind generally associated
with passions of a looser character.[3]   If, as a literal interpretation of Martial [4] would lead us to infer, Calenus was
her husband, the poems of Sulpicia confront us with a
spectacle unique in ancient literature—a wife writing love-
poems to her husband.   Her language came from the heart,
not from book-learning ; she was a poetess such as Martial
delighted to honour.

> omnes Sulpiciam legant puellae,   [1]
> uni quae cupiunt viro placere ;
> omnes Sulpiciam legant mariti,
> uni qui cupiunt placere nuptae.
> non haec Colchidos adserit furorem,
> diri prandia nec refert Thyestae ;

[1]   Read your Sulpicia, maidens all,
> Whose husband shall your sole love be ;
> Read your Sulpicia, husbands all,
> Whose wife shall reign, and none but she.
> No theme for her Medea's fire,
> Nor orgy of Thyestes dire ;

[1] Schol. Vall. *ad Iuv.* vi. 537, unde ait Sulpicia :
> si me cadurcis dissolutis fasciis
> nudam Caleno concubantem proferat.

[2] Mart. x. 38. 9 :
> vixisti tribus, o Calene, lustris :
> aetas haec tibi tota computatur
> et solos numeras dies mariti.

The first edition of Martial, Book x, was probably published in 95 A. D.
If Sulpicia married Calenus at the age of 18–25, her birth will therefore
fall between 55 and 62 A. D.

[3] Cp. Mart. x. 38. 4–8.

[4] Cp. Mart. x. 38. 9–11.   It is, of course, possible that *mariti* is a
euphemism.

Scyllam, Byblida nec fuisse credit :
sed castos docet et probos amores,
lusus delicias facetiasque.
cuius carmina qui bene aestimarit,
nullam dixerit esse nequiorem,
nullam dixerit esse sanctiorem.[1]

Although the thought of what *procacitas*[2] may have meant in a lady of Domitian's reign raises something of a shudder, and although it is to be feared that Martial, when he goes on to say (loc. cit.)

tales Egeriae iocos fuisse   [1]
udo crediderim Numae sub antro,

had that in his mind which would have scandalized the pious lawgiver of Rome, we may yet regret the loss of poems which, if Martial's language is not merely the language of flattery, may have breathed a fresher and freer spirit than is often to be found in the poets of the age. Catullus and Sappho would seem to have been Sulpicia's models, but her poems have left so little trace behind them that it is impossible to speak with certainty. As to their metre we are equally ill-informed. The fragment of two lines quoted above is in iambic *senarii*. If we may believe the evidence[3] of a satirical hexameter poem attributed to Sulpicia, she also wrote in hendecasyllables and scazons. The genuineness of this poem is, however, open to serious doubt. It consists of seventy hexameters denouncing the expulsion of the philosophers by Domitian, and is known by the title of

Scylla and Byblis she'd deny,
Of love she sang and purity,
Of dalliance and frolic gay ;
Who should have well appraised her lay
Had said none were more chaste than she,
Yet fuller none of amorous glee.

A. E. STREET.

[1]   Such sport I ween Egeria gave
To Numa in his spring-drenched cave.

A. E. STREET.

---

[1] Mart. x. 35. 1.   [2] See Ap. Sid. loc. cit
[3] Sulp. *Sat.*, lines 4, 5.

Sulpiciae satira.[1] That it purports to be by the poetess
beloved of Calenus is clear from an allusion to their passion.[2]
Serious doubts have, however, been cast upon its genuineness. It is urged that the work is ill-composed, insipid, and
tasteless, and that it contains not a few marked peculiarities
in diction and metre, together with more than one historical
inaccuracy. The inference suggested is that the poem is
not by Sulpicia, but at least two centuries later in date. It
may readily be admitted that the poem is almost entirely
devoid of any real merit, that its diction is obscure and
slovenly, its metre lame and unimpressive. But the critics
of the poem are guilty of great exaggeration.[3] Many of its
worst defects are undoubtedly due to the exceedingly corrupt
state of the text ; further, it is hard to see what interest a
satire directed against Domitian would possess centuries
after his death, nor is it easy to imagine what motive could
have led the supposed forger to attribute his work to Sulpicia.

---

[1] *Raph. Volaterr. comment. urban.* (fol. lvi, 1506 A. D.), ' hic (sc. at
Bobbio) anno 1493 huiuscemodi libri reperti sunt. Rutilius Namatianus.
Heroicum Sulpici carmen.' The first edition was published in 1498, with
the title *Sulpitiae carmina quae fuit Domitiani temporibus : nuper a Georgio
Merula Allexandrino, cum aliis opusculis reperta. queritur de statu reipub-
licae et temporibus Domitiani.* The MS. is now lost.

[2] Cp. line 62. Domitian's edict seems to have threatened the security
of Calenus. In the lines which follow, Domitian's death and overthrow
are foretold. The poem, therefore, if genuine, must have been published
soon after Domitian's assassination in 96, though it may have been composed in part during his lifetime.

[3] The work is generally rejected as spurious. Baehrens (*P. L. M.* v.
p. 93, and *de Sulpiciae quae vocatur satira*, Jena, 1873) holds that the work
is contemporary with Ausonius. Boot (*de Sulpiciae quae fertur satira*,
Amsterdam, 1868) goes further, and regards the work as a renaissance
forgery. He is followed by Bücheler. But there is no reason to doubt the
existence of the Bobbian MS. The metrical difficulties can be remedied
by emendation. *palare* for *palari* (43) is a solecism, but many verbs are
found in both active and deponent forms, and *palare* may be a slip, or even
an invention by analogy. *captiva* (52) does not = the Italian *cattiva* or
the French *chétive*. The most that we can say is that the work shows no
resemblance to any extant contemporary literature. That does not
necessarily prove it to be of later date. The problem cannot be answered
with certainty. On the whole, to us the difficulty of supposing it to be
a late forgery seems greater than the difficulty of supposing it to be by
Sulpicia.

The balance of probability inclines, though very slightly, in favour of the view that the work is genuine. This is unfortunate ; for the perusal of this curious satire on the hypothesis of its genuineness appreciably lessens our regret for the loss of Sulpicia's love poetry and arouses serious suspicion as to the veracity of Martial. It must, however, in justice be remembered that it does not follow that Sulpicia was necessarily a failure as a lyric writer because she had not the peculiar gift necessary for satire. The absence of the training of the rhetorical schools from a woman's education might well account for such a failure. At the worst, Sulpicia stands as an interesting example of the type of womanhood at which Juvenal levelled some of his wildest and most ill-balanced invective.

CHAPTER VIII

VALERIUS FLACCUS

THE political tendency towards retrenchment and reform that marks the reign of Vespasian finds its literary parallel in a reaction against the rhetoric of display that culminated in Seneca and Lucan. This movement is most strongly marked in the prose of Quintilian and the *Dialogus* of Tacitus, but finds a faint echo in the world of poets as well. The three epic poets of the period—Valerius Flaccus, Statius, and Silius Italicus—though they, too, have suffered much from their rhetorical training, are all clear followers of Vergil. They, like their predecessors, find it hard to say things naturally, but they do not to the same extent go out of their way with the deliberate intention of saying things unnaturally.[1] We may condemn them as phrase-makers, though many a modern poet of greater reputation is equally open to the charge. But their phrase-making has not the flamboyant quality of the Neronian age. If it is no less wearisome, it is certainly less offensive. They do not lack invention; their mere technical skill is remarkable; they fail because they lack the supreme gifts of insight and imagination.

Valerius Flaccus chose a wiser course than Lucan and Silius Italicus. He turned not to history, but to legend, for his theme; and the story of the Argonauts, on which his choice lighted, possessed one inestimable advantage. Well-worn and hackneyed as it was, it possessed the secret of eternal youth. ' Age could not wither it nor custom stale its infinite variety.' The poorest of imitative poetasters could never have made it wholly dull, and Valerius Flaccus was more than a mere poetaster.

Of his life and position little is known. His name is

---

[1] An exception must be made of the *Silvae* of Statius.

given by the MSS. as Gaius Valerius Flaccus Setinus Balbus.[1]
The name Setinus suggests that he may have been a native
of Setia. As there were three Setias, one in Italy and two
in Spain, this clue gives us small help. It has been suggested [2]
that the peculiarities of his diction are due to his being of
Spanish origin. But we have no evidence as to the nature
of Spanish Latin, while the authors of known Spanish birth,
who found fame in the Silver Age—Seneca, Lucan, Martial,
Quintilian, Columella—show no traces of their provenance.
No more helpful is the view that he is one Flaccus of
Patavium, the poet-friend to whom two of Martial's epigrams
are addressed.[3] For Martial's acquaintance was poor and
is exhorted to abandon poetry as unlucrative, whereas
Valerius Flaccus had some social standing and, not improb-
ably, some wealth. From the opening of the *Argonautica* we
learn that he held the post of *quindecimvir sacris faciundis.*[4]
But there our knowledge of the poet ends, save for one
solitary allusion in Quintilian, the sole reference to Valerius
in any ancient writer. In his survey of Latin literature [5]
he says *multum in Valerio Flacco nuper amisimus.* The
work of Quintilian having been published between the
years 93 and 95 A. D., the death of Valerius Flaccus may
be placed about 90 A. D.

The poem seems to have been commenced shortly after
the capture of Jerusalem in 70 A. D. At the opening of
the first book [6] Valerius addresses Vespasian in the conventional language of courtly flattery with appropriate
reference to his voyages in northern seas during his service
in Britain, a reference doubly suitable in a poem which
is largely nautical and geographical. He excuses himself
from taking the obvious subject of the Jewish war on the

---

[1] Or Balbus Setinus.
[2] Schenkl, *Stud. zu V. F.* 272. [3] Mart. i. 61 and 76.
[4] i. 5:
> Phoebe mone, si Cymaeae mihi conscia vatis
> stat casta cortina domo.

In *Cymaeae vatis* there is an allusion to the custody of the Sibylline
books.
[5] x. 1. 90. [6] i. 7–12.

ground that that theme is reserved for the inspired pen of Domitian. It is for him to describe Titus, his brother, dark with the dust of war, launching the fires of doom and dealing destruction from tower to tower along the ramparts of Jerusalem.[1] The progress of the work was slow. By the time the third book is reached we find references to the eruption of Vesuvius that buried Pompeii and Herculaneum in 79 A.D.,[2] while in the two concluding books there seem to be allusions to Roman campaigns in the Danube lands, perhaps those undertaken by Domitian in 89 A.D.[3] At line 468 of the eighth book the poem breaks off suddenly. It is possible that this is due to the ravages of time or to the circumstances of the copyist of our archetype, but consideration of internal evidence points strongly to the conclusion that Valerius died with his work uncompleted.

Not only do the words of Quintilian (l. c.) suggest a poet who left a great work unfinished, but the poem itself is full of harshnesses and inconsistencies of a kind which so slow and careful a craftsman would assuredly have removed had the poem been completed and received its final revision.[4]

---

[1] i. 13, 14 :

Solymo nigrantem pulvere fratrem
spargentemque faces et in omni turre furentem.

Domitian pretended to be a poet and connoisseur of poetry. See p. 167.

[2] iii. 207 :

ut mugitor anhelat
Vesvius, attonitas acer cum suscitat urbes

[3] vii. 645 ; viii. 228. If these allusions be to events of 89 A.D. they point to the view that the last two books were composed shortly before the poet's death, and confirm the opinion that the *Argonautica* was never finished.

[4] A few instances will suffice. In iii. 302 Jason asserts that seers had prophesied his father's death ; this is nowhere else mentioned ; on the contrary, at the beginning of the second book, it is specially told us that Juno concealed from Jason the fact of his father's death, while in vii. 494 Jason speaks of him as still alive. In vii. 394 Venus is represented as leaving Medea in terror at the sound of her magic chant, while five lines later it is implied that she is still holding Medea's hand. In viii. 24 Jason goes to the grove of Mars to meet Medea and to steal the fleece of gold ; but no arrangement to this effect has been made between Jason and Medea at their previous meeting (vii. 516). Instances might be multiplied. See

These blemishes leave us little room for doubt. The poem
that has come down to us is a fragment lacking the *limae
labor*. Like the *Thebais* of Statius and the *Aeneid* itself, the
work was probably planned to fill twelve books. The poem
breaks off with the marriage of Medea and Jason on the Isle
of Peuce at the mouth of the Danube, where they are over-
taken by Medea's brother Absyrtus, who has come in anger
to reclaim his sister and take vengeance on the stranger who
has beguiled her. It is clear that the Argonauts[1] were, as
in Apollonius Rhodius, to escape up the Danube and reach
another sea. In Apollonius they descended from the head
waters of the Danube by some mythical river to the Adriatic ;
it is in the Adriatic that Absyrtus is encountered and slain ;
it is in Phaeacia that Jason and Medea are married. In
Valerius both these incidents take place in the Isle of Peuce,
at the Danube's mouth. The inference is that Valerius
contemplated a different scheme for his conclusion. It has
been pointed out[2] that a mere 'reproduction of Apollonius'
episodes could not have occupied four books '; and it is suggested that Valerius definitely brought his heroes into relation
to the various Italian places[3] connected with the Argonautic
legend, while he may even, as a compliment to Vespasian,[4]
have brought them back ' by way of the North Sea past
Britain and Gaul '. This ingenious conjectural reconstruction has some probability, slight as is the evidence on which
it rests. Valerius was almost bound to give his epic a
Roman tinge. More convincing, however, is the suggestion
of the same critic[5] that the poem was designed to exceed

Schenkl, op. cit. 12 sqq. ; Summers' *Study of Argonautica of Valerius
Flaccus*, p. 2 sqq. The inconsistency which makes the *Argo* to be at once
the first ship and to meet many other ships by the way is perhaps the most
glaring, but its rectification would have involved very radical alterations.

[1] Cp. viii. 189 :

                                        inde sequemur
          ipsius amnis iter, donec nos flumine certo
          perferat inque aliud reddat mare.

[2] Summers, op. cit. 6.

[3] e. g. Argous Portus, Cales, the portico of the Argonauts at Rome.

[4] i. 7–12.   [5] Summers, p. 7.

the scope of the epic of Apollonius and to have included the
death of Pelias, the malignant and usurping uncle, who, to
get rid of Jason, compels him to the search of the golden
fleece.   To the retribution that came upon him there are
two clear references[1] and only the design to describe it
could justify the introduction of the suicide of Jason's
parents at the outset of the first book, a suicide to which
they are driven to avoid death at the hands of Pelias.

The scope of the unwritten books is, however, of little
importance in comparison with the execution of the existing
portion of the poem.   The Argonaut Saga has its weaknesses
as a theme for epic.   It is too episodic, it lacks unity and
proportion.   Save for the struggle in Colchis and the loves
of Jason and Medea, there is little deep human interest.
These defects, however, find their compensation in the variety
and brilliance of colour, and, in a word, the romance that
is inseparable from the story.   The scene is ever changing,
each day brings a new marvel, a new terror.   Picturesqueness atones for lack of epic grandeur.   For that reason the
theme was well suited to the Silver Age, when picturesqueness and rich invention of detail predominated at the expense
of poetic dignity and kindling imagination.   In many ways
Valerius does justice to his subject, in spite of the initial
difficulty with which he was confronted.   Apollonius Rhodius
had made the story his own ; Varro of Atax had translated
Apollonius : both in its Greek and Latin forms the story
was familiar to Roman readers.   It was hard to be original.

Much as Valerius owes to his greater predecessor, he yet
succeeds in showing no little originality in his portrayal of
character and incident, and in a few cases in his treatment
of plot.[2]   In one particular indeed he has markedly improved

---

[1] i. 806 ; ii. 4.

[2] Valerius was no slavish imitator of Apollonius.   Some of his incidents
are new, such as the rescue of Hesione (ii. 450 sqq.).   Many of the incidents
in Apollonius are omitted (e. g. Stymphalian birds, A. R. ii. 1033, and the
encounter with the sons of Phrixus, A. R. ii. 1093).   Other incidents
receive a fresh turn.   In both poets the Argonauts see traces of the doom
of Prometheus.   But in A. he is still being devoured, in V. he is being
freed by Hercules amid an earthquake.   Again V. often expands or con-

on his model ; he has made Jason, the hero of his epic, a
real hero ; conventional he may be, but he still is a leader of
men. In Apollonius, on the other hand, he plays a curiously
inconspicuous part ; he is, in fact, the weakest feature of
the poem ; he is in despair from the outset, and at no point
shows genuine heroic qualities ; he is at best a peerless
wooer and no more. Here, however, he is exalted by the
two great battles of Cyzicus and Colchis ; it is in part his
prowess in the latter battle that wins Medea's heart. In
this connexion we may also notice a marked divergence from
Apollonius as regards the plot. Aeetes has promised Jason
the fleece if he will aid him against his brother Perses, who
is in revolt against him with a host of Scythians at his back.
Jason aids him, does prodigies of valour, and wins a glorious
victory. Aeetes refuses the reward. This act of treachery
justifies Jason in having recourse to Medea's magic arts and
in employing her to avenge him on her father. In Apollonius
we find a very different story. The sons of Phrixus, who,
to escape the wrath of Aeetes, have thrown in their lot with
the Argonauts, urge Jason to approach Medea ; they themselves work upon the feelings of their mother, Chalciope,
till she seeks her sister Medea—already in love with Jason
and only too ready to be persuaded—and induces her to
save her nephews, whose fate is bound up with that of the
strangers. This incident is wholly absent from Valerius
Flaccus, with the result that the loves of Jason and Medea

---

tracts an incident related by A. E. g. Contraction: The launching of *Argo*,
V. F. i. 184–91 ; A. R. i. 362–93. Expansion : The story of Lemnos
V. ii. 72–427 ; A. i. 591–884 : here there is not much difference in length,
but V. tells us much more. The visit to Cyzicus, V. iii. 1–361 ; A. i. 947–
1064 : note also that in V. the purification of the Argonauts, 362–459,
takes the place of the irrelevant founding of the temple of Rhea on Dindy-
mus, A. i. 1103 sqq. The debate as to whether to abandon Hercules, who
has gone in search of Hylas, V. iii. 598–714 ; in A. the Argonauts sail
without noticing the absence of Hercules and Hylas, and the debate takes
place at sea, A. i. 1273–1325. As a rule, however, V. is longer than A.,
partly owing to longer descriptions, partly owing to the greater compli-
cation of the plot at Colchis. On the other hand, there is much imitation
of A. Cp. V. F. i. 255 ; A. R. i. 553 ; V. F. iii. 565–97 ; A. i. 1261–72 ;
V. F. iv. 733 ; A. ii. 774 ; V. F. v. 73–100 ; A. ii. 911–929.

assume a somewhat different character. Jason's conduct becomes more natural and dignified. Medea, on the other hand, is shown in a less favourable light. In the Greek poet she has for excuse the desire to save her sister from the loss of her sons, which gives her half a right to love Jason. In the Latin epic she is without excuse, unless, indeed, the hackneyed supernatural machinery,[1] put in motion to win her for Jason, can be called an excuse. This crude employment of the supernatural leaves Valerius small room for the subtle psychological analysis wherein the Greek excels, and this, coupled with the love of the Silver Age for art magic, tends to make Medea—as in Seneca— a sorceress first, a woman after. In Apollonius she is bar- baric, unsophisticated, a child of nature ; in Valerius she is a figure of the stage, not without beauty and pathos, but essentially melodramatic.

But Apollonius had concentrated all his powers upon Medea, and dwarfs all his other characters, Jason not excepted. It is Medea alone that holds our interests. The little company of heroes embarked on unsailed seas and beset with strange peril are scarcely more than a string of names, that drop in and out, as though the work were a ship's log rather than an epic. In Valerius, though he attempts no detailed portraiture, they are men who can at least fight and die. He has, in a word, a better general conception as to how the story should be told ; he is less perfunctory, and strives to fill in his canvas more evenly, whereas Apollonius, although by no means concise, leaves much of his canvas covered by sketches of the slightest and most insignificant character. In the Greek poem, though half the work is consumed in describing the voyage to Colchis, the first two books contain scarcely anything of real poetic interest, if we except the story of Phineus and

---

[1] In Apollonius the aid of Aphrodite and Eros is requisitioned to make Medea fall in love with Jason, but there is no further conventional super- natural interference. In Valerius, Juno (v. 350, vi. 456-660, vii. 153-90) kindles Medea's passion with Venus's aid. In vii. 190 sqq., Venus goes in person.

the Harpies, a few splendid similes, and two or three descriptive passages, as brief as they are brilliant. In Valerius, on the contrary, there is abundance of stirring scenes and rich descriptive passages before the Argonauts reach their goal. His superiority is particularly noticeable at the outset of the poem. Apollonius plunges *in medias res* and fails to give an adequate account of the preliminaries of the expedition. He has no better method of introducing us to his heroes than by giving us a dreary catalogue of their names. Valerius, too, has his catalogue, but later ; we are not choked with indigestible and unpalatable fare at the very opening of the feast. And though both authors take five hundred lines to get their heroes under way, Valerius tells us far more and in far better language ; Apollonius does not find his stride till the second book, and forgets that it is necessary to interest the reader in his characters from the very beginning.

But though in these respects Valerius has improved on his predecessor, and though his work lacks the arid wastes of his model, he is yet an author of an inferior class, and comes ill out of the comparison. For he has little of the rich, almost oriental, colouring of Apollonius at his best, lacks his fire and passion, and fails to cast the same glamour of romance about his subject. While the Dido and Aeneas of Vergil are in some respects but a pale reflection of the Medea and Jason of Apollonius, the loves of Jason and Medea in Valerius are fainter still. His heroine is not the tragic figure that stands out in lines of fire from the pages of Apollonius. His lovers' speeches have a certain beauty and tenderness of their own, but they lack the haunting melody and the resistless passion that make the Rhodian's lines immortal. And while to a great extent he lacks the peculiar merits of the Greek,[1] he possesses his most serious blemish, the blemish that is so salient a characteristic of both Alexandrian and Silver Latin literature, the passion

---

[1] As evidence for Apollonius' superiority cp. V. F. v. 329 sqq. ; A. R. iii. 616 sq. ; V. F. vii. 1–25 ; A. R. iii. 771 sq. ; V. F v. 82–100 ; A. R. ii. 911–21.

for obscure learning. A good example is the huge, though most ingenious, catalogue of the tribes of Scythia at the opening of the sixth book, with its detailed inventory of strange names and customs, and its minute descriptions of barbaric armour. His love of learning lands him, moreover, in strange anachronisms. We are told that the Colchians are descended from Sesostris ;[1] the town of Arsinoe is spoken of as already in existence ; Egypt is already connected with the house of Lagus.[2]

In addition, Valerius possesses many of the faults from which Apollonius is free, but with which the post-Augustan age abounds. The dangerous influence of Seneca has, it is true, decayed ; we are no longer flooded with epigram or declamatory rhetoric. Rhetoric there is, and rhetoric that is not always effective ;[3] but it is rather a perversion of the rhetoric of Vergil than the descendant of the brilliant rant of Lucan and Seneca. From the gross lack of taste and humour that characterizes so many of his contemporaries he is comparatively free, though his description of the historic ' crab ' caught by Hercules reaches the utmost limit of absurdity :

                laetus et ipse   [1]
Alcides : Quisnam hos vocat in certamina fluctus ?
dixit, et, intortis adsurgens arduus undis,
percussit subito deceptum fragmine pectus,
atque in terga ruens Talaum fortemque Eribotem
et longe tantae securum Amphiona molis
obruit, inque tuo posuit caput, Iphite, transtro. (iii. 474–80.)

---

[1] Alcides gladdened in his heart and cried : ' Who challenges these waves to combat ? ' and as he rose against those buffeting waves, sudden with broken oar he smote his baffled breast, and, falling headlong back, o'erthrows Talaus and brave Eribotes and far-off Amphion, that never feared so vast a bulk should fall on him, and laid his head against thy thwart, O Iphitus.

---

[1] v. 418. Cp. Apollon. iv. 272 ; Herod. ii. 103 ; Strab. xvi. 4. 4 ; Plin. *N. H.* xxxiii. 52.

[2] vi. 118. Cp. also v. 423 :

           Arsinoen illi tepidaeque requirunt
    otia laeta Phari.

[3] Cp. vii. 35 sqq.

This unheroic episode is a relic of the comic traditions associated with Hercules, traditions which obtrude themselves from time to time in serious and even tragic surroundings.[1] Apollonius describes the same incident[2] with the quiet humour that so strangely tinges the works of the pedants of Alexandria. Valerius, on the other hand, has lost touch with the broad comedy of these traditions, and his attempt to be humorous only succeeds in making him ridiculous.[3]

His worst fault, however, lies in his obscurity and preciosity of diction. The error lies not so much in veiling simple facts under an epigram, as in a vain attempt to imitate the 'golden phrases' of Vergil. The strange conglomeratior of words with which Valerius so often vexes his readers resembles the 'chosen coin of fancy' only as the formless designs of the coinage of Cunobelin resemble the exquisite staters of Macedon from which they trace their descent. It requires more than a casual glance to tell that (i. 411)

> it quem fama genus non est decepta Lyaei
> Phlias inmissus patrios de vertice crines

means that Phlias was 'truly reported the son of Bacchus with streaming locks like to his sire's '; or that (vi. 553)

> Argus utrumque ab equis ingenti porrigit arvo

signifies no more than that the victims of Argus covered a large space of ground when they fell.[4] How miserable is such a phrase compared with the κεῖτο μέγας μεγαλωστί of Homer ! And though there is less serious obscurity, nothing can be more awkward than the not infrequent inversion of the natural order of words that we find in phrases such as *nec pereat quo scire malo* (vii. 7).[5]

---

[1] As, for instance, in the *Alcestis* of Euripides and Callimachus' Hymn to Artemis.

[2] A. R. i. 1167 δὴ τότ' ἀνοχλίζων τετρηχότος οἴδματος ὁλκοὺς | μεσσόθεν ἆξεν ἐρετμόν· ἀτὰρ τρύφος ἄλλο μὲν αὐτὸς | ἄμφω χερσὶν ἔχων πέσε δόχμιος, ἄλλο δὲ πόντος | κλύζε παλιρροθίοισι φέρων. ἀνὰ δ' ἕζετο σιγῇ | παπταίνων· χεῖρες γὰρ ἀήθεον ἠρεμέουσαι.

[3] Cp. also V. F. iv. 682–5 ; viii. 453–7.

For obscurity cp. also iii. 133–7, 336–7 ; vii. 55.

[5] Valerius is fond of such inversions, especially in the case of particles, pronouns, &c. ; cp. v. 187 *iuxta* ; ii. 150 *sed* ; vi. 452 *quippe*; vi. 543 *sed*.

Of mere preciosity and phrase-making without any special obscurity examples abound.[1] Pelion sinks below the horizon (ii. 6)—

> iamque fretis summas aequatum Pelion ornos.

A fight at close quarters receives the following curious description (ii. 524)—

> iam brevis et telo volucri non utilis aer.

A spear flying through the air and missing its mark is a *volnus raptum per auras* (iii. 196). More startling than these is the picture of a charge of trousered barbarians (vi. 702)—

> improba barbaricae procurrunt tegmina plantae.

One more peculiarity remains to be noticed. Here and there in the *Argonautica* we meet with a strange brevity and compression resulting not from the desire to produce phrases of curious and original texture, but rather from a praiseworthy though misdirected endeavour to be concise. The most remarkable example is found in the first book, where Mopsus, the official prophet of the expedition, falls into a trance and beholds a vision of the future (211):

> heu quaenam aspicio ! nostris modo concitus ausis   [1]
> aequoreos vocat ecce deos Neptunus et ingens
> concilium. fremere et legem defendere cuncti
> hortantur. sic amplexu, sic pectora fratris,
> Iuno, tene ; tuque o puppem ne desere, Pallas :
> nunc patrui nunc flecte minas. cessere ratemque
> accepere mari. per quot discrimina rerum
> expedior ! subita cur pulcher harundine crines
> velat Hylas ? unde urna umeris niueosque per artus
> caeruleae vestes ? unde haec tibi volnera, Pollux ?

---

[1] Alas ! what do I see ! Even now, stirred by our daring, lo ! Neptune calls the gods to a vast conclave. They murmur, and one and all urge him to defend his rights. Hold as thou holdest now, Juno, hold thy brother in thine embrace : and thou, Pallas, forsake not our ship : now, even now, appease thy brother's threats. They have yielded: they give Argo entrance to the sea. Through what perils am I whirled along! Why does fair Hylas veil his locks with a sudden crown of reeds ? Whence comes the pitcher on his shoulder and the azure raiment on his limbs of snow ? Whence, Pollux,

---

[1] Cp. i. 436–8 ; ii. 90 ; iii, 434 ; vi. 183, 260–4.

quantus io tumidis taurorum e naribus ignis !
tollunt se galeae sulcisque ex omnibus hastae
et iam iamque umeri. quem circum vellera Martem
aspicio ? quaenam aligeris secat anguibus auras
caede madens ? quos ense ferit ? miser eripe parvos,
Aesonide. cerno et thalamos ardere iugales.

These lines form a kind of abridgement or *précis* of the whole *Argonautica*, or even more, for we can hardly believe that the scheme of it included the murder of Medea's children and her vengeance on the house of Creon.[1] They are also far too obscure to be interesting to any save a highly-trained literary audience, while their extreme compression could only be justified by their having been primarily designed for recitation in a dramatic and realistic manner with suitable pauses between the different visions.[2] A yet worse and less excusable example of this peculiar brevity is the jerky and prosaic enumeration of Medea's achievements in the black art (vi. 442)—

mutat agros fluviumque vias; suus alligat ingens   [1]
cuncta sopor, recoquit fessos aetate parentes,
datque alias sine lege colus.

The attempt to be concise and full [3] at one and the same time fails, and fails inevitably.

But for all these faults Valerius Flaccus offends less than any of the Silver Latin writers of epic. He rants less and he exaggerates less ; above all, he has much genuine poetic

---

come these wounds of thine ? Ah ! what a flame streams from the wide-spread nostrils of the bulls. Helmets and spears rise from every furrow, and now see ! shoulders too ! What warfare for the fleece do I see ? Who is it cleaves the air with winged snakes, reeking with slaughter ? Whom smites she with the sword ? Ah ! son of Aeson, hapless man, save thy little ones. I see, too, the bridal chamber all aflame.

[1] She changes crops of fields and course of rivers. [At her bidding] deep clinging slumber binds all things; fathers outworn with age she seethes to youth again, and to others she gives new span of life against fate's ordinance.

1 See p. 183.
2 The passage may conceivably be only a rough draft, cp p. 197 note.
3 Cp. also i. 130–48, 251–4.

merit. He has been strangely neglected, both in ancient[1] and
modern times, and unduly depreciated in the latter.   There
has been a tendency to rank him with Silius Italicus, whereas
it would be truer criticism to place him close to Statius, and
not far below Lucan.   He is more uneven than the former,
has a far less certain touch, and infinitely less command of
his instrument.   He has less mastery of words, but a more
kindling and penetrating imagination.   His outlines are less
clear, but more suggestive.   He has less rhetoric ; beneath
an often obscure diction he reveals a greater simplicity and
directness of thought, and he has been infinitely more happy
in his theme.   Only the greatest of poets could achieve a
genuine success with the Theban legend, only the worst of
poets could reduce the voyage of the Argonauts to real
dullness.   On the other hand, in an age of *belles-lettres* such
as the Silver Age, and by the majority of scholars, whose
very calling leads them to set a perhaps abnormally high
value on technical skill, Statius is almost certain to be preferred to Valerius.   About the relative position of Lucan
there is no doubt.   He is incomparably the superior of
Valerius, both in genius and intellect.   But Valerius never
sins against taste and reason to the same extent, and though
he has less fire, possesses a finer ear for music and rhythm,
and more poetic feeling as distinct from rhetoric.   Vergil was
his master ; it has been said with a little exaggeration that
Valerius stands in the same relation to Vergil as Persius to
Horace.   This statement conveys but a half-truth. Valerius
is as superior to Persius in technique as he is inferior in
moral force and intellectual power.   He is, however, full of
echoes from Vergil,[2] and if his verse has neither the ' ocean

---

[1] There is little evidence that he had any influence on posterity, though
there may be traces of such influence in Hyginus and the Orphic Argonautica. Of contemporaries Statius and Silius seem to have read him and
at times to imitate him. See Summers, pp. 8, 9. Blass, however (*J. f. Phil.
und Päd.* 109, 471 sqq.), holds that Valerius imitates Statius.

[2] Cp. V. F. i. 833 sqq. ; *Aen.* vi. 893, 660 sqq., 638 sqq. ; V. F. i. 323 ;
A. viii. 560 sqq. ; V. F. vi. 331 ; A. ix. 595 sqq. ; V. F. iii. 136 ; A. xii.
300 sqq. ; V. F. viii. 358 ; A. x. 305 ; V. F. vi. 374 ; A. xi. 803. See
Summers, pp. 30–3. His echoes from Vergil are perhaps more obvious

roll ' of the greater poets, nor the same tenderness, he yet
has something of the true Vergilian glamour.   But he has
weakened his hexameter by succumbing to the powerful
influence of Ovid.   His verse is polished and neat to the
verge of weakness.   Like Ovid, he shows a preference for the
dactyl over the spondee, shrinks from elision, and does not
understand how to vary his pauses.[1]   Too many lines close
with a full-stop or colon, and where the line is broken, the
same pause often recurs again and again with wearisome
monotony.   In this respect Valerius, though never mono-
tonously ponderous like Lucan, compares ill with Statius.
As a compensation, his individual lines have a force and
beauty that is comparatively rare in the *Thebais*.   The poet
who could describe a sea-cave thus (iv. 179)—

> non quae dona die, non quae trahat aetheris ignem ;   [1]
> infelix domus et sonitu tremibunda profundi,

is not to be despised as a master of metre.   And whether
for picturesqueness of expression or for beauty of sound,
lines such as (iii. 596)

> rursus Hylan et rursus Hylan per longa reclamat   [2]
> avia ; responsant silvae et vaga certat imago,

or (i. 291)

> quis tibi, Phrixe, dolor, rapido cum concitus aestu   [3]
> respiceres miserae clamantia virginis ora
> extremasque manus sparsosque per aequora crines !

---

[1] That receiveth never daylight's gifts nor the light of the heavenly
fires, the home of gloom all a-tremble with the sound of the deep.

[2] ' Hylas', and again ' Hylas ', he calls through the long wilderness;
the woods reply, and wandering echo mocks his voice.

[3] Phrixus, what grief was thine when, swept along by the swirling
tide, thou lookedst back on the hapless maiden's face as she cried for
thine aid, her sinking hands, her hair streaming o'er the deep.

---

in some respects than similar echoes in Statius, owing to the fact that he
had a more Vergilian imagination than Statius, and lacked the extreme
dexterity of style to disguise his pilferings.   But in his general treatment
of his theme he shows far greater originality ; this is perhaps due to the
fact that the Argonaut saga is not capable of being ' Aeneidized ' to the
same extent as the Theban legend.   But let Valerius have his due.   He is
in the main unoriginal in diction, Statius in composition.

[1] Cp. Summers, p. 49.   See also note, p. 123.

are not easily surpassed outside the pages of Vergil. But it is above all on his descriptive power that his claim to consideration rests.[1] For it is there that he finds play for his most remarkable gifts, his power of suggestion of mystery, and his keen sense of colour. These gifts find their most striking manifestation in his description of the Argonauts' first night upon the waters. They

> were the first that ever burst
> Into that silent sea.

All is strange to them. Each sight and sound has its element of terror:

> auxerat hora metus, iam se vertentis Olympi   [1]
> ut faciem raptosque simul montesque locosque
> ex oculis circumque graves videre tenebras.
> ipsa quies rerum mundique silentia terrent
> astraque et effusis stellatus crinibus aether.
> ac velut ignota captus regione viarum
> noctivagum qui carpit iter non aure quiescit,
> non oculis, noctisque metus niger auget utrimque
> campus et occurrens umbris maioribus arbor,
> haud aliter trepidare viri (ii. 38).

There are few more vivid pictures in Latin poetry than that of the benighted wanderer lost on some wide plain studded with clumps of trees that seem to throng upon him in the gloom, seen greater through the darkness. Not less imaginative, though less clear cut and precise, is his picture of the underworld in the third book:

---

[1] The dark hour deepened their fears when they saw heaven's vault wheel round, and the peaks and fields of earth snatched from their view, and all about them the horror of darkness. The very stillness of things and the deep silence of the world affright them, the stars and heaven begemmed with streaming locks of gold. And as one benighted in a strange place 'mid paths unknown pursues his devious journey through the night and finds rest neither for eye nor ear, but all about him the blackness of the plain, and the trees that throng upon him seen greater through the gloom, deepen his terror of the dark—even so the heroes trembled.

[1] Cp. beside the passages quoted below iii. 558 sqq., 724, 5; iv. 16-50, 230, 1; v. 10-12; vii. 371-510, 610, 648-53.

est procul ad Stygiae devexa silentia noctis   [1]
Cimmerium domus et superis incognita tellus,
caeruleo tenebrosa situ, quo flammea numquam
Sol iuga sidereos nec mittit Iuppiter annos.
stant tacitae frondes inmotaque silva comanti
horret Averna iugo ; specus umbrarumque meatus
subter et Oceani praeceps fragor arvaque nigro
vasta metu et subitae post longa silentia voces (iii. 398).

It is a more theatrical underworld than that of Vergil, and
the picture is not clearly conceived, but its very vagueness
is impressive. The poet gives us, as it were, the scene for
the enactment of some dim dream of terror. He is equally
at home in describing the happy calm of Elysium. Though
the picture lacks originality, it has no lack of beauty :

hic geminae infernum portae, quarum altera dura   [2]
semper lege patens populos regesque receptat ;
ast aliam temptare nefas et tendere contra ;
rara et sponte patet, siquando pectore ductor
volnera nota gerens, galeis praefixa rotisque
cui domus aut studium mortales pellere curas,
culta fides, longe metus atque ignota cupido ;
seu venit in vittis castaque in veste sacerdos.
quos omnes lenis plantis et lampada quassans
progenies Atlantis agit. lucet via late

---

[1] Far hence by the deep sunken silence of the Stygian night lies the
Cimmerians' home, a land unknown to denizens of upper air, all dark with
gloomy squalor. Thither the sun hath never driven his flaming car nor
Jupiter sent forth his starry seasons. Silent are the leaves of its groves,
and all along its leafy hill bristles unmoved Avernus' wood: thereunder
are caverns, and the shades go to and fro; there Ocean plunges roaring
to its fall, there are plains with dark fear desolate, and after long
silences sudden voices thunder out.

[2] Here lie the twin gates of Hell, whereof the one is ever open by stern
fate's decree, and through it march the peoples and princes of the world.
But the other may none essay nor beat against its bars. Rarely it opens
and untouched by hand, if e'er a chieftain comes with glorious wounds
upon his breast, whose halls were decked with helm and chariots, or
who strove to cast out the woes of mankind, who honoured truth and bade
farewell to fear and knew no base ambition. Then, too, it opens when
some priest comes wearing sacred wreath and spotless robe. All such the
child of Atlas leads along with gentle tread and waving torch. Far shines

igne dei, donec silvas et amoena piorum
deveniant camposque, ubi sol totumque per annum
durat aprica dies thiasique chorique virorum
carminaque et quorum populis iam nulla cupido (i. 833).

Many lines might be quoted that startle us with their
unforeseen vividness or some unexpected blaze of colour ;
when the fleece of gold is taken from the tree where it had
long since shone like a beacon through the dark, the tree
sinks back into the melancholy night,

tristesque super coiere tenebrae (viii. 120).

At their bridal on the desolate Isle of Peuce under the
shadow of approaching peril, Jason and Medea gleam star-
like amid the company of heroes (viii. 257) :

ipsi inter medios rosea radiante iuventa   [1]
altius inque sui sternuntur velleris auro.

This characteristic is most evident in the similes over
which Valerius, like other poets of the age, would seem to
have expended particular labour. He scatters them over
his pages with too prodigal a hand, and they suffer at times
from over-elaboration and ingenuity.[1] Desire for originality
has led him to such startling comparisons as that between a
warrior drawn from his horse and a bird snared by the limed
twig of the fowler,[2] surely as inappropriate a simile as was

---

the road with the fire of the god until they come to the groves and plains,
the pleasant mansions of the blest, where the sun ceases not, nor the warm
daylight all the year long, nor dancing companies of heroes, nor song,
nor all the innocent joys that the peoples of the earth desire no more.

[1] Themselves in their comrades' midst, bright with the rosy glow of
youth, above them all, lie on the fleece of gold that they had made their
own.

---

[1] One is tempted at times to account for the profusion and lack of
spontaneity of similes in poets of this age by the supposition that they
kept commonplace books of similes and inserted them as they thought fit.
[2] vi. 260 :

qualem populeae fidentem nexibus umbrae
siquis avem summi deducat ab aere rami,
ante manu tacita cui plurima crevit harundo ;
illa dolis viscoque super correpta sequaci
inplorat ramos atque inrita concitat alas.

ever framed.   More distressing still is the maudlin pathos of
the simile which likens Medea to a dog on the verge of madness.[1]   But such gross aberrations are rare ; against them
may be set some of the freshest and most beautiful similes
in the whole range of Latin poetry.   The silence that follows
on the wailing of the women of Cyzicus is like the silence of
Egypt when the birds that wintered there have flown to
more temperate lands.   'And now they had paid due
honour to their ashes ; with weary feet, wives with their
babes wandered away and the waves had rest, the waves
long torn by their wakeful lamentation, even as when the
birds in mid-spring have returned to the north that is their
home, and Memphis and their yearly haunt by sunny Nile
are dumb once more '—

> qualiter Arctos
> ad patrias avibus medio iam vere revectis
> Memphis et aprici statio silet annua Nili (iii. 358).

The beauty of Medea among her Scythian maidens is likened
to that of Proserpine leading her comrades over Hymettus'
hill or wandering with Pallas and Diana in the Sicilian
mountains—

> altior ac nulla comitum certante, prius quam   [1]
> palluit et viso pulsus decor omnis Averno (v. 346).

The relief of the Argonauts, when at last they reach haven
after their fearful passage of the Symplegades, is like that of
Theseus and Hercules, when they have forced a way through
the gates of hell to the light of day once more.[2]   Most
remarkable of all is the strange accumulation of similes that

---

[1] Taller than all her comrades and fairer than them all or ever she
turned pale, and at the sight of Hell all beauty was banished from her face.

---

[1] vii. 124 :

> sic adsueta toris et mensae dulcis erili,
> aegra nova iam peste canis rabieque futura,
> ante fugam totos lustrat queribunda penates.

[2] iv. 699 :

> discussa quales formidine Averni
> Alcides Theseusque comes pallentia iungunt
> oscula vix primas amplexi luminis oras.

describe the meeting of Jason and Medea. Medea is going
through the silent night chanting a song of magic, whereat all
nature trembles. At last, when she has come ' to the shadowy
place of the triune goddess ', Jason shines forth before her
in the gloom, ' as when in deepest night panic bursts on herd
and herdsman, or shades meet blind and voiceless in the
deep of Chaos ; even so, in the darkness of the night and of
the grove, the two met astonied, like silent pines or motion-
less cypress, ere yet the whirling breath of the south wind
has caught and mingled their boughs ' [1]—

> obvius ut sera cum se sub nocte magistris
> inpingit pecorique pavor, qualesve profundum
> per chaos occurrunt caecae sine vocibus umbrae ;
> ·haut secus in mediis noctis nemorisque tenebris
> inciderant ambo attoniti iuxtaque subibant,
> abietibus tacitis aut immotis cyparissis
> adsimiles, rapidus nondum quas miscuit Auster (vii. 400).

These similes suffer from sheer accumulation.[2] Taken
individually they are worthy of many a greater poet.

In his speeches Valerius is less successful, though rarely
positively bad. But with few exceptions they lack force
and interest. At times, however, his rhetoric is effective, as
in the speech of Mopsus (iii. 377), where he sets forth the
punishment of blood-guiltiness, or in the fierce invective in
which the Scythian, Gesander, taunts a Greek warrior with
the inferiority of the Greek race (vi. 323 sqq.). This latter

---

[1] This simile is a free translation from Apollonius, iii. 966 τὼ δ'
ἄνεῳ καὶ ἄναυδοι ἐφέστασαν ἀλλήλοισιν, | ἢ δρυσίν, ἢ μακρῆσιν ἐειδόμενοι
ἐλάτῃσιν, | αἵ τε παράσσον ἔκηλοι ἐν οὔρεσιν ἐρρίζωνται, | νηνεμίῃ· μετὰ δ' αὖτις
ὑπὸ ῥιπῆς ἀνέμοιο | κινύμεναι ὁμάδησαν ἀπείριτον· ὡς ἄρα τώγε | μέλλον ἅλις
φθέγξασθαι ὑπὸ πνοιῇσιν Ἔρωτος. Valerius has compressed the last three
lines into *rapidus nondum quas miscuit Auster*. The effective *miscuit*
conveys nearly as much as the longer and not less beautiful version in
the Greek.

[2] This accumulation is probably due to the lack of revision. *obvius . . .
pavor* fits the context ill and is curiously reminiscent of l. 392 ('iam stabulis
gregibusque pavor strepitusque sepulcris inciderat'), while ll. 400-2 would
probably have been considerably altered had the poem undergone its final
correction. There are other indications of the unfinished character of the
work to be found in this passage (p. 181, note).

speech is closely modelled on Vergil (*A.* ix. 595 sqq.), and although it is somewhat out of place in the midst of a battle, is not wholly unworthy of its greater model. But it is to the speeches of Jason and Medea that we naturally turn to form the estimate of the poet's mastery of the language of passion. These speeches serve to show us how far he falls below Vergil (*A.* iv) and Apollonius (bk. iii). They offer a noble field for his powers, and it cannot be said that he rises to the full height of the occasion. On the other hand, he does not actually fail. There is a note of deep and moving appeal in all that Medea says as she gradually yields to the power of her passion, and the thought of her father and her home fades slowly from her mind.

[1] ' " Why," ' she cries (vii. 438), ' " why, I beseech thee, Thessalian, camest thou ever to this land of ours ? Whence hadst thou any hope of me ? And why didst thou seek these toils with faith in aught save thine own valour ? Surely hadst thou perished, had I feared to leave my father's halls—aye, and so surely had I shared thy cruel doom. Where now is thy helper Juno, where now thy Tritonian maid, since I, the queen of an alien house, have come to help thee in thy need ? Aye, even thyself thou marvellest, methinks, nor any more does this grove know me for Aeetes' daughter. Nay, 'twas thy cruel fate overcame me ; take now, poor suppliant, these my gifts, and, if e'er again Pelias seek to destroy thee and send thee forth to other cities, ah ! put not too fond trust in thy beauty ! " ' Yet again, before she puts the saving

---

[1]   quid, precor, in nostras venisti, Thessale, terras ?
        unde mei spes ulla tibi ? tantosque petisti
        cur non ipse tua fretus virtute labores ?
        nempe, ego si patriis timuissem excedere tectis,
        occideras ; nempe hanc animam sors saeva manebat
        funeris. en ubi Iuno, ubi nunc Tritonia virgo,
        sola tibi quoniam tantis in casibus adsum
        externae regina domus ? miraris et ipse,
        credo, nec agnoscunt hae nunc Aeetida silvae.
        sed fatis sum victa tuis ; cape munera supplex
        nunc mea ; teque iterum Pelias si perdere quaeret,
        inque alios casus alias si mittet ad urbes,
        heu formae ne crede tuae.

charms into his hands, she appeals to him (452): [1] ' " If
thou hast any hope of safety from these goddesses, that are
thine helpers, or if perchance thine own valour can snatch thee
from the jaws of death, even now, I pray thee, stranger, let
me be, and send me back guiltless to my unhappy sire."
She spake, and straightway—for now the stars outworn sank
to their setting, and Bootes in the furthest height of heaven
had turned him towards his rest—straightway she gave the
charms to the young hero with wailing and with lamentation,
as though therewith she cast away her country and her own
fair fame and honour.' And then, 'when her guilt was
accomplished and the blush of shame had passed from her
face for evermore,' she saw as in a vision (474) ' the Minyae
spreading their sails for flight without her. Then in truth
bitter anguish laid hold of her spirit, and she grasped the
right hand of the son of Aeson and humbly spake: "Remember me, I pray, for I, believe me shall forget thee never.
When thou art hence, where on all the vault of heaven shall
I bear to gaze? Ah! do thou too, where'er thou art, through
all the years ne'er let the thought of me slip from thy heart.
Remember how thou stood'st to-day, tell of the gifts I gave,

---

[1]   si tamen aut superis aliquam spem ponis in istis,
        aut tua praesenti virtus educere leto
        si te forte potest, etiam nunc deprecor, hospes,
        me sine, et insontem misero dimitte parenti.
        dixerat; extemploque (etenim matura ruebant
        sidera, et extremum se flexerat axe Booten)
        cum gemitu et multo iuveni medicamina fletu
        non secus ac patriam pariter famamque decusque
        obicit. ille manu subit, et vim conripit omnem.
          inde ubi facta nocens, et non revocabilis umquam
        cessit ab ore pudor, ...
          .   .   .   pandentes Minyas iam vela videbat
        se sine. tum vero extremo percussa dolore
        adripit Aesoniden dextra ac submissa profatur:
        sis memor, oro, mei, contra memor ipsa manebo,
        crede, tui. quando hinc aberis, dic quaeso, profundi
        quod caeli spectabo latus ? sed te quoque tangat
        cura mei quocumque loco, quoscumque per annos ;
        atque hunc te meminisse velis, et nostra fateri

and feel no shame that thou wast saved by a maiden's guile. Alas! why stream no tears from thine eyes? Knowest thou not that the death I have deserved waits me at my father's hand? For thee there waits a happy realm among thine own folk, for thee wife and child; but I must perish deserted and betrayed." ' [1]

All this lacks the force and passion of the corresponding scene in Apollonius. This Medea could never have cried, ' I am no Greek princess, gentle-souled,' [2] nor have prayed that a voice from far away or a warning bird might reach him in Iolcus on the day when he forgot her, or that the stormwind might bear her with reproaches in her eyes to stand by his hearth-stone and chide him for his forgetfulness and ingratitude. The Medea of Apollonius has been softened and sentimentalized by the Roman poet. Valerius knows no device to clothe her with power, save by the narration of her magic arts (vii. 463-71 ; viii. 68-91). Yet she has a charm of her own ; and it needed true poetic feeling to draw even the Medea of Valerius Flaccus.

In no age would Valerius have been a great poet, but under happier circumstances he would have produced work that would have ranked high among literary epics. As it is, there is no immeasurable distance between the *Argonautica* and works such as the *Gerusalemme liberata*, or much of *The Idylls of the King*. He is a genuine poet whose genius was

---

munera ; servatum pudeat nec virginis arte.
hei mihi, cur nulli stringunt tua lumina fletus ?
an me mox merita morituram patris ab ira
dissimulas ? te regna tuae felicia gentis,
te coniunx natique manent ; ego prodita obibo.

---

[1] Cp. also viii. 10, where Medea bids farewell to her home. 'O my father, would thou mightest give me now thy last embrace, as I fly to exile, and mightest behold these my tears. Believe me, father, I love not him I follow more than thee : would that the stormy deep might whelm us both. And mayest thou long hold thy realm, grown old in peace and safety, and mayest thou find thy children that remain more dutiful than me.'

[2] Ap. Rh. iii. 1105 sqq.; cp. also Murray on Apollonius in his *History of Greek Literature*, p. 382.

warped by the spirit of the age, stunted by the inherent difficulties besetting the Roman writer of epic, overweighted by his admiration of his two great predecessors, Ovid and Vergil. He is obscure, he is full of echoes, he staggers beneath a burden of useless learning, he overcrowds his canvas and strives in vain to put the breath of life into bones long dry; in addition, his epic suffers from the lack of the reviser's hand. And yet, in spite of all, his characters are sometimes more than lay-figures, and his scenes more than mere stage-painting. He has the divine fire, and it does not always burn dim. Others have greater cunning of hand, greater force of intellect, and have won a higher place in the hierarchy of poets. He—though, like them, he lacks the ' fine madness that truly should possess a poet's brain'—yet gives us much that they cannot give, and sees much that they cannot see. With Quintilian, though with altered meaning, we too may say *multum in Valerio Flacco amisimus*.

CHAPTER IX

STATIUS

OUR information as to the life of P. Papinius Statius is drawn almost exclusively from his minor poems entitled the *Silvae*. He was born at Naples, his father was a native of Velia, came of good family,[1] and by profession was poet and schoolmaster. The father's school was at Naples,[2] and, if we may trust his son, was thronged with pupils from the whole of Southern Italy.[3] He had been victorious in many poetic contests both in Naples and in Greece.[4] He had written a poem on the burning of the Capitol in 69 A. D., had planned another on the eruption of Vesuvius in 79 A. D., but apparently died with the work unfinished.[5] It was to his father that our poet attributed all his success as a poet. It was to him he owed both education and inspiration, as the *Epicedion in patrem* bears pathetic witness (v. 3. 213):

> sed decus hoc quodcumque lyrae primusque dedisti   [1]
> non volgare loqui et famam sperare sepulcro.

The *Thebais* was directly due to his prompting (loc. cit., 233):

>   te nostra magistro   [2]
> Thebais urgebat priscorum exordia vatum;
> tu cantus stimulare meos, tu pandere facta
> heroum bellique modos positusque locorum
> monstrabas.

---

[1] Thou wert the first to give this glory, whate'er it be, that my lyre hath won; thine was the gift of noble speech and the hope that my tomb should be famous.

[2] At thy instruction my Thebais trod the steps of elder bards; thou taughtest me to fire my song, thou taughtest me to set forth the deeds of heroes and the ways of war and the position of places.

---

1 *Silv.* v. 3. 116 sqq.
2 Ib. 146 sqq.   3 Ib. 163.   4 Ib. 141.
5 Ib. 195–208. This passage suggests that the elder Statius died soon after 79 A. D. On the other hand, he probably lived some years longer

The poet-father lived long enough to witness his son well on the way to established fame. He had won the prize for poetry awarded by his native town, the crown fashioned of ears of corn, chief honour of the Neapolitan Augustalia.[1] Early in the reign of Domitian he had received a high price from the actor Paris for his libretto on the subject of Agave,[2] and he had already won renown by his recitations at Rome,[3] recitations in all probability of portions of the *Thebais*[4] which he had commenced in 80 A.D.[5] But it was not till after his father's death that he reached the height of his fame by his victory in the annual contest instituted by Domitian at his Alban palace,[5] and by the completion and final publication in 92 A.D. of his masterpiece, the *Thebais*.[6] This poem was the outcome of twelve years' patient labour, and it was on this that he based his claim to immortality.[6] He had now made himself a secure position as the foremost poet of his age. His failure to win the prize at the quin-quennial Agon Capitolinus in 94 A.D. caused him keen morti-fication, but was in no way a set-back to his career.[7] By this time he had already begun the publication of his *Silvae*. The first book was published not earlier than 92 A.D.,[8] the second and third between that date and 95 A.D. The fourth appeared in 95 A.D.,[8] the fifth is unfinished. There is no

as the *Thebais*, inspired and directed by him, was not begun till 80 A.D. He must, however, have died before 89 A.D., the earliest date assignable to Statius' victory at the Alban contest.

[1] *Silv.* v. 3. 225.

[2] Juv. vii. 86. Paris had fallen from imperial favour by 83 A.D. Dio. lxvii. 3. 1.

[3] *Silv.* v. 3. 215.   [4] Juv. vii. 82.

[5] *Silv.* v. 3. 227. The subject of his prize recitation was the triumph of Domitian over the Germans and Dacians; i. e. after 89 A.D.

[6] Praef. *Silv.* i. 'pro Thebaide quamvis me reliquerit timeo.' The first book of the *Silvae* was published in 92 A.D. For the time taken for its composition and the poet's anticipations of immortality see *Th.* xii. 811 sqq.

[7] *Silv.* iii. 5. 28, v. 3. 232. The Agon Capitolinus was instituted in 86 A.D. The contests falling in Statius' lifetime are those of 86, 90, 94 A.D. As his failure is always mentioned after the Alban victory, 94 A.D. would seem the most probable date.

[8] Rutilius Gallicus had just died when the first book was published;

allusion to any date later than 95 A.D., no indication that the
poet survived Domitian (d. 96 A. D.).   These facts, together
with the fragmentary state of his ambitious *Achilleis*, begun
in 95 A.D.,[1] point to Statius having died in that year, or at
least early in 96 A. D.   He left behind him, beside the works
already mentioned, a poem on the wars of Domitian in
Germany,[2] and a letter to one Maximus Vibius, which may
have served as a preface to the *Thebais*.[3]   He had spent the
greater portion of his life either at Rome, Naples, or in the
Alban villa given him by Domitian.   In his latter years he
seems to have resided almost entirely at Rome, though he
must have paid not infrequent visits to the Bay of Naples.[4]
But in 94 A. D., whether through failing health or through
chagrin at his defeat in the Capitoline contest, he retired
to his native town.[5]   He had married a widow named
Claudia,[6] but the union was childless ;   towards the end of
his life he adopted the infant son of one of his slaves,[7] and
the child's premature death affected him as bitterly as
though it had been his own son that died.   Of his age we
know little ;   but in the *Silvae* there are allusions to the

---

cp. Praef., bk. i.   This took place in 92 A. D.;   cp. *C. I. L.* v. 6988, vi. 1984.
8.   *Silv.* iv. 1 celebrates Domitian's seventeenth consulate (95 A. D.).

[1] Such at least is a legitimate inference from the fact that it is not
mentioned before the fourth and fifth books of the *Silvae*; cp. iv. 4. 94,
iv. 7. 23, v. 2. 163.

[2] Written probably in 95 A. D.   Statius promises such a work in
Silv. iv. 4. 95.   Four lines are quoted from it in G. Valla's scholia on
Juv. iv. 94:

> lumina : Nestorei mitis prudentia Crispi
> et Fabius Veiento (potentem signat utrumque
> purpura, ter memores implerunt nomine fastos),
> et prope Caesareae confinis Acilius aulae.

[3] Praef. *Silv.* iv ' Maximum Vibium et dignitatis et eloquentiae nomine
a nobis diligi satis eram testatus epistula quam ad illum de editione
Thebaidos meae publicavi.'

[4] Witness poems such as the Villa Surrentina Pollii.   *Silv.* ii. 2. 3, 1.

[5] *Silv.* iii. 5. 13.

[6] Praef. *Silv.* iii. and iii. 5.   He was married soon after beginning the
Thebais, i. e. about 82 A. D. (cp. *S.* iii. 5. 35).   Claudia had a daughter by
her first husband, iii. 5. 52–4.

[7] v. 5. 72–5.

approach of old age and the decline of his physical powers.[1]
He can scarcely have been born later than 45 A. D., and may
well have been born considerably earlier. His life, as far
as we can judge, was placid and uneventful. The position
of his father seems to have saved him from a miserable
struggle for his livelihood, such as vexed the soul of Martial.[2]
There is nothing venal about his verse. If his flattery of
the emperor is fulsome almost beyond belief, he hardly
overstepped the limits of the path dictated by policy and
the custom of the age ; his conduct argues weakness rather
than any deep moral taint. In his flattery towards his
friends and patrons his tone is, at its worst, rather that of
a social inferior than of a mere dependent.[3] And under-
lying all the preciosity and exaggeration of his praises and
his consolations, there is a genuine warmth of affection that
argues an amiable character. And this warmth of feeling
becomes unmistakable in the *epicedia* on his father and his
adopted son, and again in the poem addressed to his wife.
The feeling is genuine, in spite of the suggestion of insincerity

---

[1] iii. 5. 13, iv. 4. 69, v. 2. 158. It is worth noting how late in life all his
best work was done, i. e. 80–95 A. D.

[2] The well-known passage of Juvenal, vii. 86 (' cum fregit subsellia versu, |
esurit, intactam Paridi nisi vendit Agaven '), as has been pointed out, is
only Juvenal's exaggerated way of saying that the *Thebais* brought Statius
no material gain. The family was not, however, rolling in wealth ; cp.
v. 3. 116 sqq.

[3] His friendships do not throw much light on his life, though they show
that he moved in high circles. Rutilius Gallicus (i. 4) had had a distinguished career and rose to be *praefectus urbis* ; Claudius Etruscus (i. 5),
originally a slave from Smyrna, had risen to the imperial post *a rationibus* ;
Abascantus (v. 1) held the office known as *ab epistulis*; Plotius Grypus
(iv. 9) came of senatorial family ; Crispinus (v. 2) was the son of Vettius
Bolanus, Governor of Britain and afterwards of Asia ; Vibius Maximus
(iv. 7) became praefect of Egypt under Trajan ; Polla Argentaria (ii. 7) was
the widow of Lucan ; Arruntius Stella (i. 2) was a poet, and rose to the
consulship. Most of these persons must have been possessed of strong
literary tastes. Some are mentioned by Martial, e. g. Stella, Claudius
Etruscus, Polla Argentaria. Atedius Melior and Novius Vindex were also
friends of the two poets. Both must have moved in the same circles, yet
neither ever mentions the other. They were probably jealous of one
another and on bad terms.

created by the artificiality of his language. No less noteworthy is his enthusiasm for the beauties of his birthplace,
which shines clear through all the obscure legends beneath
which he buries his topography.[1] These qualities, if any,
must be set against his lack of intellectual power ; his mind
is nimble and active, but never strong either in thought or
emotion : of sentiment he has abundance, of passion none.
Considering the corruption of the society of which he consti-
tuted himself the poet, and of which there are not a few
glimpses in the *Silvae*, despite the tinselled veil that is thrown
over it, the impression of Statius the man is not unpleasing :
it is not necessary to claim that it is inspiring.

Of Statius the poet it is harder to form a clear judgement.
His masterpiece, the *Thebais*, from the day of its publication
down to comparatively recent times, possessed an immense
reputation.[2] Dante seems to regard him as second only to
Vergil ; and it was scarcely before the nineteenth century that
he was dethroned from his exalted position. Before the verdict
of so many ages one may well shrink from passing an unfavourable criticism. That he had many of the qualifications of a
great poet is undeniable; his technical skill is extraordinary ;
his variety of phrase is infinite ; his colouring is often brilliant. And even his positive faults, the faults of his age, the
crowding of detail, the rhetoric, the bombast, offend rather
by their quantity than quality. Alone of the epic [3] writers
of his age he rarely raises a derisive laugh from the irreverent
modern. Again, his average level is high, higher than that
of any post-Ovidian poet. And yet that high level is due
to the fact that he rarely sinks rather than that he rises to

---

[1] e. g. ii. 2. Cp. also i. 3. 64–89.

[2] Dante regards him also as a Christian. This compliment was paid
by the Middle Ages to not a few of the great classical authors. It was not
even a fatal obstacle to have lived before the birth of Christ. Cicero, for
instance, was believed to have been a Christian. The description of the
Altar of Mercy at Athens (*Th*. xii. 493) has been regarded as a special
reason for the Christianizing of Statius : cp. Verrall, *Oxford and Cambridge
Review*, No. 1 ; Arturo Graf, *Roma nella memoria del medio evo*, vol. ii,
ch. 17.

[3] This statement does not, however, apply to the *Silvae*.

sublime heights. His brilliant metre, always vivacious and
vigorous, seldom gives us a line that haunts the memory ;
and therefore, though its easy grace and facile charm may
for a while attract us, we soon weary of him. He lacks
warmth of emotion and depth of colour. In this respect he
has been not inaptly compared to Ovid. Ovid said of Callimachus *quamvis ingenio non valet, arte valet*.[1] Ovid's detractors apply the epigram to Ovid himself. This is unjust, but
so far as such a comprehensive dictum can be true of any
distinguished writer, it is true of Statius.

Scarcely inferior to Ovid in readiness and fertility, he
ranks far below the earlier writer in all poetic essentials.
Ovid's gifts are similar but more natural ; his vision is
clearer, his imagination more penetrating. ' The paces of
Statius are those of the *manège*, not of nature ';[2] he loses
himself in the trammels of his art. He lacks, as a rule, the
large imagination of the poet ; and though his detail may
often please, the whole is tedious and disappointing. Merivale sums him up admirably :[2] ' Statius is a miniature
painter employed on the production of a great historic
picture : every part, every line, every shade is touched and
retouched ; approach the canvas and examine it with
glasses, every thread and hair has evidently received the
utmost care and taken the last polish ; but step backwards
and embrace the whole composition in one gaze, and the
general effect is confused from want of breadth and largeness
of treatment.'

He was further handicapped by his choice of a subject.[3]

---

[1] Ov. *Am.* i. 15. 14.   [2] Merivale, *Rom. Emp.* viii. 80, 1.

[3] The sources for his story were the old Cyclic poem, the later epic of
Antimachus, the plays of Aeschylus, Sophocles, and Euripides, that draw
their plots from the Theban cycle of legend. The material thus given
him he worked over in the Vergilian manner, remoulding incidents or
introducing fresh episodes in such a fashion as to provide precise parallels
to many episodes in the *Aeneid*. He also drew certain hints from the
Phoenissae and *Oedipus* of Seneca : for details see Legras, *Étude sur la
Thébaïde de Stace*, part i, ch. 2, part ii, chh. 1 and 2. The subject had
been treated also by one Ponticus, the friend of Propertius (Prop. i. 7. 1,
Ov. *Tr.* iv. 10. 47) and possibly by Lynceus (Prop. ii. 34).

The Theban legend is unsuitable for epic treatment for
more reasons than one. In the first place the story is unpleasant from beginning to end. Horror accumulates on
horror, crime on crime, and there are but three characters
which evoke our sympathy, Oedipus, Jocasta, and Antigone.
These characters play only subsidiary parts in the story of
the expedition of the Seven against Thebes, round which the
Theban epic turns. The central characters are almost of
necessity the odious brothers Eteocles and Polynices :
Oedipus appears only to curse his sons. Antigone and
Jocasta come upon the scene only towards the close in a
brief and futile attempt to reconcile the brothers. The deeds
and deaths of the Argive chiefs may relieve the horror and
at times excite our sympathy, but we cannot get away from
the fact that the story is ultimately one of almost bestial
fratricidal strife, darkened by the awful shadow of the woes
of the house of Labdacus. The old Greek epic assigned great
importance to the character of Amphiaraus [1] persuaded by
his false wife, Eriphyla, to go forth on the enterprise that
should be his doom ; it has even been suggested that he
formed the central character of the poem. If this suggestion
be true—and its truth is exceedingly doubtful—we are confronted with what was in reality only a false shift, the
diversion of the interest from the main issues of the story
to a side issue. The *Iliad* cannot be quoted in his defence ;
there we have an episode of a ten years' siege, which in itself
possesses genuine unity and interest. But the Theban epic
comprises the whole story of the expedition of the seven
chieftains, and it is idle to make Amphiaraus the central
figure. In any case the prominence given to the fortunes of
the house of Labdacus by the great Greek dramatists, and
the genius with which they brought out the genuinely

---

[1] Legras, *Les Légendes Théb.*, ch. iii. 4. The Ἀμφιαράου ἐξέλασις mentioned by Suidas s.v. Ὅμηρος is sometimes identified with the *Thebais* ;
but it is more probably merely the title of a book of that epic. Still the
fact that the Ἀμφ. ἐξέλ. is given such prominence by Suidas does lend
some support to the view that he was the chief character of the epic. He
is certainly the most tragic figure.

dramatic issues of the legend, had made it impossible for after-comers to take any save the Labdacidae for the chief actors in their story. And so from Antimachus onward Polynices and Eteocles are the tragic figures of the epic.

To give unity to this story all our attention must be concentrated on Thebes. The enlistment of Adrastus in the cause of Polynices must be described, and following this the gathering of the hosts of Argos. But when once the Argive demands are rejected by Thebes, the poet's chief aim must be to get his army to Thebes with all speed, and set it in battle array against the enemy. Once at Thebes, there is plenty of room for tragic power and stirring narrative. First comes the ineffectual attempt of Jocasta to reconcile her scarce human sons ; then comes the battle, with the gradual overthrow of the chieftains of Argos, the turning of the scale of battle in favour of Thebes by the sacrifice of Menoeceus, and last the crowning combat between the brothers. There, from the artistic standpoint, the story finds its ending. It could never have been other than forbidding, but it need not have lacked power. Unfortunately, precedent did not allow the story to end there. The Thebans forbid burial to the Argive dead ; Antigone transgresses the edict by burying her brother Polynices, and finds death the reward of her piety ; Theseus and the Athenians come to Adrastus' aid, defeat the Thebans, and bury the Argive dead, while as a sop to Argive feeling they are promised their revenge in after years, when the children of the dead have grown to man's estate. If it were felt that the deadly struggle between the two brothers closed the epic on a note of unrelieved gloom and horror, there was perhaps something to be said for introducing the story of Antigone's self-sacrifice, and closing on a note of tragic beauty. Unhappily, the story of Antigone involved the introduction of material sufficient for one, if not two fresh epics in the legend of the Athenian War and the triumphant return of Argos to the conflict. Antimachus [1] fell into the snare. His vast

---

[1] Porphyr. ad Hor. *A. P.* 146.

Thebais told the whole story from the arrival of Polynices
at Argos to the victory of the Epigoni. Nor was he content
with this alone, but must needs clog the action of his poem
with long descriptions of the gathering of the host at Argos,
and of their adventures on the march to Thebes. And so it
came about that he consumed twenty-four books in getting
his heroes to Thebes !

The precedent of Antimachus proved fatal to Statius. He
did not, it is true, run to such prolixity as his Greek predecessor ; he eliminated the legend of the Epigoni altogether,
only alluding to it once in vague and general terms ; he
ucceeded in getting the story, down to the burial of the
Argive dead, within the compass of twelve books of not
inordinate length. But it is possible to be prolix without
being an Antimachus, and the prolixity of Statius is quite
sufficient. The Argives do not reach Thebes till half-way
through the seventh book,[2] the brothers do not meet till
half-way through the eleventh book. The result is that the
compression of events in the last 300 lines of the eleventh
book and in the last book is almost grotesque ; for these
1,100 lines contain the death of Jocasta, the banishment of
Oedipus, the flight of the Argives, the prohibition to bury
the Argive dead, the arrival of the wives of the vanquished,
the devotion of Antigone and Argia, the wife of Polynices,
their detection and sentencing to death, the arrival of the
Athenians under Theseus, the defeat and death of Creon, and
the burial of the fallen. The effect is disastrous. As we
have seen, this appendix to the main story of the feud
between the brothers cannot form a satisfactory conclusion
to the story. Treated with the perfunctory compression
of Statius, it becomes flat and ineffective ; even the reader
who finds Statius at his best attractive is tempted to throw
down the *Thebais* in disgust.

It is perhaps in his concluding scenes that we see Statius
at his worst, but his capacity for irrelevance and digression is

---

[1] Vergil had given six books to the wanderings of Aeneas ; Statius must
give six to the preparation and march of the Thebans !

an almost equally serious defect. That he should use the
conventional supernatural machinery is natural and permissible, though tedious to the modern reader, who finds it
hard to sympathize with outworn literary conventions.
But there are few epics where divine intervention is carried
to a greater extent than in the *Thebais*.[1] And not content
with the intervention of the usual gods and furies, on two
occasions Statius brings down frigid abstractions from the
skies in the shape of Virtus [2] and Pietas.[3] Again, while au-
guries and prophecies play a legitimate part in such a work,
nothing can justify, and only the passion of the Silver Age
for the supernatural can explain, the protraction of the scenes
of augury at Thebes and Argos to 114 and 239 lines respectively. Equally disproportionate are the catalogues of the
Argive and the Theban armies, making between them close
on 400 lines.[4] Nor is imitation of Vergil the slightest justi-
fication for introducing a night-raid in which Hopleus and
Dymas are but pale reflections of Nisus and Euryalus,[5] for
expending 921 lines over the description of the funeral rites
and games in honour of the infant Opheltes,[6] or putting the
irrelevant history of the heroism of Coroebus in the mouth
of Adrastus, merely that it may form a parallel to the tale of
Hercules and Cacus told by Evander.[7] Worst of all is the
enormous digression,[8] consuming no less than 481 lines, where
Hypsipyle narrates the story of the Lemnian massacre.

---

[1] See Legras, op. cit., pp. 183 ff.   [2] x. 632.

[3] xi. 457. Cp. also the strange and stilted description of the cave of
sleep, x. 84, where Quies, Oblivio, Ignavia, Otium, Silentium, Voluptas,
and even Labor and Amor are to be found. But with the exception of
Amor these abstract personages are inventions of Statius. Virtus and
Pietas had temples at Rome.

[4] iv. 32–308 ; vii. 250–358.

[5] x. 262–448.

[6] vi. 1–921. Two other funerals are to be found, iii. 114–217, xii. 22–104.

[7] *Th.* i. 557 sqq. ; Verg. *Aen.* viii. 190 sqq.

[8] v. 17–498 : with this compare the version of the story given by
Valerius Flaccus, ii. 78–305 ; except in point of brevity there is little to
choose between the two versions. But it is not a digression in Valerius,
and it is told at less inordinate length. The versions differ much in
detail, and Statius owes little or nothing to Valerius.

And yet this is hardly more than a digression in the midst of a digression. The Argive army are marching on Thebes. Bacchus, desirous to save his native town, causes a drought in the Peloponnese. The Argives, on the verge of death, and maddened with thirst, come upon Hypsipyle, the nurse of Opheltes, the son of Lycurgus, King of Nemea. Hypsipyle leaves her charge to show them the stream of Langia, which alone has been unaffected by the drought, and so saves the Argive host. She then at enormous length narrates to Adrastus the story of her life, how she was daughter of Thoas, King of Lemnos, and how, when the women of Lesbos slew their mankind, she alone proved false to their hideous compact, and saved her father. After describing the arrival of the Argonauts at Lemnos, and her amour with Jason, to whom she bore two sons, she tells how she was banished from Lesbos on the discovery that Thoas, her father, still lived, how she was captured by pirates, and twenty long years since sold into slavery to Lycurgus. This prodigious narration finished, it is discovered that a serpent sacred to Jupiter has killed Opheltes. Lycurgus, hearing the news, would have slain Hypsipyle, but she is protected by the Argives whom she has saved. Then follows the burial of Opheltes—henceforth known as Archemorus—and his funeral games.

Now it is not improbable that the story of Opheltes and Hypsipyle occurred in the old cyclic poem.[1] But that scarcely justifies Statius in devoting the whole of the fifth and sixth books and some 200 lines of the fourth to the description of an episode so alien to the main interest of the poem. But if we cannot justify these copious digressions and irrelevances we can explain them. The *Thebais* was written primarily for recitation ; many of these episodes which are hopelessly superfluous to the real story are admirably designed for the purpose of recitation. The truth is that

---

[1] Cp. Legras, *Les légendes Thébaines*, ch. ii. 4, Welcker, *Ep. Cycl.* ii. 350. The story was well known. Aeschylus probably treated it in his Νεμέα, Euripides certainly in his Ὑψιπύλη. The legend gives the origin of the Nemean games.

Statius had many qualifications for the writing of *epyllia*, few
for writing epic on a large scale. He has therefore sacrificed
the whole to its parts, and relies on brilliance of description
to catch the ear of an audience, rather than on sustained
epic dignity and ordered development of his story. But
although he cannot give real unity to his epic, he succeeds,
by dint of his astonishing fluency and his mastery over his
instrument, in giving a specious appearance of unity. The
sutures of his story are well disguised and his inconsistencies
of no serious importance. He fails as an epic writer, but
he fails gracefully.

It is, however, possible for an epic to be structurally
ineffective and yet possess high poetic merit. Statius'
episodes do not cohere ; how far have they any splendour
in their isolation ? The answer to the question must be on
the whole unfavourable. The reasons for this are diverse.
In the first place the characters for the most part fail to
live. Statius can give us a vivid impression of the outward
semblance of a man ; we see Parthenopaeus and Atys, we
see Jocasta and Antigone, we see the struggle of Eteocles and
Polynices vividly enough. But we see them as strangers,
standing out, it is true, from the crowd in which they move,
but still wholly unknown to us. We cannot differentiate
Polynices and Eteocles save that the latter, from the very
situation in which he finds himself, is necessarily the more
odious of the two ; Polynices would have shown himself the
same, had the fall of the lot given him the first year of
kingship. Jocasta and Antigone, Creon and Menoeceus,
Hypsipyle and Lycurgus, play their parts correctly enough,
but they do not live, nor people our brain with moving
images. We are told that they behaved in such and such a
way under such and such circumstances ; we are told, and
admit, that such conduct implies certain moral qualities,
but Statius does not make us *feel* that his characters possess
such qualities. The reason for this lies partly in the fact
that they all speak the same brilliant rhetoric,[1] partly in the

---

[1] The speeches in the *Thebais*, though they lack variety, are almost

fact that Statius lacks the direct sincerity of diction that is
required for the expression of strong and poignant emotion.
Anger he can depict ; anger suffers less than other emotions
from rhetoric.　Hence it is that he has succeeded in drawing the character of Tydeus, whose brutality is redeemed
from hideousness by the fact that it is based on the most
splendid physical courage, and fired by strong loyalty to his
comrade and sometime foe Polynices.　His accents ring
true.　When he has gone to Thebes to plead Polynices'
cause, and his demands have been angrily refused by Eteocles,
who concludes by saying (ii. 449),

nec ipsi,　　　　　[1]

> si modo notus amor meritique est gratia, patres
> reddere regna sinent,

Tydeus will hear no more, but breaks in with a cry of
fury (ii. 452) :

' reddes,'　　　　　[2]

> ingeminat ' reddes ; non si te ferreus agger
> ambiat aut triplices alio tibi carmine muros
> Amphion auditus agat, nil tela nec ignes
> obstiterint, quin ausa luas nostrisque sub armis
> captivo moribundus humum diademate pulses.
> tu merito ; ast horum miseret, quos sanguine viles
> coniugibus natisque infanda ad proelia raptos
> proicis excidio, bone rex. o quanta Cithaeron
> funera sanguineusque vadis, Ismene, rotabis !
> haec pietas, haec magna fides ! nec crimina gentis

---

always exceedingly clever and quite repay reading ; see esp. i. 642 ;
iii. 59, 151, 348 ; iv. 318 ; vi. 138 ; vii. 497, 539 ; ix. 375 ; xi. 155, 677, 708.

[1] Nor will the fathers of the city, if they but know the love I bear them
or if they have aught of gratitude, allow me to give back the kingship.

[2] 'Thou shalt give it back,' he cries, 'thou shalt give it back.　Though
thou wert girdled with a wall of bronze, or Amphion's voice be heard and
with a new song raise triple bulwarks about thee ; fire and sword should
not save thee from the doom of thy daring, and, struck down by our swords,
thy diadem should smite the ground as thou fallest dying, our captive.
Thus shouldst *thou* have thy desert ; but *these* I pity, whose blood thou
ratest lightly, and whom thou snatchest from their children and their
wives to give them over to death, thou virtuous king.　What vast slaughter,
Cithaeron, and thou, Ismenus, shalt thou see whirl down thy blood-stained
shallows.　This is thy piety, this thy true faith ! nor marvel I at the

mira equidem duco : sic primus sanguinis auctor
incestique patrum thalami ; sed fallit origo :
Oedipodis tu solus eras, haec praemia morum
ac sceleris, violente, feres ! nos poscimus annum ;
sed moror.' haec audax etiamnum in limine retro
vociferans iam tunc impulsa per agmina praeceps
evolat.

As he is here, so is he always, unwavering in decision,
prompt of speech and of action. Caught in ambush, ill-
armed and solitary, by the treacherous Thebans, as he
returns from his futile embassy, he never hesitates ; he
seizes the one point of vantage, crushes his foes, and when
he speaks, speaks briefly and to the point. He spares the
last of his fifty assailants and sends him back to Thebes
with a message of defiance, brief, natural, and manly
(ii. 697) :

quisquis es Aonidum, quem crastina munere nostro   [1]
manibus exemptum mediis Aurora videbit,
haec iubeo perferre duci : cinge aggere portas,
tela nova, fragiles aevo circum inspice muros,
praecipue stipare viros densasque memento
multiplicare acies ! fumantem hunc aspice late
ense meo campum : tales in bella venimus.

On his return to Argos he bursts impetuously into the
palace, crying fiercely for war.[1] When Lycurgus would slay
Hypsipyle for her neglect of her nursling, he saves her.[2] She

crimes of such a race : 'twas for this that thou hadst such an author of
thy being, for this thy father's marriage-bed was stained with incest. But
thou art deceived as to thine own birth and thy brother's ; thou alone
wast begotten of Oedipus, that shall be the reward for thy nature and
thy crime, fierce man. We ask but for a year ! But I tarry over long.'
These words he shouted back at him while he still lingered on the threshold ;
then headlong burst through the crowd of foemen and sped away.

[1] Whoe'er thou art of the Aonides, whom to-morrow's dawn shall see
saved from the world of the dead by my boon, I bid thee bear this message
to thy chief : ' Raise mounds about the gates, forge new weapons, look
to your walls that crumble with years, and above all be mindful to marshal
thick and multiply thine hosts ! Behold this plain smoking with the work
of my sword. Such men are we when we enter the field of battle.'

---

[1] iii. 348.   [2] v. 660.

has preserved the Argive army, and Tydeus, if he never
forgives an enemy, never forgets a friend. He alone defeats
the entreaties of Jocasta[1] and launches the hosts of Argos
into battle ; and when his own doom is come, he dies as he
had lived, *impiger, iracundus, inexorabilis* ; he has no
thought for himself ; he cares nought for due burial (viii.
736) :

> non ossa precor referantur ut Argos   [1]
> Aetolumve larem ; nec enim mihi cura supremi
> funeris : odi artus fragilemque hunc corporis usum,
> desertorem animi.

His one thought is for vengeance on the dead body of the
man who has slain him[2] and for the victory of his comrades
in arms.

Only one other of the heroes has any real existence, the
prophet Amphiaraus. Statius does not give him the prominence that he held in the original epic, and misses a noble
opportunity by almost ignoring the dramatic story of
Eriphyla and the necklace that won her to persuade her
husband to go forth to certain death. But the heroic warrior
priest of Apollo, who knows his doom and yet faces it fear-
lessly, could not fail to be a picturesque figure, and at least
in the hour of his death Statius has done him full justice.
Apollo, disguised as a mortal, mounts the chariot of Amphiaraus and drives him through the midst of the battle,
dealing destruction on this side and that (vii. 770) :

> tandem se famulo summum confessus Apollo   [2]
> ' utere luce tua longamque ' ait, ' indue famam,

---

[1] I ask not that my bones be borne home to Argos or Aetolia; 1 care
not for my last rites of funeral ; I hate these limbs and this frail tene-
ment, my body, that fails my spirit in its hour of need.

[2] At length Apollo revealed himself to his servant. 'Use,' he said, 'the
light of life that is left thee and win an age of fame while thy doom still

---

[1] vii. 538.

[2] viii. 751. Tydeus bites the severed head of Melanippus to the brain,
thereby losing the gift of immortality that Pallas was hastening to bring
him. The incident is revolting, but Statius has merely followed the old
legend recorded by Aesch. *Sept.* 587 ; Soph. *Fr.* 731 ; Eurip. *Fr.* 357.

dum tibi me iunctum mors inrevocata veretur.
vincimur : immites scis nulla revolvere Parcas
stamina ; vade, diu populis promissa voluptas
Elysiis, certe non perpessure Creontis
imperia aut vetito nudus iaciture sepulcro.'
ille refert contra, et paulum respirat ab armis :
' olim te, Cirrhaee pater, peritura sedentem
ad iuga (quis tantus miseris honor ?) axe trementi
sensimus ; instantes quonam usque morabere manes ?
audio iam rapidae cursum Stygis atraque Ditis
flumina tergeminosque mali custodis hiatus.
accipe commissum capiti decus, accipe laurus,
quas Erebo deferre nefas. nunc voce suprema,
si qua recessuro debetur gratia vati,
deceptum tibi, Phoebe, larem poenasque nefandae
coniugis et pulchrum nati commendo furorem.'
desiluit maerens lacrimasque avertit Apollo.

An earthquake shakes the plain ; the warriors shrink from
battle in terror at the thunder from under-ground ; when
(816)—

             ecce alte praeceps humus ore profundo   [1]
dissilit, inque vicem timuerunt sidera et umbrae.
illum ingens haurit specus et transire parantes
mergit equos ; non arma manu, non frena remisit :

---

unrepealed shrinks back in awe of me. The foemen conquer : thou
knowest the cruel fates never unravel the threads they weave : go forward,
thou, the promised darling of the peoples of Elysium ; for surely thou
shalt ne'er endure the tyranny of Creon, or lie naked, denied a grave.'
He answered, pausing awhile from the fray : ' Long since, lord of Cirrha,
the trembling axle told me that 'twas thou sat'st by my doomed steeds.
Why honourest thou a wretched mortal thus ? How long wilt thou delay
the advancing dead ? Even now I hear the course of headlong Styx,
and the dark streams of death, and the triple barking of the accursed
guard of hell. Take now thine honours bound about my brow, take
now the laurel crown I may not bear down unto Erebus : now with
my last utterance, if aught of thanks thou owest thy seer that now
must pass away, to thee I trust my wronged hearth, the doom of my
accursed wife, and the noble madness of my son (Alcmaeon).' Apollo
leapt from the car in grief and strove to hide his tears.

[1] Lo ! the earth gaped sheer and deep with vast abyss, and the stars of
heaven and the shades of the dead trembled with one accord : a vast
chasm drew him down and swallowed his steeds as they made ready to

sicut erat, rectos defert in Tartara currus
respexitque cadens caelum campumque coire
ingemuit, donec levior distantia rursus
miscuit arva tremor lucemque exclusit Averno.

Here we see Statius at his highest level, whether in point of
metre, diction, or poetic imagination.

Of the other characters there is little to be said. For all
the wealth of detail that Statius has lavished on them, they
are featureless. Adrastus is a colourless and respectable
old king, strongly reminiscent of Latinus. Capaneus and
Hippomedon are terrific warriors of gigantic stature and
truculent speech, but they are wholly uninteresting. Argia
and Jocasta are too rhetorical, Antigone too slight a figure
to be really pathetic ; Oedipus can do little save curse,
which he does with some rhetorical vigour ; but the gift of
cursing hardly makes a character. Parthenopaeus, however,
is a pathetic figure ; he is an Arcadian, the son of Atalanta,
a mere boy whom a romantic ambition has hurried into
war ere his years were ripe for it. His dying speech is
touching, though it errs on the side of triviality and mere
prettiness (ix. 877) :

at puer infusus sociis in devia campi   [1]
tollitur (heu simplex aetas !) moriensque iacentem
flebat equum ; cecidit laxata casside vultus,
aegraque per trepidos exspirat gratia visus,
.   .   .   .
ibat purpureus niveo de pectore sanguis.
tandem haec singultu verba incidente profatur :
' labimur, i, miseram, Dorceu, solare parentem.

---

leap the gulf : he loosed not the grip on rein or spear, but, as he was,
carried his car steadfast to Tartarus, and, as he fell, gazed up to heaven
and groaned to see the plain close above him, till a lighter shock once more
united the gaping fields and shut out the light from hell.

[1] But the boy fell into his comrades' arms and they bore him to a place
apart. Alas for his tender years ! As he died, he wept for his fallen horse :
his face drooped as they unbound his helmet, and a fading grace passed
faintly o'er his quivering visage. . . .

The purple blood flowed from his breast of snow. At length he spake
these words through sobs that checked his utterance : ' My iife is falling
from me ; go, Dorceus, comfort my unhappy mother : she indeed, if care

illa quidem, si vera ferunt praesagia curae,
aut somno iam triste nefas aut omine vidit.
tu tamen arte pia trepidam suspende diuque
decipito ; neu tu subitus neve arma tenenti
veneris, et tandem, cum iam cogere fateri,
dic : " Merui, genetrix, poenas invita capesse ;
arma puer rapui, nec te retinente quievi,
nec tibi sollicitae tandem inter bella peperci.
vive igitur potiusque animis irascere nostris,
et iam pone metus. frustra de colle Lycaei
anxia prospectas, si quis per nubila longe
aut sonus aut nostro sublatus ab agmine pulvis :
frigidus et nuda iaceo tellure, nec usquam
tu prope, quae vultus efflantiaque ora teneres.
hunc tamen, orba parens, crinem "—dextraque secandum
praebuit—" hunc toto capies pro corpore crinem,
comere quem frustra me dedignante solebas.
huic dabis exsequias, atque inter iusta memento,
ne quis inexpertis hebetet mea tela lacertis
dilectosque canes ullis agat amplius antris.
haec autem primis arma infelicia castris
ure, vel ingratae crimen suspende Dianae." '

When we have said that Parthenopaeus is almost too

---

and sorrow can give foreknowledge, has seen my woeful fate in dreams
or through some omen ; yet do thou with loving art keep her terrors in
suspense and long hold back the truth ; and come not upon her suddenly,
nor when she hath a weapon in her hands ; but when at last the truth
must out, say: " Mother, I deserved my doom ; I am punished, though my
punishment break thy heart. I rushed to arms too young, and abode not
at home when thou wouldst restrain me : nor had I any pity for thine
anguish in the day of battle. Live on then, and keep thine anger for my
headstrong courage and fear no more for me. In vain thou gazest from
the Lycaean height, if any sound perchance may be borne from far to
thine ear through the clouds, or thine eye have sight of the dust raised
by our homeward march. I lie cold upon the bare earth, and thou art
nowhere nigh to hold my head as my lips breathe farewell. Yet, childless
mother, take this lock of hair "—and in his right hand he stretched it out
to be cut away—"take this poor lock in place of my whole body, this lock
of that hair which thou didst tire in my despite. To it shalt thou give
due burial and remember this also as my due ; let no man blunt my spears
with unskilful cast, nor any more drive the hounds I loved through any
caverned glen. But this mine armour, whose first battle hath brought
disaster, burn thou, or hang it to be a reproach to Dian's ingratitude." '

young to have been accepted as a leader, or have performed
the feats of war assigned to him, we have said all that can
be said against this beautiful speech. Parthenopaeus is for
the *Thebais* what Camilla is for the *Aeneid*, though he
presents at times hints both of Pallas and Euryalus. But
he is little more than a child, and fails to carry the conviction or awaken the deep emotion excited by the Amazon
of Vergil.[1]

Statius then, with a few striking exceptions, fails in his
portrayal of life and character. On the whole—one says it
with reluctance in view of his brilliant variety, his boundless
invention, his wealth of imagery—the same is true of his
descriptions. The picture is too crowded ; he has not the
unerring eye for the relevant or salient points of a scene.
Skilful and faithful touches abound, but, as in the case of
certain pre-Raphaelite pictures, extreme attention to detail
causes him to miss the full scenic effect. He is not sufficiently the impressionist ; he cannot suggest—a point in
which he presents a strong contrast to Valerius Flaccus.
And too many of his incidents, in spite of ingenious variation
of detail, are but echoes of Vergil. The foot-race and the
archery contest at the funeral games of Archemorus, together
with the episode of Dymas and Hopleus,[2] to which we have

---

[1] Cp. in this context Atalanta's beautiful lament on his departure for
the war, iv. 318.

[2] Every book, however, abounds in echoes of Vergil, both in matter and
diction ; e.g. *Aen.* vii. 475, Allecto precipitates the war by making Ascanius
kill a tame stag. *Theb.* vii. 562, an Erinnys brings about the war by
causing the death of two pet tigers sacred to Bacchus. *Aen.* xi. 591, Diana
orders one of her nymphs to kill the slayer of Camilla. *Theb.* ix. 665, she
tells Apollo that the slayer of Parthenopaeus shall perish by her arrows,
for which see *Th.* ix. 875. Cp. also *Th.* ii. 205 ; *Aen.* iv. 173, 189 ;
Th. ii. 162 ; *Aen.* xi. 581. The passage previously referred to concerning
the exploits of Dymas and Hopleus is especially noteworthy as openly
challenging comparison with Vergil ; cp. x. 445. For verbal imitations
cp. *Aen.* v. 726, 7 ; *Th.* ii. 115 ; *Aen.* i. 106 ; *Th.* v. 366 ; *Aen.* vii. 397;
Th. iv. 379, &c. It is no defence to urge that the ancients held different
views on plagiarism, that Vergil and Ovid pilfered from their predecessors.
For *they* made their appropriations their own, and set the stamp of their
genius upon what they borrowed. And, further, the process of borrowing cannot continue indefinitely. The cumulative effect of progressive

already referred, are perhaps the most marked examples of
this unfortunate characteristic. We are continually saying
to ourselves as we read the *Thebais*, ' All this has been before !'
We weary at times of the echoes of Homer in Vergil, and the
combats that stirred us in the *Iliad* make us drowsy in the
Aeneid. Homer knew what fighting was from personal
experience, or at least from being in touch with warriors who
had killed their man. Vergil had come no nearer these things
than ' in the pages of a book '. Statius is yet one remove
further from the truth than Vergil. He is tied hand and
foot by his intimate acquaintance with previous poetic
literature. If he is less the victim of the schools of rhetoric
than many post-Augustan writers, he is more than most the
victim of the poetic training of the schools. But with all
these faults there are passages which surprise us by their
effectiveness. It would be hard to imagine anything more
vigorous and exciting than the fight of Tydeus ambushed
by his fifty foes. The opening passage is splendidly successful in creating the requisite atmosphere (ii. 527) :

> coeperat umenti Phoebum subtexere palla   [1]
> Nox et caeruleam terris infuderat umbram.
> ille propinquabat silvis et ab aggere celso
> scuta virum galeasque videt rutilare comantes,
> qua laxant rami nemus adversaque sub umbra
> flammeus aeratis lunae tremor errat in armis.
> obstipuit visis, ibat tamen, horrida tantum
> spicula et inclusum capulo tenus admovet ensem.
> ac prior ' unde, viri, quidve occultatis in armis ? '

---

[1] Night began to shroud Phoebus with her humid pall and shed her blue
darkness o'er the earth. He drew nigh the forest, and from a high knoll
espied the gleam of warriors' shields and plumed helmets, where the boughs
of the wood left a space, and in the shadow before him the quivering fire
of the moonbeam played o'er their brazen armour. Dumbstruck at what he
saw, he yet pursued his way, only he made ready for the fight his bristling
javelins and the sword sheathed to its hilt. He was the first to speak :
' Whence come ye ? ' he asked, in fear, yet haughty still. ' And why hide

---

plagiarism is distressing. For Statius' imitation of other Latin poets,
notably Lucan, Seneca, and Ovid, see Legras, op. cit., i. 2. Such imitations,
though not very rare, are of comparatively small importance.

non humili terrore rogat. nec reddita contra
vox, fidamque negant suspecta silentia pacem.

The fight that follows, though it occupies more than 160
lines, is intensely rapid and vigorous ; indeed it is the one
genuinely exciting combat in Latin epic, and forms a refreshing contrast to the pseudo-Homeric or pseudo-Vergilian
combats before the walls of Thebes. In no other portion
of the *Thebais* does Statius attain to such success, with the
exception of the passage already quoted descriptive of the
death of Amphiaraus. But there are other passages of
sustained merit, such as the vigorous description of the
struggle of Hippomedon with the waters of Ismenus and
Asopus.[1] While it is not particularly interesting to those
acquainted with the corresponding passage in the *Iliad*, it
would be unjust to deny the gifts of vigour and invention
to the Latin poet's imitation.

It is, however, rather in smaller and more minute pictures
that Statius as a rule excels. The picture of the baby
Opheltes left by his nurse is pretty enough (iv. 787) :

> at puer in gremio vernae telluris et alto   [1]
> gramine nunc faciles sternit procursibus herbas
> in vultum nitens, caram modo lactis egeno
> nutricem plangore ciens iterumque renidens
> et teneris meditans verba inluctantia labris
> miratur nemorum strepitus aut obvia carpit
> aut patulo trahit ore diem nemorisque malorum
> inscius et vitae multum securus inerrat.

Fine, too, in a different way is the sinister picture of
Eteocles left sole king in Thebes (i. 165) :

ye thus armoured for the fray ? ' There came no answer, and their ominous
silence told him no peace nor loyalty was there.

[1] But the child, lying face downward in the bosom of the vernal earth,
now as he crawls in the deep herbage lays low the yielding grass ; now cries
for his loved nurse athirst for milk, and then, all smiles again, with infant
lips frames words in stumbling speech, marvels at the sounds of the
woods, gathers what lies before him, or open-mouthed drinks in the day;
and knowing naught of the dangers of the woods, with ne'er a care in life,
roams here and there.

[1] ix. 315 sqq.

quis tunc tibi, saeve,   [1]
quis fuit ille dies, vacua cum solus in aula
respiceres ius omne tuum cunctosque minores
et nusquam par stare caput?

Less poetical, but scarcely less effective, is the description
of the compact between the brothers (i.138):

alterni placuit sub legibus anni   [2]
exsilio mutare ducem. sic iure maligno
fortunam transire iubent, ut sceptra tenentem
foedere praecipiti semper novus angeret heres.
haec inter fratres pietas erat, haec mora pugnae
sola nec in regem perduratura secundum.

But far beyond all other portraits in Statius is the description of Jocasta as she approaches the Argive camp on her
mission of reconciliation (vii. 474):

ecce truces oculos sordentibus obsita canis   [3]
exsangues Iocasta genas et bracchia planctu
nigra ferens ramumque oleae cum velleris atri
nexibus, Eumenidum velut antiquissima, portis
egreditur magna cum maiestate malorum.

In this last line we have one of the very few lines in Statius
that attain to real grandeur.   In the lack of such lines, and
in the lack of real breadth of treatment lies Statius' chief
defect as a narrator. All that dexterity can do he does;
but he lacks the supreme gifts, the selective eye and the
penetrating imagination of the great poet.

---

[1] Ah! what a day was that for thee, fierce heart, when, sitting alone
amid thy courtiers, thy brother gone from thee, thou sawest thyself
enthroned above all men, with all things in thy power, without a peer.

[2] It was resolved that in alternate years the king should quit his throne
for exile. Thus with baneful ordinance they bade fortune pass from one
to the other, that he who held the sceptre on these brief terms should ever
be vexed by the thought of his successor's coming. Such was the brothers'
love, such the sole bond that kept them from conflict, a bond that should
not last till the kingship changed.

[3] Lo! Jocasta, her white hair streaming unkempt over her wild eyes,
her cheeks all pale, her arms bruised by the beating of her anguished hands,
bearing an olive-branch hung with black wool, came forth from the gates
in semblance like to the eldest of the Eumenides, in all the majesty of her
many sorrows.

Of his actual diction and ornament little need be said.
Without being precisely straightforward, he is not, as a rule,
obscure.   But his language gradually produces a feeling of
oppression.   He can be read in short passages without this
feeling ; the moment, however, the reader takes his verse in
.considerable quantities, the continued, though only slight,
over-elaboration of the work produces a feeling of strain.
Throughout there runs a vein of artificiality which ultimately
gives the impression of insincerity.   He can turn out phrases
of the utmost nicety.   Nothing can be more neatly turned
than the description of the feelings of Antigone and Ismene
on the outbreak of the war (viii. 614) :

> nutat utroque timor, quemnam hoc certamine victum, [1]
> quem vicisse velint : tacite praeponderat exsul ;

or than the line describing the parting of the Lemnian
women from the Argonauts, their second husbands (v. 478) :

> heu iterum gemitus, iterumque novissima nox est.   [2]

But this neatness often degenerates into preciosity, *bellator
campus* means a field suitable for battle (viii. 377). Nisus, the
king of Megara, with the talismanic purple lock, becomes
a *senex purpureus* (i. 334) ; an embrace is described by the
words *alterna pectora mutant* (v. 722) ; a woman nearing
her time is one *iustos cuius pulsantia menses vota tument*
(v. 115).   We have already noted a similar tendency in
Valerius Flaccus ; such phrase-making is not a badge of
any one poet, it is a sign of the times.   In the case of Statius
there is perhaps less obscurity and less positive extravagance
than in any of his contemporaries, but whether as regards
description or phrase-making, there is always a suspicion
of his work being pitched—if the phrase is permissible—
a tone too high.   This is, perhaps, particularly noticeable in
his similes.   They are very numerous, and he has obviously

---

[1] Their fears incline this way and that : whom would they have the
conqueror in the strife, whom the vanquished ?   All unconfessed the exile
has their prayers.

[2] Alas ! once more the hour of lamentation is near, once more is come
the last night of wedded sleep.

expended great trouble over them. But, with very few exceptions, they are failures. The cause lies mainly in their lack of variety. There are, for instance, no less than sixteen similes drawn from bulls, twelve from lions, six from tigers.[1] None of these similes show any close observance of nature, and in any case the poetic interest of bulls, lions, and tigers is far from inexhaustible. It is less reprehensible that twenty similes should be drawn from storms, which have a more cogent interest and greater picturesque value. But even here Statius has overshot the mark. This lack of variety testifies to a real dearth of poetic imagination, and this failing is noticeable also in the execution. There is rarely a simile containing anything that awakens either imagination, emotion, or thought. Still, to give Statius his due, there *are* exceptions, such as the simile comparing Parthenopaeus, seen in all his beauty among his comrades, to the reflections of the evening star outshining the reflections of the lesser stars in the waveless sea (vi. 578):

> sic ubi tranquillo perlucent sidera ponto   [1]
> vibraturque fretis caeli stellantis imago,
> omnia clara nitent, sed clarior omnia supra
> Hesperus exsertat radios, quantusque per altum
> aethera, caeruleis tantus monstratur in undis.

The comparison is a little strained and far-fetched. The reflection of stars in the sea is not quite so noticeable or impressive as Statius would have us believe. But there is real beauty both in the conception and the execution of the simile. Of more indisputable excellence is the comparison in the eleventh book (443), where Adrastus, flying from Thebes in humiliation and defeat, is likened to Pluto, when

---

[1] So when the stars are glassed in the tranquil deep and the reflection of the starry sky quivers in the waves, all the stars shine clear, but clearer than all doth Hesperus send forth his rays ; and as he gleams in the high heavens, even so bright do the blue waters show him forth.

---

[1] Statius is imitating early Greek epic. That might excuse him if these similes possessed either truth or beauty.

he first entered on his kingdom of the underworld, his lord-
ship over the strengthless dead—

                              qualis   [1]
        demissus curru laevae post praemia sortis
        umbrarum custos mundique novissimus heres
        palluit, amisso veniens in Tartara caelo.

The picture is Miltonic, and Pluto is for a brief moment
almost an anticipation of the Satan of *Paradise Lost*.

The metre, like that of Valerius Flaccus, draws its primary
inspiration from Vergil, but has been strongly influenced
by the *Metamorphoses* of Ovid.   There are fewer elisions
in Statius than in Vergil, and more dactyls.[1]   He is, however,
less dactylic than Valerius Flaccus and Ovid.   In his management of pauses he is far more successful than any epic
writer, with the exception of Vergil.   As a result, he is far
less monotonous than Ovid, Lucan, or Valerius.   The one
criticism that can be levelled against him is that his verse,
while possessing rapidity and vigour, is not sufficiently
adapted to the varying emotions that his story demands, and
that it shows a consequent lack of nobility and stateliness.
For the *Silvae* his metre is admirably adapted.   It is light
and almost sprightly, and the poet can let himself go.   He
was not blind to the requirements of the epic metre even
if he did not satisfy them, and in his lighter verse there is
a notable increase of fluency and ease.

The *Thebais* is a work whose value it is difficult to estimate.
Its undeniable merits are never quite such that we can accord it whole-hearted praise ; its cleverness commands our
wonder, while its defects are not such as to justify a sweeping
condemnation.   But it must be remembered that epic must
be very good if it is to avoid failure, and it is probable that
there are few works on which such skill and labour have been

---

[1] Even as the warden of the shades, the third heir of the world, when he
entered on the realm that the unkind lot had given him, leapt from his
car and turned pale, for heaven was lost and he was at the gate of hell.

---

1 See p. 123, note.

expended without any proportionate success. An attempt has been made in the preceding pages to indicate the main reasons for the failure of the *Thebais*. One more reason may perhaps be added here. Over and above the poet's lack of originality and the highest poetic imagination, over and above his distracting echoes and his artificiality, there is a lack of moral fire and insight about the poem. Statius gives us but a surface view of life. He had never plumbed the depths of human passion nor realized anything of the mystery of the world. His reader never derives from him the consciousness, that he so often derives from Vergil, of a ' deep beyond the deep, and a height beyond the height '. He has neither the virtues of the mystic nor of the realist. Ultimately, life is for him a pageant with intervals for sentimental threnodies and rhetorical declamation.

The same qualities characterize the *Achilleis* and still more the *Silvae*. The *Achilleis* was to have comprised the whole life of Achilles. Only the first book and 167 lines of the second were composed. They tell how Thetis endeavoured to withhold Achilles from the Trojan War by disguising him as a girl and sending him to Scyros, how he became the lover of Deidamia, the king's daughter, was discovered by the wiles of Ulysses, and set forth on the expedition to Troy. The fragment is not unpleasant reading, but contains little that is noteworthy.[1] The style is simpler, less precious, and less rhetorical than that of the *Thebais*. But it lacks the vigour as well as many of the faults of the earlier poem. There is nothing to make us regret that the poet died before its completion ; there is something to be thankful for in the fact that he did not live to challenge direct comparison with Homer.

The *Silvae*, on the other hand, is a work of considerable interest. The meaning of the word *silva*, in the literary sense, is ' raw material' or ' rough draft '. It then came to be used to mean a work composed at high speed on the spur

---

[1] i. 841–85 gives a good idea of the *Achilleis* at its best. The passage describes the unmasking of the disguised Achilles.

of the moment, differing in fact but little from an improvisa-
tion.[1] That these poems correspond to this definition will
be seen from Statius' preface to book i : ' hos libellos, qui
mihi subito calore et quadam festinandi voluptate fluxerunt....
Nullum ex illis biduo longius tractum, quaedam et in singulis
diebus effusa.' There are thirty-two poems in all, divided
into five books. The fifth is incomplete ; and, if we may
judge from the unfinished state of its preface, was published
after the author's death. The poems are extremely varied
in subject, and to a lesser degree in metre, hendecasyllables,
alcaics, and sapphics being found as well as hexameters.
They comprise poems in praise of the appearance and the
achievements of Domitian,[2] consolations to friends and
patrons for the loss of relatives or favourite slaves,[3] lamenta-
tions of the poet or his friends for the death of dear ones,[4]
letters on various subjects,[5] thanksgivings for the safety of
friends,[6] and farewells to them on their departure,[7] descriptions of villas and the like built by his acquaintances,[8] an
epithalamium,[9] an ode commemorating the birthday of
Lucan,[10] the description of a statuette of Hercules,[11] poems on
the deaths of a parrot and a lion,[12] and a remarkable invocation to Sleep.[13] One and all, these poems show abnormal
cleverness. These slighter subjects were far better suited
to the poet's powers. His miniature painting was in place,
his sprightly and dexterous handling of the hexameter and
the hendecasyllable could be more profitably employed.
Yet here, too, his artificiality is a serious blemish, his lamen-
tations for the loss of the *pueri delicati* of friends do not, and
can hardly be expected to, ring true, and the same blemish
affects even the poems where he laments his own loss.
Further, the poems addressed to Domitian are fulsome to the
verge of nausea ; [14] the beauty of the emperor is such that

---

[1] Quint. x. 3. 17.
[2] *Silv.* i. 1. 6 ; iii. 4 ; iv. 1. 2, 3.   [3] ii. 1. 6 ; iii. 3.   [4] v. 1. 3, 5.
[5] iii. 5 ; iv. 4. 5, 7 ; v. 2.   [6] i. 4.   [7] iii. 2.
[8] i. 3. 5 ; ii. 2 ; iii. 1.   [9] i. 2.   [10] ii. 7.
[11] iv. 6.   [12] ii. 4. 5.   [13] v. 4.
[14] Cp. also the extravagant dedication of the *Thebais*.

all the great artists of the past would have vied with one another in depicting his features ; his eyes are like stars ; his equestrian statue is so glorious that at night (i. 1. 95)

> cum superis terrena placent, tua turba relicto   [1]
> labetur caelo miscebitque oscula iuxta.
> ibit in amplexus natus fraterque paterque
> et soror : una locum cervix dabit omnibus astris.

The poem on the emperor's sexless favourite, Earinus, can scarcely be quoted here. Without being definitely coarse, it succeeds in being one of the most disgusting productions in the whole range of literature. The emperor who can accept flattery of such a kind has certainly qualified for assassination. The lighter poems are almost distressingly trivial, and it is but a poor excuse to plead that such triviality was imposed by the artificial social life of the day and the jealous tyranny of Domitian. Moreover, the tendency to preciosity, which was kept in check in the *Thebais* by the requirements of epic, here has full play. The death of a boy in his fifteenth year is described as follows (ii. 6, 70) :

> vitae modo cardine adultae   [2]
> nectere temptabat iuvenum pulcherrimus ille
> cum tribus Eleis unam trieterida lustris.

Writers of elegiac verse are addressed as (i. 2. 250)

> ' qui nobile gressu   [3]
> extremo fraudatis opus '.

A new dawn is expressed by an astounding periphrasis (iv. 6. 15) :

---

[1] When heaven takes its joy of earth, thy kin shall leave heaven and glide down to earth and kiss thee face to face. Thy son and sister, thy brother and thy sire, shall come to thy embrace ; and about thy sole neck shall all the stars of heaven find a place.

[2] Come now to the turning-point where boyhood becomes manhood, he, the fairest of youths, was on the point of linking three olympiads (twelve years) with a space of three years.

[3] Ye that cheat the noble march of your verse of its last stride.

ab Elysiis prospexit sedibus alter   [1]
Castor et hesternas risit Tithonia mensas.

There is, in fact, no limit in these poems to Statius' luxuriance
in far-fetched and often obscure mythological allusions.
In spite, however, of such cardinal defects as these, the *Silvae*
present a brilliant though superficial picture of the cultured
society of the day and contain much that is pretty, and
something that is poetic.[1] Take, for instance, the poem
in which the poet writes to console Atedius Melior for the
death of his favourite Glaucias, a *puer delicatus*. The work
is hopelessly clever and hopelessly insincere. Statius exaggerates at once the charms of the dead boy and the grief of
Atedius and himself. But at the conclusion he works up
an old commonplace into a very pretty piece of verse. He
has been describing the reception of Glaucias in the underworld (ii. 1. 208):

hic finis rapto ! quin tu iam vulnera sedas   [2]
et tollis mersum luctu caput ? omnia functa
aut moritura vides : obeunt noctesque diesque
astraque, nec solidis prodest sua machina terris.
nam populos, mortale genus, plebisque caducae
quis fleat interitus ? hos bella, hos aequora poscunt ;
his amor exitio, furor his et saeva cupido,
ut sileam morbos ; hos ora rigentia Brumae,

---

[1] Castor in turn looked forth from the halls of Elysium and Tithonus'
bride made merry over yesterday's feasts. [Castor and Pollux lived on
alternate days.]

[2] Such is the rest thy lost darling has won. Come, soothe thine anguish
and lift up thy head that droops with woe. Thou seest all things dead or soon
to die. Day and night and stars all pass away, nor shall its massive fabric
save the world from destruction. As for the tribes of earth, this mortal race,
and the death of multitudes all doomed to pass away, why bewail them ?
Some war, some ocean, demands for its prey : some die of love, others of
madness, others of fierce desire, to say naught of pestilence : some winter's

---

[1] It is hard to select from the *Silvae*. Beside those poems from which
quotations are given, iii. 5, v. 3 and 5 are best worth reading. But the
average level is high. The Sapphic and Alcaic poems (iv. 5 and 7) and the
hexameter poems in praise of Domitian (i. 1, iii. 4, iv. 1 and 2) are the
least worth reading.

illos implacido letalis Sirius igni,
hos manet imbrifero pallens Autumnus hiatu.
quicquid init ortus, finem timet. ibimus omnes,
ibimus : immensis urnam quatit Aeacus ulnis.
ast hic quem gemimus, felix hominesque deosque
et dubios casus et caecae lubrica vitae
effugit, immunis fatis. non ille rogavit,
non timuit meruitve mori : nos anxia plebes,
nos miseri, quibus unde dies suprema, quis aevi
exitus incertum, quibus instet fulmen ab astris,
quae nubes fatale sonet.

There is nothing great about such work, but it is a neat
and elegant treatment of a familiar theme, while the phrase
non ille rogavit, non timuit meruitve mori has a pathos worthy
of a better cause.[1]   Far more suited, however, to the genius
of Statius, with its lack of inspiration, its marvellous polish,
and its love of minutiae, are the descriptions of villas, temples,
baths, and works of art in which he so frequently indulges.
The poem on the statuette of Hercules (ii. 6) is a wonder of
cunning craftsmanship, the poems on the baths of Etruscus,
the villa of Vopiscus at Tibur, and of Pollius at Surrentum,

---

freezing breath, others the baleful Sirius' cruel fire, others again pale
autumn, gaping with rainy maw, awaits for doom : all that hath birth
must tremble before death : we all must go, must go : Aeacus shakes the
urn of fate in his vast arms.   But this child, whom we bewail, is happy,
and has escaped the power of men and gods, the strokes of chance, and
the slippery paths of our dark life : fate cannot touch him : he did not
ask, nor fear, nor deserve to die.   But we poor anxious rabble, we miserable
men, know not whence our last day shall come, what shall be the end of
life, for whom the thunderbolt shall bring death from the starry sky, nor
what cloud shall roar forth our doom.

---

[1] The poem on the death of his father (v. 3) shows genuine depth of
feeling, but its elaborate artificiality is somewhat distressing, considering
the theme. (The same is true to a less degree of v. 5.)   V. 3 must be, in
portions at any rate, the earliest of the *Silvae,* for (l. 29) the poet states
that his father has been dead but three months.   But it records (ll. 219–33)
events which took place long after that time (i.e. victory at Alba and
failure at Agon Capitolinus).   The poem must have been rewritten in
part, ll. 219–33 at least being later additions.   The inconsistency between
these lines and line 29 is probably due to the poet having died before
revising bk. v for publication.

for all their exaggeration and affectation, reveal a genuine
love for the beauties of art and nature. It is true that he
shows a preference for nature trimmed by the hand of
man, but his pleasure is genuine and its expression often
delicate. Who would not delight to live in a house such
as Pollius had built at Sorrento (ii. 2. 45) ?—

> haec domus ortus   [1]
> aspicit et Phoebi tenerum iubar ; illa cadentem
> detinet exactamque negat dimittere lucem,
> cum iam fessa dies et in aequora montis opaci
> umbra cadit vitreoque natant praetoria ponto.
> haec pelagi clamore fremunt, haec tecta sonoros
> ignorant fluctus terraeque silentia malunt.
>
> . . . .
>
> quid mille revolvam
> culmina visendique vices ? sua cuique voluptas
> atque omni proprium thalamo mare, transque iacentem
> Nerea diversis servit sua terra fenestris.

We cannot, perhaps, share his enthusiasm in the minute
description that follows of the coloured marbles used in the
decoration of the house, and his panegyric of Pollius leaves
us cold, but we quit the poem with a pleasant impression
of the Bay of Naples and of the poet who loved it so well.
It recalls in its way the charming, if over-elaborate and
exaggerated, landscapes of the younger Pliny in his letters
on the source of the Clitumnus and on his Tuscan and Laurentine villas.[1] But it is in two poems of a very different kind
that the *Silvae* reach their high-water mark. The *Genethliacon*

---

[1] One chamber looks to the east and the young beam of Phoebus; one
stays him as he falls and will not part with the expiring light, when the
day is outworn and the shadow of the dark mount falls athwart the deep,
and the great castle swims reflected in the glassy sea. These chambers
are full of the sound of ocean, those know not the roaring waves, but rather
love the silence of the land. . . . Why should I recount thy thousand
roofs and every varied view ? Each has a joy that is its own : each
chamber has its own sea, and each several window its own tract of land
seen across the sea beneath.

---

1 viii, 8 ; ii. 17 ; v. 6,

Lucani, despite its artificial form and the literary conventions
with which it is overloaded, reveals a genuine enthusiasm for
the dead poet, and is couched in language of the utmost
grace and verse of extraordinary melody ; the hendecasyllables of Statius lack the poignant vigour of the Catullan
hendecasyllables, but they have a music of their own which
is scarcely less remarkable.[1]   The lament of Calliope for her
lost nursling will hold its own with anything of a similar
kind produced by the Silver Age (ii. 7. 88) :

> ' o saevae nimium gravesque Parcae !   [1]
> o numquam data longa fata summis !
> cur plus, ardua, casibus patetis ?
> cur saeva vice magna non senescunt ?
> sic natum Nasamonii Tonantis
> post ortus obitusque fulminatos
> angusto Babylon premit sepulcro.
> sic fixum Paridis manu trementis
> Peliden Thetis horruit cadentem.
> sic ripis ego murmurantis Hebri
> non mutum caput Orpheos sequebar
> sic et tu (rabidi nefas tyranni !)
> iussus praecipitem subire Lethen,
> dum pugnas canis arduaque voce
> das solatia grandibus sepulcris,
> (o dirum scelus ! o scelus !) tacebis.'
> sic fata est leviterque decidentes
> abrasit lacrimas nitente plectro.

[1] 'Ah ! fates severe and all too cruel ! O life that for our noblest ne'er
is long ! Why are earth's loftiest most prone to fall ? Why by hard fate do
her great ones ne'er grow old ?   Even so the Nasamonian Thunderer's son
like lightning rose, like lightning passed away, and now is laid in a narrow
tomb at Babylon.   So Thetis shuddered, when the son of Peleus fell trans-
fixed by Paris' coward hand.   So I, too, by the banks of murmuring
Hebrus followed the head of Orpheus that could not cease from song.
So now must thou—out on the mad tyrant's crime !—go down untimely
to the wave of Lethe, and while thou singest of war and with lofty strain
givest comfort to the sepulchres of the mighty,—O infamy, O monstrous
infamy !—art doomed to sudden silence.' So spake she, and with gleaming
quill wiped away the tears that gently fell.

[1] With Statius, as with Martial, the hendecasyllable always begins
with a spondee.   The Alcaics of iv. 5 and Sapphics of iv. 7 call for no

But more beautiful as pure poetry, and indeed unique in
Latin, is the well-known invocation to Sleep (v. 4):

> crimine quo merui iuvenis,[1] placidissime divum, [1]
> quove errore miser, donis ut solus egerem,
> Somne, tuis ? tacet omne pecus volucresque feraeque
> et simulant fessos curvata cacumina somnos,
> nec trucibus fluviis idem sonus ; occidit horror
> aequoris, et terris maria acclinata quiescunt.
> septima iam rediens Phoebe mihi respicit aegras
> stare genas ; totidem Oetaeae Paphiaeque revisunt
> lampades et totiens nostros Tithonia questus
> praeterit et gelido spargit miserata flagello.
> unde ego sufficiam ? non si mihi lumina mille
> quae sacer alterna tantum statione tenebat
> Argus et haud umquam vigilabat corpore toto.
> at nunc heus ! aliquis longa sub nocte puellae
> bracchia nexa tenens ultro te, Somne, repellit :
> inde veni ! nec te totas infundere pennas
> luminibus compello meis (hoc turba precetur

---

[1] By what crime, O Sleep, most gentle of gods, or by what error, have
I, that am young, deserved—woe's me !—that I alone should lack thy
blessing ? All cattle and birds and beasts of the wild lie silent; the curved
mountain ridges seem as though they slept the sleep of weariness, and wild
torrents have hushed their roaring. The waves of the deep have fallen
and the seas, reclined on earth's bosom, take their rest. Yet now Phoebe
returning gazes for the seventh time on my sleepless weary eyes. For the
seventh time the lamps of Oeta and Paphos (i. e. Hesperus and Venus)
revisit me, for the seventh time Tithonus' bride sweeps over my complaint
and all her pity is to touch me with her frosty scourge. How may I find
strength to endure ? I needs must faint, even had I the thousand eyes
which divine Argos kept fixed upon his prey in shifting relays (so only
could he wake, nor watched he ever with all his body). But now—woe's
me !—another, his arms locked about his love, spurneth thee from him
all the long night. Leave him, O Sleep, for me. I bid thee not sweep
upon my eyes with all the force of thy fanning pinions. That is the prayer

---

special comment. They are closely modelled on Horace. The two poems
fail because they are prosy and uninteresting, not through any fault of
the metre, but it may be that Statius felt his powers hampered by an
unfamiliar metre.

1 If *iuvenis* be taken to refer to Statius, the poem must be an early work
or depict an imaginary situation. The alternative is to take it as a vocative
referring to Sleep.

laetior) : extremo me tange cacumine virgae
(sufficit) aut leviter suspenso poplite transi.

Here Statius far surpasses himself. Had all else that he
wrote been merely mediocre, this one short poem would
have given him a claim on the grateful memory of posterity.
The note it strikes is one that has never been heard before
in Latin poetry and is never heard again. We have wavered
before as to Statius' title to the name of true poet ; this
should turn the balance in his favour. Great he is not for
a moment to be called ; Lucan, with all his faults, stands
high above him ; Valerius Flaccus, aided largely by his
happier choice of subject, is in some respects his superior ;
but for finish, dexterity, and fluency, Statius is unique among
the post-Augustans. Just as an actor who has acquired
a perfect mastery of all the tricks and technique of the
stage may sometimes cheat us into believing him to be a
great actor, though in reality neither intellect, presence, nor
voice qualify him for such high praise, so it is with Statius.
His facility and cunning workmanship hold us amazed,
and at times the reader is on the verge of yielding up his
saner judgement before such charm. But the revulsion of
feeling comes inevitably. Statius had not learned the art
of concealing his art. The unreality of his work soon
makes itself felt, and his skill becomes in time little better
than a weariness and a mockery.

---

of happier souls than I. Touch me only with the tip of thy wand—that
shall suffice—or lightly pass over my head with hovering feet.

CHAPTER X

SILIUS ITALICUS

TITUS CATIUS SILIUS ITALICUS [1] is best known to us as the author of the longest and worst of surviving Roman epics. But by a strange irony of fate we have a fuller knowledge of his life and character than is granted us in the case of any other poet of the Silver Age, with the exception of Seneca and Persius. His social position, his personal character, his cultured and artistic tastes, rather than any merit possessed by his verse, have won him a place in the picture-gallery of Pliny the younger.[2] We would gladly sacrifice the whole of the ' obituary notice ' transmitted to us by the kindly garrulity of Pliny, for a few more glimpses into the life of Juvenal, or even of Valerius Flaccus, but the picture is interesting and even attractive, and awakens feelings of a less unfriendly nature than are usually entertained for the plodding poetaster who had the misfortune to write the seventeen books of *Punica*.

Silius was born in the year 25 or 26 A.D.[3]; of his family and place of birth we know nothing.[4] He first appears in the unpleasing guise of a ' delator ' in the reign of Nero, in the last year of whose principate he filled the position of consul (68 A.D.).

In the ' year of the four emperors ' (69 A.D.) he is found

---

[1] *C. I. L.* vi. 1984. 9, in the ' fasti sodalium Augustalium Claudialium '. In MSS. Pliny and Tacitus, he is Silius Italicus, in Martial simply Silius or Italicus.

[2] Plin. *Ep.* iii. 7. In the description of his life which follows, Pliny is the authority, where not otherwise stated.

[3] Pliny writes in 101 A.D. to record Silius' death. Silius was over seventy-five when he died.

[4] *Italicus* might suggest that he came from the Spanish town of *Italica*. But Martial, who addresses him in several epigrams of almost servile flattery, would surely have claimed him as fellow-countryman had this been the case.

as the friend and counsellor of Vitellius ;[1] his conduct, we are told, was wise and courteous.   He subsequently won renown by his admirable administration of the province of Asia, and then retired from the public gaze to the seclusion of a life of study.[2]   The amiability and virtue which marked the leisure of his later years wiped out the dark stain that had be-smirched his youth.   ' Men hastened to salute him and to do him honour.   When not engaged in writing, he would pass the day in learned converse with the friends and acquaintances—no mere fortune-hunters—who continually thronged the chambers where he would lie for long hours upon his couch.   His verses, which he would sometimes sub-mit to the judgement of the critics by giving recitations, show diligence rather than genius.   The increasing infirmities of age led him to forsake Rome for Campania ; not even the accession of a new princeps induced him to quit his retire-ment.   It is not less creditable to Caesar to have permitted than to Silius to have ventured on such a freedom.   He was a connoisseur even to the verge of extravagance.   He had several country houses in the same district, and often abandoned those which he already possessed, if some new house chanced to catch his fancy.   He had a large library, and a fine collection of portraits and statues, and was an enthusiastic admirer of works of art which he was not fortunate enough to possess.   He kept Vergil's birthday with greater care than his own, especially when he was at Naples, where he would visit the poet's tomb with all the veneration

---

[1] Pliny, loc. cit. ; Tac. *Hist.* iii. 65.

[2] His poem was already planned in 88 ; cp. Mart. iv. 14 (published 88 A. D.).   Some of it was already written in 92 ; cp. *legis*, M. vii. 62 (pub-lished 92 A. D.).   But the allusion to Domitian, iii. 607, must have been inserted after that date, while xiv. 686 points to the close of Nerva's principate.   Statius, *Silv.* iv. 7. 14 (published 95 A. D.) seems to imitate Silius :

> Dalmatae montes ubi Dite viso
> pallidus fossor redit erutoque
> concolor auro.

Sil. i. 233 ' et redit infelix effosso concolor auro.'   The last five books, compressed and markedly inferior to i–xii, may have been left unrevised.

due to the temple of a god.' He died [1] in his Neapolitan villa of self-chosen starvation. His health had failed him. He was afflicted by an incurable tumour, and ran to meet death with a fortitude that nothing could shake. ' His life was happy and prosperous to his last hour ; his one sorrow was the death of his younger son ; the elder (and better) of his sons, who survives him, has had a distinguished career, and has even reached the consulate.' From Epictetus [2] we gather, what we might infer from the manner of his death, that he was a Stoic. From Martial,[3] who addresses him in the interested language of flattery as the leading orator of his day, and as the maker of immortal verse, we learn that he was the proud possessor of the Tusculan villa of Cicero, and that he actually owned the tomb of the poet whom he loved so well.

Silius' life is more interesting than his verse. Like Lucan, he elected to write historical epic, and in his choice of a subject was undoubtedly wiser than his younger contemporary. For instead of selecting a period so dangerously recent as the civil strife in which the republic perished, he went back to the Second Punic War, to a time sufficiently remote to permit of greater freedom of treatment and to enable him to avoid the peril of unduly republican ecstasies. In making this choice he was in all probability influenced by his reverence for Vergil. He, too, would sing of Rome's rise to greatness, would write a truly national epic on the great theme which Vergil so inimitably foreshadowed in the dying words of the Carthaginian queen, would link the most stirring years of Rome's history with the past, just as Vergil had

---

[1] In 101 A. D. at the age of seventy-five. [2] Epict. *diss*. iii. 8. 7.

[3] Mart. xi. 48 :

> Silius haec magni celebrat monumenta Maronis,
>   iugera facundi qui Ciceronis habet.
> heredem dominumque sui tumulive larisve
>   non alium mallet nec Maro nec Cicero.

That it was the Tusculanum and not the Cumanum of Cicero that Silius possessed is an inference from *C. I. L.* xix. 2653, found at Tusculum : ' D.M. Crescenti Silius Italicus Collegium salutarem '

linked the epic of Rome's founder to the greatness of the
years that were to come.   Ennius had been before him, but
he might well aspire to remodel and develop the rude anna-
listic work of the earlier poet.[1]   The brilliant history of
Livy, with its vivid battle-scenes and its sonorous speeches,
was a quarry that might provide him with the richest
material.   Unhappily, less wise than Lucan, he made the
fatal mistake of adopting the principles set forth by Eumolpus, the dissolute poet in the novel of Petronius.[2]

The intrusion of the mythological method into historical
epic is disastrous.   It is barely tolerable in the pseudo-
historical epic of Tasso.   In the military narrative of Silius
it is monstrous and insufferable.   His reverence for Vergil
led him to control, or attempt to control, every action of
the war by divine intervention.

Juno reappears in her old rôle as the implacable enemy of
Rome.   It is she that kindles Hannibal's hatred for Rome,
causes the outbreak of the war,[3] and, disguised as the lake-god
Trasimenus, spurs him on to Rome.[4]   It is at her instigation
that Anna Perenna kindles him to fresh effort by the news
that Fabius Cunctator is no longer in command against him,[5]
that Somnus moderates his designs after Cannae.[6]   It is Juno
that conceals the Carthaginian forces in a cloud at Cannae,[7]
and that rescues Hannibal from the fury of Scipio at Zama.[8]
Against Juno is arrayed Venus, the protector of the sons of
Aeneas.   She persuades her husband Vulcan to dry up the
Trebia, whose flood threatens the Romans with yet greater
disaster than they have already suffered,[9] she unnerves and
demoralizes the Punic army by the luxury of Capua.[10]
Minerva and Mars play minor parts, the former favouring
Carthage, the latter Rome.[11]   Nothing is gained by this
dreary and superannuated mechanism, while the poem is
yet further hampered by the other encumbrances of epic
commonplace.

---

[1] Enn. *Ann.* vii, viii, ix.   [2] See p. 103.   [3] i. 55.   [4] iv. 727.
[5] viii. 28.   [6] x. 349.   [7] ix. 484.   [8] xvii. 523.
[9] iv. 675.   [10] xi. 387.   [11] ix. 439.

The *Thebais* of Statius is full of episodes that only find
a place because Vergil had borrowed similar episodes from
Homer.   But the *Thebais* is a professedly mythological epic,
and Statius commands a light touch and brilliant colours.
The reader merely groans when the heavy-handed Silius
introduces his wondrously engraven shield,[1] his funeral
games,[2] his Amazon,[3] his dismal catalogues,[4] his Nekuia.[5]
In the latter episode, he even introduces the Vergilian Sibyl
of Cumae ; it is a redeeming feature that Scipio does not
make a ' personally conducted tour ' through the nether
world ; such a direct challenge to the Sixth Aeneid was
perhaps impossible for so true a lover of Vergil as Silius.
The Homeric method of necromancy is wisely preferred,
and the Sibyl reveals the past and future of Rome as the
spirits pass before them.   But there are no illuminating
flashes of imagination ; the best feature of the episode is
an uninspired and frigid appropriateness.   Nothing serves
better than the failure of Silius to show at once the daring
and the genius of Vergil, when he ransacked the wealth of
Homer and

> from a greater Greek
> Borrowed as beautifully as the moon
> The fire o' the sun.

Apart from these unintelligent plagiarisms and vexatious
absurdities, the actual form and composition of the work
show some skill.   The poet passes from scene to scene, from
battle to battle, with ease and assurance in the earlier books.
It is only with the widening of the area of conflict that the
work loses its connexion.   The earlier and less important
exploits of the elder Scipios were wisely dismissed in a few
words.[6]   The poet avoided the mistake of undue scrupulosity
in respect of chronology and makes no attempt to pose as
a scientific military historian.   But it is a serious defect
that he should fail to show the significance of the successful

---

[1] ii. 395.   [2] xvi. 288.   [3] ii. 56.
[4] iii. 222 and viii. 356.   [5] xiii. 395.
[6] e. g. the Funeral Games, the choice of Scipio (xv. 20), the Nekuia.

' peninsular campaign ' of the younger Scipio. Here, as in
the descriptions of the siege of Syracuse, the reader is
haunted by the feeling that these great events are regarded
as merely episodic. Even the thrilling march of Hasdrubal,
ending in the dramatic catastrophe of the Metaurus, is
hardly given its full weight. There is more true historical
and dramatic appreciation in Horace's

> Karthagini iam non ego nuntios
> mittam superbos : occidit, occidit
>   spes omnis et fortuna nostri
>   nominis Hasdrubale interempto

than in all the ill-proportioned verbiage of Silius. The
task of setting forth the course of a conflict that flamed all
over the Western Mediterranean world was not easy, and
Silius' failure was proportionately great. Nay—if it be
not merely the hallucination of a weary reader—he seems to
have tired of his task. The first twelve books take us
no further than Hannibal's appearance before the walls of
Rome, and the war is summarily brought to a close in the
last five books, although these, it should be noted, are by
no means free from irrelevant matter. The last three books
above all are jejune and perfunctory, and it has been suggested that they lack the final revision that the rest of the
work had received. Be this as it may, the result of the
inadequate treatment of the close of the war is that the
reader lays down the poem with no feeling of the greatness
of Rome's triumph.

Yet even with these faults of composition, a genuine poet
might have wrought a great work from the rough ore of
history. The scene is thronged with figures as remarkable and
inspiring as history affords. There is the fierce irresistible
Hannibal, the sagacious Fabius, the elder Scipios, tragic
victims of disaster, the younger Scipio, glorious with the light
of victory as the clouds of defeat are rolled away, Hasdrubal
hurled to ruin at the supreme crisis of the war, Marcellus
the victorious, beleaguered [1] and beleaguerer, the ill-starred

---

[1] At Nola.

Paulus, the Senate of Rome that thanked the fugitive Varro because he had not despaired of the republic,[1] and above all the gigantic figure of Rome herself, unshaken, indomitable, triumphant. These are no dry bones that the breath of the poet alone should make them live. They breathe immortal in the prose of Livy, in the verse of Silius they are vain ' shadows of men foredone '. The Hannibal of Silius is not the dazzling villain of Livy, the incarnation of military daring and ' Punic faith '. Mistaken patriotism does not lead Silius to blacken the character of Rome's great antagonist ; he strives to do him justice ; he is as true a patriot, as chivalrous[2] a warrior, as any of the Roman leaders. But he does not live ; he is merely the stock warrior of epic, and his exploits fail to compel belief.

Fabius, the least romantic, though not the least interesting figure in the war, stands forth more clearly. The prosaic Silius is naturally most successful with his most prosaic hero. The younger Scipio is the embodiment of *pietas*, an historical Aeneas, without his prototype's most distressing weaknesses, but with all his dullness, and lacking the halo of legend and the splendour of the founder of the race to glorify him. Paulus has the merit of true courage, and his consciousness of his colleague's folly invests him with a certain pathos. He makes the best death of any Silian warrior, and deserves the eulogy passed on him by Hannibal. The rest are lay-figures, with even less individuality and life. Silius failed to depict character. He fails, too, to show any true sense of the political greatness of Rome. The genius of Rome and the genius of Carthage are never confronted or contrasted ; the greatness of Rome in defeat, the scenes of Rome agonizing in the grip of unexpected disaster, are never brought home to the reader with the least degree of vividness.

---

[1] Cp. x. 628 ' quod . . . Laomedontiadum non desperaverit urbi '. The tasteless *Laomedontiadum* as a learned equivalent for *Romanorum* is characteristic. Silius has the *Aeneid* in his mind when he chooses this word : his literary proclivities lead him astray ; where he should be most strong he is most feeble.

[2] *Vide infra* for his treatment of Paulus' dead body after Cannae.

The great battles are described at tedious length[1] and rendered ridiculous by the lavish introduction of Homeric single
combats. If Silius is rarely bombastic or rendered absurd
by the grossness of his exaggeration, he yet fails to see what
Lucan saw plainly—that for the author of a military historical epic, it is the issues of the war, big with the fate of
generations to come, the temper of the combatants, the
character of the chief actors, that are the really interesting
elements. Almost alone of Silver Latin poets he shows no
real gifts of rhetoric and epigram, no virtuosity of diction,
no brilliance of description. We lack the declamation of
Lucan, the apostrophes on the issues of the war, the vivid
character-sketches of the generals, the political enthusiasm,
the thunder of the oratory of general and statesman. The
battle-speeches of Livy, whose glow and vigour half atone
for their theatricality, have been made use of by Silius, but
find only a feeble echo in his lifeless verse. Nothing stands
out sharply defined; the epic lacks impetus and has no
salient points; outlines are blurred in an unpoetic haze.
The history of Tacitus has been described as history ' seen
by lightning flashes '. Such should be the history of historical epic. In its stead Silius presents us with a confused
welter of archaistic battle, learned allusion, and epic commonplace.

'Aequalis liber est, Cretice, qui malus est,' cries Martial [2]
to a friend. The epigram would apply to the *Punica*.
There is scarcely a passage in the whole work that reveals
genuine poetic imagination. Silius is free from many of
the faults of his contemporaries, the faults that spring
from aspirations towards originality. He is content to be
an imitator. In his style, as in his composition, Vergil is
an obsession. But the echoes are muffled or unmusical.
Gifted with ease and fluency and—for his age—comparative
lucidity of diction, Silius has no true ear for music, nor true
eye for beauty. His verse moves naturally but heavily.

---

[1] Trebia, iv. 480–703 ; Trasimene, v. 1–678 ; Cannae, ix. 178—x. 578.
[2] Mart, vii. 90.

He is the most spondaic poet[1] of his age, and the spondaic
rhythm is not alleviated by artistic variety of pause or
judicious use of elision. Lucan is heavy, but he hits hard
and is weighty in the best sense. Silius rolls on lumbering
and unperturbed, never rising or falling. He has all the
faults of Ovid, and, in spite of his laboured imitation, none
of the merits of Vergil. Nothing can kindle him. The
most heroic and the most tragic of all the stories of the
struggle for the empire of the western world is that of
Regulus, the famous captive of Carthage in the first Punic
War.[2] The episode is skilfully and naturally introduced.
The story is told by an aged veteran of the first Punic War
to a descendant of Regulus, who has fled wounded from the
rout of Trasimene. Silius succeeds in making one of the
noblest stories in history lifeless and dull. The narration
opens with the description of a melodramatic struggle between Regulus and a monstrous serpent in Africa, scarcely
an harmonious prelude for the simple and solemn climax
of the hero's life, his return to his home to fix ' the Senate's
wavering will ', his departure unmoved to Carthaginian
captivity, with the certainty of death and torture before
him. Silius treats this tragic episode simply and severely ;
there is nothing to offend the taste, but there is equally
nothing to move the heart ; the description is merely
dull ; it lacks the fire of life and the finer imagination.
Here, again, we turn for relief to Horace with his brief but
incomparable

> atqui sciebat quae sibi barbarus
> tortor pararet, non aliter tamen
> dimovit obstantes propinquos
> et populum reditus morantem
> quam si clientum longa negotia
> diiudicata lite relinqueret,
> tendens Venefranos in agros
> aut Lacedaemonium Tarentum (iii. 5. 49).

Take the corresponding passage in Silius. Regulus concludes his speech to the Senate as follows (vi. 485) :

[1] See p. 123, note. [2] Bk. vi.

exposcunt Libyes nobisque dedere   [1]
haec referenda, pari libeat si pendere bellum
foedere et ex aequo geminas conscribere leges.
sed mihi sit Stygios ante intravisse penates
talia quam videam ferientes pacta Latinos.
　haec fatus Tyriae sese iam reddidit irae,
nec monitus spernente graves fidosque senatu
Poenorum dimissa cohors. quae maesta repulsa
ac minitans capto patrias properabat ad oras.
prosequitur volgus, patres, ac planctibus ingens
personat et luctu campus. revocare libebat
interdum et iusto raptum retinere dolore.

Criticism is needless.　One passage is in the grand style, the
other is not ; one is mere verse-making, the other the purest
poetry.　Silius has nothing of *curiosa felicitas* or even of
the more common gift of vague sensuous charm.　Even
on such hackneyed themes as the choice of Hercules, with
Scipio playing the part of Hercules, he fails to rise to the
conventional prettiness of which even a Calpurnius Siculus
would have been capable.　Virtue and pleasure are rendered equally unattractive, and we pity Scipio for having
to make the choice.　With the other poets of the age it
is easy to select passages to illustrate their characteristic
merits and defects.　But from the dull monotony of
Silius it is hard to choose.　He does not read well even
in selections.　Apart from the general absurdity of the
conception of the poem he is rarely grotesque.　His taste is
chastened by his love of Vergil, and the absence of genuine
rhetorical power saves him from dangerous exuberance.

---

[1] 'The Libyans ask whether you will cease from war on equal terms
and draw up a treaty wherein each side keeps its own. They bid me bring
back your reply.　But may I sooner enter the gates of hell than see the
Latins make such a compact!'　He spake, and yielded himself back once
more to the mercies of the Tyrian's hate : the Senate spurned not his words
of weight, his loyal warning. The Punic embassy was dismissed. Cast
down at their rebuff, and threatening their captive, they hastened homeward to their native shores. The people, the fathers, follow them : the whole
vast plain resounds with weeping and beating of breasts, and ever and
again they strove to recall the hero and with just grief to retain him as
he was snatched away from them.

The tricks of rhetoric are there, but the edge of his wit is
dull, and he has no speed nor energy. For similar reasons
he never attains sublimity. There are faint traces of the
Romana gravitas in lines such as

> iamque tibi veniet tempus quo maxima rerum   [1]
> nobilior sit Roma malis (iii. 584).

The idea that the trials of Rome shall be as a ' refiner's fire '
has a certain grandeur, but the expression of the idea is
commonplace. The same is true of the elaboration of the
Vergilian *parcere subiectis*, where the poet describes Marcellus' clemency to the vanquished Syracusans, and makes
brief allusion to the unhappy death of Archimedes (xiv.
673):

>   sic parcere victis   [2]
> pro praeda fuit et sese contenta nec ullo
> sanguine pollutis plausit Victoria pennis.
> tu quoque ductoris lacrimas, memorande, tulisti,
> defensor patriae, meditantem in pulvere formas
> nec turbatum animi tanta feriente ruina.

To find Silius at his best—not a very exalted best—we
must turn to the passage where he depicts the feelings of
Hannibal on finding the body of Paulus on the field of
Cannae (x. 513):

> quae postquam aspexit, geminatus gaudia ductor   [3]
> Sidonius ' Fuge, Varro,' inquit ' fuge, Varro, superstes,
> dum iaceat Paulus. patribus Fabioque sedenti
> et populo consul totas edissere Cannas.
> concedam hanc iterum, si lucis tanta cupido est,

---

[1] And the time shall come when Rome, the greatest thing in all the
world, shall be yet more ennobled by her woes.

[2] So mercy toward the conquered took the place of rapine, and Victory
was content with herself and clapped her wings unstained by any blood.
Thou, too, immortal sage, defender of thy country, didst win the meed
of the conqueror's tears, thou whom ruin smote down, all unmoved, as
thou broodedst o'er figures traced in the dust.

[3] When this he saw, the Sidonian chief was filled with double joy and
cried, ' Fly, Varro, fly and survive defeat ; enough that Paulus lieth low !
Go, consul, tell all the tale of Cannae to the fathers, to laggard Fabius,
to the people. If so thou long'st to live, I will grant thee, Varro, to flee

concedam tibi, Varro, fugam. at, cui fortia et hoste
me digna haud parvo caluerunt corda vigore,
funere supremo et tumuli decoretur honore.
quantus, Paule, iaces! qui tot mihi milibus unus
maior laetitiae causa est. cum fata vocabunt,
tale precor nobis salva Karthagine letum.'

.   .   .   .

'i. decus Ausoniae, quo fas est ire superbas (572)
virtute et factis animas. tibi gloria leto
iam parta insigni. nostros Fortuna labores
versat adhuc casusque iubet nescire futuros.'
haec Libys, atque repens crepitantibus undique flammis
aetherias anima exultans evasit in auras.

The picture of the soul of Paulus soaring heavenward from
the funeral pyre, exultant at the honour paid him by his
great foe, is the nearest approach to pure poetic imagination
in the whole weary length of the *Punica*.[1] But the pedestrian muse of Silius is more at home in the ingenious description of the manœuvres and counter-manœuvres of Fabius
and Hannibal in the seventh book ; the similes with which
the passage closes are hackneyed, but their application is
both new and clever :

(vii. 91) iam Fabius tacito procedens agmine et arte   [1]
     bellandi lento similis, praecluserat omnes

---

once more as thou fleest to-day. But let him, whose heart was bold and
worthy to be my foe, and all aflame with mighty valour, be honoured with
the last rites of burial and all the honour of the tomb. How great, Paulus,
art thou in the death! Thy fall alone gives greater cause for joy than the
fall of so many thousands. Such, when the fates shall summon me, such
I pray be my fate, so Carthage stand unshaken.' . . . 'Go, Ausonia's glory,
where the souls of those whom valour and noble deeds make proud may
go. *Thou* hast won great glory by thy death. For *us*, Fortune still tosses
us too and fro in weltering labour and forbids us to see what chance the
future hath in store.' So spake the Libyan, and straightway from the
crackling flame the exulting spirit soared skyward through the air.
  [1] Now Fabius advanced, leading his host in silence and—such was his
cunning—like to a laggard in war ; so closed he all the paths whereby

---

1 xii. 212–67, where the death of Cinyps clad in Paulus' armour is
described, are pretty enough, but too frankly an imitation of Vergil to be
worth quoting. The simile 247–50 is, however, new and quite picturesque.

fortunaeque hostique vias. discedere signis
haud licitum summumque decus, quo tollis ad astra
imperii, Romane, caput, parere docebat

. . . .

(123) cassarum sedet irarum spectator et alti
celsus collę iugi domat exultantia corda
infractasque minas dilato Marte fatigat
sollers cunctandi Fabius, ceu nocte sub atra
munitis pastor stabulis per ovilia clausum
impavidus somni servat pecus : effera saevit
atque impasta truces ululatus turba luporum
exercet morsuque quatit restantia claustra.
inritus incepti movet inde atque Apula tardo
arva Libys passu legit ac nunc valle residit
conditus occulta, si praecipitare sequentem
atque inopinata detur circumdare fraude ;
nunc nocturna parat caecae celantibus umbris
furta viae retroque abitum fictosque timores
adsimulat, tum castra citus deserta relicta
ostentat praeda atque invitat prodigus hostem :
qualis Maeonia passim Maeandrus in ora,
cum sibi gurgitibus flexis revolutus oberrat.
nulla vacant incepta dolis : simul omnia versat
miscetque exacuens varia ad conamina mentem,

fortune or the foe might fall on him. No soldier might quit the standards,
and he taught that the height of glory, even that glory, Roman, that raises
thine imperial head to the stars, was obedience. . . . Fabius sits high
on the mountain slopes watching the foeman's rage and tames his impetuous ardour, humbles his threats, and, with skilful delay, postpones the
day of battle and wears out his patience : as when through the darkness of
the night a shepherd, fearless and sleepless in his well-guarded byre, keeps
his flock penned within the fold : without, the wolf-pack, fierce and
famished, howls fiercely, and with its teeth shakes the gates that bar its
entrance. Baffled in his enterprise, the Libyan departs thence and slowly
marches across the Apulian fields and pitches his camp deep in a hidden
vale, if perchance he may hurl the Roman to ruin as he follows in his
track and surround him by hidden guile. Now he prepares a midnight
ambush in some dark pass beneath the shelter of the gloom, and falsely
feigns retreat and fear ; then, swiftly leaving his camp and booty, he displays
them to the foe, and lavishly invites a raid. Even as on Maeonian shores
Maeander with winding channel turns upon himself and wanders far and
wide, now here, now there. Naught he attempts, but has some guile in it.
He weighs every scheme, sharpens his mind for divers exploits, and blends

> sicut aquae splendor radiatus lampade solis
> dissultat per tecta vaga sub imagine vibrans
> luminis et tremula laquearia verberat umbra.

There is in this passage nothing approaching real excellence, but its dexterity may reasonably command some respect. It is dexterity of which Silius has little to show. He is well-read in history and its bastard sister mythology. At his best he can string together his incidents with some skill, and he makes use of his learning in the accepted fashion of his day.[1] The poem is deluged with proper names and learned aetiology, though he has no conception of that magical use of proper names and legendary allusions which is the secret of the masters of literary epic.[2]

But the absence of any true poetic genius makes him the most tedious of Latin authors, and his unenviable reputation is well deserved. For the poetry of the struggle with Carthage for the

> plumed troops and the big wars
> That make ambition virtue,

for ' all quality, pride, pomp, and circumstance of glorious war ', we must go to the inspired prose of Livy.

And yet it is well that the *Punica* should have been preserved. It is well to know that as France has its *Henriade* and England its *Madoc*, so Rome had its *Punica*. It is our one direct glimpse into the work of that cultured society, devastated by the 'scribendi cacoethes', as Juvenal puts it, or, from the point of view of the facile Pliny, adorned by the number of its poets.[3] The *Punica* have won an immortality far other than that prophesied for them by

---

contrivance with contrivance, even as the gleam of water lit by the sun's torch dances through a house quivering, and the reflected beam goes wandering and lashes the roof with tremulous reflection.

---

[1] Sights of Naples, xii. 85 ; Tides at Pillars of Hercules, iii. 46 ; Legend of Pan, xiii. 313 ; Sicily, xiv. 1–50 ; Fabii, vii. 20 ; Anna Perenna, viii. 50 ; Bacchus at Falernum, vii. 162 ; Trasimenus, v. ad init.

[2] See note on p. 13.   [3] Plin. *Ep.* i. 13.

Martial,[1] but they show us the work of a cultured Roman gentleman of his day, who, if he had small capacity, had a high enthusiasm for letters, who had diligence if he had not genius, and was possessed by a love for the supreme poet in whose steps he followed, a passion so sincere that it may win from his scanty readers at least a partial forgiveness for the inadequacy of his imitation and for the suffering inflicted on all those who have essayed the dreary adventure of reading the seventeen books that bear his name.

---

[1] Mart. vii. 63.

CHAPTER XI

MARTIAL

MARCUS VALERIUS MARTIALIS, like Quintilian, Seneca, and Lucan, was a Spaniard by birth, and, unlike those writers, never became thoroughly reconciled to life at Rome. He was born at Bilbilis,[1] a small town of Hispania Tarraconensis. The exact year of his birth is uncertain; but as the tenth book of his epigrams, written between 95 and 98 A.D., contains a reference (24) to his fifty-seventh birthday, he must have been born between 38 and 41 A.D. His birthday was the 1st of March, a fact to which he owes his name Martialis.[2] Of the position of his parents, Valerius Fronto and Flaccilla,[3] we have no evidence. That they were not wealthy is clear from the circumstances of their son. But they were able to give him a regular literary education,[4] although, unlike his fellow-countrymen whom we have mentioned above, he was educated in his native province. But the life of a provincial did not satisfy him. Conscious, perhaps, of his literary gifts, he went, in 64 A.D.,[5] like so many a young provincial, to make his fortune at Rome. There he attached himself as client to the powerful Spanish family of the Senecas, and found a friendly reception also in the house of Calpurnius Piso.[6] But fortune was against him ; as he was congratu-lating himself on his good luck in starting life at Rome under such favourable auspices, the Pisonian conspiracy (65 A.D.) failed, and his patrons fell before the wrath of Nero.[7] His

---

[1] On the modern Cerro de Bambola near the Moorish town of El Cala-tayud.

[2] Cp. ix. 52, x. 24, xii. 60.   [3] Cp. v. 34.   [4] ix. 73. 7.

[5] In x. 103. 7, written in 98 A.D., he tells us that it is thirty-four years since he left Spain.

[6] iv. 40, xii. 36.

[7] He is found rendering poetic homage to Polla, the wife of Lucan, as late as 96 A.D., x. 64, vii. 21-3. For his reverence for the memory of Lucan, cp. i. 61. 7 ; vii. 21, 22 ; xiv. 194.

career must be commenced anew.   Of his life from this point
to the reign of Domitian we know little.   But this much is
certain, that he endured all the indignities and hardships
of a client's life,[1] and that he chose this degrading career in
preference to the active career of the Roman bar.   He had
no taste for oratory, and rejected the advice of his friend
Gaius [2] and his distinguished compatriot Quintilian to seek
a livelihood as an advocate or as a politician.   ' That is not
life ! ' he replies to Quintilian :

> vivere quod propero pauper nec inutilis annis,
>   da veniam : properat vivere nemo satis.
> differat hoc patrios optat qui vincere census
>   atriaque immodicis artat imaginibus (ii. 90. 3).

His ideals and ambitions were low, and his choice had, as
we shall see, a degrading effect upon his poetry.   He chose
rather to live on such modest fortune as he may have possessed, on the client's dole, and such gifts as his complimentary epigrams may have won from his patrons.   These gifts
must have been in many cases of a trifling description,[3] but
they may occasionally have been on a more generous scale.
At any rate, by the year 94 A. D., we find him the possessor
of a little farm at Nomentum,[4] and a house on the Quirinal.[5]
Although he must presumably have written a considerable
quantity of verse in his earlier years, it is not till 80 A. D. that
he makes an appearance on the stage of literature.   In that
year the Flavian amphitheatre was consecrated by the
Emperor Titus, and Martial celebrated the fact by the
publication of his first book, the *Spectaculorum Liber*.   It is
of small literary value, but it was his first step on the ladder
of fame.   Titus conferred on him the *ius trium liberorum*,

---

[1] Cp. his regrets for the ease of his earlier clienthood and the generosity
of the Senecas, xii. 36.

[2] ii. 30 ; cp. l. 5 :

> is mihi ' dives eris, si causas egeris ' inquit.
>   quod peto da, Gai : non peto consilium.

[3] Vide his epigrams *passim*.

[4] xiii. 42, xiii. 119.   Perhaps the gift of Seneca, cp. Friedländer on
Mart. i. 105.   [5] ix. 18, ix. 97. 7, x. 58. 9.

although he seems not to have entered on the enjoyment of this privilege till the reign of Domitian.[1] He thus first came in touch with the imperial circle. From this time forward we get a continual stream of verse in fulsome praise of Domitian and his freedman. But his flattery met with small reward. There are many poems belauding the princeps, but few that thank him. The most that he acquired by his flattery was the honorary military tribunate and his elevation to the equestrian order.[2] Of material profit he got little,[3] save such as his improved social position may have conferred on him indirectly.

Four years after the publication of the *Spectaculorum Liber* (i.e. later in 84 and 85)[4] he published two books, the thirteenth and fourteenth, composed of neat but trifling poems on the presents (Xenia and Apophoreta) which it was customary to give at the feast of the Saturnalia. From this point his output was continuous and steady, as the following table will show : [5]

I, II. 85 or early in 86.	VIII. 93.
III. 87 or early in 88.	IX. Summer, 94.
IV. December (Saturnalia) 88.	X. 1. December, 95.
V. Autumn, 89.	X. 2. 98.
VI. Summer or Autumn, 90.	XI. 97.
VII. December, 92.	XII. Late in 101.

---

[1] Such is the most plausible interpretation of iii. 95. 5, ix. 97. 5 :

tribuit quod Caesar uterque

ius mihi natorum (uterque, i. e. Titus and Domitian).

[2] iii. 95, v. 13, ix. 49, xii. 26.   [3] iii. 95. 11, vi. 10. 1.

[4] xiii. 4 gives Domitian his title of Germanicus, assumed after war with Chatti in 84 ; xiv. 34 alludes to peace ; no allusion to subsequent wars.

[5] I, II. Perhaps published together. This would account for length of preface. II. Largely composed of poems referring to reigns of Vespasian and Titus. Reference to Domitian's censorship shows that I was not published before 85. There is no hint of outbreak of Dacian War, which raged in 86.

III. Since bk. IV contains allusion to outbreak of revolt of Antonius Saturninus towards end of 88 (11) and is published at Rome, whereas III was published at *Cornelii forum* (1), III probably appeared in 87 or 88.

IV. Contains reference to birthday of Domitian, Oct. 24 (1. 7), and seems then to allude to *ludi saeculares* (Sept. 88). Reference to snowfall

His life during this period was uneventful. He lived expensively and continually complains of lack of funds and of the miseries of a client's life. Once only (about 88) the discomfort of his existence seems to have induced him to abandon Rome. He took up his residence at Forum Cornelii, the modern Imola, but soon returned to Rome.[1] It was not till 98 that he decided to leave the capital for good and to return to his Spanish home. A new princeps was on the throne. Martial had associated his work too closely with Domitian and his court to feel at his ease with

at Rome (2 and 13) suggests winter. Perhaps therefore published in *Saturnalia* of 88.

V. Domitian has returned to Italy (1) from Dacian War, but there is no reference to his triumph (Oct. 1, 89 A. D.). Book therefore probably published in early autumn of 89.

VI. Domitian has held his triumph (4. 2 and 10. 7). Julia (13) is dead (end of 89). Book probably published in 90, perhaps in summer. Friedländer sees allusion to Agon Capitolinus (Summer, 90) in vi. 77.

VII. 5–8 refer to Domitian's return from Sarmatic War. He has not yet arrived. These epigrams are among last in book. He returned in January 93. His return was announced as imminent in Dec. 92.

VIII. 21 describes Domitian's arrival; 26, 30, and others deal with festivities in this connexion. 65 speaks of temple of Fortuna Redux and triumphal arch built in Domitian's honour. They are mentioned as if completed. 66 speaks of consulate of Silius Italicus' son beginning Sept. 1, 93.

IX. 84 is addressed to Appius Norbanus Maximus, who has been six years absent from Rome. He went to Upper Germany to crush Antonius Saturninus in 88. 35 refers to Agon Capitolinus in summer of 94.

X. Two editions published. We possess later and larger. Cp. x. 2. 70. 1 suggests a year's interval between IX and X. X, ed. 1 was therefore perhaps published in Dec. 95. X, ed. 2 has references to accession of Trajan, Jan. 25, 98 A. D. (6, 7 and 34). Martial's departure for Spain is imminent.

XI. 1 is addressed to Parthenius, executed in middle of 97 A. D. xii. 5 refers to a selection made from X and XI, perhaps from presentation to Nerva ; cp. xii. 11.

XII. In preface Martial apologizes for three years' silence (l. 9) from publication of X, ed. 2. xii. 3. 10 refers to Stella's consulship, Oct. 101 or 102. Three years' interval points to 101. It was published late in the year ; cp. 1 and 62. Some epigrams in this book were written at Rome. But M. says that it was written *paucissimis diebus*. This must refer only to Spanish epigrams, or the book must have been enlarged after M.'s death.

For the whole question see Friedländer Introd., pp. 50 sqq.

[1] iii, 1 and 4.

Nerva. He sent the new emperor a selection from his tenth
and eleventh books, which we may, perhaps, conjecture to
have been expurgated. He denounced the dead Domitian
in a brilliant epigram which may have formed part of that
selection, but which has only been preserved to us by the
scholiast on Juvenal (iv. 38):

> Flavia gens, quantum tibi tertius abstulit heres !   [1]
>   paene fuit tanti non habuisse duos.

But he felt that times were changed and that there was no
place now for his peculiar talent for flattery (x. 72. 8):

> non est hic dominus sed imperator,   [2]
> sed iustissimus omnium senator,
> per quem de Stygia domo reducta est
> siccis rustica Veritas capillis.
> hoc sub principe, si sapis, caveto
> verbis, Roma, prioribus loquaris.

Let flattery fly to Parthia. Rome is no place for her
(ib. 4). Martial had made his name : he was read far and
wide throughout the Empire.[1] He could afford to retire from
the city that had given him much fame and much pleasure,
but had balanced its gifts by a thousand vexations and indignities. Pliny assisted him with journey-money, and after
a thirty-four years' sojourn in Italy he returned to Bilbilis
to live a life of *dolce far niente*. The kindness of a wealthy
friend, a Spanish lady named Marcella,[2] gave him an estate

---

[1] How much thy third has wronged thee, Flavian race !
    'Twere better ne'er to have bred the other brace.   ANON.

[2]   an emperor
    Is ours, no master as of yore,
    Himself the Senate's very crown
    Of justice, who has called from down
    In her deep Stygian duress
    The hoyden Truth, with tangled tress.
    Be wise, Rome, see you shape anew
    Your tongue ; your prince would have it true.
                                A. E. STREET.

---

1 Cp. xi. 3.
2 xii. 21, xii. 31. There is no reason to suppose with some critics that
she was his wife.

on which he lived in comfort, if not in affluence. He published
but one book in Spain, the twelfth, written, he says in the
preface, in a very few days. He lived in peace and happiness, though at times he sighed for the welcome of the public
for whom he had catered so long,[1] and chafed under the lack
of sympathy and culture among his Spanish neighbours.[2]
He died in 104. 'Martial is dead,' says Pliny, 'and I am
grieved to hear it. He was a man of genius, with a shrewd
and vigorous wit. His verses are full of point and sting, and
as frank as they are witty. I provided him with money for
his journey when he left Rome ; I owed it to my friendship
for him, and to the verses which he wrote in my honour '—
then follows Mart. x. 20—'Was I not right to speed him on
his way, and am I not justified in mourning his death, seeing
that he wrote thus concerning me ? He gave me what he
could, he would have given more had he been able. And yet
what greater gift can one man give another than by handing
down his name and fame to all eternity. I hear you say
that Martial's verses will not live to all eternity ? You may
be right ; at any rate, he hoped for their immortality when
he wrote them ' (Plin. *Ep.* iii. 21).

Of Martial's character we shall have occasion to speak
later. There is nothing in the slight, but generous, tribute
of Pliny that has to be unsaid.

Of the circles in which he moved his epigrams give us
a brilliant picture ; of his exact relations with the persons
whom he addresses it is hard to speak with certainty. Many
distinguished figures of the day appear as the objects of his
flattery. There are Spaniards, Quintilian, Lucinianus Maternus and Canius Rufus, all distinguished men of letters, the
poets Silius Italicus, Stertinius Avitus, Arruntius Stella, the
younger Pliny, the orator Aquilius Regulus, Lentulus Sura,
the friend of Trajan, the rich knights, Atedius Melior, and
Claudius Etruscus, the soldier Norbanus, and many others.
With Juvenal also he seems to have enjoyed a certain

---

[1] xii. praef. 'civitatis aures quibus adsueveram quaero.'
[2] Ib. 'accedit his municipalium robigo dentium.'

intimacy. Statius he never mentions, although he must have moved in the same circles.[1] His intimates—as might be expected—are for the most part, as far as we can guess, of lower rank. There are the centurions Varus and Pudens, Terentius Priscus his compatriot, Decianus the Stoic from the Spanish town of Emerita, the self-sacrificing Quintus Ovidius, Martial's neighbour at Nomentum and a fellow-client of Seneca, and, above all, Julius Martialis. His enemies and envious rivals are attacked and bespattered with filth in many an epigram, but Martial, true to his promise in the preface to his first book, conceals their true names from us.

Of his *vie intime* he tells us little. As far as we may judge, he was unmarried. It is true that several of his epigrams purport to be addressed to his wife. But two facts show clearly that this lady is wholly imaginary. Even Martial could not have spoken of his wife in such disgusting language as, for instance, he uses in xi. 104, while in another poem (ii. 92) he clearly expresses his intention not to marry:

> natorum mihi ius trium roganti
> Musarum pretium dedit mearum
> solus qui poterat. valebis, uxor,
> non debet domini perire munus.

The honorary *ius trium liberorum* had given him, he says, all that marriage could have brought him. He has no intention of making the emperor's generosity superfluous by taking a wife. He preferred the untrammelled life of a bachelor. So only could he enjoy the pleasures which for him meant ' life '. He is neither an impressive nor a very interesting figure. He has many qualities that repel, even if we do not take him too seriously ; and though he may have been a pleasant and in many respects most amiable companion, he has few characteristics that arrest our attention or compel our respect. More will be said of his virtues and his vices in the pages that follow. It is the artist rather than the man that wakens our interest.

---

[1] See p. 271. It is hard to avoid the conclusion that this silence was due to dislike or jealousy.

In Martial we have a poet who devoted himself to the
one class of poetry which, apart from satire, the conditions
of the Silver Age were qualified to produce in any real
excellence — the epigram.   In a period when rhetorical
smartness and point were the predominant features of
literature, the epigram was almost certain to flourish. But
Roman poets in general, and Martial in particular, gave a
character to the epigram which has clung to it ever since,
and has actually changed the significance of the word itself.

In the best days of the Greek epigram the prime consideration was not that a poem should be pointed, but that it
should be what is summed up in the untranslatable French
epithet *lapidaire* ;   that is to say, it should possess the
conciseness, finish, and relevance required for an inscription
on a monument.   Its range was wide ; it might express the
lover's passion, the mourner's grief, the artist's skill, the
cynic's laughter, the satirist's scorn.   It was all poetry in
miniature.   Point is not wanting, but its chief characteristics
are delicacy and charm.   ' No good epigram sacrifices its
finer poetical substance to the desire of making a point, and
none of the best depend on having a point at all.' [1]   Trans-
planted to the soil of Italy the epigram changes.   The less
poetic Roman, with his coarse tastes, his brutality, his tendency to satire, his appreciation of the incisive, wrought it to
his own use.   In his hands it loses most of its sensuous and
lyrical elements and makes up for the loss by the cultivation
of point.   Above all, it becomes the instrument of satire,
stinging like a wasp where the satirist pure and simple uses
the deadlier weapons of the bludgeon and the rapier.

The epigram must have been exceedingly plentiful from
the very dawn of the movement which was to make Rome
a city of *belles-lettres*.   It is the plaything of the dilettante
littérateur, so plentiful under the empire.[2]   Apart from the
work of Martial, curiously few epigrams have come down to
us ; nevertheless, in the vast majority of the very limited

---

[1] Mackail, *Greek Anthol.*, Introd., p. 5.
[2] Domitius Marsus was famous for his epigrams, as also Calvus, Gaetulicus, Pedo, and others.

number we possess the same Roman characteristics may be traced. In the non-lyrical epigrams of Catullus, in the shorter poems of the *Appendix Vergiliana*, there is the same vigour, the same coarse humour, the same pungency that find their best expression in Martial. Even in the epigrams attributed to Seneca in the *Anthologia Latina*,[1] something of this may be observed, though for the most part they lack the personal note and leave the impression of mere juggling with words. It is in this last respect, the attention to point, that they show most affinity with Martial. Only the epigrams in the same collection attributed to Petronius[2] seem to preserve something of the Greek spirit of beauty untainted by the hard, unlovely, incisive spirit of Rome.

Martial was destined to fix the type of the epigram for the future. For pure poetry he had small gifts. He was endowed with a warm heart, a real love for simplicity of life and for the beauties of nature. But he had no lyrical enthusiasm, and was incapable of genuine passion. He entered heartwhole on all his amatory adventures, and left them with indifference. Even the cynical profligacy of Ovid shows more capacity for true love. At their best Martial's erotic epigrams attain to a certain shallow prettiness,[3] for the most part they do not rise above the pornographic. And even though he shows a real capacity for friendship, he also reveals an infinite capacity for cringing or impudent vulgarity in his relations with those who were merely patrons or acquaintances. His needy circumstances led him, as we shall see, to continual expressions of a peevish mendicancy, while the artificiality and pettiness of the life in which he moved induced an excessive triviality and narrowness of outlook.

He makes no great struggle after originality. The slightness of his themes and of his *genre* relieved him of that

---

[1] See p. 36. [2] See p. 134.

[3] The best of his erotic poems is the pretty vi. 34, but it is far from original; cp. the last couplet:

> nolo quot (sc. basia) arguto dedit exorata Catullo
> Lesbia: pauca cupit qui numerare potest.

necessity.   Some of his prettiest poems are mere variations
on some of the most famous lyrics of Catullus.[1]   He pilfers
whole lines from Ovid.[2]   Phrase after phrase suggests something that has gone before.   But his plagiarism is effected
with such perfect frankness and such perfect art, that it
might well be pardoned, even if Martial had greater claims
to be taken seriously.   As it is, his freedom in borrowing
need scarcely be taken into account in the consideration
of our verdict.   At the worst his crime is no more than petty
larceny.   With all his faults, he has gifts such as few poets
have possessed, a perfect facility and a perfect finish.   Alone
of poets of the period he rarely gives the impression of
labouring a point.   Compared with Martial, Seneca and
Lucan, Statius and Juvenal are, at their worst, stylistic
acrobats.   But Martial, however silly or offensive, however
complicated or prosaic his theme, handles his material with
supreme ease.   His points may often not be worth making ;
they could not be better made.   Moreover, he has a perfect
ear ; his music may be trivial, but within its narrow limits
it is faultless.[3]   He knows what is required of him and he
knows his own powers.   He knows that his range is limited,
that his sphere is comparatively humble, but he is proud to

---

[1] Cp. Cat. 5 and 7 ; Mart. vi. 34 ; Cat. 2 and 3 ; Mart. i. 7 and
109 (it is noteworthy that this last poem has itself been exquisitely
imitated by du Bellay in his poem on his little dog Peloton).

[2] Cp. Ov. *Tr.* ii. 166 ; Mart. vi. 3. 4 ; Ov. *F.* iii. 192 ; Mart. vi. 16. 2 ;
Ov. *A.* i. 1. 20 ; Mart. vi. 16. 4 ; Ov. *Tr.* i. 5. 1, iv. 13. 1 ; Mart. i. 15. 1.
His imitations of other poets are not nearly so marked.   There are a good
many trifling echoes of Vergil, but little wholesale borrowing.   A very
large proportion of the parallel passages cited by Friedländer are unjust
to Martial.   No poet could be original judged by such a test.

[3] There is little of any importance to be said about Martial's metre.
The metres most often employed are elegiac, hendecasyllabic, and the
scazon.   In the elegiac he is, on the whole, Ovidian, though he is naturally
freer, especially in the matter of endings both of hexameter and penta-
meter.   He makes his points as well, but is less sustainedly pointed.
His verse, moreover, has greater variety and less formal symmetry than
that of Ovid.   On the other hand his effects are less sparkling, owing to
his more sparing use of rhetoric.   In the hendecasyllable he is smoother
and more polished.   It invariably opens with a spondee.

excel in it. He has the artist's self-respect without his vanity.

His themes are manifold. He might have said, with even greater truth than Juvenal, ' quidquid agunt homines, nostri est farrago libelli.' He does not go beneath the surface, but almost every aspect of the kaleidoscopic world of Rome receives his attention at one time or another. His attitude is, on the whole, satirical, though his satire is not inspired by deep or sincere indignation. He is too easy in his morals and too good-humoured by temperament. He is often insulting, but there is scarcely a line that breathes fierce resentment, while his almost unparalleled obscenity precludes the intrusion of any genuine earnestness of moral scorn in a very large number of his satiric epigrams. On these points he shall speak for himself ; he makes no exacting claims.

' I hope,' he says in the preface to his first book, ' that I have exercised such restraint in my writings that no one who is possessed of the least self-respect may have cause to complain of them. My jests are never outrageous, even when directed against persons of the meanest consideration. My practice in this respect is very different from that of early writers, who abused persons without veiling their invective under a pseudonym. Nay more, their victims were men of the highest renown. My *jeux d'esprit* have no *arrières-pensées*, and I hope that no one will put an evil interpretation on them, nor rewrite my epigrams by infusing his own malignance into his reading of them. It is a scandalous injustice to exercise such ingenuity on what another has written. I would offer some excuse for the freedom and frankness of my language—which is, after all, the language of epigram—if I were setting any new precedent. But all epigrammatists, Catullus, Marsus, Pedo, Gaetulicus, have availed themselves of this licence of speech. But if any one wishes to acquire notoriety by prudish severity, and refuses to permit me to write after the good Roman fashion in so much as a single page of my work, he may stop short at the preface, or even at the title. Epigrams are written for such

persons as derive pleasure from the games at the Feast of
Flowers. Cato should not enter my theatre, but if he does
enter it, let him be content to look on at the sport which
I provide. I think I shall be justified in closing my preface
with an epigram

To Cato

Once more the merry feast of Flora's come,
With wanton jest to split the sides of Rome;
Yet come you, prince of prudes, to view the show.
Why come you? merely to be shocked and go?'

He reasserts the kindliness of his heart and the excellence
of his intentions elsewhere :

hunc servare modum nostri novere libelli ;   [1]
parcere personis, dicere de vitiis (x. 33).

Malignant critics *had* exercised their ingenuity in the manner
which he deprecated.[1] Worse still, libellous verse had been
falsely circulated as his :

quid prodest, cupiant cum quidam nostra videri   [2]
si qua Lycambeo sanguine tela madent,
vipereumque vomant nostro sub nomine virus
qui Phoebi radios ferre diemque negant? (vii. 12. 5).

In this respect his defence of himself is just. When he
writes in a vein of invective his victim is never mentioned
by name. And we cannot assert in any given case that his
pseudonyms mask a real person. He may do no more than
satirize a vice embodied and typified in an imaginary personality.

---

[1]   For in my verses 'tis my constant care
         To lash the vices, but the persons spare.
                                              HAY.
[2]   But what does't avail,
         If in bloodfetching lines others do rail,
         And vomit viperous poison in my name,
         Such as the sun themselves to own do shame?
                                              ANON., 1695.

---

1 Cp. vii. 72. 12, x. 3.

He is equally concerned to defend himself against the
obvious charges of prurience and immorality :

> innocuos censura potest permittere lusus :   [1]
>   lasciva est nobis pagina, vita proba[1] (i. 4. 7).

This is no real defence, and even though we need not take
Martial at his word, when he accuses himself of the foulest
vices, there is not the slightest reason to suppose that
chastity was one of his virtues.   In Juvenal's case we have
reason to believe that, whatever his weaknesses, he was a
man of genuinely high ideals.   Martial at his best shows
himself a man capable of fine feeling, but he gives no evidence
of moral earnestness or strength of character.   On the other
hand, to give him his due, we must remember the standard
of his age.   Although he is lavish with the vilest obscenities,
and has no scruples about accusing acquaintances of every
variety of unnatural vice, it must be pointed out that such
accusations were regarded at Rome as mere matter for
laughter.   The traditions of the old *Fescennina locutio* survived, and with the decay of private morality its obscenity
increased.   Caesar's veterans could sing ribald verses unre-
buked at their general's triumph, verses unquotably obscene
and casting the foulest aspersions on the character of one
whom they worshipped almost as a god.   Caesar could invite
Catullus to dine in spite of the fact that such accusations
formed the matter of his lampoons.   Catullus could insert
similar charges against the bridegroom for whom he was
writing an *epithalamium*.   The writing of Priapeia was
regarded as a reputable diversion.   Martial's defence of his
obscenities is therefore in all probability sincere, and may
have approved itself to many reputable persons of his day.
It was a defence that had already been made in very similar
language by Ovid and Catullus,[2] and Martial was not the

---

[1]   Let not these harmless sports your censure taste !
My lines are wanton, but my life is chaste.
                              ANON., seventeenth century.

---

[1] Cp. vii. 12. 9, iii. 99. 3.
[2] Catull. xvi. 5 ; Ov. *Tr.* ii. 354 ; Apul. *Apol.* 11 ; Auson. 28, *cento nup.* ;
Plin. *Ep.* vii. 8.

last to make it. But the fact that Martial felt it necessary to defend himself shows that a body of public opinion—even if not large or representative—did exist which refused to condone this fashionable lubricity. Extenuating circumstances may be urged in Martial's defence, but even to have conformed to the standard of his day is sufficient condemnation; and it is hard to resist the suspicion that he fell below it. His obscenities, though couched in the most easy and pointed language, have rarely even the grace—if grace it be—of wit; they are puerile in conception and infinitely disgusting.

It is pleasant to turn to the better side of Martial's character. No writer has ever given more charming expression to his affection for his friends. It is for Decianus and Julius Martialis that he keeps the warmest place in his heart. In poems like the following there is no doubting the sincerity of his feeling or questioning the perfection of its expression:

> si quis erit raros inter numerandus amicos, [1]
> quales prisca fides famaque novit anus,
> si quis Cecropiae madidus Latiaeque Minervae
> artibus et vera simplicitate bonus,
> si quis erit recti custos, mirator honesti,
> et nihil arcano qui roget ore deos,
> si quis erit magnae subnixus robore mentis:
> dispeream si non hic Decianus erit (i. 39).

Even more charming, if less intense, is the exhortation to Julius Martialis to live while he may, ere the long night come that knows no waking:

---

[1]   Is there a man whose friendship rare
       With antique friendship may compare;
       In learning steeped, both old and new,
       Yet unpedantic, simple, true;
       Whose soul, ingenuous and upright,
       Ne'er formed a wish that shunned the light,
       Whose sense is sound? If such there be,
       My Decianus, thou art he.

                          PROFESSOR GOLDWIN SMITH

o mihi post nullos, Iuli, memorande sodales,   [1]
    si quid longa fides canaque iura valent,
bis iam paene tibi consul tricensimus instat,
    et numerat paucos vix tua vita dies.
non bene distuleris videas quae posse negari,
    et solum hoc ducas, quod fuit, esse tuum.
exspectant curaeque catenatique labores :
    gaudia non remanent, sed fugitiva volant.
haec utraque manu complexuque adsere toto :
    saepe fluunt imo sic quoque lapsa sinu.
non est, crede mihi, sapientis dicere ' vivam '.
    sera nimis vita est crastina : vive hodie (i. 15).

Best of all is the retrospect of the long friendship which
has united him to Julius. It is as frank as it is touching :

triginta mihi quattuorque messes   [2]
tecum, si memini, fuere, Iuli.
quarum dulcia mixta sunt amaris
sed iucunda tamen fuere plura ;
et si calculus omnis huc et illuc
diversus bicolorque digeratur,
vincet candida turba nigriorem.

---

[1]   Friend of my heart—and none of all the band
      Has to that name older or better right :
   Julius, thy sixtieth winter is at hand,
      Far-spent is now life's day and near the night.
   Delay not what thou would'st recall too late ;
      That which is past, that only call thine own :
   Cares without end and tribulations wait,
      Joy tarrieth not, but scarcely come, is flown.
   Then grasp it quickly firmly to thy heart,—
      Though firmly grasped, too oft it slips away ;—
   To talk of living is not wisdom's part :
      To-morrow is too late : live thou to-day !
                        PROFESSOR GOLDWIN SMITH.

[2]   My friend, since thou and I first met,
      This is the thirty-fourth December ;
   Some things there are we'd fain forget,
      More that 'tis pleasant to remember.
   Let for each pain a black ball stand,
      For every pleasure past a white one,
   And thou wilt find, when all are scanned,
      The major part will be the bright one.

si vitare voles acerba quaedam
et tristes animi cavere morsus,
nulli te facias nimis sodalem :
gaudebis minus et minus dolebis (xii. 34).[1]

He does not pour the treasure of his heart at his friend's
feet, as Persius does in his burning tribute to Cornutus.
He has no treasure of great price to pour. But it is only
natural that in the poems addressed to his friends we should
find the statement of his ideals of life :

vitam quae faciunt beatiorem,   [1]
iucundissime Martialis, haec sunt :
res non parta labore sed relicta ;
non ingratus ager, focus perennis ;
lis numquam, toga rara, mens quieta ;
vires ingenuae, salubre corpus ;
prudens simplicitas, pares amici,
convictus facilis, sine arte mensa ;
nox non ebria sed soluta curis.

He who would heartache never know,
   He who serene composure treasures,
Must friendship's chequered bliss forego ;
   Who has no pain hath fewer pleasures.
                              PROFESSOR GOLDWIN SMITH.
[1]   What makes a happy life, dear friend,
         If thou would'st briefly learn, attend—
         An income left, not earned by toil ;
         Some acres of a kindly soil ;
         The pot unfailing on the fire ;
         No lawsuits ; seldom town attire ;
         Health ; strength with grace ; a peaceful mind ;
         Shrewdness with honesty combined ;
         Plain living ; equal friends and free ;
         Evenings of temperate gaiety ;

---

[1] We might also quote the beautiful
         extra fortunam est quidquid donatur amicis :
         quas dederis solas semper habebis opes (v. 42).

   What thou hast given to friends, and that alone,
   Defies misfortune, and is still thine own.
                              PROFESSOR GOLDWIN SMITH.
   But the needy poet may have had some *arrière-pensée*. We do not
know to whom the poem is addressed.

> non tristis torus et tamen pudicus ;
> somnus qui faciat breves tenebras :
> quod sis esse velis nihilque malis ;
> summum nec metuas diem nec optes (x 47).

This exquisite echo of the Horatian ' beatus ille qui procul negotiis' sets forth no very lofty ideal. It is frankly, though restrainedly, hedonistic. But it depicts a life that is full of charm and free from evil. Martial, in his heart of hearts, hates the Rome that he depicts so vividly. Rome with its noise, its expense, its bustling snobbery, its triviality, and its vice, where he and his friend Julius waste their days :

> nunc vivit necuter sibi, bonosque   [1]
> soles effugere atque abire sentit,
> qui nobis pereunt et imputantur (v. 20. 11).

He longs to escape from the world of the professional lounger and the parasite to an ampler air, where he can breathe freely and find rest. He is no philosopher, but it is at times a relief to get away from the rarified atmosphere and the sense of strain that permeates so much of the aspirations towards virtue in this strange age of contradictions.

Martial at last found the ease and quiet that his soul desired in his Spanish home :

> hic pigri colimus labore dulci   [2]
> Boterdum Plateamque (Celtiberis
> haec sunt nomina crassiora terris) :
> ingenti fruor inproboque somno

> A wife discreet, yet blythe and bright ;
> Sound slumber, that lends wings to night.
> With all thy heart embrace thy lot,
> Wish not for death and fear it not.
>
> Professor Goldwin Smith.

[1]   Dead to our better selves we see
          The golden hours take flight,
      Still scored against us as they flee.
          Then haste to live aright.
>
> Professor Goldwin Smith.

[2]   Busy but pleas'd and idly taking pains,
      Here Lewes Downs I till and Ringmer plains,
      Names that to each South Saxon well are known,
      Though they sound harsh to powdered beaux in town.

quem nec tertia saepe rumpit hora,
et totum mihi nunc repono quidquid
ter denos vigilaveram per annos.
ignota est toga, şed datur petenti
rupta proxima vestis a cathedra.
surgentem focus excipit superba
vicini strue cultus iliceti,

. . . .

sic me vivere, sic iuvat perire. (xii. 18. 10).

Martial has a genuine love for the country. Born at a
time when detailed descriptions of the charms of scenery
had become fashionable, and the cultivated landscape at
least found many painters, he succeeds far better than any
of his contemporaries in conveying to the reader his sense
of the beauties which his eyes beheld. That sense is limited,
but exquisite. It does not go deep ; there is nothing of the
almost mystical background that Vergil at times suggests ;
there is nothing of the feeling of the open air and the wild
life that is sometimes wafted to us in the sensuous verse of
Theocritus. But Martial sees what he sees clearly, and he
describes it perfectly. Compare his work with the affected
prettiness of Pliny's description of the source of the Clitumnus
or with the more sensuous, but over-elaborate, craftsmanship of Statius in the *Silvae*. Martial is incomparably their
superior. He speaks a more human language, and has a far
clearer vision. Both Statius and Martial described villas
by the sea. We have already mentioned Statius' description of the villa of Pollius at Sorrento ; Martial shall speak
in his turn :

> None can enjoy a sounder sleep than mine ;
> I often do not wake till after nine ;
> And midnight hours with interest repay
> For years in town diversions thrown away.
> Stranger to finery, myself I dress
> In the first coat from an old broken press.
> My fire, as soon as I am up, I see
> Bright with the ruins of some neighbouring tree.
>
> . . . .
> Such is my life, a life of liberty ;
> So would I wish to live and so to die.   HAY.

    o temperatae dulce Formiae litus,   [1]
    vos, cum severi fugit oppidum Martis
    et inquietas fessus exuit curas,
    Apollinaris omnibus locis praefert.

    .   .   .   .

    hic summa leni stringitur Thetis vento :
    nec languet aequor, viva sed quies ponti
    pictam phaselon adiuvante fert aura,
    sicut puellae non amantis aestatem
    mota salubre purpura venit frigus.
    nec saeta longo quaerit in mari praedam,
    sed a cubili lectuloque iactatam
    spectatus alte lineam trahit piscis.

    .   .   .   .

    frui sed istis quando, Roma, permittis ?
    quot Formianos imputat dies annus
    negotiosis rebus urbis haerenti ?
    o ianitores vilicique felices !
    dominis parantur ista, serviunt vobis [1] (x. 30).

These are surely the most beautiful *scazons* [2] in the Latin

---

[1]   O strand of Formiae, sweet with genial air,
        Who art Apollinaris' chosen home
        When, taking flight from his task-mistress Rome,
        The tired man doffs his load of troubling care.

        .   .   .   .   .   .

        Here the sea's bosom quivers in the wind ;
        'Tis no dead calm, but sweet serenity,
        Which bears the painted boat before the breeze,
        As though some maid at pains the heat to ban,
        Should waft a genial zephyr with her fan.
        No fisher needs to buffet the high seas,
        But whiles from bed or couch his line he casts,
        May see his captive in the toils below.

        .   .   .   .   .   .

        But, niggard Rome, thou giv'st how grudgingly !
        What the year's tale of days at Formiae
        For him who tied by work in town must stay ?
        Stewards and lacqueys, happy your employ,
        Your lords prepare enjoyment, you enjoy.
                           A. E. STREET.

---

[1] Cp. the description of the villa of Faustinus, iii. 58.
[2] Their only rival is the famous Sirmio poem of Catullus.

tongue ; the metre limps no more ; a master-hand has
wrought it to exquisite melody ; the quiet undulation of the
sea, the yacht's easy gliding over its surface, live before us
in its music. Even more delicate is the homelier description
of the gardens of Julius Martialis on the slopes of the Janiculum. It is animated by the sincerity that never fails
Martial when he writes to his friend :

> Iuli iugera pauca Martialis　　　　　　　　　　[1]
> hortis Hesperidum beatiora
> longo Ianiculi iugo recumbunt :
> lati collibus imminent recessus
> et planus modico tumore vertex
> caelo perfruitur sereniore
> et curvas nebula tegente valles
> solus luce nitet peculiari :
> puris leniter admoventur astris
> celsae culmina delicata villae.
> hinc septem dominos videre montes
> et totam licet aestimare Romam,
> Albanos quoque Tusculosque colles
> et quodcumque iacet sub urbe frigus (iv. 64).

Such a picture is unsurpassed in any language.[1] Statius,
with all his brilliance, never came near such perfect success;

---

[1]　　　　Martial's few acres, e'en more blest
　　　　　Than those famed gardens of the West,
　　　　　Lie on Janiculum's long crest ;
　　　　　Above the slopes wide reaches hang recessed.
　　　　　The level, gently swelling crown
　　　　　Breathes air from purer heavens blown ;
　　　　　When mists the hollow valleys drown
　　　　　'Tis radiant with a light that's all its own.
　　　　　The clear stars almost seem to lie
　　　　　On the wrought roof that's built so high ;
　　　　　The seven hills stand in majesty,
　　　　　And Rome is summed in one wide sweep of eye.
　　　　　Tusculan, Alban hills unfold,
　　　　　Each nook which holds its store of cold.
　　　　　　　　　　　　　　　　　　　A. E. STREET.

---

[1] Even Tennyson's remarkable poem addressed to F. D. Maurice fails
to reach greater perfection.

he lacks sincerity ; he can juggle with words against any one, but he never learned their truest and noblest use.

There are many other themes beside landscape painting in which the *Silvae* of Statius challenge comparison with the epigrams of Martial. Both use the same servile flattery to the emperor, both celebrate the same patrons,[1] both console their noble friends for the loss of relatives, or favourite slaves; both write *propemptica*. Even in the most trivial of these poems, those addressed to the emperor, Statius is easily surpassed by his humbler rival. His inferiority lies largely in the fact that he is more ambitious. He wrote on a larger scale. When the infinitely trivial is a theme for verse, the epigrammatist has the advantage of the author of the more lengthy *Silvae*. Perfect neatness vanquishes dexterous elaboration. Moreover, if taste can be said to enter into such poems at all, Martial errs less grossly. Even Domitian—one might conjecture—may have felt that Statius' flattery was 'laid on with a trowel'. Martial may have used the same instrument, but had the art to conceal it.[2] There are even occasions where his flattery ceases to revolt the reader, and where we forget the object of the flattery. In a poem describing the suicide of a certain Festus he succeeds in combining the dignity of a funeral *laudatio* with the subtlest and most graceful flattery of the princeps :

> indignas premeret pestis cum tabida fauces,   [1]
>   inque suos voltus serperet atra lues,
> siccis ipse genis flentes hortatus amicos
>   decrevit Stygios Festus adire lacus.

----

[1]   When the dire quinsy choked his guiltless breath,
           And o'er his face the blackening venom stole,
       Festus disdained to wait a lingering death,
           Cheered his sad friends and freed his dauntless soul.

----

[1] e. g. Arruntius Stella and Atedius Melior. Cp. p. 205.
[2] Cp. the poems on the subject of Earinus, Mart. ix. 11, 12, 13, and esp. 16 ; Stat. *Silv.* iii. 4.

> nec tamen obscuro pia polluit ora veneno
> aut torsit lenta tristia fata fame,
> sanctam Romana vitam sed morte peregit
> dimisitque animam nobiliore via.
> hanc mortem fatis magni praeferre Catonis
> fama potest ; huius Caesar amicus erat (i. 78).

The unctuous dexterity of Statius never achieved such a master-stroke.

So, too, in laments for the dead, the superior brevity and simplicity of Martial bear the palm away. Both poets bewailed the death of Glaucias, the child favourite of Atedius Melior. Statius has already been quoted in this connexion; Martial's poems on the subject,[1] though not quite among his best, yet ring truer than the verse of Statius. And Martial's epitaphs and epicedia at their best have in their slight way an almost unique charm. We must go to the best work of the Greek Anthology to surpass the epitaph on Erotion (v. 34) :

> hanc tibi, Fronto pater, genetrix Flaccilla, puellam　　[1]
> oscula commendo deliciasque meas,
> parvola ne nigras horrescat Erotion umbras
> oraque Tartarei prodigiosa canis.
> inpletura fuit sextae modo frigora brumae,
> vixisset totidem ni minus illa dies.

> No meagre famine's slowly-wasting force,
> 　Nor hemlock's gradual chillness he endured,
> But like a Roman chose the nobler course,
> 　And by one blow his liberty secured.
> His death was nobler far than Cato's end,
> For Caesar to the last was Festus' friend.
> 　　　　　　　　　　　　HODGSON (slightly altered).

[1]　Fronto, and you, Flaccilla, to you, my father and mother,
　　Here I commend this child, once my delight and my pet,
So may the darkling shades and deep-mouthed baying of hellhound
　Touch not with horror of dread little Erotion dear.
Now was her sixth year ending, and melting the snows of the winter,
　Only a brief six days lacked to the tale of the years.

---

1 Mart. vi. 28 and 29.

inter tam veteres ludat lasciva patronos
et nomen blaeso garriat ore meum.
mollia non rigidus caespes tegat ossa nec illi,
terra, gravis fueris : non fuit illa tibi.

Another poem on a like theme shows a different and more
fantastic, but scarcely less pleasing vein (v. 37) :

puella senibus dulcior mihi cycnis,   [1]
agna Galaesi mollior Phalantini,
concha Lucrini delicatior stagni,
cui nec lapillos praeferas Erythraeos
nec modo politum pecudis Indicae dentem
nivesque primas liliumque non tactum ;
quae crine vicit Baetici gregis vellus
Rhenique nodos aureamque nitellam ;
fragravit ore quod rosarium Paesti,
quod Atticarum prima mella cerarum,
quod sucinorum rapta de manu gleba ;
cui conparatus indecens erat pavo,

Young, amid dull old age, let her wanton and frolic and gambol,
  Babble of me that was, tenderly lisping my name.
Soft were her tiny bones, then soft be the sod that enshrouds her,
  Gentle thy touch, mother Earth, gently she rested on thee !
A. E. STREET.

[1]   Little maiden sweeter far to me
      Than the swans are with their vaunted snows,
  Maid more tender than the lambkins be
      Where Galaesus by Phalantus flows ;
  Daintier than the daintiest shells that lie
      By the ripples of the Lucrine wave ;
  Choicer than new-polished ivory
      That the herds in Indian jungles gave ;
  Choicer than Erythrae's marbles white,
      Snows new-fallen, lilies yet unsoiled :
  Softer were your tresses and more bright
      Than the locks by German maidens coiled :
  Than the finest fleeces Baetis shows,
      Than the dormouse with her golden hue :
  Lips more fragrant than the Paestan rose,
      Than the Attic bees' first honey-dew,
  Or an amber ball, new-pressed and warm ;
      Paled the peacock's sheen in your compare ;

inamabilis sciurus et frequens phoenix,
adhuc recenti tepet Erotion busto,
quam pessimorum lex amara fatorum
sexta peregit hieme, nec tamen tota,
nostros amores gaudiumque lususque.

Through all the playful affectations of the lines we get the
portrait of a fairy-like child, light-footed as the squirrel,
golden-haired and fair as ivory or lilies.[1] Martial was a
child-lover before he was a man of letters.

Beautiful as these little poems are, there is in Martial
little trace of feeling for the sorrows of humanity in general.
He can feel for his intimate friends, and his tears are ready
to flow for his patron's sorrows. But the general impression
given by his poetry is that of a certain hardness and lack of
feeling, of a limited sympathy, and an unemotional temperament. It is a relief to come upon a poem such as
that in which he describes a father's poignant anguish for
the loss of his son (ix. 74):

effigiem tantum pueri pictura Camoni   [1]
  servat, et infantis parva figura manet.
florentes nulla signavit imagine voltus,
  dum timet ora pius muta videre pater.

or to find a sudden outbreak of sympathy with the sorrows
of the slave (iii. 21):

> E'en the winsome squirrel lost his charm,
>   And the Phoenix seemed no longer rare.
> Scarce Erotion's ashes yet are cold;
>   Greedily grim fate ordained to smite
> E'er her sixth brief winter had grown old—
>   Little love, my bliss, my heart's delight.
>
> A. D. INNES.

> [1]   Here as in happy infancy he smiled
>   Behold Camonus—painted as a child;
>   For on his face as seen in manhood's days
>   His sorrowing father would not dare to gaze.
>
> W. S. B.

---

[1] The remaining lines of the poem are tasteless and unworthy of the
portion quoted, and raise a doubt as to the poet's sincerity in the particular
case. But this does not affect his *general* sympathy for childhood.

proscriptum famulus servavit fronte notata,   [1]
non fuit haec domini vita sed invidia.[1]

Of the *gravitas* or dignity of character specially associated with Rome he shows equally few traces. His outlook on life is not sufficiently serious, he shows little interest in Rome of the past, and has nothing of the retrospective note so prominent in Lucan, Juvenal, or Tacitus; he lives in and for the present. He writes, it is true, of the famous suicide of Arria and Caecina Paetus,[2] of the death of Portia the wife of Brutus,[3] of the bravery of Mucius Scaevola.[4] But in none of these poems does he give us of his best. They lack, if not sincerity, at least enthusiasm; emotion is sacrificed to point. He is out of sympathy with Stoicism, and the suicide doctrinaire does

---

[1]   When scarred with cruel brand, the slave
       Snatched from the murderer's hand
    His proscript lord, not life he gave
       His tyrant, but the brand.

                        PROFESSOR GOLDWIN SMITH.

---

[1] i. 101 provides an instance of Martial's sympathy for his own slaves. Cp. l. 5:—

        ne tamen ad Stygias famulus descenderet umbras,
          ureret implicitum cum scelerata lues,
        cavimus et domini ius omne remisimus aegro ;
          munere dignus erat convaluisse meo.
        sensit deficiens mea praemia meque patronum
          dixit ad infernas liber iturus aquas.

[2] i. 13.   [3] i. 42.

[4] i. 21.   He is perhaps at his best on the death of Otho (vi. 32):

        cum dubitaret adhuc belli civilis Enyo
          forsitan et posset vincere mollis Otho,
        damnavit multo staturum sanguine Martem
          et fodit certa pectora tota manu.
        sit Cato, dum vivit, sane vel Caesare maior :
          dum moritur, numquid maior Othone fuit ?

      When doubtful was the chance of civil war,
      And victory for Otho might declare ;
      That no more Roman blood for him might flow,
      He gave his breast the great decisive blow.
      Caesar's superior you may Cato call :
      Was he so great as Otho in his fall ?   HAY.

not interest him. 'Live while you may' is his motto,
'and make the best of circumstances.' It is possible to
live a reasonably virtuous life without going to the lengths
of Thrasea :

> quod magni Thraseae consummatique Catonis   [1]
>   dogmata sic sequeris salvus ut esse velis,
> pectore nec nudo strictos incurris in enses,
>   quod fecisse velim te, Deciane, facis.
> nolo virum facili redimit qui sanguine famam ;
>   hunc volo, laudari qui sine morte potest (i. 8).

The sentiment is full of common sense, but it is undeniably
unheroic. Martial is not quixotic, and refuses to treat life
more seriously than is necessary. Our complaint against him
is that he scarcely takes it seriously enough. It would be
unjust to demand a deep fund of earnestness from a professed epigrammatist dowered with a gift of humour and a
turn for satire. But it is doing Martial no injustice to style
him the laureate of triviality. For his satire is neither genial
nor earnest. His kindly temper led him to avoid direct
personalities, but his invective is directed against vice, not
primarily because it is wicked, but rather because it is grotesque or not *comme il faut*. His humour, too, though often
sparkling enough, is more often strained and most often
filthy. Many of his epigrams were not worth writing, by
whatever standard they be judged.[1] The point is hard to
illustrate, since a large proportion of his inferior work is
fatuously obscene. But the following may be taken at
random from two books :

---

[1]   That you, like Thrasea or Cato, great,
        Pursue their maxims, but decline their fate ;
        Nor rashly point the dagger to your heart ;
        More to my wish you act a Roman's part.
        I like not him who fame by death retrieves,
        Give me the man who merits praise and lives.   HAY.

---

1 It is to be noted that even in the most worthless of his epigrams he
never loses his sense of style. If childish epigrams are to be given to the
world, they cannot be better written.

> Eutrapelus tonsor dum circuit ora Luperci   [1]
>   expingitque genas, altera barba subit (vii. 83).

> invitas ad aprum, ponis mihi, Gallice, porcum.   [2]
>   hybrida sum, si das, Gallice, verba mihi (viii. 22).

> pars maxillarum tonsa est tibi, pars tibi rasa est,   [3]
>   pars volsa est. unum quis putet esse caput ? (viii. 47).

> tres habuit dentes, pariter quos expuit omnes,   [4]
>   ad tumulum Picens dum sedet ipse suum ;
> collegitque sinu fragmenta novissima laxi
>   oris et adgesta contumulavit humo.
> ossa licet quondam defuncti non legat heres :
>   hoc sibi iam Picens praestitit officium (viii. 57).

> summa Palatini poteras aequare Colossi,   [5]
>   si fieres brevior, Claudia, sesquipede (viii. 60).

Without wishing to break a butterfly on the wheel, we may
well quote against Martial the remark made in a different
context to a worthless poet :

> tanti non erat esse te disertum (xii. 43).   [6]

There is much also which, without being precisely pointless
or silly, is too petty and mean to be tolerable to modern
taste. Most noticeable in this respect are the epigrams in
which Martial solicits the liberality of his patrons. The
amazing relations existing at this period between patron
and client had worked a painful revolution in the manners
and tone of society, a revolution which meant scarcely less

---

[1]   Eutrapelus the barber works so slow,
          That while he shaves, the beard anew does grow.
                               ANON., 1695.

[2] You invite me to partake of a wild boar, you set before me a
home-grown pig. I'm half-boar, half-pig, if you can cheat me thus.

[3] Part of your jaws is shaven, part clipped, part has the hair pulled
out. Who'd think you'd only one head ?

[4] Picens had three teeth, which he spat out altogether while he was
sitting at the spot he had chosen for his tomb. He gathered in his robe the
last fragments of his loose jaw and interred them in a heap of earth. His
heir need not gather his bones when he is dead, Picens has performed
that office for himself.

[5] Had you been eighteen inches shorter, Claudia, you would have
been as tall as the Colossus on the Palatine.

[6]   'Twas scarce worth while to be thus eloquent.

than the pauperization of the middle class. The old sacred and almost feudal tie uniting client and patron had long since disappeared, and had been replaced by relations of a professional and commercial character. Wealth was concentrated in comparatively few hands, and with the decrease of the number of the patrons the throng of clients proportionately increased. The crowd of clients bustling to the early morning *salutatio* of the patronus, and struggling with one another for the *sportula* is familiar to us in the pages of Juvenal and receives fresh and equally vivid illustration from Martial. The worst results of these unnatural relations were a general loss of independence of character and a lamentable growth of bad manners and cynical snobbery. The patron, owing to the increasingly heavy demands upon his purse, naturally tended to become close-fisted and stingy, the needy client too often was grasping and discontented. The patron, if he asked his client to dine, would regale him with food and drink of a coarser and inferior quality to that with which he himself was served.[1] The client, on the other hand, could not be trusted to behave himself ; he would steal the table fittings, make outrageous demands on his patron, and employ every act of servile and cringing flattery to improve his position.[2] The poor poet was in a sense doubly dependent. He would stand in the ordinary relation of *cliens* to a *patronus*, and would be dependent also for his livelihood on the generosity of his literary patrons. For, in spite of the comparative facilities for the publication and circulation of books, he could make little by the public sale of his works, and living at Rome was abnormally expensive. The worst feature of all was that such a life of servile dependence was not clearly felt to be degrading. It was disliked for its hardship, annoyance, and monotony, but the client too often seems to have regarded it as beneath his dignity to attempt to escape from it by industry and manly independence.

---

[1] Cp. Juv. 5 ; Mart. iii. 60, vi. 11, x. 49 ; Plin. *Ep.* ii. 6.
[2] v. 18. 6.

As a result of these conditions, we find the pages of Martial full of allusions to the miserable life of the client. His skill does not fail him, but the theme is ugly and the historical interest necessarily predominates over the literary, though the reader's patience is at times rewarded with shrewd observations on human nature, as, for instance, the bitter expression of the truth that ' To him that hath shall be given '—

semper pauper eris, si pauper es, Aemiliane;   [1]
dantur opes nullis nunc nisi divitibus (v. 81);

or the even more incisive

pauper videri Cinna vult : et est pauper (viii. 19).

But we soon weary of the continual reference to dinners and parasites, to the snobbery and indifference of the rich, to the tricks of toadyism on the part of needy client or legacy hunter. It is a mean world, and the wit and raillery of Martial cannot make it palatable. Without a moral background, such as is provided by the indignation of Juvenal, the picture soon palls, and the reader sickens. Most unpleasing of all are the epigrams where Martial himself speaks as client in a language of mingled impertinence and servility. His flattery of the emperor we may pass by. It was no doubt interested, but it was universal, and Martial's flattery is more dexterous without being either more or less offensive than that of his contemporaries. His relations towards less exalted patrons cannot be thus easily condoned. He feels no shame in begging, nor in abusing those who will not give or whose gifts are not sufficient for his needs. His purse is empty; he must sell the gifts that Regulus has given him. Will Regulus buy ?

aera domi non sunt, superest hoc, Regule, solum   [2]
ut tua vendamus munera : numquid emis ? (vii. 16).

---

[1]   Poor once and poor for ever, Nat, I fear,
      None but the rich get place and pension here.
                          N. B. HALHEAD.
[2] I have no money, Regulus, at home. Only one thing is left to do—
sell the gifts you gave me. Will you buy ?

Stella has given him some tiles to roof his house ; he would like a cloak as well :

> cum pluvias madidumque Iovem perferre negaret   [1]
>   et rudis hibernis villa nataret aquis,
> plurima, quae posset subitos effundere nimbos,
>   muneribus venit tegula missa tuis.
> horridus ecce sonat Boreae stridore December :
>   Stella, tegis villam, non tegis agricolam (vii. 36).[1]

This is not the way a gentleman thanks a friend, nor can modern taste appreciate at its antique value abuse such as—

> primum est ut praestes, si quid te, Cinna, rogabo ;   [2]
>   illud deinde sequens ut cito, Cinna, neges.
> diligo praestantem ; non odi, Cinna, negantem :
>   sed tu nec praestas nec cito, Cinna, negas (vii. 43).

The poet's poverty is no real excuse for this petulant mendicancy.[2] He had refused to adopt a profession,[3] though professional employment would assuredly have left him time for writing, and no one would have complained if his output had been somewhat smaller. Instead, he chose a life which involved moving in society, and was necessarily expensive. We can hardly attribute his choice merely to the love of his

---

[1]   When my crased house heaven's showers could not sustain,
      But flooded with vast deluges of rain,
      Thou shingles, Stella, seasonably didst send,
      Which from the impetuous storms did me defend :
      Now fierce loud-sounding Boreas rocks doth cleave,
      Dost clothe the farm, and farmer naked leave ?

ANON., 1695.

[2]   The kindest thing of all is to comply :
      The next kind thing is quickly to deny.
      I love performance nor denial hate :
      Your ' Shall I, shall I ? ' is the cursed state.

---

[1] This is doubly offensive if addressed to the poor Cinna of viii. 19. Cp. the similar vii. 53, or the yet more offensive viii. 33 and v. 36.

[2] More excusable are poems such as x. 57, where he attacks one Gaius, an old friend (cp. ii. 30), for failing to fulfil his promise, or the exceedingly pointed poem (iv. 40) where he reproaches Postumus, an old friend, for forgetting him. Cp. also v. 52.

[3] See p. 252.

art. If he must beg, he might have done so with better
taste and some show of finer feeling. Macaulay's criticism
is just : ' I can make large allowance for the difference of
manners ; but it can never have been *comme il faut* in any
age or nation for a man of note—an accomplished man—a
man living with the great—to be constantly asking for
money, clothes, and dainties, and to pursue with volleys of
abuse those who would give him nothing.'

In spite, however, of the obscenity, meanness, and exaggerated triviality of much of his work, there have been few
poets who could turn a prettier compliment, make a neater
jest, or enshrine the trivial in a more exquisite setting. Take
the beautifully finished poem to Flaccus in the eighth book
(56), wherein Martial complains that times have altered since
Vergil's day. ' Now there are no patrons and consequently
no poets '—

> ergo ego Vergilius, si munera Maecenatis   [1]
>   des mihi ? Vergilius non ero, Marsus ero.

Here, at least, Martial shows that he could complain of his
poverty with decency, and speak of himself and his work
with becoming modesty. Or take a poem of a different type,
an indirect plea for the recall of an exile (viii. 32) :

> aera per tacitum delapsa sedentis in ipsos   [2]
>   fluxit Aratullae blanda columba sinus.
> luserat hoc casus, nisi inobservata maneret
>   permissaque sibi nollet abire fuga.
> si meliora piae fas est sperare sorori
>   et dominum mundi flectere vota valent,
> haec a Sardois tibi forsitan exulis oris,
>   fratre reversuro, nuntia venit avis.

---

[1] Shall I then be a Vergil, if you give me such gifts as Maecenas
gave ? No, I shall not be a Vergil, but a Marsus.

[2] A gentle dove glided down through the silent air and settled even in
Aratulla's bosom as she was sitting. This might have seemed but the sport
of chance had it not rested there, though undetained, and refused to
part even when flight was free. If it is granted to the loving sister to hope
for better things, and if prayers can move the lord of the world, this bird
perchance has come to thee from Sardinia's shore of exile to announce
the speedy return of thy brother.

Nothing could be more conventional, nothing more perfect
in form, more full of music, more delicate in expression.
The same felicity is shown in his epigrams on curiosities
of art or nature, a fashionable and, it must be confessed,
an easy theme.¹   Fish carved by Phidias' hand, a lizard
cast by Mentor, a fly enclosed in amber, are all given
immortality :

> artis Phidiacae toreuma clarum   [1]
> pisces aspicis : adde aquam, natabunt (iii. 35).
>
> inserta phialae Mentoris manu ducta   [2]
> lacerta vivit et timetur argentum (iii. 41).
>
> et latet et lucet Phaethontide condita gutta,   [3]
>   ut videatur apis nectare clusa suo.
> dignum tantorum pretium tulit illa laborum :
>   credibile est ipsam sic voluisse mori (iv. 32).

Always at home in describing the trifling amenities of life,
he is at his best equally successful in dealing with its trifling
follies.   An acquaintance has given his cook the absurd
name of Mistyllos in allusion to the Homeric phrase μίστυλλόν
τ' ἄρα τἆλλα.   Martial's comment is inimitable :

> si tibi Mistyllos cocus, Aemiliane, vocatur,
>   dicatur quare non Taratalla mihi ? (i. 50).

He complains of the wine given him at a dinner-party with
a finished whimsicality :

---

[1]   These fishes Phidias wrought : with life by him
        They are endowed : add water and they swim.
                              PROFESSOR GOLDWIN SMITH.
[2]   That lizard on the goblet makes thee start.
        Fear not : it lives only by Mentor's art.
                              PROFESSOR GOLDWIN SMITH.
[3]   Here shines a bee closed in an amber tomb,
        As if interred in her own honey-comb.
        A fit reward fate to her labours gave ;
        No other death would she have wished to have.   MAY.

---

¹ Cp. the elaborate and long-winded poem of Statius on a statuette of
Hercules (*Silv.* iv. 6) with Martial on the same subject, ix. 43 and 44.

potavi modo consulare vinum.   [1]
quaeris quam vetus atque liberale ?
Prisco consule conditum : sed ipse
qui ponebat erat, Severe, consul (vii. 79).

Polycharmus has returned Caietanus his IOU's. ' Little
good will that do you, and Caietanus will not even be
grateful ' :

quod Caietano reddis, Polycharme, tabellas,   [2]
    milia te centum num tribuisse putas ?
' debuit haec ' inquis. tibi habe, Polycharme, tabellas
et Caietano milia crede duo (viii. 37).

Chloe, the murderess of her seven husbands, erects monu-
ments to their memory, and inscribes *fecit Chloe* on the
tombstones :

inscripsit tumulis septem scelerata virorum   [3]
    ' se fecisse ' Chloe. quid pote simplicius ? (ix. 15).

Vacerra admires the old poets only. What shall Martial
do ?
miraris veteres, Vacerra, solos   [4]
nec laudas nisi mortuos poetas.
ignoscas petimus, Vacerra : tanti
non est, ut placeam tibi, perire (viii. 69).

All this is very slight, *merae nugae* ; but even if the
humour be not of the first water, it will compare well with
the humour of epigrams of any age. Martial knows he is
not a great poet.[1]   He knows, too, that his work is uneven :

---

[1] I have just drunk some consular wine. How old, you ask, and
how generous ? It was bottled in Priscus' consulship : and he who set it
before me was the consul himself.

[2] In giving back Caietanus his IOU's, Polycharmus, do you think you
are giving him 100,000 sesterces ? ' He owed me that sum,' you say.
Keep the IOU's and lend him two thousand more !

[3] On her seven husbands' tombs she doth impress
    ' This Chloe did.' What more can she confess ?   WRIGHT.

[4] Vacerra lauds no living poet's lays,
    But for departed genius keeps his praise.
    I, alas, live, nor deem it worth my while
    To die that I may win Vacerra's smile.
                                        PROFESSOR GOLDWIN SMITH.

---

[1] Cp. viii. 3 and 56.

> iactat inaequalem Matho me fecisse libellum :   [1]
>   si verum est, laudat carmina nostra Matho.
> aequales scribit libros Calvinus et Vmber :
>   aequalis liber est, Cretice, qui malus est (vii. 90).

If there are thirty good epigrams in a book, he is satisfied
(vii. 81). His defence hardly answers the question, ' Why
publish so many ? ' but should at least mollify our judgement. Few poets read better in selections than Martial,
and of few poets does selection give so inadequate an idea.
For few poets of his undoubted genius have left such a large
bulk of work which, in spite of its formal perfection, is
morally repulsive or, from the purely literary standpoint,
uninteresting. But he is an important figure in the history
of literature, for he is the father of the modern epigram.
Alone of Silver Latin poets is he a perfect stylist. He has
the gift of *felicitas* to the full, but it is not *curiosa*. Inferior
to Horace in all other points, he has greater spontaneity.
And he is free from the faults of his age. He is no *virtuoso*,
eaten up with self-conscious vanity ; he attempts no impossible feats of language; he is clear, and uses his mythological
and geographical knowledge neatly and picturesquely ; but
he makes no display of obscure learning. ' I would please
schoolmasters,' he says, ' but not *qua* schoolmasters ' (x.
21. 5). So, too, he complains of his own education :

> at me litterulas stulti docuere parentes :   [2]
>   quid cum grammaticis rhetoribusque mihi ? (ix. 73. 7).

As a result, perhaps, of this lack of sympathy with the
education of his day, we find that, while he knows and
admires the great poets of the past, and can flatter the rich
poetasters of the present, his bent is curiously unliterary.
He gives us practically no literary criticism. It is with the
surface qualities of life that he is concerned, with its pleasures

---

[1] Matho makes game of my unequal verse ;
     If it 's unequal it might well be worse.
     Calvinus, Umber, write on one dead level,
     The book that 's got no up and down 's the devil !
[2] My learning only proves my father fool !
     Why would he send me to a grammar school ?   HAY.

and its follies, guilty or innocent. He has a marvellously
quick and clear power of observation, and of vivid presentation. He is in this sense above all others the poet of his
age. He either does not see or chooses to ignore many of the
best and most interesting features of his time, but the
picture which he presents, for all its incompleteness, is wider
and more varied than any other. We both hate him and
read him for the sake of the world he depicts. ' Ugliness is
always bad art, and Martial often failed as a poet from his
choice of subject.' [1] There are comparatively few of his
poems which we read for their own sake. Remarkable as
these few poems are, the main attraction of Martial is to be
found not in his wit or finish, so much as in the vividness with
which he has portrayed the life of the brilliant yet corrupt
society in which his lot was cast. It lives before us in all
its splendour and in all its squalor. The court, with its
atmosphere of grovelling flattery, its gross vices veiled and
tricked out in the garb of respectability; the wealthy
official class, with their villas, their favourites, their circle of
dependants, men of culture, wit, and urbanity, through all
which runs, strangely intermingled, a vein of extreme coarseness, vulgarity, and meanness; the lounger and the reciter,
the diner-out and the legacy-hunter; the clients struggling
to win their patrons' favour and to rise in the social scale,
enduring the hardships and discomfort of a sordid life un-
illumined by lofty ideals or strength of will, a life that under
cold northern skies would have been intolerable; the freedman and the slave, with all the riff-raff that support a para-
sitic existence on the vices of the upper classes; the noise and
bustle of Rome, its sleepless nights, its cheerless tenements,
its noisy streets, loud with the sound of traffic or of revelry;
the shows in the theatre, the races in the circus, the inter-
change of presents at the Saturnalia; the pleasant life in
the country villa, the simplicity of rural Italy, the sights and
sounds of the park and the farm-yard; and dimly seen
beyond all, the provinces, a great ocean which absorbs from

---

[1] Bridge and Lake, Introd., *Select Epigrams of Martial.*

time to time the rulers of Rome and the leaders of society, and from which come faint and confused echoes of frontier wars ; all are there. It is a great pageant lacking order and coherence, a scene that shifts continually, but never lacks brilliance of detail and sharply defined presentment. Martial was the child of the age ; it gave him his strength and his weakness. If we hate him or despise him, it is because he is the faithful representative of the life of his times ; his gifts we cannot question. He practised a form of poetry that at its best is not exalted, and must, even more than other branches of art, be conditioned by social circumstance. Within its limited sphere Martial stands, not faultless, but yet supreme.

CHAPTER XII

JUVENAL

OUR knowledge of the life of the most famous of Roman satirists is strangely unsatisfactory. Many so-called lives of Juvenal have come down to us, but they are confused, contradictory, inadequate, and unreliable.[1] His own work and allusions in other writers help us but little in our attempt to reconstruct the story of the poet's life.

Only by investigating the dates within which the satires seem to fall is it possible to arrive at some idea of the dates within which falls the life of their author. The satires were published in five books at different times. The first book (1-5), which is full of allusions to the tyranny of Domitian, cannot have been published before 100 A.D., since the first satire contains an allusion to the condemnation of Marius Priscus,[2] which took place in that year. The fifth book (13-16) must, from references in the thirteenth and fifteenth[3] satires to the year 127, have been published not much later than that date. The publication of the satires falls, therefore, between 100 and 130.

With these data it is possible to approach the question of the dates of Juvenal's birth and death. The main facts to guide us are the statements of the best of the biographies that he did not begin to write satire till on the confines of middle age, that even then he delayed to publish, and that he died at the age of eighty.[4] The inference is that he was

---

[1] The ancient biographies of the poet all descend from the same source : their variations spring largely from questionable or absurd interpretations of passages in the satires themselves. The best of them, if not their actual source, is the life found at the end of the codex Pithoeanus, the best of the MSS. of Juvenal. It was in all probability written by the author of the scholia Pithoeana—to whom Valla, on the authority of a MS. now lost, gave the name of Probus—and dates from the fourth or fifth century.

[2] L. 41. Cp. Plin. *Ep.* ii. 11.

[3] xiii. 17 ' sexaginta annos Fonteio consule natus '. xv. 27 ' nuper consule Iunco '.

[4] *Vita* 1 (O. Jahn ed.): 1a (Dürr, *Das Leben Juvenals*). A life contained

born between 50 and 60 A. D., and died between 130 and
140 A. D.[1]

As to the facts of his life we are on little firmer ground.
But concerning his name and birthplace there is practical
certainty. Decimus Junius Juvenalis [2] was born at Aquinum,[3] a town of Latium, and is said to have been the son or
adopted son of a rich freedman. His education was of the
usual character, literary and rhetorical, and was presumably
carried out at Rome.[4] He acquired thus early in youth a
taste for rhetoric that never left him. For he is said to
have practised declamation up till middle age, not with a
view to obtaining a position as professor of rhetoric or as
advocate, but from sheer love of the art.[5] It is probable that
he combined his passion for rhetoric with service as an
officer in the army. Not only does he show considerable
intimacy in his satires with a soldier's life,[6] but interesting
external evidence is afforded by an inscription discovered
near Aquinum. It runs :

> CERERI . SACRVM
> D. IVNIVS . IVVENALIS
> TRIB . COH . I . DELMATARVM
> II . VIR . QVINQ . FLAMEN
> DIVI . VESPASIANI
> VOVIT . DEDICAVITQVE
> SVA   PEC.[7]

in Cod. Barberin. viii. 18 (fifteenth century), says *Iunius Iuvenalis Aquinas
Iunio Iuvenale patre, matre vero Septumuleia ex Aquinati municipio, Claudio
Nerone et L. Antistio consulibus* (55 A. D.) *natus est ; sororem habuit Septu-
muleiam, quae Fuscino nupsit.* This may be mere invention on the part
of a humanist of the fifteenth century. The life contains many improba-
bilities and the MS. is of suspiciously late date. But see Dürr, p. 28.

[1] *Vitae* 2 and 3 'oriundus temporis Neronis Claudii imperatoris'.
Vit. 4 'decessit sub Antonino Pio '.

[2] So Cod. Paris. 9345; Vossian. 18 and 64; Bodl. (Canon Lat. 41);
Schol. Pith. ad *vit.* 1.

[3] So all ancient biographies except 1. In *Sat.* iii, Umbricius,
addressing Juvenal, speaks of *tuum Aquinum*: cp. also the inscription
found near Aquinum and quoted later.

[4] This is only conjecture, but the son of a rich citizen of Aquinum
would naturally be sent to Rome for his education. For his rhetorical
education cp. i. 15–17.   [5] *Vita* 1.

[6] Cp. especially the whole of xvi ; also i. 58, ii. 165, iii. 132, vii. 92,
xiv. 193–7.   [7] *C. I. L.* x. 5382.

If this inscription refers, as well it may, to the poet, it will
follow that he served as tribune of the first Dalmatian cohort,
probably in Britain,[1] held high municipal office in his native
town, and was priest of the deified Vespasian. But the
praenomen is wanting in the original, and the inscription
may have been erected not by the satirist but by one of his
kinsfolk. That he spent the greater portion of his life at
Rome is evident from his satires. Of his friends we know
little. Umbricius, Persicus, Catullus, and Calvinus[2] are
mere names. Of Quintilian[3] he speaks with great respect,
and may perhaps have studied under him ; of Statius he
writes with enthusiasm, but there is no evidence that he had
done more than be present at that poet's recitations.[4] Martial, however, was a personal friend, and writes affectionately
of him and to him in three of his epigrams.[5] Unlike Martial,
whose life was a continual struggle against poverty, Juvenal,
though he had clearly endured some of the discomforts and
degradations involved by a client's attendance on his rich
patronus, was a man of some means, possessing an estate at
Aquinum,[6] a country house at Tibur,[7] and a house at Rome.[8]
At what date precisely he began to write is uncertain. We
are told that his first effort was a brief poem attacking the
actor Paris, which he afterwards embodied in the seventh
satire. But it was long before he ventured to read his satires
even to his intimate friends.[9] This suggests that portions,
at any rate, of the satires of the first book were composed
during the reign of Domitian.[10] Juvenal had certainly
every reason for concealing their existence till after the
tyrant's death. The first satire was probably written later
to form a preface to the other four, and the whole book may
have been published in 101. It is noteworthy, however,
that Martial, writing to him in that year, mentions merely

---

[1] *C. I. L.* vii, p. 85 ; Hübner, *Rhein. Mus.* xi (1857), p. 30 ; *Hermes*,
xvi (1881), p. 566.

[2] Satt. 3, 11, 12, 13. Trebius in 5 is perhaps an imaginary character.

[3] vi. 75, 280, vii. 186.   [4] vii. 82.   [5] Mart. vii. 24, 91, xii. 18.

[6] vi. 57.   [7] xi. 65.   [8] xi. 190, xii. 87.   [9] *Vita* 1.

[10] There are, however, allusions to Domitian as dead in ii. 29–33, iv. 153.

his gifts as a declaimer, and seems not to know him as a satirist. The second book, containing only the sixth satire, was probably published about 116, since it contains allusions to earthquakes in Asia and to a comet boding ill to Parthia and Armenia (ll. 407–12). Such a comet was visible in Rome in the autumn of 115, on the eve of Trajan's campaign against Parthia, while in December an earthquake did great damage to the town of Antioch. The third book (7–9) opens with an elaborate compliment to Hadrian as the patron of literature at Rome. As Hadrian succeeded to the principate in 117 and left Rome for a tour of the provinces in 121, this book must fall somewhere between our dates. The fourth book (10–12) contains no indication as to its date, but must lie between the publication of the third book and of the fifth (after 127). Beyond these facts it is hardly possible to go in our reconstruction of the poet's life. As far as may be judged it was an uneventful career save for one great calamity. The ancient biographies assert that Juvenal's denuncia-tion of actors embodied in the seventh satire offended an actor who was the favourite of the princeps. They are sup-ported by Apollinaris Sidonius,[1] who speaks of Juvenal as the ' exile-victim of an actor's anger ', and by Johannes Malala.[2] The latter writer, with certain of the ancient biographies, identifies the actor with Paris, the favourite of Domitian; others, again, say that the poet was banished by Nero [3]—a manifestly absurd statement—others by Trajan,[4] while our best authority asserts that he was eighty years old when banished, and that he died of grief and mortification.[5] The place of exile is variously given. Most of the biographies place it in Egypt, the best of them asserting that he was given a military command in that province.[5] Others mention Britain,[6] others the Pentapolis of Libya.[7] Amid such dis-

---

[1] Ap. Sid. ix. 269.

[2] Joh. Mal. *Chron.* x, p. 341, *Chilm.*

[3] *Vita* 7. Schol. ad vii. 92.   [4] *Vita* 6.

[5] *Vitae* 1, 2, 4, 7. Perhaps an inference from *Sat.* xv. 45.

[6] *Vitae* 5 and 6. If the inscription (see p. 288) refers to the poet, this view has further support.   [7] Joh. Mal., loc. cit.

crepancies it is impossible to give any certain answer. But
it is certain that the actor who caused Juvenal's banishment
was not Paris, who was put to death by Domitian as early
as 83, and almost equally certain that Domitian is guiltless
of the poet's exile. It is, however, possible that he was
banished by Trajan or Hadrian, though it would surprise us
to find Trajan, for all the debauchery of his private life, so
far under the influence of an actor [1] as to sacrifice a Roman
citizen to his displeasure ; while as regards Hadrian it is
noteworthy that the very satire said to have offended the
pantomimus contains an eloquent panegyric of that emperor.
Further, it is hard to believe the story that Juvenal was
banished to Egypt at the advanced age of eighty under the
pretext of a military command.   The problem is insoluble.[2]
The most that can be said is that the persistence of the
tradition gives it some claim to credibility, though the details
handed down to us are wholly untrustworthy, and probably
little better than clumsy inferences from passages in the
satires.

The scope of Juvenal's work and the motives that spur
him are set forth in the first satire. He is weary of the
deluge of trivial and mechanical verse poured out by the
myriad poetasters of the day :

> Still shall I hear and never quit the score,
> Stunned with hoarse Codrus' Theseid, o'er and o'er ?
> Shall this man's elegies and t'other's play
> Unpunished murder a long summer's day ?
> . . . since the world with writing is possest,
> I'll versify in spite ; and do my best
> To make as much waste-paper as the rest.[3]

---

[1] Trajan had, however, a favourite in the *pantomimus* Pylades. Dio.
Cass. lxviii. 10.

[2] The simplest suggestion is that Juvenal was at some time banished,
that the reason for his banishment was forgotten and supplied by conjecture. Cp. Friedländer's ed., p. 44.   There is no real evidence to prove
that Juvenal was ever in Egypt or Britain.   His topography in *Sat.* xv is
faulty, and allusion to the oysters of Richborough (*ostrea Rutupina*, iv. 141)
would be possible even in a poet who had never visited Britain.

[3] i. 1–3, 17, 18 (Dryden's translation).

He will write in a different vein from his rivals. Satire
shall be his theme. In such an age, when virtue is praised
and vice practised, the age of the libertine, the *parvenu*,
the forger, the murderer, it is hard not to write satire.
'Facit indignatio versum!'[1] he cries. 'All the daily life of
Rome shall be my theme':

> quidquid agunt homines votum timor ira voluptas   [1]
> gaudia discursus nostri est farrago libelli.[2]

Never was vice so rampant; luxury has become monstrous;
the rich lord lives in pampered and selfish ease, while those
poor mortals, his clients, jostle together to receive the paltry
dole of the *sportula* ; that is all the help they will get from
their patron :

> No age can go beyond us ; future times
> Can add no further to the present crimes.
> Our sons but the same things can wish and do ;
> Vice is at stand and at the highest flow.
> Then, Satire, spread thy sails, take all the winds that blow.[3]

And yet the satirist must be cautious ; the days are past
when a Lucilius could lash Rome at his will :

> When Lucilius brandishes his pen
> And flashes in the face of guilty men,
> A cold sweat stands in drops on every part,
> And rage succeeds to tears, revenge to smart.
> Muse, be advised ; 'tis past considering time,
> When entered once the dangerous lists of rhyme :
> Since none the living villains dare implead,
> Arraign them in the persons of the dead.[4]

No better preface has ever been written ; it gives a perfect
summary of the motives, the objects, and the methods of the
poet's work in language which for vigour and brilliance he

---

[1] What human kind desires and what they shun,
Rage, passion, pleasure, impotence of will,
Shall this satirical collection fill.   DRYDEN.

---

[1] i. 79.   [2] Ib. 85.
[3] Ib. 147–50.   [4] i. 165–71.

never surpassed. The closing lines show us his literary parentage. It is Lucilius who inspires him; it is the fierce invective of the father of Roman satire that appeals to him. Lucilius had scourged Rome, when the inroads of Hellenism and oriental luxury, the fruits of foreign conquest, were beginning to make themselves felt. To Juvenal it falls to denounce the triumph of these corroding influences. He has nothing of the almost pathetic philosophic detachment of Persius, nor of the easy-going compromise of Horace. He does not palter with problems of right and wrong, nor hesitate over his moral judgements ; casuistry is wholly alien to his temper. It is indignation makes the verse, and from this fact, together with his rhetorical training, his chief merits and his chief failings spring. He introduces no novelty into satire save the almost unvarying bitterness and ferocity of his tone. Like Horace and Persius, he employs the dactylic hexameter to the exclusion of other metres, while, owing in the main to his taste for declamation, he is far more sparing in the use of the dialogue-form than either of his predecessors.

Before further discussing his general characteristics, it is necessary to take a brief survey of the remaining satires. The second and ninth are savage and, as was almost inevitable, obscene denunciations of unnatural vice. In the third, the most orderly in arrangement and the most brilliant in execution of all his satires, he describes all the dangers and horrors of life at Rome. Umbricius, a friend of the poet, is leaving the city. It is no place for a man of honour ; it has become a city for Greeks ; the worthless and astute *Graeculus* is everywhere predominant, and, stained though he be with a thousand vices, has outwitted the native-born, and, by the arts of the panderer and the flatterer, has made himself their master. The poor are treated like slaves. Houses fall, or are burned with fire. Sleep is impossible, so loud with traffic are the streets. By day it is scarcely safe to walk abroad for fear of being crushed by one of the great drays that throng the city ; by night there are the lesser perils of slops and broken crockery cast from the windows, the greater perils of roisterers and thieves. Rome is no place for Umbricius. He must go.

The fourth satire opens with a violent attack on the *parvenu* Egyptian Crispinus, so powerful at the court of Domitian, and goes on by a somewhat clumsy transition to tell the story of the huge turbot caught near Ancona and presented to the emperor. So large was it that a cabinet council must needs be called to decide what should be done with it. This affords excuse for an inimitable picture of Domitian's servile councillors. At last it is decided that the turbot is to be served whole and a special dish to be constructed for it. 'Ah! why,' the poet concludes, 'did not Domitian devote himself entirely to such trifles as these ? '

In the fifth satire Juvenal returns to the subject of the hardships and insults which the poor client must endure. He pictures the host sitting in state with the best of everything set before him and served in the choicest manner, while the unhappy client must be content with food and drink of the coarsest kind. Virro, the rich man, does this not because he is parsimonious, but because the humiliation of his client amuses his perverted mind. But the satirist does not spare the client, whose servile complaisance leads him to put up with such treatment. ' Be a man ! ' he cries, ' and sooner beg on the streets than degrade yourself thus.'

The sixth satire, the longest of the collection, is a savage denunciation of the vices of womankind. The various types of female degradation are revealed to our gaze with merciless and often revolting portrayal. The unchastity of woman is the main theme, but ranked with the adulteress and the wanton are the murderess of husband or of child, the torturer of the slave, the client of the fortune-teller or the astrologer, and even the more harmless female athlete and blue-stocking. For vigour and skill the satire ranks among Juvenal's best, but it is marred by wanton grossness and at times almost absurd exaggeration.

The seventh satire deals with the difficulties besetting a literary career. It opens with a dexterous compliment to Hadrian ; the poet qualifies his complaints by saying that

they apply only to the past. The accession of Hadrian has
swept all the storm-clouds from the author's sky. But in
the unhappy days but lately passed away, the poet's lot was
most miserable. His work brings him no livelihood ; his
patron's liberality goes but a little way. The historian is in
no less parlous plight. The advocate makes some show of
wealth, but it is, as a rule, the merest show ; only the man
already wealthy succeeds at the bar ; many a struggling
lawyer goes bankrupt in the struggle to advertise himself
and push his way. The teacher of rhetoric and the schoolmaster receive but a miserable fee, yet they have all the
drudgery of discipline and all the responsibility of moulding
the characters of the young placed upon their shoulders.
They are expected to be omniscient, and yet they starve.

The eighth satire treats the familiar theme that without
virtue birth is of small account. Many examples of the
degeneracy of the aristocracy are given, some trivial, some
grave, but above all the satirist denounces the cruelty and
oppression of nobly-born provincial governors. He concludes in his noblest vein in praise of the great plebeians of
the past, Cicero, Marius, the Decii, and Servius Tullius. It
is in deeds, not in titles, that true nobility lies. Better
be the son of Thersites and possess the valour of Achilles,
than live the life of a Thersites and boast Achilles for
your sire.

The eighth satire may be regarded as the presage of a
distinct change of type. Instead of the vivid pictures of
Roman life and the almost dramatic representation of vice
personified, Juvenal seems to turn for inspiration to the
scholastic declamation which had fascinated his youth.
Moral problems are treated in a more abstract way, and
the old fierce onset of indignation, though it has by no
means disappeared, seems to have lost something of its
former violence. There are also traces of declining powers,
a greater tendency to digression, a lack of concentration
and vigour, and even of dexterity of language. But the
change is due in all probability not merely to advance in
years nor to the calming and mellowing influence of old age.

but also to a change that was gradually passing over the
Roman world. The material for savage satire was appreciably less. Evil in its worst forms had triumphed under
Domitian. With Nerva, Trajan, and Hadrian virtue began
slowly and uncertainly to reclaim part of her lost dominions.

The fourth book opens with the famous tenth satire on
the vanity of human wishes. What should man pray for ?
The theme is hackneyed and the treatment shows no special
originality. But the thought is elevated, the rhetoric
superb, and the verse has a resounding tread such as is only
found in Persius and Juvenal among the later poets of Rome.
' What shall man pray for ? ' Power ? Think of Sejanus,
Pompey, Demosthenes, Cicero ! To each one greatness
brought his doom. Think of Hannibal and Alexander, how
they, and with them all their high schemings, came to die ;
Long life ? What ? Should we pray to outlive our bodily
powers, to bewail the death of our nearest and dearest, to
fall from the high place where once we stood ? Beauty ?
Beauty is beset by a thousand perils in these vile days, and
rarely do beauty and chastity go hand in hand. Rather
than pray for boons like these, ' entrust thy fortune to the
gods above,' or, if pray thou must,

> stand confined
> To health of body and content of mind ;
> A soul that can securely death defy,
> And count it nature's privilege to die ;
> Serene and manly, hardened to sustain
> The load of life and exercised in pain :
> Guiltless of hate and proof against desire,
> That all things weighs and nothing can admire ;
> That dares prefer the toils of Hercules,
> To dalliance, banquet, and ignoble ease.
> The path to peace is virtue ; what I show,
> Thyself may freely on thyself bestow ;
> Fortune was never worshipped by the wise,
> But, set aloft by fools, usurps the skies.[1]

In the eleventh satire we drop from these splendid heights

---

[1] x, 356–66 (Dryden's translation).

of rhetoric to a declamatory invitation to dinner, which
affords occasion for a denunciation of the extravagant indul-
gence in the pleasures of the table and for the praise of the
good old days when Romans clave to the simple life.   The
dinner to which Juvenal invites his friend will be of simple
fare simply served—

> You'll have no scandal when you dine,
> But honest talk and wholesome wine.

And instead of lewd dance and song, a slave shall read aloud
Homer and Homer's one rival, Vergil.

The twelfth satire opens with a thanksgiving for the escape
of a friend, Catullus, from a great storm at sea, and ends
with a denunciation of legacy hunters, the connecting link
between these somewhat remote themes being that Juvenal,
at any rate, is disinterested in his joy at his friend's escape.

The thirteenth and fourteenth satires deal with more
abstract themes, the pangs of the guilty conscience and
the importance of parental example.   In the first, Juvenal
consoles his friend, Calvinus, who has been defrauded of
a sum of money.   The loss, he says, is small, and, after all,
honesty is rare nowadays.   Men have so little care for the
gods that they shrink from no perjury.   Besides, what is
such loss compared with the many worse crimes that darken
life.   Why thirst for revenge ?   It is the doctrine of the
common herd.   Philosophy teaches otherwise.   The torment
of conscience will be a worse penalty than any you can
inflict, and at last justice will claim its own.   In the next
satire, to emphasize the value of parental example, the
poet illustrates his point from the vice of avarice, and
finally, forgetting his original theme, lashes the avaricious
man in words such as would never suggest that the question
of parental example had been raised at all.   It is noteworthy
that throughout these two satires the poet draws his illustrations from the themes of the schools rather than from
the scenes of contemporary life.

In the fifteenth satire, however, he returns to depict and
discuss actual occurrences, but in how altered and strange a

manner. His theme is a case of cannibalism in Egypt,[1] the
result of a collision between religious fanatics of neighbouring
townships. The aged poet spurs himself into one last fury
against the hated Oriental, regardless of the fact that the
denunciation of cannibalism to a civilized audience must
necessarily be insipid. Last comes a fragment expatiating
bitterly on the shameful advantages of a military career. The
unhappy civilian assaulted by a soldier cannot get redress, for
the case must be heard in camp before a bench of soldiers.
The soldier, on the other hand, can get summary settlement
of all his disputes, and alone of Romans is exempt from the
patria potestas, can control his earnings and bequeath them
to whom he will. At this point the satire breaks off abruptly,
and we have no means of judging the extent of the loss. It
is a striking reversion to his earlier manner. Once more the
satire takes the form of a series of sketches from actual life.

   Both of these satires, notably the fifteenth, show a marked
falling off alike in style and matter. Both, in fact, have
been branded as spurious, the latter from times as early
as those of the scholia. But there is no real ground for
such a suspicion. Both satires have all the characteristics
of Juvenal, excepting only the vigour and brilliance of his
earlier days. No poet's powers are proof against the advance
of old age, and there is no vein of poetry more exhausting
or more easily exhausted than satire. And, as has already
been remarked, there are signs of a falling away before these
satires are reached. Even the famous tenth satire, for all
its indisputable greatness, does not demand or reveal such
special gifts of style and observation as the first and third.
It is less in touch with actual life : it is a theme from the
schools, and the illustrations, effective as they are, are as
trite as the theme itself. Were it his only work, the tenth
satire would give Juvenal high rank among Roman poets :

---

[1] There is nothing in this satire to suggest that Juvenal had or had not
visited Egypt. The legend of his banishment to Egypt may be true, but
it is quite as likely that this satire caused the scholiast to localize his
traditional exile in Egypt. The theme of cannibalism was sometimes
dealt with by the rhetoricians. Cp. Quintilian, *Decl.* 12.

it will always, thanks to the brilliance of its rhetoric and the wide applicability of its moral, be his most popular work : it is not his highest achievement.

It will have been obvious from this brief survey that the themes chosen by Juvenal are for the most part of a commonplace nature. It could hardly be otherwise. Satire, to be effective, must choose obvious themes. But in some respects the treatment of them is surprisingly commonplace. There is little freshness or originality about Juvenal's way of thinking. His morality is neither satisfying nor profound. His ideal is the old narrow Roman republican ideal of a chaste, vigorous, and unluxurious life, wherein publicity is for man alone, while woman is confined to the cares of the family and the household ; the ideal of a society wholly Italian and free-born, untainted by the importations of Greece and Asia ; of a state stern and exclusive, though just and merciful, sparing the subject and beating down the proud. The nobility of this ideal is not to be denied, but it is inadequate because it is wholly unpractical. There is no denying that the emancipation of women had led to gross evils, some of them imperilling the very existence of the State ; nor can it be doubted that much of the Greek influence had been wholly for the bad, and that in many cases the introduction of the cults of the East served merely to cloak debauchery. The rich freedman, also, for whom Juvenal reserves his bitterest shafts, was often of vicious and degraded character and had risen to power by repulsive means. But there is another side to the picture, the existence of which Juvenal sometimes, by his vehemence, seems to deny. The freedman class supplied some of the most valuable of civil servants, and many must have been worthy of their emancipation and of their rise to power.[1] There was a higher Hellenism, which Juvenal ignored. The intellectual movements of the Empire still found their chief source in Greece, and the great Sophistic movement was already setting in,

---

[1] e.g. Claudius Etruscus, who held the imperial secretaryship of finance under Nero and Vespasian, and Abascantus, the secretary *ab epistulis* to Domitian. Stat. *Silv.* iii. 3, v. 1.

as a result of which Greek literature was to revive and the
Greek language to supersede the Latin as the chief vehicle
of literary expression even at Rome itself. The greater
freedom accorded to women had its compensations ; in
spite of Juvenal, woman does not become worse or less
attractive because she is cultured and well educated, and if
there was much dissipation and debauchery in the high
society of his day, even high society contained many noble
women of fine intellect and pure character. The spread of
Roman citizenship and the breaking down of the old exclusive tradition were potent factors for good in the history of
civilization. It may be urged in Juvenal's defence that satire
must necessarily deal with the darker side of life, that his
silence as to the better and more hopeful elements in society
does not mean that he ignored them, and that it is absurd
to attack a satirist because he is not a scientific social historian. All this is true ; but it is possible to have plenty
of material for the bitterest satire and to indict gross and
rampant vice without leaving the impression that the life
of the day has no redeeming elements, without generalizing
extravagantly from the vices of one section of society, even
though that section be large and influential. The weakness
of Juvenal is that he is too retrospective, both in his praise
and in his blame. He dare not satirize the living, but will
attack the dead. But it would be wrong to assume that in
the dead he always attacks types of the living. There is
always the impression that he is in reality attacking the
first century rather than the second, the reigns of Nero and
Domitian rather than the society governed by Trajan and
Hadrian. He had lived through a night of terror and would
not recognize the signs of a new dawn. Directing his attention too exclusively on Rome itself and on the past, he forgets
the larger world and the future hope. It is to the impossible
Rome of the past that he turns his eyes for inspiration.
Hence comes his hatred, often merely racial, for Greek and
Asiatic importations,[1] hence his dislike and contempt for

---

[1] For a fine picture of the exclusive Roman spirit, cp. *Le procurateur de
Judée*, by Anatole France in *L'Étui de nacre*.

the new woman. Moreover, he had lived on the fringe of high society and not in it ; he had drunk in the bitterness of the client's life, and had lived in the enveloping atmosphere of scandal that always surrounds society for those who are excluded from it. A man of an acrid and jealous temperament, easily angered and not readily appeased, he yields too lightly and indiscriminately to that indignation, which, he tells us, is the fountain-head of all he writes. Satire should be something more than a wild torrent sweeping away obstacles great and small with one equal violence ; it should have its laughing shallows and its placid deeps. But Juvenal's laughter rings harsh and wild, and wounds as deeply as his invective ; he drives continually before the fierce gale of his spirit, and there are no calm havens where he may rest and contemplate the ideal that so much denunciation implies. He knows no gradations : all failings suffer beneath the same remorseless lash. The consul Lateranus has a taste for driving : bad taste, perhaps, yet hardly criminal. But Juvenal thunders at him as though he were guilty of high treason (viii. 146) :

> praeter maiorum cineres atque ossa volucri   [1]
> carpento rapitur pinguis Lateranus, et ipse,
> ipse rotam adstringit sufflamine mulio consul,
> nocte quidem, sed Luna videt, sed sidera testes
> intèndunt oculos. finitum tempus honoris
> cum fuerit, clara Lateranus luce flagellum
> sumet et occursum numquam trepidabit amici
> iam senis.

---

[1]   See ! by his great progenitor's remains
       Fat Lateranus sweeps, with loosened reins.
       Good Consul ! he no pride of office feels,
       But stoops, himself, to clog his headlong wheels.
       ' But this is all by night,' the hero cries,
       Yet the moon sees ! yet the stars stretch their eyes
       Full on your shame !—A few short moments wait,
       And Damasippus quits the pomp of state :
       Then, proud the experienced driver to display,
       He mounts the chariot in the face of day,
       Whirls, with bold front, his grave associate by,
       And jerks his whip, to catch the senior's eye.   GIFFORD.

Elsewhere (i. 55–62) the ' horsy ' youth is spoken of as
worse than the husband who connives at his wife's dis-
honour and pockets the reward of her shame. Among
the monstrous women of the sixth satire we come with
a shock of surprise upon the learned lady (434) :

> illa tamen gravior, quae cum discumbere coepit   [1]
> laudat Vergilium, periturae ignoscit Elissae,
> committit vates et comparat, inde Maronem
> atque alia parte in trutina suspendit Homerum.

She figures strangely among the poisoners and adulteresses.
Juvenal is misogynist by temperament as well as by conviction.   Nero is a matricide like Orestes, but—

> in scaena numquam cantavit Orestes,   [2]
> Troica non scripsit. quid enim Verginius armis
> debuit ulcisci magis aut cum Vindice Galba,
> quod Nero tam saeva crudaque tyrannide fecit ? (viii. 220).

It is almost a crime to be a foreigner.   The Greek is a liar,
a base flatterer, a monster of lust, a traitor, a murderer.[1]
The Jew is the sordid victim of a narrow and degrading
superstition.[2]   The Oriental is the defilement of Rome ;
worst of all are the Egyptians ;[3] they even eat each other.
The freedman, the *nouveau riche*, the *parvenu*[4] are hated
with all a Roman's hatred.   The old patriotism of the city
state is not yet merged in the wider imperialism.   It is bitter
to hear one of alien blood say ' Civis Romanus sum '.

---

[1]   But of all plagues the greatest is untold ;
       The book-learned wife, in Greek and Latin bold ;
       The critic dame, who at her table sits,
       Homer and Virgil quotes and weighs their wits,
       And pities Dido's agonizing fits.   DRYDEN.
[2]   Besides, Orestes in his wildest mood
       Sung on no public stage, no Troics wrote.—
       This topped his frantic crimes ! This roused mankind !
       For what could Galba, what Virginius find,
       In the dire annals of that bloody reign,
       Which called for vengeance in a louder strain ?   GIFFORD.

---

[1] iii. 60–125.   [2] xiv. 96 sqq.
[3] i. 130 sqq , and the whole of xv.   Above all, he hates the Egyptian
Crispinus, cp. iv. 2.   [4] i. 102 sqq.

This strange violence and lack of proportion are due in part to the poet's rhetorical training, which had warped still further a naturally biased temperament. He had been taught and loved to use the language of hyperbole. And he had lived through the principate of Domitian ; it was that above all else which made him cry *difficile est saturam non scribere*. To this same tendency to exaggeration may be in part attributed the extreme grossness of so much of his work. It is true that vices flaunted themselves before his eyes that it would be hard to satirize without indecency. There is excuse to some extent for the second, sixth, and ninth satires. But even there Juvenal oversteps the mark and is often guilty of coarseness for coarseness' sake. It is easy to plead the custom of the age,[1] but it is doubtful whether such pleading affords any real palliation for a writer who sets out to be a moralist. It is easy in an access of admiration to say that Juvenal is never prurient : but it is hard to be genuinely convinced that such a statement is true, or that Juvenal's coarseness is never more than mere plain speaking.[2]

For not a few readers, this tenseness of language, this violence of judgement, and this occasional unclean handling of the unclean, make Juvenal an exhausting and a depressing poet to read in any large quantity at a time. Worse still, they lead the reader at times to harbour doubts as to the genuineness of Juvenal's indignation. Such doubts are not in reality justifiable. Juvenal sometimes goads himself into inappropriate frenzies and sometimes betrays a suspiciously close acquaintance with the most disgusting details of the worst vices of the age. But though he had something of the unreality of the rhetorician, and though his character may, perhaps, not have been free from serious blemish, he is never a hypocrite ; nor, though he paints exclusively the darkest side of society, is there the least reason to accuse

---

[1] For the tradition of coarseness see chapter on Martial, p. 263.

[2] It has been pointed out that the epigrams of Martial addressed to Juvenal are disfigured by gross obscenities. It is, however, a little unfair to make Juvenal responsible for his friend's observations.

him of culpable misrepresentation of actual facts. He has
selected the material most suited to his peculiar genius :
we may complain of his principle of selection, and of his
tendency to generalize. There our criticism must end.

These defects are largely the defects of his qualities and
may be readily forgiven. We have Pliny the younger and
the inscriptions to modify his sombre picture. When all is
said, Juvenal had a matchless field for satire and matchless
gifts, against which his defects will not weigh in the balance
for a moment. His unrivalled capacity for declamation,
for mordant epigram and scathing wit, more than compensate for his often ill-balanced ferocity ; the extraordinary
vividness of his pictures of the life of Rome makes up for
lack of perspective and proportion, the richness and variety
of his imagination for its too frequent superficiality, the
vigour and trenchancy of his blows for the absence of the
rapier thrust, the fervour of his teaching for its lack of
breadth and depth. These qualities make him the greatest
of the satirists of Rome, if not of the world.

It is, perhaps, his vividness that makes the most immediate impression. It would be hard to find in any literature
a writer with such a power to make the scenes described
live before his readers. The salient features of a scene or
character are seized at once.[1] There is no irrelevant detail ;
the picture may be crowded, but it is never obscure ; if
there is a fault it is that the colouring is sometimes too
crude and glaring to please. But before such word-paint-
ing as the description of Domitian's privy council criticism
is dumb :

> nec melior vultu quamvis ignobilis ibat   [1]
> Rubrius, offensae veteris reus atque tacendae.

.   .   .   .

[1]   Rubrius, though not, like these, of noble race,
        Followed with equal terror in his face ;

.   .   .   .

[1] The sixth satire abounds throughout its great length with sketches
of the most appalling clearness and power, though they tend to crudeness
of colour and   few of them suitable for quotation.

Montani quoque venter adest abdomine tardus,
et matutino sudans Crispinus amomo
quantum vix redolent duo funera, saevior illo
Pompeius tenui iugulos aperire susurro,
et qui vulturibus servabat viscera Dacis
Fuscus marmorea meditatus proelia villa,
et cum mortifero prudens Veiento Catullo,
qui numquam visae flagrabat amore puellae,
grande et conspicuum nostro quoque tempore monstrum,
caecus adulator, dirusque a ponte satelles
dignus Aricinos qui mendicaret ad axes
blandaque devexae iactaret basia raedae (iv. 104).

Figure after figure they live before us, till the procession
culminates with the crowning horror of the blind delator,
L. Valerius Catullus Messalinus. Equally vivid is Juvenal's
description of places. There is the rude theatre of the
country town with its white-robed audience *en négligé* :—

ipsa dierum   [1]

festorum herboso colitur si quando theatro
maiestas tandemque redit ad pulpita notum

Montanus' belly next, and next appeared
The legs on which that monstrous pile was reared.
Crispinus followed, daubed with more perfume,
Thus early! than two funerals consume.
Then bloodier Pompey, practised to betray,
And hesitate the noblest lives away.
Then Fuscus, who in studious pomp at home,
Planned future triumphs for the arms of Rome.
Blind to the event! those arms a different fate,
Inglorious wounds and Dacian vultures wait.
Last, sly Veiento with Catullus came,
Deadly Catullus, who at beauty's name
Took fire, although unseen : a wretch, whose crimes
Struck with amaze even those prodigious times.
A base, blind parasite, a murderous lord,
From the bridge-end raised to the council-board,
Yet fitter still to dog the traveller's heels,
And whine for alms to the descending wheels.   GIFFORD.

[1]   Some distant parts of Italy are known,
Where none but only dead men wear a gown,
On theatres of turf, in homely state,
Old plays they act, old feasts they celebrate;

.   .   .   .

exodium, cum personae pallentis hiatum
in gremio matris formidat rusticus infans,
aequales habitus illic similesque videbis
orchestram et populum, clari velamen honoris
sufficiunt tunicae summis aedilibus albae (iii. 172).

There is the poor gentleman's garret high on the topmost
story of some tottering *insula*, close beneath the tiles, where
the doves nest:

lectus erat Codro Procula minor, urceoli sex   [1]
ornamentum abaci nec non et parvulus infra
cantharus, et recubans sub eodem marmore Chiro
iamque vetus graecos servabat cista libellos,
et divina opici rodebant carmina mures (iii. 203).

There is the hurrying throng of the streets of Rome with
all its dangers and discomforts:

      .   nobis properantibus opstat   [2]
unda prior, magno populus premit agmine lumbos
qui sequitur; ferit hic cubito, ferit assere duro
alter, at hic tignum capiti incutit, ille metretam.

The mimic yearly gives the same delights;
And in the mother's arms the clownish infant frights.
Their habits (undistinguished by degrees)
Are plain alike; the same simplicity
Both on the stage and in the pit you see.
In his white cloak the magistrate appears;
The country bumpkin the same livery wears.   DRYDEN.

[1]   Codrus had but one bed, so short to boot,
That his short wife's short legs go dangling out;
His cupboard's head six earthen pitchers graced,
Beneath them was his trusty tankard placed;
And to support this noble plate, there lay
A bending Chiron cast from honest clay;
His few Greek books a rotten chest contained,
Whose covers much of mouldiness complained;
Where mice and rats devoured poetic bread,
And on heroic verse luxuriously were fed.   DRYDEN.

[2]   The press before him stops the client's pace;
The crowd that follows crush his panting sides,
And trip his heels; he walks not but he rides.
One elbows him, one jostles in the shoal,
A rafter breaks his head or chairman's pole;

pinguia crura luto, planta mox undique magna
calcor et in digito clavus mihi militis haeret.
nonne vides quanto celebretur sportula fumo ?
centum convivae, sequitur sua quemque culina.
Corbulo vix ferret tot vasa ingentia, tot res
inpositas capiti, quas recto vertice portat
servulus infelix et cursu ventilat ignem.
scinduntur tunicae sartae modo, longa coruscat
serraco veniente abies, atque altera pinum
plaustra vehunt, nutant alte populoque minantur (iii. 243).

Even in the later satires, where with the advance of age
this pictorial gift begins to fail him and he tends to rely
rather on brilliant rhetorical treatment of philosophical
commonplaces, there are still flashes of the old power. The
well-known description of the fall of Sejanus in the tenth
satire is in his best manner, while even the humbler picture
of the rustic family of primitive Rome in the fourteenth
satire shows the same firmness of touch, the same eye for
vivid and direct representation :

saturabat glaebula talis [1]
patrem ipsum turbamque casae, qua feta iacebat
uxor et infantes ludebant quattuor, unus

Stockinged with loads of fat town dirt he goes,
And some rogue-soldier with his hob-nailed shoes
Indents his legs behind in bloody rows.
  See, with what smoke our doles we celebrate !
A hundred guests invited walk in state ;
A hundred hungry slaves with their Dutch-kitchens wait :
Huge pans the wretches on their heads must bear,
Which scarce gigantic Corbulo could rear ;
Yet they must walk upright beneath the load,
Nay run, and running blow the sparkling flames abroad,
Their coats from botching newly brought are torn.
Unwieldy timber-trees in waggons borne,
Stretched at their length, beyond their carriage lie,
That nod and threaten ruin from on high.   DRYDEN.

[1] For then the little glebe, improved with care,
Largely supplied with vegetable fare,
The good old man, the wife in childbed laid,
And four hale boys, that round the cottage played,

X 2

  vernula, tres domini, sed magnis fratribus horum
  a scrobe vel sulco redeuntibus altera cena
  amplior et grandes fumabant pultibus ollae (166).

His handling of the essential weapons of satire, scathing
epigram, and impetuous rhetoric, contribute equally to his
success. He has the capacity of branding a character with
eternal shame in a few terse trenchant lines. Who can
forget the Greek adventurer of the third satire ?—

  grammaticus rhetor geometres pictor aliptes   [1]
  augur schoenobates medicus magus, omnia novit
  Graeculus esuriens ; in caelum miseris, ibit (iii. 76);

or the summary of Domitian's reign with which he dates
the story of the gigantic turbot ?—

  cum iam semianimum laceraret Flavius orbem   [2]
  ultimus et calvo serviret Roma Neroni (iv. 37);

or the curse upon the legacy-hunter Pacuvius ?—

  vivat Pacuvius quaeso vel Nestora totum,   [3]
  possideat quantum rapuit Nero, montibus aurum
  exaequet, nec amet quemquam nec ametur ab ullo (xii. 128).

Not less mordant in a different way is the savage and
sceptical melancholy of the conclusion of the second satire,
where he contrasts the degenerate Roman, tainted by the

  Three free-born, one a slave : while, on the board,
  Huge porringers, with wholesome pottage stored,
  Smoked for their elder brothers, who were now,
  Hungry and tired, expected from the plough. GIFFORD.
[1] A cook, a conjurer, a rhetorician,
  A painter, pedant, a geometrician,
  A dancer on the ropes and a physician ;
  All things the hungry Greek exactly knows,
  And bid him go to heaven, to heaven he goes. DRYDEN.
[2] When the last Flavius, drunk with fury, tore
  The prostrate world, which bled at every pore,
  And Rome beheld, in body as in mind,
  A bald-pate Nero rise to curse mankind. GIFFORD.
[3] Health to the man ! and may he thus get more
  Than Nero plundered ! pile his shining store
  High, mountain high : in years a Nestor prove,
  And, loving none, ne'er know another's love ! GIFFORD.

foulest lusts, with the noble Romans of the past, and even
with the barbarians, newly conquered, on the confines of
empire (149) :

> esse aliquos manes et subterranea regna [1]
> et contum et Stygio ranas in gurgite nigras
> atque una transire vadum tot milia cumba
> nec pueri credunt, nisi qui nondum aere lavantur.
> sed tu vera puta : Curius quid sentit et ambo
> Scipiadae, quid Fabricius manesque Camilli,
> quid Cremerae legio et Cannis consumpta iuventus,
> tot bellorum animae, quotiens hinc talis ad illos
> umbra venit ? cuperent lustrari, si qua darentur
> sulpura cum taedis et si foret umida laurus.
> illic heu miseri traducimur. arma quidem ultra
> litora Iuvernae promovimus et modo captas
> Orcadas ac minima contentos nocte Britannos,
> sed quae nunc populi fiunt victoris in urbe,
> non faciunt illi quos vicimus.

[1]   That angry Justice formed a dreadful hell,
That ghosts in subterranean regions dwell,
That hateful Styx his sable current rolls,
And Charon ferries o'er unbodied souls,
Are now as tales or idle fables prized ;
By children questioned and by men despised.
Yet these, do thou believe. What thoughts, declare,
Ye Scipios, once the thunderbolts of war !
Fabricius, Curius, great Camillus' ghost !
Ye valiant Fabii, in yourselves an host !
Ye dauntless youths at fatal Cannae slain !
Spirits of many a brave and bloody plain !
What thoughts are yours, whene'er with feet unblest,
An unbelieving shade invades your rest ?
Ye fly, to expiate the blasting view ;
Fling on the pine-tree torch the sulphur blue,
And from the dripping bay dash round the lustral dew.
And yet—to these abodes we all must come,
Believe, or not, these are our final home ;
Though now Ierne tremble at our sway,
And Britain, boastful of her length of day ;
Though the blue Orcades receive our chain,
And isles that slumber in the frozen main.
But why of conquest boast ? the conquered climes
Are free, O Rome, from thy detested crimes.   GIFFORD.

In the same bitter spirit, Umbricius is made to cry:

> quid Romae faciam ? mentiri nescio ; librum,　　　　[1]
> si malus est, nequeo laudare et poscere ; motus
> astrorum ignoro ; funus promittere patris
> nec volo nec possum ; ranarum viscera numquam
> inspexi ; ferre ad nuptam quae mittit adulter,
> quae mandat, norunt alii ; me nemo ministro
> fur erit, atque ideo nulli comes exeo tamquam
> mancus et extinctae, corpus non utile, dextrae (iii. 41).

This bitterness Juvenal seasons at times with saturnine jests of a type that is all his own. Virro gives rancid oil to his poor guests as dressing to their salad:

> illud enim vestris datur alveolis quod　　　　[2]
> canna Micipsarum prora subvexit acuta,
> propter quod Romae cum Boccare nemo lavatur,
> quod tutos etiam facit a serpentibus atris (v. 88).

When the blind *delator*, Catullus Messalinus, is summoned to give his advice concerning the gigantic turbot:

> nemo magis rhombum stupuit ; nam plurima dixit　　　[3]
> in laevom conversus, at illi dextra iacebat

---

[1]　What's Rome to me, what business have I there ?
　I who can neither lie nor falsely swear ?
　Nor praise my patron's undeserving rhymes,
　Nor yet comply with him nor with his times ?
　Unskilled in schemes by planets to foreshow,
　Like canting rascals, how the wars will go ;
　I neither will nor can prognosticate
　To the young gaping heir his father's fate ;
　Nor in the entrails of a toad have pried,
　Nor carried bawdy presents to a bride :
　For want of these town-virtues, thus alone
　I go conducted on my way by none ;
　Like a dead member from the body rent,
　Maimed and unuseful to the government.　　　　DRYDEN.

[2]　　　　　　　Such oil to you is thrown,
　Such rancid grease, as Afric sends to town ;
　So strong that when her factors seek the bath,
　All wind and all avoid the noisome path.　　　　GIFFORD.

[3]　None dwelt so largely on the turbot's size,
　Or raised with such applause his wondering eyes ;
　But to the left (O treacherous want of sight)
　He poured his praise ;—the fish was on the right.

> belua. sic pugnas Cilicis laudabat et ictus
> et pegma et pueros inde ad velaria raptos (iv. 119).

Grimmest of all is the jest on the mushrooms set before
Virro :

> vilibus ancipites fungi ponentur amicis,   [1]
> boletus domino, sed quales Claudius edit
> ante illum uxoris, post quem nihil amplius edit (v. 146).

But Juvenal is not always bitter, nor always angry. His
indignation is never absent, but takes at times a graver
and a nobler tone. At times he preaches virtue directly,
instead of doing so indirectly through the denunciation of
vice. He has no new secret of morality to reveal, no fresh
lights to throw upon problems of conduct ; his advice is
obvious and straightforward ; neither in form nor matter is
there anything paradoxical. He was no student of philosophy,[1] though naturally familiar with the more important
philosophic creeds and disposed by temperament to fall in
with the views of the stern Stoic school. The conclusion
of the tenth satire quoted above owes much to the Stoics.
' Leave the ordering of your fortunes to the powers above.
Man is dearer to them than to himself. The wise man is
free from all desire, all anger and all fear of death.'[2]
' Revenge is an unworthy and degrading passion.'[3] ' Fate[4]
and the revolution[5] of the stars in heaven rule all with
unchanging law.' All these maxims have their counterpart

> Thus would he at the fencer's matches sit,
> And shout with rapture at some fancied hit ;
> And thus applaud the stage machinery, where
> The youths were rapt aloft and lost in air.   GIFFORD.

[1] You champ on spongy toadstools, hateful treat !
> Fearful of poisons in each bit you eat :
> He feasts secure on mushrooms, fine as those
> Which Claudius for his special eating chose,
> Till one more fine, provided by his wife,
> Finished at once his feasting and his life !   GIFFORD.

---

[1] xiii. 120 sqq.   [2] x. 346 sqq.   [3] xiii. 180.
[4] ix. 32, xii. 63.   [5] vii. 194 sqq., ix. 33.

in the Stoic creed.   But there is no need of the philosophy
of the schools to guide man to the paths of virtue.

> numquam aliud natura, aliud sapientia dicit (xiv. 321). [1]

Philosophy has its value, but the good man is no less good
for not being a philosopher :

> magna quidem, sacris quae dat praecepta libellis,   [2]
> victrix fortunae sapientia, ducimus autem
> hos quoque felices, qui ferre incommoda vitae
> nec iactare iugum vita didicere magistra (xiii. 19).

He agrees with the Stoics just because their practical teaching
harmonizes so entirely with the old *virtus Romana* that is
his ideal.

No more profound are his religious views : he hates the
alien cults that work as insidious poison in the life of Rome ;
he rejects the picturesque legends of the afterworld, bred
of the fertile imagination of the Greeks. But he is no
unbeliever :

> separat hoc nos   [3]
> a grege mutorum, atque ideo venerabile soli
> sortiti ingenium divinorumque capaces
> atque exercendis pariendisque artibus apti
> sensum a caelesti demissum traximus arce,
> cuius egent prona et terram spectantia. mundi

---

[1] Nature and wisdom never are at strife.   GIFFORD.
[2] Wisdom, I know, contains a sovereign charm,
  To vanquish fortune or at least disarm :
  Blest they who walk in her unerring rule !
  Nor those unblest who, tutored in life's school,
  Have learned of old experience to submit,
  And lightly bear the yoke they cannot quit.   GIFFORD.
[3]   This marks our birth
  The great distinction from the beasts of earth !
  And therefore—gifted with superior powers
  And capable of things divine—'tis ours
  To learn and practise every useful art ;
  And from high heaven deduce that better part,
  That moral sense, denied to creatures prone
  And downward bent, and found with man alone !—

principio indulsit communis conditor illis
tantum animas, nobis animum quoque, mutuus ut nos
adfectus petere auxilium et praestare iuberet (xv. 142).

God is over all and guides and guards the world, and has
ordained torment of conscience and slow retribution for sin.[1]
Yet Juvenal does not definitely reject the gods of his native
land ; nor do these exalted beliefs cause him to refuse
sacrifice to Jupiter, Juno, Minerva, and his household gods.[2]
It is the creed, not of a theologian, but of a man with high
ideals, a staunch patriotism, and a deep reverence for the
past.

But this lack of profundity and philosophical training
does not, as may be inferred from passages already quoted,
prevent him from being intensely effective as a moral
teacher.   His platitudes are none the worse for not having
a Stoic label and all the better for their simplicity and
directness of expression.   They do not reveal the hunger
and thirst after righteousness that breathe from the lines
of Persius, but they have at least an equal appeal to the
plain man, and they are matchlessly expressed.   His pleading against revenging the wrong done, if not on the very
highest moral plane, possesses a grave dignity and beauty
that brings it straight home to the heart :

at vindicta bonum vita iucundius ipsa.   [1]
nempe hoc indocti, quorum praecordia nullis
interdum aut levibus videas flagrantia causis.

.   .   .   .

For He, who gave this vast machine to roll,
Breathed life in them, in us a reasoning soul :
That kindred feelings might our state improve,
And mutual wants conduct to mutual love.   GIFFORD.
[1]   ' Revenge,' they say, and I believe their words,
' A pleasure sweeter far than life affords.'
Who say ?   The fools, whose passions prone to ire
At slightest causes or at none take fire.
.   .   .   .   .   Chrysippus said not so ;

---

[1] xiii. 192–249.   [2] xii. 3–6, 89 sqq.

Chrysippus non dicet idem nec mite Thaletis
ingenium dulcique senex vicinus Hymetto,
qui partem acceptae saeva inter vincla cicutae
accusatori nollet dare. plurima felix
paulatim vitia atque errores exuit omnes,
prima docet rectum sapientia. quippe minuti
semper et infirmi est animi exiguique voluptas
ultio. continuo sic collige, quod vindicta
nemo magis gaudet quam femina. cur tamen hos tu
evasisse putes, quos diri conscia facti
mens habet attonitos et surdo verbere caedit
occultum quatiente animo tortore flagellum ?
poena autem vehemens ac multo saevior illis
quas et Caedicius gravis invenit et Rhadamanthus,
nocte dieque suum gestare in pectore testem (xiii. 180).

The same characteristics mark his praise of nobility of
character as opposed to nobility of birth :

tota licet veteres exornent undique cerae   [1]
atria, nobilitas sola est atque unica virtus.

Nor Thales, to our frailties clement still ;
Nor that old man, by sweet Hymettus' hill,
Who drank the poison with unruffled soul,
And, dying, from his foes withheld the bowl.
Divine philosophy ! by whose pure light
We first distinguish, then pursue the right,
Thy power the breast from every error frees
And weeds out every error by degrees :—
Illumined by thy beam, revenge we find
The abject pleasure of an abject mind,
And hence so dear to poor, weak womankind.
But why are those, Calvinus, thought to 'scape
Unpunished, whom in every fearful shape
Guilt still alarms, and conscience ne'er asleep
Wounds with incessant strokes 'not loud but deep',
While the vexed mind, her own tormentor, plies
A scorpion scourge, unmarked by human eyes ?
Trust me, no tortures which the poets feign,
Can match the fierce, the unutterable pain
He feels, who night and day, devoid of rest,
Carries his own accuser in his breast.   GIFFORD.

[1]   Fond man, though all the heroes of your line
         Bedeck your halls, and round your galleries shine

Paulus vel Cossus vel Drusus moribus esto,
hos ante effigies maiorum pone tuorum,
praecedant ipsas illi te consule virgas.
prima mihi debes anima bona. sanctus haberi
iustitiaeque tenax factis dictisque mereris ?
adgnosco procerem ; salve Gaetulice, seu tu
Silanus, quocumque alio de sanguine, rarus
civis et egregius patriae contingis ovanti (viii. 19).

This is rhetoric, but rhetoric of the noblest kind. Of pure
poetry there is naturally but little in Juvenal. Neither
his temperament nor his subject would admit it. He had
too keen an eye for the hideous and the grotesque, too
strong a passion for the declamatory style. Hence it is
rather his brilliant sketches of a vicious society, his fiery
outbursts of rhetoric, his striking *sententiae* that primarily
impress the reader :

expende Hannibalem : quot libras in duce summo [1]
invenies ? (x. 147).

finem animae quae res humanas miscuit olim,   [2]
non gladii, non saxa dabunt nec tela, sed ille
Cannarum vindex et tanti sanguinis ultor

In proud display : yet take this truth from me,
' Virtue alone is true nobility.'
Set Cossus, Drusus, Paulus, then, in view,
The bright example of their lives pursue ;
Let these precede the statues of your race,
And these, when consul, of your rods take place,
O give me inborn worth ! Dare to be just,
Firm to your word and faithful to your trust.
Then praises hear, at least deserve to hear,
I grant your claim and recognize the peer.
Hail from whatever stock you draw your birth,
The son of Cossus or the son of Earth,
All hail ! in you exulting Rome espies
Her guardian power, her great Palladium rise.   GIFFORD.

[1]   Great Hannibal within the balance lay,
And count how many pounds his ashes weigh.   DRYDEN.

[2]   What wondrous sort of death has heaven designed
For so untamed, so turbulent a mind ?
Nor swords at hand, nor hissing darts afar,
Are doomed to avenge the tedious bloody war ;

anulus. i demens et saevas curre per Alpes,
ut pueris placeas et declamatio fias (x. 163).

nemo repente fuit turpissimus (ii. 83). [1]

summum crede nefas animam praeferre pudori [2]
et propter vitam vivendi perdere causas (viii. 83).

si natura negat, facit indignatio versum (i. 79).

It is lines such as these that first rise to the mind at the
mention of Juvenal. But he was no mere declaimer. Here
and there we may find phrases of the purest poetry and
of the most perfect form. Far above all others come the
wonderful lines of the ninth satire:

                 festinat enim decurrere velox [3]
flosculus angustae miseraeque brevissima vitae
portio ; dum bibimus, dum serta unguenta puellas
poscimus, obrepit non intellecta senectus (ix. 126).

Of a very different character, but of a beauty that is nothing
less than startling in its sombre surroundings, is the blessing
that he invokes on the good men of old who ' enthroned
the teacher in the revered parent's place '.

di maiorum umbris tenuem et sine pondere terram [4]
spirantesque crocos et in urna perpetuum ver,

But poison drawn through a ring's hollow plate,
Must finish him—a sucking infant's fate.
Go, climb the rugged Alps, ambitious fool,
To please the boys, and be a theme at school.   DRYDEN.

[1]   For none become at once completely vile.   GIFFORD.
[2]   Think it a crime no tears can e'er efface,
To purchase safety with compliance base,
At honour's cost a feverish span extend,
And sacrifice for life, life's only end !   GIFFORD.

[3]   For youth, too transient flower ! of life's short day
The shortest part, but blossoms—to decay.
Lo ! while we give the unregarded hour
To revelry and joy in Pleasure's bower,
While now for rosy wreaths our brow to twine,
While now for nymphs we call, and now for wine,
The noiseless foot of time steals swiftly by,
And, ere we dream of manhood, age is nigh !   GIFFORD.

[4]   Shades of our sires ! O sacred be your rest,
And lightly lie the turf upon your breast !
Flowers round your urns breathe sweets beyond compare,
And spring eternal shed its influence there !

qui praeceptorem sancti voluere parentis
esse loco (vii. 207).

The sensuous appeal of the 'fragrant crocus and the spring
that dies not in the urn of death' is unique in Juvenal.
This slender stream of definitely poetic imagination reveals
itself suddenly and unexpectedly in strange forms and
circumstances.   At the close of the passage in the third
satire describing the perils of the Roman streets, Juvenal
imagines the death of some householder in a street accident.
All is bustle and business at home in expectation of his
return :

> domus interea secura patellas   [1]
> iam lavat et bucca foculum excitat et sonat unctis
> striglibus et pleno componit lintea guto.
> haec inter pueros varie properantur, at ille
> iam sedet in ripa taetrumque novicius horret
> porthmea nec sperat caenosi gurgitis alnum
> infelix nec habet quem porrigat ore trientem (iii. 261).

Out of the grotesque there gradually looms the horror of
death and the friendless ghost sitting lost and homeless
by the Stygian waters.

That there is small scope in his work for such distinctively
poetic imagination is not Juvenal's fault, nor can we complain of its absence.   But in technical accomplishment he
shows himself a writer of the first rank.   His treatment
of the hexameter exactly suits his declamatory type of
satire.   The conversational verse of Horace, with its easy-

---

[1]
> You honoured tutors, now a slighted race,
> And gave them all a parent's power and place.   GIFFORD.
> Meantime, unknowing of their fellow's fate,
> The servants wash the platter, scour the plate,
> Then blow the fire with puffing cheeks, and lay
> The rubbers and the bathing-sheets display,
> And oil them first, each handy in his way.
> But he for whom this busy care they take,
> Poor ghost ! is wandering by the Stygian lake ;
> Affrighted by the ferryman's grim face,
> New to the horrors of the fearful place,
> His passage begs, with unregarded prayer,
> And wants two farthings to discharge his fare.   DRYDEN.

going rambling gait, was unsuitable for the thunders of
Juvenal's rhetoric. Something more massive in structure,
more vigorous in movement, was needed as the vehicle of
so much rhetoric and invective. The delicate tripping
hexameter of contemporary epic was equally unsuitable.

Unlike the majority of post-Augustan poets, Juvenal is
almost untouched by the Ovidian influence. As far as his
metre has any ancestry, it is descended from the Vergilian
hexameter, though with the licence of satire it claims greater
liberty in its treatment of pauses and of elision. The post-
Augustan poet with whom in this respect Juvenal has
greatest affinity is Persius. For vigour and variety he far
surpasses all other poets of the age ; while even Persius,
although at his best and in his more declamatory passages
he is at least Juvenal's equal, does not maintain the same
level of excellence, and his more frequent employment of the
traditional dialogue of satire gives him fewer opportunities
for striking metrical effect.

As regards his diction Juvenal is equally remarkable.
He has suffered little from the schools of rhetoric and has
gained much. He is pointed and clear, without being
either obscure [1] or mechanical. There is no vain striving
after antithesis and no epigram for epigram's sake. Grotesque he is not seldom, but the grotesqueness is deliberate
and effective, and no mere affectation.

His one serious weakness is his lack of constructive
power and his incapacity to preserve due proportion between
the parts of his satires. The most glaring instances of
this failing are to be found in the fourth, twelfth, and
fourteenth satires, but except the third there is hardly
a satire that can be regarded as wholly successful in point
of construction. This defect, it may be admitted, is less
serious in satire than in almost any other branch of literature. Such discursiveness was justified by the tradition

---

[1] Such obscurity as he presents is due almost entirely to the fact that
we have lost the key to his topical allusions. He has a strong affection for
ingenious periphrases (e.g. v. 139, vi. 159, x. 112, xii. 70), but they are as
a rule effective and amusing.

and by the inherent nature of satire. But Juvenal offends
in this respect beyond due reason, and only his extraordinary merits in other directions save him from the
penalties of this failing.

Juvenal is the last of the poets of the Silver Age, and
the only one of them to whom the epithet ' great ' can
reasonably be applied. He is no faultless writer, but he
has genius and power, and has risen superior to the besetting
sins of the age. He is a rhetorician, it is true, but he chose
a form of literature where his rhetoric could have legitimate
play. But he is no plagiarist or imitator ; though, as in
any other poet, we may find in him many traces and even
echoes of his predecessors, he is in the best sense original.
He is never a mere juggler in words and phrases, he is a true
artist. Form and matter are indissolubly welded and inter-
fused one with another. And this is because, unlike other
writers of the age, he has something to say. He is poet
by inspiration, not by profession. His excessive pessimism,
his tendency to bias and exaggeration, cannot on the worst
estimate obscure his merits either as artist or moralist.
His picture of society has large elements of truth, and we
can no more blame him for his tendency to caricature than
we can blame Hogarth. Satire, especially the satire of
declamatory invective, must be one-sided, and the satirist
must select the features of life which he desires to denounce.
And if this leads us at times into unpleasant places and
among unpleasant people unpleasantly described, that does
not justify us in denouncing the satirist. It must be
remembered that the true satirist is not likely to be a man
of perfect character. He must have seen much and experienced much ; if his character has in the process become
not merely unduly embittered, but perhaps somewhat
smirched, these failings may be redeemed by other qualities.
And in the case of Juvenal they are so redeemed.

He has not the lucid judgement of Horace nor the pure
fervour of Persius. He is more positive than the former,
more negative than the latter. But he has lived in a sense
in which Persius never had, and possesses the gift of direct

and lucid expression ; therefore, when he strikes, he strikes home. He cannot, like Horace, ' play about the hearts of men,' he will have nothing of compromise, he cannot and will not adapt himself to his environment. . The doctrine of μηδὲν ἄγαν, the *aurea mediocritas*, have no attractions for him. Hence his ideal is often unpractical ; ' the times were out of joint,' and Juvenal was not precisely the man to ' set them right '. But at least he sets forth an ideal, that any honest man must admit to be noble. It is precisely because he is no casuist, because he hits hard and unsparingly, and is translucently honest, and because his weapon is the most fervid and trenchant rhetoric, that Juvenal is the most quoted and one of the most popular of Latin poets. He has contributed little to the thought of the world, but he has taught men to hate iniquity. He does not rise to the height of such an immortal saying as

virtutem videant intabescantque relicta;

he is no philosopher, and his ideals have neither the exaltation nor the stimulating power of the Stoic ideal. But he unveils vice and folly, so that men may fly from their utter hideousness, in such burning words as it has fallen to few poets to utter. He is ' dowered with the hate of hate, the scorn of scorn ' ; had he possessed also the ' love of love ', he might have reached greater heights of pure poetry, but he would not have been Juvenal, and the world would have been the loser.

INDEX OF NAMES